Global Development Finance

Striving for Stability in Development Finance

I: ANALYSIS AND STATISTICAL APPENDIX 2003

THE WORLD BANK

1818 H Street, NW
Washington, DC 20433
Telephone: 202-473-1000
Internet: www.worldbank.org
E-mail: feedback@worldbank.org

1 2 3 4 05 04 03

Cover photo of the Calcutta Stock Exchange taken by Viviane Moos/CORBIS.
Cover design by Fletcher Design.

ISBN 0-8213-5428-0
ISSN 1020-5454

The cutoff date for data used in this report was March 12, 2003. Dollars are current U.S. dollars unless otherwise specified.

Table of Contents

Tables

Figures

Boxes

Foreword

GLOBAL DEVELOPMENT FINANCE IS THE World Bank's annual review of global financial conditions facing developing countries. The current volume provides analysis and a statistical appendix. A separate volume contains detailed, standardized external debt statistics for 138 countries.

The background to this year's report is a difficult one. The global economy has been struggling to recover from a recession in 2001. Even though macroeconomic policies in the major economies have been very supportive, the recovery that has been underway for almost 18 months remains disappointingly anemic. A key hindrance to global recovery has been the financial imbalances that built during the expansion of the 1990s, and there has been a wide incidence of debt difficulties across both developed and developing countries. On top of this already challenging environment, current geopolitical uncertainties add an overlay of uncertainty for both financial markets and policymakers.

Against this difficult backdrop, developing countries are struggling to adjust to a major shift in the pattern of external financing that has been underway since the middle of 1998. Since that time, the flow of private sector *debt* finance to developing countries has plunged. At the same time, however, the flow of private sector *equity* finance—primarily foreign direct investment (FDI)—has remained remarkably robust. Countries that have adjusted in order to live with less debt and that have opened themselves to the flow of FDI funding have been the relatively strong performers in recent years. In turn, this solid economic performance has translated into tangible benefits in the area of poverty alleviation.

Creating the right conditions to benefit, rather than suffer, from the shifts in private-sector financing for developing countries is primarily the responsibility of developing countries. This means building conditions that both promote domestic productivity and investment, and attract FDI. And it has become all the more important for governments to run prudent debt-management policies, especially in nascent local-currency debt markets.

However, the high-income countries also have an important role to play if the pattern of international development finance in coming years is to be more stable than the volatile, growth-inhibiting one of recent years. With private capital flows low, raising the flow of official development assistance—as agreed to at the Monterrey Conference in 2001—is of key importance to the poorest countries. Moreover, the rich countries need to foster an open, competitive world-trading system, especially in goods such as textiles and agricultural products, in which developing countries have an obvious comparative advantage. Not only would this give countries that are under pressure to pay down debt the opportunity to generate the necessary export revenue (through export growth, rather than by relying on import compression), but it would also help create conditions fostering the continuation of a steady and significant flow of FDI to developing countries.

Nicholas Stern
Chief Economist and Senior Vice President
The World Bank
March 12, 2003

Acknowledgments

THIS REPORT WAS PREPARED BY THE INTERnational Finance Team of the Development Prospects Group (DECPG) but drew on resources throughout the Development Economics Vice-Presidency, the World Bank operational regions, the International Finance Corporation, and the Multilateral Investment Guarantee Agency.

The principal author was Philip Suttle, with direction by Uri Dadush. The report was prepared under the general direction of Nicholas Stern. The lead authors are identified on the opening page of each chapter. The statistical appendix was prepared by Philip Suttle, Eung Ju Kim, and Fernando Martel-Garcia of DECPG, and Punam Chuhan, Nevin Fahmy, Shelley Fu, Ibrahim Levent, and Gloria Moreno of the Financial Data Team of the Development Data Group (DECDG). The financial flow and debt estimates were developed in a collaborative effort between DECPG and DECDG. The main macroeconomic forecasts were prepared by the Global Trends Team of DECPG, led by Hans Timmer and including John Baffes, Betty Dow, Caroline Farah, Robert Keyfitz, Annette I. De Kleine, Fernando Martel-Garcia, Donald Mitchell, Mick Riordan, Shane Streifel, and Bert Wolfe. The analysis and forecasts were also prepared in conjunction with the Bank's regional chief economists: Guillermo Perry (Latin America and the Caribbean), Alan Gelb (Sub-Saharan Africa), Homi Kharas (East Asia and Pacific), Sadiq Ahmed (South Asia), Pradeep K. Mitra (Europe and Central Asia), and Mustapha Nabli (Middle East and North Africa).

The report also benefited from the comments of the Bank's Executive Directors made at informal board meetings on March 6 and 10, 2003.

Many others from inside and outside the Bank provided input, comments, guidance and support at various stages of the report's publication. Jack Glen (International Finance Corporation), Barbara Mierau-Klein, Sharon Stanton Russell (Massachusetts Institute of Technology), Gregory Toulmin, and Hung Tran (International Monetary Fund) were discussants at the Bankwide review. Within the Bank, comments and help were provided by Ivar Alexander, Amarendra Bhattacharya, Anthony Bottrill, Asli Demirguc-Kunt, Jean-Jacques Dethier, Mark Dorfman, Shahrokh Fardoust, Norbert Fiess, Lisa Finneran, Ian Goldin, James Hanson, Demet Kaya, Yung Chul Kim, Leora Klapper, Steven Knack, Stefan Koeberle, Frank Lysy, Pilar Maisterra, Raymundo Morales, Vikram Nehru, Richard Newfarmer, Brian Ngo, Luis Periera da Silva, Guy Pfeffermann, Malvina Pollock, Michael Pomerleano, Sanjivi Rajasingham, David Rosenblatt, Luis Serven, Emily Sinnott, Mark Sundberg, Graeme Wheeler, and John Wilton.

Outside the Bank, invaluable help was received from Charles Blitzer, Matthew Fisher, Alexander Lehmann and Krishna Srinivasan (International Monetary Fund), John Clark (Federal Reserve Bank of New York), Elizabeth Kelderhouse (Federal Deposit Insurance Corporation), Philip Wooldridge (Bank for International Settlements), William Cline (Institute of International Economics), Jeff Anderson and Greg Fager (Institute of International Finance), Eric Beinstein and Joyce Chang (JP Morgan Chase), Arturo Porzecanski (ABN-Amro), David Sekiguchi (Deutsche Bank), and Susan Martin (Georgetown University).

Steven Kennedy edited the report. Sarah Crow and Awatif Abuzeid provided assistance to the team. Dorota Nowak managed production and dissemination activities by DECPG. Book design, editing, and production were coordinated by Cindy Fisher, Melissa Edeburn, and Ilma Kramer of the World Bank Office of the Publisher.

Overview and Policy Messages: Striving for Stability in Development Finance

Although 2002 was a year of hesitant global recovery, financial conditions facing many developing countries were once again challenging, especially for those countries (mainly middle-income countries) dependent on international financial markets. Conditions have improved a little in the early months of 2003, although the uncertainties surrounding Iraq have cast a shadow over both the global economy and financial markets.

Concern over the recent pattern of financial flows for global development that has prevailed in recent years is widespread—and understandably so.

Since 1998, developing countries have repaid external debt to private creditors in developed countries. In some cases these net repayments of debt have been required by timorous capital markets grown wary of overexposure to developing-country debt. In others they reflect reduced demand for debt by countries that have either found alternative forms of external finance or have reduced their overall demand for external investment funds. Combined with developing countries' steady accumulation of financial assets in high-income economies, however, these debt repayments mean that the developing world has become a net capital *exporter* to the developed world.

On a net basis, therefore, capital is no longer flowing from high-income countries to economies that need it to sustain their progress toward the Millennium Development Goals. The shortage is compounded in the poorest countries by a significant drop in official development assistance from bilateral donors.

What can or should be done to promote access by developing countries to external capital? What can be done to prevent growing economies from the disruptive effects of sharp reversals in financing? These are the central concerns of this year's *Global Development Finance*.

On the bright side, the steady drop in external debt financing has been cushioned by resilience in foreign direct investment (FDI). A further positive sign is the growth of local-currency bond markets in several emerging economies and the development of several promising innovations to manage credit risk. These issues, too, are covered in this report.

The developing world is learning to live with less external debt

The supply of debt capital to the developing world, which swelled in the early 1990s, was first reduced by the shock of the East Asian crisis of 1997–98, then by the turmoil in global fixed-income markets in the summer of 1998, and most recently by the problems in global high-yield markets in the aftermath of the 2001 slowdown. However, this broad-based decline in debt flows, first evident in East Asia and the Russian Federation, is now focused on Latin America.

Some early signs of improvement in the external-debt market cropped up as 2002 came to a close. The forecasts in this publication point to a further, gradual rise in debt flows in 2003 and 2004 (see chapters 1 and 3). It is unlikely, however, that private debt flows to developing countries will return to the levels of the 1990s. Nor would such a rebound necessarily be desirable.

While external bond and bank financing should continue to play an important role in the financing strategies of governments and private-sector borrowers in developing countries, the fixed commitments of debt service are not well suited to the swings in nominal income experienced by many developing countries, especially those dependent on primary commodities. Market reactions to debt-servicing strains add a whole new layer of volatility that can be severely damaging to growth and poverty reduction.

The movement from debt to equity has been underway in private financial markets since 1998. Policymakers should recognize the consequences of this important shift—and respond to the opportunities and policy challenges it poses.

Measures to promote the inflow of foreign equity capital are critical

FDI is less volatile than external debt. Its focus on long-term returns makes it clearly more appropriate for developing countries. And it can bring advantages both in technology and in operational and financial management. In this context, the resilience of FDI in the face of the sustained weakness in debt flows is a hopeful sign (see chapter 4).

In contrast to debt investors, companies have been willing to raise their exposures in the developing world, in part because their holdings in developing countries are a relatively small part of their overall capital stock, and in part because many mature companies now expect a large portion of their revenue growth and cost reduction (and thus their profit growth) to come from operations in developing countries, whether they are producing for export or for local sale.

FDI usually brings with it important benefits such as access to markets and transfers of technology and skills. In a world of volatile private capital flows, however, it is the financial aspects of FDI that are particularly desirable. Companies tend to invest in developing countries for the long haul. They see their returns rise and fall with the overall performance of the host economy and generally keep a significant share of earnings in the country.

A solid flow of FDI to developing countries should not be taken for granted, however. Indeed, net FDI to developing countries has already fallen from its peak of $179 billion in 1999 to $143 billion in 2002. With the bulk of net cross-border capital flows now coming in this form, it becomes increasingly important for policymakers and market participants to focus on sustaining FDI—and that depends critically on improvements in the investment climate. A healthy operating environment for the corporate sector—including a sound domestic institutional framework—is a necessary condition for profitable investment and the mitigation of risk, and therefore for the attraction of FDI (see chapter 5). It is also required to promote productivity, entrepreneurship, and investment for domestic firms and farms, the sources of 90 percent of developing-country investment and the main drivers of growth. Finally, it is the key determinant of whether domestic capital stays at home or flees abroad.

Growth and poverty reduction depend on prudent management of sovereign financial risks

Financial markets react swiftly to adverse news, making it all the more important to plan carefully to mitigate risk. Fortunately, bond markets in developing countries have moved in recent years toward issues denominated in local currency, although such issues tend to have shorter maturities, at least in the early years of market development. During such a transition, it is all too easy for a sovereign borrower to shift, rather than mitigate, its risk, with currency risks giving way to the rollover risks that occur when domestic debt is linked to a foreign currency (see chapter 3). The fact that the epicenter of most middle-income debt problems in recent years has been the local short-term money and bond markets serves as a graphic reminder of the case for prudent debt management.

Workers' remittances are an increasingly important source of external financing

An under-recognized trend in the external finances of developing countries—especially some of the smallest and poorest—is the steadily growing importance of workers' remittances (see chapter 7). Such flows now rank second in importance only to FDI in the overall external financing of developing countries (see chapter 1). At $80 billion in 2002, remittances were about double the level of official aid–related inflows and showed a remarkably steady growth through the 1990s. The strong U.S. labor market was especially important in fueling the growth of remittances, and the United States is now by far the largest source of remittance flows.

Demographic trends suggest that remittance flows from high-income countries will grow over the medium term, with the demographic dependency ratio falling in poor countries and rising in rich ones. However, heightened security concerns and a softening labor market in the high-income economies will probably check these flows over the next year or two. This prospect highlights the importance of the issues of trade in services and migration.

The international community must help borrowers manage pressures to reduce debt

Intense pressures to pay down external debt have placed many countries under severe stress in recent years, usually with particularly adverse consequences for poor people. There is now a growing consensus that the mechanisms available to cushion these debt pressures are in need of reform.

For low-income economies, significant progress has been made in providing debt relief under the Heavily Indebted Poor Countries Initiative. However, continued weakness in commodity prices, and thus in the export earnings of many poor countries, means that several countries will require additional resources before their debt can be considered sustainable (see chapter 6).

For highly indebted middle income countries, the International Monetary Fund (IMF) has proposed the creation of a sovereign debt restructuring mechanism that would provide an orderly framework for restructuring external sovereign bond debt (see chapter 3).

The proposed framework is intended to be useful not only *after* a sovereign default, but also ahead of such an event, as its existence would make both debtors and creditors act in a more measured fashion, avoiding some of the extreme actions that have complicated recent defaults on sovereign debt.

The discussion of this proposal reminds us that the current set-up has not worked well and that the debt difficulties of middle-income countries are likely to persist in a world of low nominal income growth (see chapter 2).

Policymakers in the industrial countries can help stabilize development financing—

—by improving aid and trade policies—

Although much of the policy and many of the institutional reforms needed to stabilize development financing must come from governments in developing countries, the authorities in the developed world can play an important role. The major economies can support development most directly through coherent aid and trade policies that promote development. The commitments made in advance of the United Nations Conference on Financing for Development in Monterrey in March 2002 promised a modest increase in aid flows. These point to a welcome reversal of the downward trend through most of the 1990s, but their scale is incommensurate with the commitment to reach the Millennium Development Goals by 2015.

The effectiveness of aid can be improved by reallocating funds to poorer countries that have the policies, institutions, and governance that can be expected to reduce poverty. In those same countries, aid is also likely to be more productive if channeled through government institutions, with the close involvement of civil society, rather than through project-oriented institutions with intrusive management by donors.

Most important of all, industrial countries can spur development by reducing agricultural subsidies and trade barriers that discriminate against developing countries' exports. Industrial countries spend more than $300 billion each year in agricultural subsidies, about six times the amount they spend on foreign aid. Unless progress is made on agricultural protection and subsidies, negotiations within the World Trade Organization (WTO) are likely to be stalled, to the detriment of growth and development.

—and by ensuring broader macroeconomic stability

The major economies also play an important role through their macroeconomic policies and performances, which shape the global opportunities open to developing countries (see chapter 2). Developing countries benefit most when the major economies achieve steady, sustainable growth, avoiding booms and busts. Central banks in the major economies have established conditions favorable for the growth of global liquidity. With nominal interest rates within the Organisation for Economic Co-operation and Development (OECD) at their lowest levels in 50 years and real short-term interest rates generally close to zero, the core condition for reversing the flow of capital from developing to developed countries is in place. Through the 1990s, the countries of the OECD made important gains in reducing budget deficits, but much of this progress has been reversed in the past two years. The expectation of large, continuing budget deficits may further reduce developing countries' access to funds, while fiscal stimulus packages, which provided an important near-term boost to growth, have now generally reached their limits of effectiveness.

The widespread debt difficulties of the corporate sector in the United States and Europe were an important feature of the global downturn in 2001, contributing not only to a pronounced, sustained downturn in capital spending, but also to a rise in spreads in high-yield debt markets. Given the large number of investors who are active in both industrial and emerging markets, the rise in spreads on high-yield debt helped lift interest-rate spreads in markets for the external debt of developing countries (see chapter 3). In Japan, corporate-debt woes and their effects on the banking system held back growth throughout the 1990s and added to deflationary pressures throughout the economy.

Japan serves as a graphic example of the costs of delaying necessary corporate adjustments. By contrast, the high-profile corporate bankruptcies in other mature economies—especially the United States—in 2002 can be seen as a mixed blessing. On the one hand, they underlined the severity of the downturn and the magnitudes of the necessary adjustments in corporate spending. On the other, they served to highlight that corporate restructuring is proceeding.

1

Financial Flows to Developing Countries: Recent Trends and Near-Term Prospects

Philip Suttle

NET CAPITAL FLOWS TO DEVELOPING countries were down last year for the second year in a row (see table 1.1 on page 8 and box 1.1 on page 10). In 2002, the sum of net private debt and equity and net official flows was $192 billion, or 3.2 percent of developing countries' nominal gross domestic product (GDP), down from $210 billion in 2001 (3.6 percent of GDP) and $215 billion in 2000 (3.7 percent of GDP).[1] The slide has been a steady one since 1997, when net flows to developing countries peaked at about $325 billion (5.5 percent of GDP).

The decline since 1997 has occurred primarily in net capital flows from the private sector (figure 1.1), particularly in the debt component (both banks and bonds). From the peak years of 1995–96, when net debt inflows from the private sector were about $135 billion per year, they have dropped steadily (figure 1.2), becoming net outflows in 2001 and 2002.

Unprecedented weakness in debt flows

This weakness in the growth of private-sector debt flows is unprecedented in the post-1965 period (figure 1.3). Already strong debt growth to developing countries in the late 1960s exploded in the 1970s, as commercial banks furiously recycled oil surpluses from oil producers to other developing countries (Cline 1995).[2] In the decade of the 1970s, developing-country debt growth posted a compound annual growth rate of 24 percent (or 16 percent in real terms).

The debt crisis of the early 1980s slowed this growth but did not end it. The widespread efforts to

Figure 1.1 Net financial flows to developing countries, 1995–2002

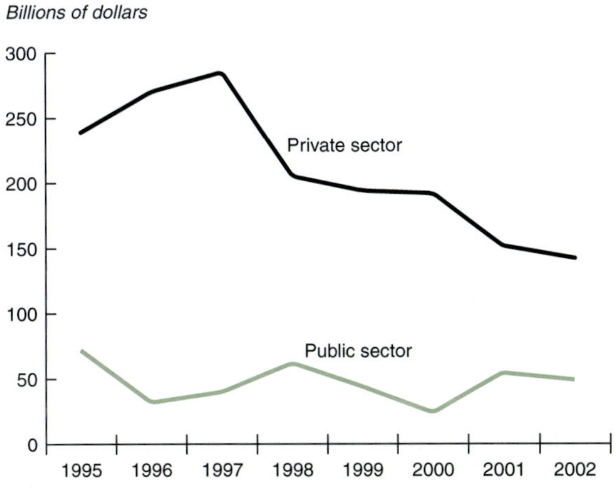

Source: World Bank Debtor Reporting System and staff estimates.

Figure 1.2 Net financial flows to developing countries from the private sector, 1995–2002

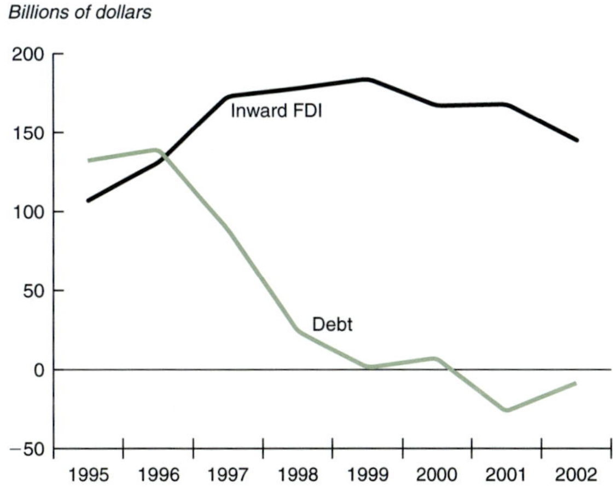

Source: World Bank Debtor Reporting System and staff estimates.

Table 1.1 Net capital flows to developing countries, 1997–2003
(billions of dollars)

	1997	1998	1999	2000	2001	2002e	2003f	For more detail
Current account balance	−91.4	−113.6	−10.7	61.9	27.6	48.3	26.2	→ Chapter 2
as % GDP	−1.5	−2.0	−0.2	1.0	0.5	0.8	0.4	
Financed by:								
Net equity flows	196.4	181.9	194.3	186.7	177.6	152.3	158.0	→ Chapter 4
Net FDI inflows	169.3	174.5	179.3	160.6	171.7	143.0	145.0	Chapter 5
Net portfolio equity inflows	26.7	7.4	15.0	26.0	6.0	9.4	13.0	
Net debt flows	102.1	57.4	13.9	−1.0	3.2	7.2	5.0	
Official creditors	13.0	34.1	13.5	−6.2	28.0	16.2	0.0	→ Chapter 6
World Bank	9.2	8.7	8.8	7.8	7.5	1.5	—	
IMF	3.4	14.1	−2.2	−10.6	19.5	14.5	—	
Others	0.5	11.2	6.9	−3.4	1.0	0.2	—	
Private creditors	89.1	23.3	0.5	5.1	−24.8	−9.0	5.0	→ Chapter 3
Net M-L term debt flows	84.0	87.4	21.9	14.5	−8.6	2.9	—	
Bonds	38.4	39.7	29.6	17.4	10.1	18.6	—	
Banks	43.1	51.4	−5.9	2.6	−11.8	−16.0	—	
Others	2.5	−3.6	−1.8	−5.5	−7.0	−5.5	—	
Net short-term debt flows	5.3	−64.2	−21.4	−9.4	−16.2	−6.1	—	
Balancing item[a]	−153.8	−109.0	−160.1	−192.5	−128.2	−97.8	−81.2	
Change in reserves (− = increase)	−52.9	−16.6	−37.3	−55.1	−80.3	−110.0	−108.0	→ Chapter 1
Memo items:								
Bilateral aid grants (ex technical co-operation grants)	26.7	28.2	29.4	29.6	29.5	32.9	32.0	→ Chapter 6
Net private flows (debt+equity)	285.1	205.2	194.7	191.8	152.8	143.3	163.0	
Net official flows (aid+debt)	39.7	62.3	42.9	23.4	57.5	49.0	32.0	
Workers' remittances	62.7	59.5	64.6	64.5	72.3	80.0	—	→ Chapter 7

Note: e = estimate; f = forecast
a. Combination of errors and omissions and net acquisition of foreign assets (including FDI) by developing countries.

Figure 1.3 Developing countries' total external debt, 1966–2002

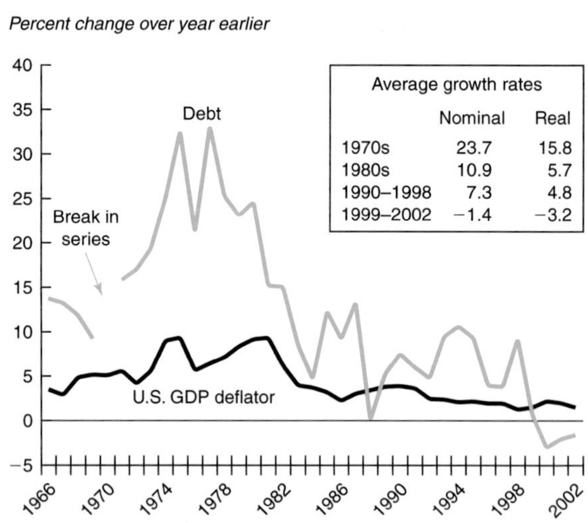

Sources: World Bank Debtor Reporting System and staff estimates; U.S. Commerce Department.

reschedule debt (and add new money) meant that exposures to problem debtors were generally maintained, while net new credits were extended in other parts of the developing world. When market confidence returned in the 1990s in the aftermath of the Brady Plan, real debt grew at a steady pace.

Since the middle of 1998, however, the whole context for development financing has shifted. As borrowers have chosen or been required by their creditors to pay down their debts, the external debt of developing countries has fallen in dollar terms, even as the cost of debt (as measured by OECD interest rates) fell and remained at very low levels.

Rotation from debt to equity

As debt is being repaid to private-sector creditors, net equity inflows to developing countries remain significant, mainly through the route of FDI. Net inward FDI flows did slow in 2002,

Figure 1.4 Developing countries' external debt and FDI stocks, 1980–2000

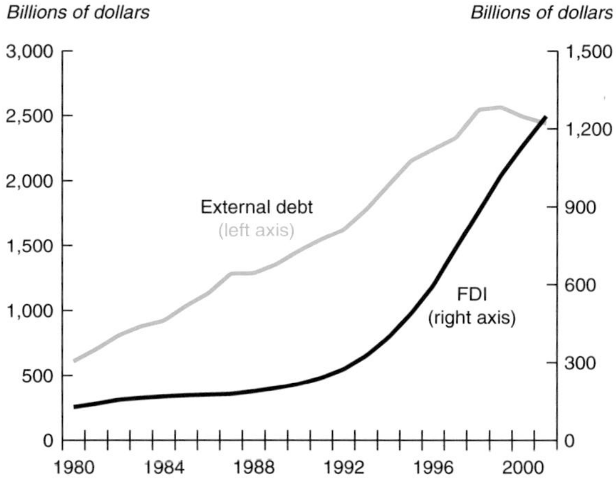

Sources: World Bank Debtor Reporting System and staff estimates; IMF *Balance of Payments Yearbook.*

with most of the slowdown occurring in Latin America. By contrast, flows to China picked up in response to strong growth and optimism following China's accession to the WTO.

The shifting pattern of private flows—debt down, equity up—has had an important implication for the associated stocks of debt (figure 1.4). While the stock of developing-country external debt outstanding from all sources has fallen since 1998, the stock of equity capital owned and controlled by foreigners has risen sharply over the past decade.

The drop in what might be called the external debt-equity ratio, from more than 300 percent at the end of 1997 to less than 200 percent at the end of 2001, has been spread across all regions of the developing world (table 1.2). The relative

Table 1.2 Developing countries' external debt-equity ratios, 1997 and 2001
(percent)

	1997	2001	Ext.liabs. % GDP[a]
East Asia and Pacific	218	134	65.0
Europe and Central Asia	505	293	66.8
Latin America and the Caribbean	284	162	67.7
Middle East and North Africa	394	371	42.5
South Asia	968	613	30.5
Sub-Saharan Africa	515	303	90.6
All developing countries	316	196	61.7

a. Sum of total external debt and FDI liabilities as a percentage of 2001 GDP.
Sources: World Bank Debtor Reporting System and staff estimates; IMF, *Balance of Payments Yearbook.*

dependence on external equity is highest in East Asia and the Pacific, mainly reflecting the influence of China, where the external debt-equity ratio has now fallen below 50 percent—China's external FDI liabilities are double its external debt liabilities.

The total external liabilities, relative to GDP, of the three largest regions of the developing world (East Asia and the Pacific, Europe and Central Asia, and Latin America and the Caribbean) are all remarkably similar at about two-thirds of GDP. The region of Europe and Central Asia has the highest share of debt-based liabilities, reflecting the simple fact that equity ownership in much of this region was off limits to foreign investors until the end of the Cold War, although these countries could and did borrow on international markets. The surge in FDI in the region through the 1990s drove down the external debt-equity ratio sharply, although it remains high relative to East Asia and Latin America, which have been open to FDI much longer.

Much of the rest of this report focuses on why this external debt-equity shift is occurring, what its implications are, and how much further it has to run. Three aspects of the shift are worth noting up front:

- *The shift is partly driven by investor preferences.* Debt investors (both banks and bondholders) have become more wary of holding debt claims on developing countries, whereas nonfinancial corporations have come increasingly to believe that the developing world offers significant growth opportunities both as an export platform and as a source of domestic consumption.
- *The shift is partly driven by the preferences of developing country policymakers.* One very important lesson that many countries drew from the crises of the 1990s was that dependence on external debt financing can lead to sharp, sudden reversals of capital flows. To protect against such reversals, countries have strengthened their precautionary reserve holdings and shifted their liabilities to more stable forms of investment, especially FDI. The latter trend has been especially true of countries in East Asia (Crockett 2002), but it also has allowed Mexico, for example, to absorb the capital market shocks of the last few years much better than it could have done before 1995.

Box 1.1 Sources of information on capital flows

The World Bank's data on flows of capital and other financing to developing countries comes from several sources. Most data on FDI, portfolio equity, and workers' remittances are found in the balance-of-payments data set compiled by the IMF, although there are important exceptions (see box 4.6 and the data annex to chapter 7). Data on debt-related flows come from the Bank's Debtor Reporting System (DRS), which forms the backbone of the data set in volume 2 of *Global Development Finance.*

The DRS has its origins in the Bank's need to monitor the financial position of its borrowers. Since 1951 borrowers have been required to provide statistics, loan by loan, on their external debt and any private debt for which they have issued a guarantee. With the growth of nonguaranteed private borrowing, the Bank expanded the DRS to cover this form of debt, although these data are generally provided in a more aggregated form, not loan by loan.

Three aspects of the DRS are unique:

- *It has a long, continuous history.* As most market participants, official and private, are painfully aware, debt tends to flow in cycles, and the DRS enables analysts to study all the postwar cycles.
- *Its coverage is broad and consistent.* The same methodology is applied to data from 138 countries, large and small. Volume 2 presents a consistent array of data for all countries.
- *The loan-by-loan detail allows analysts to identify important debt characteristics* such as the currency composition of debt, terms of new debt commitments, and amortization and disbursement schedules.

An alternative to the DRS, focusing on the creditor side of the relationship, became popular in the 1980s. No single institution maintains a creditor reporting system, however, although data on banks provided by the Bank for International Settlements can be combined with data from other sources—including the DRS for data on multilateral financial institutions.

The organization that led the development of the creditor-side methodology was the Institute of International Finance (IIF), set up in 1983. Though it lacks its own data sources, the IIF combines those of other institutions (including the World Bank) to present the creditor's perspective on the external debt stocks and capital-account flows of developing countries (IIF 2003). This approach has become something of an industry standard, and the World Bank's own database is now typically analyzed from a creditor's perspective—as it is in this publication. The IMF also provides its estimates of capital flows to developing countries on a creditor basis in its semiannual *World Economic Outlook* (IMF 2002).

The latest World Bank, IIF, and IMF estimates of capital flows to developing countries are presented in the table below.

Differences in the series arise for three reasons:

- *Country coverage.* The World Bank covers 138 countries; the IMF, 125; and the IIF, 29. Note also that the IIF survey is not a subset of the World Bank coverage. The Republic of Korea, for example, is part of the IIF survey but is no longer considered by the World Bank as a developing country.
- *Different concepts.* The World Bank counts net inward FDI, whereas the IIF and IMF count net inflows less net outflows (and are thus smaller).
- *Different reporting systems.* Further discrepancies in the three institutions' measures of net capital flows occur because of differences in reporting systems. In a world of large, unregulated capital flows, measuring capital flows is as much an art as a science.

Estimates of external financing flows to developing countries, 1999–2003
(billions of dollars)

	1999	2000	2001	2002	2003
Current account					
World Bank	−11	62	28	48	26
IMF	−10	67	40	19	1
IIF	30	48	33	52	34
Net equity flows[a]					
World Bank	194	187	178	152	158
IMF	149	145	147	129	132
IIF	164	150	145	102	117
Net private debt (bonds, banks, and other)					
World Bank	0	5	−25	−9	5
IMF	−1	2	−32	1	13
IIF	−16	36	−19	11	21
Net official debt flows					
World Bank	14	−6	28	16	0
IMF	28	18	35	31	34
IIF	12	−3	15	12	10

a. IMF and IIF count net inflows less net outflows.
Sources: World Bank Debtor Reporting System and staff estimates; IMF 2002; IIF 2003.

- *On balance, the shift is a positive development.* For many countries, the fundamental rotation in capital flows is proving to be quite a challenge. For one thing, the current-account balance must move into or at least toward surplus in order to generate the foreign exchange to pay down external debt. Nevertheless, the rotation is best seen as a constructive development because it puts development finance on a stable footing. The problem with overreliance on debt financing for development is that the downside to adverse global developments has to be borne completely by developing countries: they must either pay in full or default. When macroeconomic conditions move against the country, debt markets rightly factor in more risk and thus end up charging more for debt capital.[3] The result is increased strain on the country and a greater likelihood of crisis and default. By contrast, the financing of growth and development through direct equity participation builds shock absorbers into a process that is bound to be somewhat uneven. The benefit of FDI is not just that its returns are "state contingent"—that is, they pay off for the investor when the country does well but absorb some of the hit when the country does badly—but that an adverse shock to the country does not typically produce a sudden rush for the exits. FDI investors generally emphasize that they are committed for the long haul and can absorb and tolerate a certain amount of near-term adversity.

When will it end?

This rotation in the pattern of development finance from private-sector sources has further to run under almost any scenario:

- If the global economy expands robustly in the years ahead, then foreign direct investors are likely to continue to build their holdings in developing countries. In such a scenario, debt investors would probably also return in earnest to developing countries, and the main challenge facing policymakers would be to avoid the excesses of near-term debt growth that have often led to problems in the past.
- If the global economy is weak, then FDI investors are liable to pause, but debt investors are liable to continue, and possibly accelerate, their retrenchment. This scenario is perhaps most plausible in a situation where current geopolitical tensions turn out to be a lot more severe and protracted than currently assumed (see chapter 2).
- If, as the current forecast assumes, the perfomance of the global economy is middling, then both FDI and debt investors will remain cautious. Net FDI inflows are likely to pick up in 2003–04, in line with a modest revival in global fixed investment. Net debt flows will remain subdued, although they should turn positive in 2003. The gains will be led by bond investors, for whom the high yields offered by developing country debt will be relatively attractive. By contrast, net debt repayments to commercial banks are likely to persist, as banks in the Bank for International Settlements (BIS) area remain under pressure, and are generally making strenuous efforts to reduce their risk exposures.

Official flows as buffers

Official funding for developing countries—defined as foreign aid plus debt financing from official sources—fell back in 2002, mainly because the IMF made fewer disbursements. Net official flows to developing countries, which tend to play a buffer role, are thus negatively correlated with net private flows and global growth (Ratha 2000). Indeed, with net private debt flows to developing countries likely to be once more positive in 2003, it is likely that net official flows to developing countries will fall sharply, in line with a diminished need for emergency financing. The other components of official flows are less susceptible to swings than IMF funding (see table 1.1 and chapter 6).

Trends in asset accumulation by developing countries

Although the liability flows of developing countries are important, the evolution of their external financial assets is also significant. In recent years, asset accumulation has picked up strongly and in a remarkably broad-based fashion. When combined with changes in liabilities, the net result is that developing countries overall have become net capital *exporters* to the developed world, running a modest current-account surplus in most years since 1998 (see chapter 2 for a broader discussion of the global flow of funds).

The pick-up in the acquisition of foreign assets by developing countries is evident on three dimensions, the first two of which are captured by the "balancing item" line in table 1.1.

- *An increase in FDI.* Just as globalization is leading companies in high-income countries to invest in the developing world, so many developing-country companies are investing both in high-income countries and in other developing countries. Estimates of such "South-North" or "South-South" investment vary, but it is no doubt substantial (see chapter 4).
- *An increase in private investment in other assets.* This catch-all category is difficult to measure, in part because it includes flows seeking to evade controls and taxes as well as more legitimate outward investment flows from the resident private sector.
- *An increase in official reserves.* The gross official foreign-exchange reserves of developing countries rose by about $110 billion in 2002. In the past four years, the stock of developing countries' reserves has risen by an average of about $70 billion per year to reach about $888 billion at the end of 2002.

The acquisition of substantial foreign assets by individuals, companies, and governments in developing countries has some positive features. Most significant is the opportunity to diversify away from local business cycles and other risks. Maintaining high levels of foreign-exchange reserves gives governments a cushion that can allow them to better ride out shocks in the international system. The high level of East Asian foreign-exchange reserves built up in the aftermath of the Asian financial crisis in 1997–98 helps explain why these countries were able to avoid some of the stresses and strains suffered by many Latin American countries during the most recent global downturn.

There are, however, a number of more troubling aspects to the acquisition of substantial foreign assets by the private and public sectors in developing countries.

- *Developing countries need to mobilize their savings.* Leakage of capital abroad diminishes the savings available to fund economic activity. While substantial investment abroad by the private sector is not necessarily a sign of problems, it *can* be a signal of domestic investors' distrust in their country's policies and institutions, which potential foreign investors are likely to see as a negative signal. High external reserve holdings also come with a significant interest-rate carrying cost. Most countries invest their foreign-exchange reserves in relatively safe, short-term assets, such as U.S. Treasury bills. The yields on such instruments are currently very low—well below the interest rates that developing countries pay on their debt.
- *High foreign-exchange reserves imply a fear of floating.* The move from pegged exchange rates to floating exchange rates has been generally greeted as a move to greater flexibility that gives developing countries more breathing room. While a floating-rate system does offer many advantages, especially as it avoids countries having to defend arbitrary exchange rates against speculative attack (often through extreme hikes in domestic interest rates), the move to a floating-exchange-rate regime has been accompanied by what might be called an increased precautionary demand for foreign-exchange reserves. Current holdings of foreign-exchange reserves by developing countries are generally well above benchmarks often used as guides to assess the adequacy of reserves (box 1.2). Calvo and Reinhart (2000) have highlighted that the current exchange-rate policies of many developing (and developed) countries is far from a free float in the textbook sense. For countries in East and South Asia, policy has been geared toward avoiding exchange rate appreciation through the purchase of substantial reserves.[4]
- *Accumulation of assets is a sign of global disequilibrium.* The rapid accumulation of external assets can be viewed as a stock-adjustment process. For many developing countries in Asia, for example, the determination to insulate themselves from the shocks of 1997–98 has raised the precautionary demand for official

Box 1.2 Developing countries' reserves in context

Two common benchmarks are used to assess the adequacy of foreign-exchange reserves. Applied to the most recent data on reserve holdings, these benchmarks produce the following results:

Short-term debt. For all developing countries, net foreign-exchange reserves are currently about two-and-a-half times short-term external debt. The distribution varies considerably across regions, however. Reserves are very high in East and South Asia as a consequence of the traumatic financial events in Asia in the late 1990s. Latin America's net foreign-exchange reserves are below its short-term debt.

Imports. For all developing countries, net foreign-exchange reserves are equivalent to about six months of merchandise imports. In all six regions, reserves are above the commonly assumed "safe" level of three months of imports—they are especially high in Asia and the Middle East and North Africa.

Ratio of net foreign-exchange reserves to short-term debt in World Bank regions

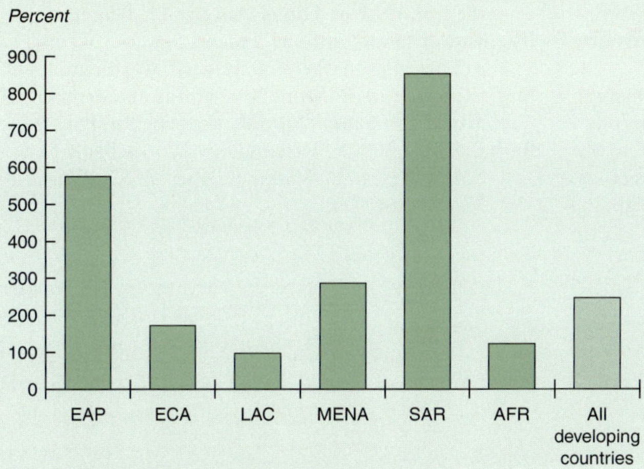

Note: EAP = East Asia and Pacific, ECA = Europe and Central Asia, LAC = Latin America and the Caribbean, MENA = Middle East and North Africa, SAR = South Asia, and AFR = Sub-Saharan Africa.
Sources: World Bank Debtor Reporting System and staff estimates; IMF International Financial Statistics.

Ratio of merchandise imports to foreign-exchange reserves in World Bank regions

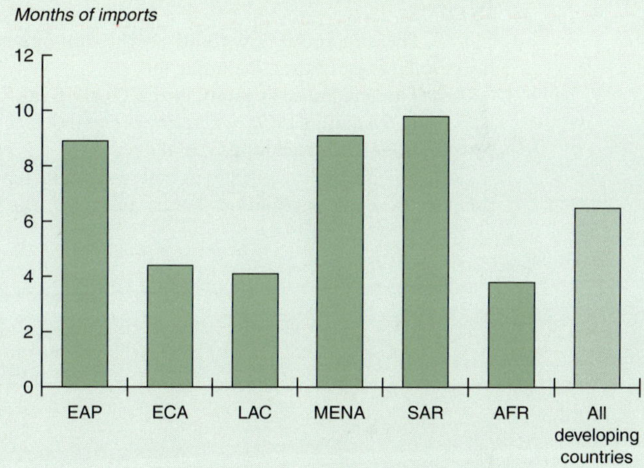

Note: EAP = East Asia and Pacific, ECA = Europe and Central Asia, LAC = Latin America and the Caribbean, MENA = Middle East and North Africa, SAR = South Asia, and AFR = Sub-Saharan Africa.
Sources: World Bank staff estimates; IMF International Financial Statistics.

reserves. At some point, however, this process will be complete and give way to pressures for the real exchange rate to rise. In the meantime, there is also a risk of overinvestment in sectors, such as the tradable goods sector in East and South Asia, that are currently benefitting from official policies to hold down the real exchange rate.

Learning to live with less debt

The pattern of overall capital flows to developing countries did not change much in 2002 over 2001. Developing countries, in aggregate, were net lenders to developed countries. They remained heavily reliant on FDI to finance both their debt repayments to private creditors and their acquisition of foreign assets, both private and official.

This relative stability is neither inevitable nor necessarily desirable, however. Key flows are adjusting to shifts in conditions that occurred in the later 1990s. The stock adjustments expressed by the changes in flows—notably the paydown of private-sector debt—continued apace in 2002, but they will have a finite life. When they are completed, capital flows will naturally move to a different pattern, probably one that again favors higher debt flows relative to equity flows. This shift is likely to begin to happen in 2003, with net debt flows to the developing world from private sources turning modestly positive once again. These shifts will not be dramatic, however, and the overall pattern of external financing for developing countries is projected to be little changed from 2002 (see table 1.1).

Meanwhile, a key role of policy will be to ensure that current shifts involve the least pain possible, and that the pattern of flows that emerges from the process of stock adjustment is one that puts development finance on a more stable footing than it was in the volatile years of the 1990s.

Notes

1. These financial flow totals are the sum of net private flows and official flows, including aid.

2. There is a discontinuity in the World Bank's Debtor Reporting System in 1970, when it was expanded to include private, nonguaranteed long-term debt.

3. For all the turbulence in emerging debt markets in the 1990s, emerging-market bonds provided the highest absolute return of any major asset class (including equities) from December 1990 to August 2002. See figure 4.18.

4. At the end of 2002, East and South Asian reserves, combined, accounted for 50 percent of total developing-country reserves, up from 45 percent at the end of 2000. See the Statistical Appendix, table A.50.

References

Calvo, G., and C. Reinhart. 2000. "Fear of Floating." NBER Working Paper 7993. National Bureau of Economic Research, Cambridge, Mass.

Cline, William R. 1995. *International Debt Reexamined*. Washington, D.C.: Institute of International Economics.

Crockett, Andrew. 2002. "Capital Flows in East Asia Since the Crisis." Address to the meeting of the deputies of the ASEAN Plus Three, October 11, Beijing.

IIF (Institute of International Finance). 2003. "Capital Flows to Emerging Market Economies." Washington, D.C.

IMF (International Monetary Fund). September 2002. *World Economic Outlook*. Washington, D.C.

Ratha, Dilip. 2000. "Demand for World Bank Lending." Policy Research Working Paper 2652. World Bank, Washington, D.C.

2

Battling the Global Headwinds of Financial Imbalances and Uncertain Geopolitics

Hans Timmer, Mick Riordan, and Robert Keyfitz

FINANCIAL IMBALANCES CONTINUE TO RE-strain the rebound in the global economy. Some of these difficulties, such as the burgeoning of nonperforming loans in Japan, have persisted for more than a decade. Others surfaced when equity bubbles deflated at the onset of the recent global slowdown, funds for many high-tech companies dried up, and financial institutions in Europe and the United States became more cautious in the wake of major defaults. Although debt overhangs have been eased through bankruptcy proceedings and improved profit rates for some, for others debt-service problems have become more severe because of low nominal growth in GDP combined with high spreads. New trouble spots have emerged as well. Against an unfavorable external environment, the debt dynamics of several governments in Latin America have become difficult.

The increasing likelihood of a military conflict in Iraq has cast its shadow over the economic and political landscape in recent months. With oil prices rising and investors waiting uneasily for events to unfold, the recovery in the global economy has likely been delayed further, while downside risks have risen, especially for countries in and around the Middle East. The baseline projections assume a quick resolution to current tensions regarding Iraq, highlighted by the quarterly pattern of the oil price assumed: $32 per barrel in the first quarter of 2003, and $29, $23, and $22 per barrel in the quarters following.

Macroeconomic stimulus measures undertaken in the high-income countries have served to cushion the global economy from an even sharper slowdown, but they have also contributed to further imbalances. By allowing automatic stabilizers to work, adding to discretionary spending, and cutting taxes, the governments of the countries of OECD saw their general balances deteriorate by an average 2.9 percent of GDP between 2000 and 2002.

The U.S. current-account deficit is now approaching 5 percent of GDP, an unprecedented level for this stage of the business cycle. At the same time, financing the deficit has become less straightforward, given the substantial weakening of the dollar over the latter months of 2002.

In this challenging financial environment, the global rebound is lacking sectoral and geographical balance. Global growth is currently projected to accelerate to 2.3 percent in 2003 from 1.7 percent in 2002 (table 2.1), but this would be very anemic for the second year of what should by now be a full-fledged, synchronized global upswing. In many parts of the world, a recovery in fixed investment is turning out to be exceptionally slow.

A worrisome characteristic of the current economic environment is that macroeconomic policies may be running up against their limits and, on balance, those policies in 2003–04 are more likely to be less stimulative—or restrictive—rather than expansive. Upside surprises are plausible, too. As the excesses of the boom of the 1990s are gradually worked out and financial markets stabilize, the fundamentals of the world economy should emerge in fairly sound condition, supporting global growth at rates nearing longer-term trends by 2004–05. Moreover, world growth potential has likely increased due to intensifying trade and financial integration, greater investment in human capital, wider availability of productivity-enhancing technology, and stronger institutional capacity throughout the world.

Table 2.1 The global outlook in summary

(percentage change from previous year, except interest rates and oil price)

						GEP 2003 forecasts	
	2001	2002e	2003f	2004f	2005f	2003	2004
Global conditions							
World trade volume	0.4	3.0	6.2	8.1	8.1	7.0	8.0
Consumer prices							
G-7 countries[a, b]	1.5	1.0	1.4	1.3	1.3	1.2	1.5
United States	2.8	1.6	2.5	2.3	2.1	2.1	2.3
Commodity prices ($ terms)							
Non-oil commodities	−9.1	5.1	8.2	2.3	1.7	5.8	4.4
Oil price (OPEC average)	24.4	24.9	26.0	21.0	20.0	23.0	20.0
Oil price (percent change)	−13.7	2.4	4.3	−19.2	−4.8	−8.0	−13.0
Manufactures unit export value[c]	−2.9	−1.4	5.6	−0.1	1.2	3.0	2.2
Interest rates							
$, 6-month (percent)	3.5	1.8	1.7	3.2	4.2	1.5	3.1
€, 6-month (percent)	4.2	3.3	2.4	2.3	3.1	3.2	3.8
Real GDP growth[d]							
World	**1.2**	**1.7**	**2.3**	**3.2**	**3.1**	**2.5**	**3.1**
Memo item: World (PPP weights)[e]	2.2	2.8	3.2	4.1	4.0	3.4	4.0
High income	**0.8**	**1.4**	**1.9**	**2.9**	**2.6**	**2.1**	**2.7**
OECD countries[f]	0.9	1.4	1.8	2.8	2.6	2.1	2.6
Euro Area	1.5	0.8	1.4	2.6	2.6	1.8	2.6
Japan	0.3	−0.3	0.6	1.6	1.4	0.8	1.3
United States	0.3	2.4	2.5	3.5	3.0	2.6	3.1
Non-OECD countries	−1.1	2.2	3.0	4.3	4.5	3.7	5.3
Developing countries	**2.8**	**3.1**	**4.0**	**4.7**	**4.8**	**3.9**	**4.7**
East Asia and Pacific[f]	5.5	6.7	6.4	6.6	5.9	6.1	6.4
Europe and Central Asia	2.3	4.1	3.7	3.7	4.1	3.4	3.6
Transition Countries	4.5	3.6	3.6	3.5	3.9	3.3	3.5
Latin America and the Caribbean	0.3	−0.9	1.7	3.8	4.5	1.8	3.7
excluding Argentina	1.1	0.8	1.6	3.7	4.7	1.9	3.6
Middle East and North Africa	3.2	2.6	3.7	3.9	3.7	3.5	3.7
Oil exporters	2.2	2.3	3.7	3.6	3.4	3.7	3.6
Diversified economies	4.1	2.5	3.1	4.2	4.2	2.7	3.6
South Asia	4.3	4.9	5.3	5.2	5.3	5.4	5.8
Sub-Saharan Africa	3.2	2.6	3.0	3.6	3.7	3.2	3.9
Memorandum items							
Developing countries							
excluding transition countries	2.6	3.1	4.1	5.0	5.0	4.0	4.9
excluding China and India	1.7	1.7	2.9	3.9	4.3	2.8	3.8

Note: PPP = purchasing power parity; GEP 2003 = *Global Economic Prospects and the Developing Countries,* World Bank, January 2003; *e* = estimate; *f* = forecast.

a. Canada, France, Germany, Italy, Japan, the United Kingdom, and the United States.

b. In local currency, aggregated using 1995 GDP weights.

c. Unit value index of manufactured exports from major economies, expressed in U.S. dollars.

d. GDP in 1995 constant dollars; 1995 prices and market exchange rates.

e. GDP measured at 1995 PPP weights.

f. Now excludes the Republic of Korea, which has been reclassified as high-income OECD.

Source: World Bank Development Prospects Group, March 2003.

Since the early 1980s, inflation has gradually been reduced in the high-income countries, while developing countries experienced a similar trend during the 1990s. Now, double-digit inflation has become an exception, and several countries are experiencing deflationary conditions. Strict and increasingly independent monetary policy, fiscal restraint, and labor-market reforms were key policies that helped to reduce inflation. A surge in innovation and increased global competition further reinforced the trend. On balance, this has been a beneficial development, as it helped foster a more stable macroeconomic environment while increasing the flexibility of relative prices and real wages. For example, sharp exchange rate devaluations no longer lead automatically to inflationary spirals, but rather to adjustments in relative prices, making possible a quick economic rebound in the wake of crises.

However, the trend toward deflation poses new challenges. Most important, debt dynamics can easily become destabilized in a deflationary environment. Against this background, monetary authorities should focus as much, if not more now, on avoiding the lower boundaries rather than the upper limits of the forward-looking inflation targets when setting policy.

A hesitant recovery in the high-income countries

The recovery among the industrial countries, which commenced in late 2001 in the United States, faltered in mid-2002 (figure 2.1). Quarterly real GDP growth in the major economies slowed from 2 percent in the first half of 2002 to just 1 percent in the fourth quarter.

The early rebound was especially evident in a strong revival of industrial production. On the demand side, a key ingredient to the turn in industrial production was the end of the process of inventory liquidation, which had severely weakened output in 2001. The boost from inventories was limited, however, especially as the underlying weakness of final demand growth in the industrial countries made producers leery of actually rebuilding inventories.

Figure 2.1 Industrial production in the Euro Area, Japan, and the United States, 2000–2002

Percentage change, 3-month/3-month, seasonally adjusted annual rate

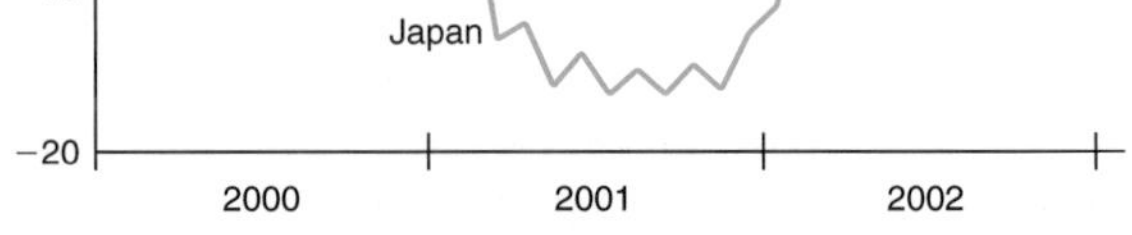

Sources: National agencies; Eurostat.

Central to this weakness in final demand growth is that the rebound in the growth of business investment from its slump in 2000–01 came more slowly and less forcefully than is usual. The debt-financed capital spending extremes of the boom years have left many companies across the industrial world with the need to scale back on spending for capital equipment. In some cases, even severe corporate retrenchment has not been sufficient, and 2002 was a year of continued high-profile corporate restructurings and bankruptcies.

During this process, growth in the industrial economies has been sustained by a sizeable stimulus from macroeconomic policies, which has, in turn, provided an important stimulus to certain components of demand, especially consumer spending and housing investment in many English-speaking economies (led by the United States). Not only has the degree of stimulus provided by macroeconomic policies likely passed its peak, but also the reliance on strong growth in U.S. consumer demand prefigures the emergence of new imbalances, as illustrated by the recent acceleration in U.S. household debt growth and the widening of the U.S. current-account deficit.

Against this background, expectations about the pace of the economic recovery in the major industrial economies are grounded in the extent of the corporate-sector adjustment. Precisely because this is a bumpy path, made more difficult by the financial market volatility and geopolitical uncertainties evident over recent months, the recovery in the major OECD blocs is likely to remain quite uneven through the first half of 2003 (table 2.2).

The pace of GDP growth is expected to ease in the United States and Japan from the second half of 2002, while the Euro Area is projected to experience little change in its recent sluggish growth.

Table 2.2 Real GDP growth in the major economies, 2001–2003

(percentage change over previous period at an annual rate)

	2001		2002		2003	
	H1	H2	H1	H2	H1f	H2f
OECD	0.5	−0.5	1.6	2.6	1.0	3.0
Euro Area	1.7	0.1	0.9	1.3	1.2	1.9
Japan	1.0	−3.9	1.0	3.3	0.3	1.2
United States	−0.4	0.1	3.5	2.7	2.2	3.1

Note: H = half, *f* = forecast.
Source: World Bank staff projections.

Growth is expected to accelerate going into the second half of the year and into 2004, however, as more progress is made to mend corporate balance sheets, and global monetary conditions remain very accommodative.

Tracking corporate-sector adjustment

The 1990s ended with a perception of health and performance in the corporate sector that was at the opposite extreme of the end of the 1980s. Then, the corporate models of Japan and Germany were held up as ideals to follow, while the corporate sector of the United States was widely seen as having fallen behind. Ten years on, however, it was the U.S. model that was viewed as best practice, especially as the spread of information technology through the economy accelerated the growth of productivity throughout the economy. Meanwhile, many of Japan's companies remained mired in the banking and debt difficulties created during what, in retrospect, came to be seen as a bubble period in the second half of the 1980s, a time when Europe's companies were held back in their own countries by rigid labor markets and inflexible distribution channels.

Two developments followed. First, capital flows to the U.S. corporate sector surged in the late 1990s, especially after the East Asian and Russian crises, producing a sharp drop in the effective cost of capital in the U.S. corporate sector, especially in (but not limited to) information technology. Second, companies outside the United States increasingly moved to follow or emulate their U.S. counterparts, either by taking outsized bets on growth in their own economies (this was especially true of European telecommunications companies), or by undertaking aggressive acquisition and expansion strategies in the United States itself (thereby helping to further fuel the U.S. equity-market surge).

When global equity markets moved down from the middle of 2000, the effect was profound on businesses across the major economies, not just in the United States. As asset prices fell, it became increasingly difficult for companies to finance capital spending at levels in excess of profits, especially since such financing was entirely dependent on debt issuance. The resultant need to cut capital spending and employment levels created something of a vicious circle, as the economic downturn and growing caution by consumers undermined profits, thus widening the corporate sector's financing gap.

Figure 2.2 U.S. business debt, 1980–2002

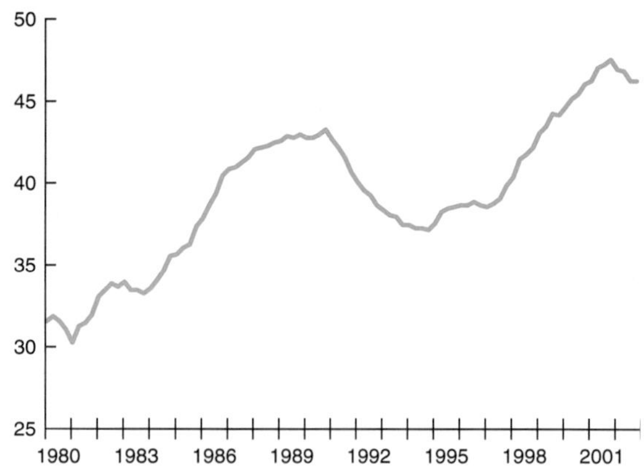

Source: U.S. Federal Reserve.

While these developments are easiest to document in the United States, given comprehensive macro-level data on the corporate sector, it is striking how widespread corporate-sector debt difficulties became in 2001–02. Business debt in the United States skyrocketed by some 25 percentage points of GDP between 1999 and 2002, presenting a formidable overhang to be addressed against a background of sluggish revenue flow (figure 2.2). Globally, telecommunications firms have suffered the consequences of building substantial excess capacity or investing in technologies not yet appropriate for the current market (such as G-3 licenses in Europe). High-tech firms and airlines have faced a collapse in demand, while financial institutions have been weakened by major corporate and sovereign defaults. And persistent weakness in construction and trades in Japan and Germany have saddled banks with nonperforming loans as business insolvencies have escalated.

The result has been a subdued private sector, with balance-sheet adjustments across the rich countries entailing a substantial contraction in capital expenditure, normally the force underpinning movement from early recovery to economic expansion. Business investment in the United States has declined at a faster rate than during the recession of the early 1990s, dropping by a cumulative 12 percent since 2000 highs, while adverse effects on employment have been quite similar (figure 2.3). The rate of unemployment has not risen to the highs

Figure 2.3 U.S. business investment and change in nonfarm payrolls, 1972–2002

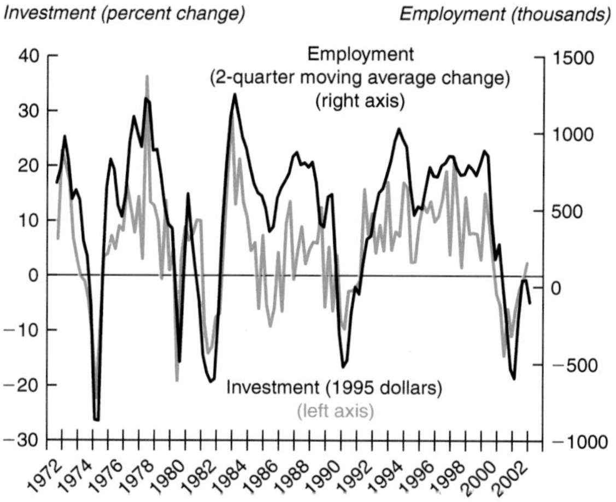

Sources: U.S. Commerce Department and Bureau of Labor Statistics.

Figure 2.4 U.S. corporate profits and the financing gap, 1989–2002

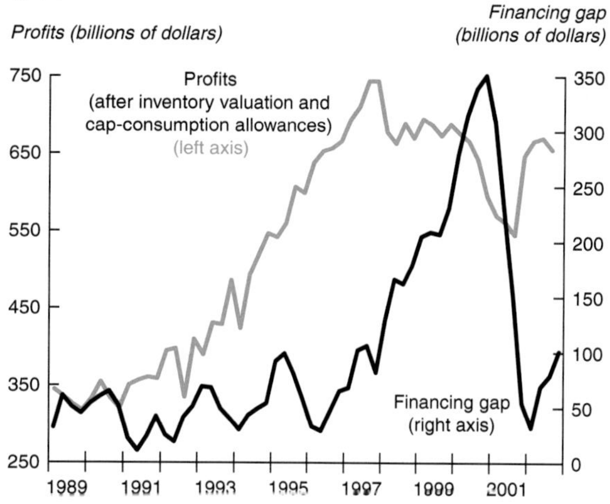

Note: Financing gap denotes capital spending less adjusted profits.
Sources: U.S. Commerce Department and Federal Reserve Board.

seen during the 1990s downturn (some 7.8 percent), due in large measure to slowing growth in the labor force. Japanese private investment has declined more than 10 percent since recent peaks, while the rate of unemployment has risen to a record 5.5 percent. And although European capital spending has contracted by a more moderate 5 percent, employment has borne a larger share of the burden, rising to 10.3 percent in Germany and to 9 percent of the labor force in France and Italy.

On an encouraging note, however, there is some evidence that corporate financial imbalances are being rectified. In the United States, corporate profits staged a recovery through 2002 and were up by 20 percent in the third quarter over a year earlier. A reacceleration in productivity growth and consequent reductions in unit labor costs have contributed, as have lower interest rates on debt. The nonfinancial corporate sector's financing gap (the difference between adjusted income and capital outlays) has narrowed substantially from the late 1990s, a signal that adjustment measures are indeed having positive financial effects (figure 2.4). Moreover, market perceptions of this progress are being reflected in narrowing spreads for the broader high-yield asset class and for the telecommunications sector in particular—which saw a drop of 1,000 basis points over the period since June 2002 (figure 2.5).

Improving signs of corporate profitability and diminished financial strains are not limited to the

Figure 2.5 Benchmark spreads for U.S. high-yield bonds, 1997–2002

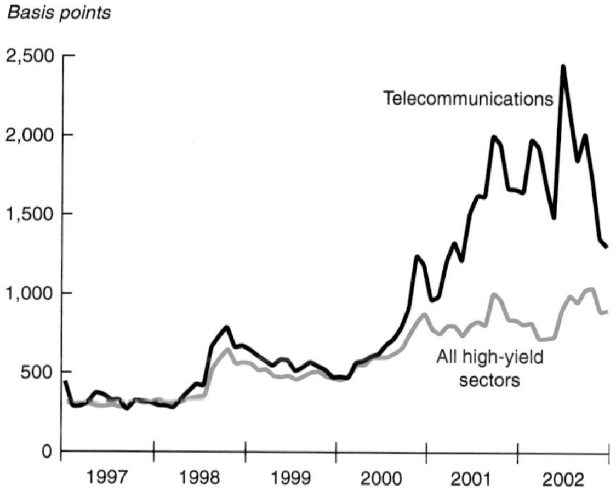

Source: Bloomberg.

United States. In Japan, profit growth has recently resumed following massive decline in 2001 (figure 2.6). The revival in profits in the Japanese economy, however, has been concentrated in the major manufacturing (and export) sectors. A return to profitability is not anticipated for industries and firms serving the domestic market, where consumer spending has been volatile and labor market conditions deteriorating. Banks continue to write off bad loans and, consequently, rack up sizeable losses.

In Europe, corporate profits have yet to turn the corner, however. German company surpluses

Figure 2.6 Corporate profits in Japan and the United States

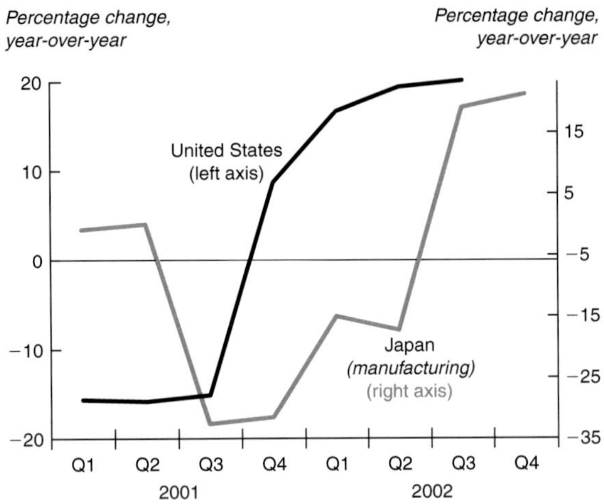

Note: The United States uses the inventory valuation and capital consumption adjusted national accounts based measure.
Sources: U.S. Department of Commerce; Japan ESRI.

Figure 2.7 Federal Reserve (Fed) and European Central Bank (ECB) target rates, 2000–2003

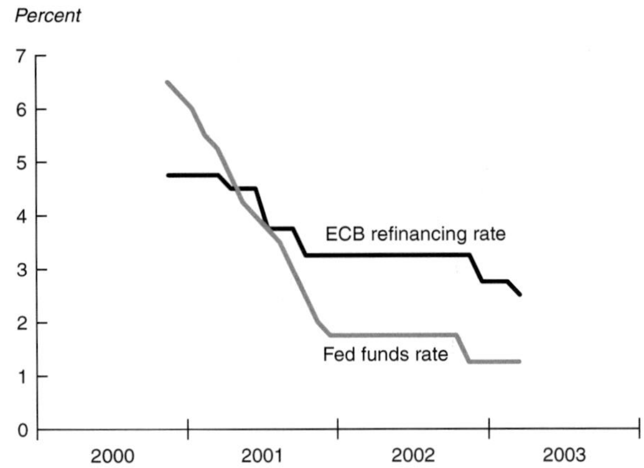

Sources: Federal Reserve; ECB.

dropped from a gain of 5 percent during 2001, to a decline of almost 4 percent in the first three quarters of 2002. Performance in France has been similar, with profit growth falling from 0.7 percent in 2001 to a decline of 3.5 percent in the first three quarters of 2002. The brightest recent signs have come in corporate debt markets, where the pace of debt downgrades has slowed and yield spreads have narrowed.

Although these generally positive signals provide some support to the view that the worst is behind the corporate sector in the industrial countries, the renewed weakening in recent months in global equity markets (although not high-yield fixed-income markets) is a reminder of both the fragility of the current situation, as well as the major adjustments still ahead.

Supportive monetary and fiscal policies

Monetary and fiscal policies were quite supportive over the course of 2001–02, limiting the downturn during 2001 and providing an important impetus to growth during the early stages of recovery.

With the effects of monetary policy expected to materialize with some lag, the degree of monetary stimulus now in the pipeline is considerable:

- The Federal Reserve's aggressive 525-basis-point reduction in target interest rates between late 2000 and late 2002 helped to underpin spending on consumer durables, while triggering large-scale mortgage refinancings that supplemented consumers' disposable incomes (figure 2.7).
- Despite having no latitude to trim short-term interest rates, the Bank of Japan has been more aggressive in expanding base money in recent months, which has helped flatten the yield curve. Unfortunately, bank credit to the private sector has continued to contract due to severe structural problems in the banking sector that stifle intermediation.
- The European Central Bank retained a cautious policy stance for much of 2002, which reflected its concerns over inflation. It too eased in December 2002, and again in March 2003, as data underlined the persistent sluggishness of economic activity in the Euro Area.

Looking ahead, the Federal Reserve has little leeway for additional interest rate reductions, and will most likely keep interest rates on hold for the rest of 2003 if growth, as expected, picks up gradually. In contrast, the European Central Bank has more room to ease and is likely to follow market expectations and possibly trim rates slightly further in the first half of 2003. The Bank of Japan is anticipated to step up its already aggressive approach to add liquidity.

Fiscal policies in the OECD shifted toward an expansionary stance in 2001, with both U.S. and European fiscal deficits widening substantially. In part this was due to the operation of automatic stabilizers. In the United States, there were also tax cuts and a sustained rise in government spending on homeland security and defense in the wake of September 11 (figure 2.8). An additional stimulus has more recently been proposed by the administration, so fiscal policy is likely to remain expansionary in the United States in 2003, especially with stepped-up spending on possible military action in Iraq.

Fiscal stimulus has already raised budget deficits significantly in many developed and developing countries around the world. These entail net dissaving and accumulation of financial liabilities by public sectors that eventually spill over to other aspects of the macroeconomic environment and begin to crowd out private-sector activity. Even if deficits are not quickly reversed, the marginal contribution of stimulus to growth will decline. Indeed, it may even turn negative on the fiscal front (box 2.1).

Figure 2.8 U.S. and German fiscal balances, 1999–2003

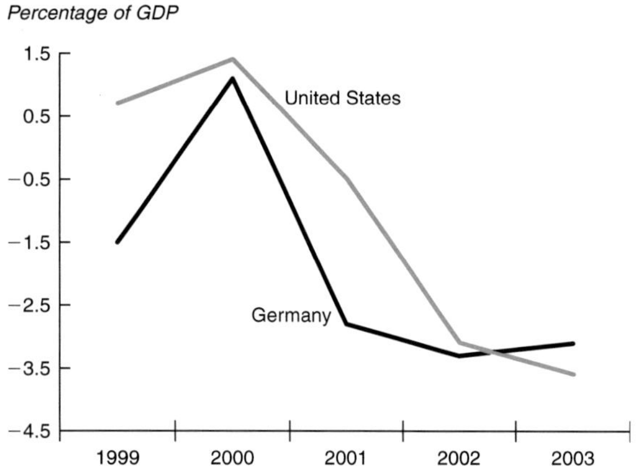

Source: OECD.

These constraints are already evident in Europe and Japan. In the Euro Area, the Growth and Stability Pact is now constraining fiscal spending, partly because of a failure by members to achieve

Box 2.1 Limits to fiscal stimulus

Average fiscal deficits in the OECD countries deteriorated by 2.9 percent of aggregate GDP between 2000 and 2002, reflecting a 1.5 percentage point of GDP increase in expenditure and 1.4 percentage point of GDP drop in revenue. Model simulations suggest that the impact on GDP was of the same order of magnitude. Indirect effects on private sector spending roughly compensate for the leakage of government spending into imports and the absorption of tax cuts into private savings. Thus fiscal policy may well have averted a sharper slowdown in the short run, but how effective is it as an engine of growth for the medium term?

Fiscal stimulus is unlikely to maintain its positive contribution to growth in the medium term, however. Two factors make fiscal stimulus a poor medium-run engine of growth:

- Even when deficits are kept at high levels, government's *direct contribution to demand growth drops.* To maintain a constant contribution to growth, the deficit has to deteriorate further each year. Instead of deterioration, there are strong pressures (economic, political, and, in some U.S. states and the European Monetary Union, statutory or normative) for more balanced fiscal positions. Under these circumstances, fiscal deficits are best used as a smoothing factor over the business cycle, but not a medium-term engine of growth.
- The positive short-run effects of fiscal stimulus on GDP tend to reverse in the medium run, when higher interest rates start to curb private expenditure and increasing indebtedness discourages foreign investors. The short-run and medium-run effects of a one-time fiscal injection tend to cancel each other out, leaving no impact in the longer term.

A fortiori these arguments apply to developing countries. Financial markets tend to punish fiscal mismanagement in developing countries quickly, making the crowding-out effects larger and more immediate and even forcing many governments into pro-cyclical fiscal policies. Moreover, governments in developing countries generally possess more limited tools and capacities than governments in rich countries. On average, government spending as a percentage of GDP in developing countries is roughly half of the corresponding share in high-income countries, making a substantial growth-stimulus program more complicated.

a more cyclically balanced fiscal stance during the late 1990s. In Japan, government debt has approached a dangerous level after an extended period of fiscal deficits of 6–7 percent of GDP, even with interest rates close to zero. According to OECD estimates, stabilizing gross debt at the relatively high level of 180 percent of GDP will require maintaining a fiscal surplus of 1.25 percent of GDP, nearly 8 percentage points higher than at present.

Rising household debt in the United States

As evidence accumulates that the corporate debt overhang is being gradually reduced, new imbalances are emerging. For example, household debt in the United States has risen to a record 320 percent of GDP as of the end of 2002, a rise of 50 percentage points of GDP since 1998 (figure 2.9). Similar trends, but of lesser magnitude, have emerged in other English-speaking countries of the OECD.

The ballooning of U.S. consumer debt primarily reflects substantial additions to household mortgage debt (some $1.5 trillion since the first quarter of 2000). In addition to financing a significant rise in the housing stock, this net new borrowing has allowed households to cash in some of the equity in their (rising) housing wealth, thus slowing the rise in personal saving rates that resulted from the collapse of household equity wealth.[1]

Figure 2.9 U.S. household debt, 1980–2002

Sources: Federal Reserve; U.S. Commerce Department.

In the aggregate balance sheet of U.S. consumers, the buildup of personal debt was overshadowed by substantial equity gains up to 2000. More recently, the appreciation of real-estate holdings has helped to lift the value of household assets. But over recent months, equity markets have remained weak, further undermining household wealth. The net effect of these asset changes over 2002 has been a decline of $1.1 trillion—a $2.2 trillion decline in equity valuation set against $1.1 trillion real-estate appreciation. Since its recent peak during the first quarter of 2000, U.S. household net financial worth has dropped by some $7.8 trillion, composed of a $6 trillion decline in the value of financial assets and a $1.8 trillion rise in liabilities. When the appreciation in the value of household tangible assets is included, this net worth decline is reduced to $4.2 trillion, or a 10 percent decline from its peak in 2000.

Although the U.S. consumer has been an impressive bulwark against global weakness, these recent developments in the household balance sheet and the labor market suggest that, in the near future, the growth contribution from this source is also likely to be more subdued. While low interest rates may allow consumers to continue to carry relatively high levels of mortgage debt, the appetite of borrowers to take on more debt, and of lenders to extend more, shows signs of fading. Notably, household delinquency rates on higher-risk instruments (so-called subprime lending) are on the rise. To date, household income growth has held up remarkably well, but the likelihood of ongoing corporate retrenchment is liable to restrain growth in labor income. Moreover, readings on consumer confidence, which capture many of these forces in a single indicator, have recently dropped sharply to levels not seen since the early 1990s.

Although less burdened than U.S. households by the legacy of debt, consumers in Japan and Europe have been adversely affected by a substantial deterioration in labor market conditions. As a result, strength in spending earlier in 2002 is now giving way to renewed declines. Particularly in Europe, consumption spending indicators were very weak in the fourth quarter of 2002.

A critical and persistent imbalance for the world economy is the large U.S. current-account

Figure 2.10 U.S. private- and public-sector financial balances and the current account, 1999–2002

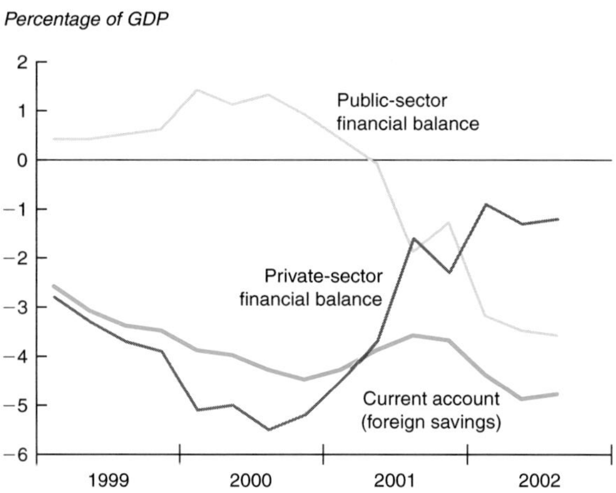

Source: Federal Reserve.

deficit. This international counterpart to earlier household and corporate exuberance has not diminished during the recent period of sluggish growth, as would normally happen in a U.S. cyclical downturn, but instead has widened to nearly 5 percent of GDP, as public-sector deficits have risen sharply.

The private-sector financial balance (gross saving less gross investment) improved as a result of the adjustments in the corporate sector noted above and the recent rise in household saving rates (figure 2.10). However, these improvements have been more than offset by the sharp swing in general government financial balance, from a surplus of 1.3 percent of GDP as recently as the third quarter of 2000 to a deficit of 3.6 percent of GDP by the third quarter of 2002. Except for World War II, this swing in the public sector's financial position is the most rapid on record. That it was produced by the working of normal cyclical elasticities and discretionary easing measures underlines the role of the boom and bust in equity prices in the U.S. government's finances (primarily through swings in the ratio of tax revenue to GDP) and in those of the private sector.

Under present economic and fiscal assumptions, the U.S. current-account deficit is projected to remain above $500 billion over the next three years, over which time foreigners will acquire more than $1.5 trillion of U.S. assets. How this imbalance, with its large global repercussions (the United States absorbs some 8–9 percent of the world's savings annually), develops over the coming years is a key issue in the outlook, not least because it raises the possibility of a significant further downward move in the dollar (as occurred in the second half of the 1980s). This issue is addressed in more detail in the last part of this chapter.

The outlook for growth in high-income countries in 2003 and beyond

Sustainable growth based on a resumption of investment spending in the high-income economies has been slow to materialize. The basic premise of the forecast, however, is that the pieces are now in place for growth to inch up over the next couple of years. There are already signs that the worst may be over on capital spending. For the OECD countries overall, quarterly statistics show a gradual return to positive growth in investment (figure 2.11). The year 2003 is likely to be one in which the pace of growth accelerates progressively as capacity use and profit rates rise and as some of the more immediate uncertainties weighing on consumers and investors, notably the issue of war in Iraq, are resolved.

The threat of a military conflict in Iraq is already acting to temper growth in the first half of 2003, as oil prices spiked by almost $15 per barrel

Figure 2.11 OECD real fixed investment spending, 2000–2002

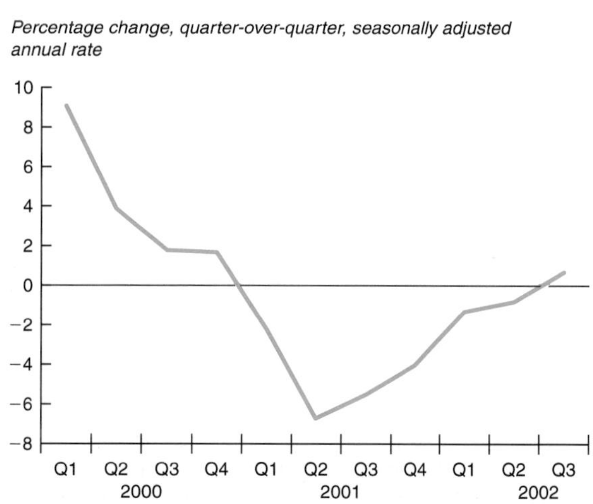

Source: OECD.

between early November and early March and investor sentiment fell anew. The rise in oil prices may well be short-lived and market sentiment may turn around quickly, even in the case of a military conflict, as was the case during the Gulf War in 1991. However, the recovery will be at best muted, and downside risks have increased.

The baseline forecast calls for growth in industrial-country GDP to accelerate from 1.4 percent in 2002 to 1.8 percent in 2003, reaching near-term peak rates of 2.8 percent by 2004 before easing to 2.6 percent in 2005. This contrasts with an average GDP advance of 3 percent during the strong years of the last upswing (1996–2000). OECD-area growth is thus likely to remain well below potential in most countries, pushing up unemployment rates. Although U.S. growth will be constrained by some of the imbalances considered above, it is likely to remain higher than that of its major OECD partners. Constraints on policy implementation in Europe and policy effectiveness in Japan are unlikely to be overcome in the near term, with the result that output growth is likely to be less in these countries.

There are obviously uncertainties in this forecast, but they are not all negative:

- The main upside risks reflect the fact that OECD monetary conditions are currently stimulative everywhere. To date, the results of this stimulus have been narrowly concentrated and slow to spread out across the global economy. As adjustments to previous excesses in both high-income and developing countries are completed, the response to easy money could become more powerful and pervasive.
- Adding to this upside is the high degree of synchronization evident across the major economies over the past few years. For most of this period, synchronization has worked to compound weakness. Once the recovery is underway in earnest, however, it should work to boost the global cycle.
- Finally, a swift resolution of geopolitical uncertainties, especially with regard to Iraq, could give a sharp lift to markets and business confidence, especially if it were combined with a significant decline in the price of oil.

Key downside risks are also evident, however. On top of the risk of protracted geopolitical uncertainty, the risk of an extreme oil price spike has risen more recently. Oil prices have increased well above $30 per barrel, as the risk of military intervention in Iraq rose and the strike in the República Bolivariana de Venezuela reduced supply by 2 million barrels per day (9 percent of OPEC [Organization of Petroleum Exporting Countries] output) through much of the first quarter of 2003.

The other main downside risk to industrial-country growth is that another round of financial turmoil or another phase of weak asset prices lies ahead:

- Despite its decline over recent years, the U.S. equity market remains highly valued when benchmarked against traditional indicators, such as actual earnings.
- Globally, corporate debt levels have been trimmed, but they remain high, and the risk of more "fallen angels"—investment-grade companies finding their debt downgraded to speculative levels by the major rating agencies—is significant.
- Japan's banks remain fragile. While the risk of more acute near-term difficulties seems to have receded, it cannot be excluded altogether.
- A degree of focus has shifted to the condition of Europe's banks, as they have been exposed to both domestic and international credit losses (in both the United States and the developing world, especially Argentina).

Developing countries: A tortuous return to stronger growth in 2003 and beyond

Output growth for the group of low- and middle-income countries was 3.1 percent in 2002, up by a small 0.3 percentage points from weak 2001 results. Growth was restrained by the lackluster recovery in the industrial countries and by financial and political uncertainties in several large emerging markets. Demand for developing-country exports grew by a small 2.2 percent, while prices for non-oil commodities rose by 5.1 percent. Net debt flows were weak, especially to Latin America, and FDI declined by $28 billion. The price of oil jumped from $19 to $28 per barrel over the course of 2002. For oil importers, this "Iraqi war premium" more than offset gains in agricultural and metals prices.

Over the past 18 months, growth performance has differed substantially across the major regions of the developing world, tied in large measure to the evolution of domestic conditions:

- China continued to make strong advances in output—some 8 percent during 2002—despite relative stagnation in Japan and volatile U.S. demand. In turn, this strong growth has increasingly helped to pull the recovery in East Asia. Together with policy stimulus in other countries, China's performance lifted the region to growth of 6.7 percent in 2002 (figure 2.12).
- At the other end of the growth spectrum, growth in Latin America and the Caribbean was held down by the government debt default and banking collapse in Argentina, uncertainty regarding Brazilian elections, a worsening of conditions in the República Bolivariana de Venezuela, and an associated $31 billion falloff in financial market flows. GDP dropped by 0.9 percent in the year, a sharp 2.4 percent fall in per-capita terms.
- Although slowing growth in the Euro Area cast a pall on those developing countries linked tightly with it, a sharp recovery of activity in Turkey following its 2001 crisis, in tandem with continued gains in the Russian Federation and the Commonwealth of Independent States (CIS) countries linked to higher oil prices, buoyed growth in Europe and Central Asia—producing a 4.1 percent rise.
- Continued strength in domestic demand in India propelled South Asia to gains of 4.9 percent, despite disruptions in regional conditions associated with the war on terrorism.
- Growth languished in Sub-Saharan Africa and the Middle East and North Africa—with the regions both registering growth rates of 2.6 percent.

Figure 2.12 GDP growth for developing countries, 1990–2002

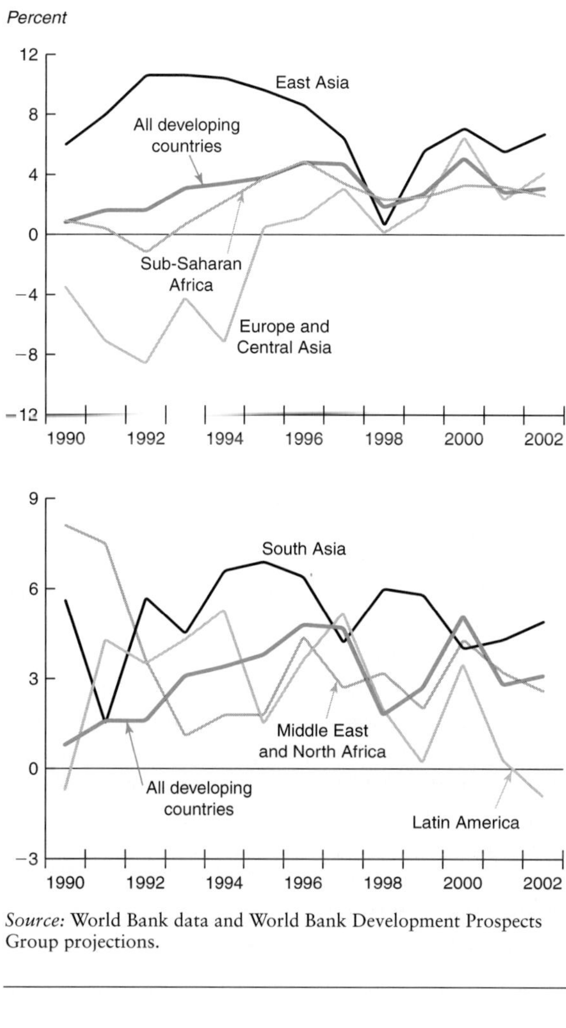

Source: World Bank data and World Bank Development Prospects Group projections.

Variability in performance across regions masks underlying similarities in the developing world. A truly global business cycle has emerged with the advancing integration of developing countries into global production, trade, and financial flows. Economic conditions in rich countries now tend to be mirrored rapidly in developing countries through enhanced trade links, just-in-time logistics, and stronger financial tie-ups with affiliates and suppliers in middle-income countries, especially those in East Asia, Central Europe, and, to a lesser degree, Latin America. Indeed, recent trends in industrial production across these regions show the effects of the general cycle—as well as the cycle of the high-tech sectors in East Asia—distinctly (figure 2.13).

Equally noteworthy is the movement into current-account surplus by the developing world. Developing countries as a group chalked up a surplus of $48 billion during 2002, up from $28 billion in 2001. The change was more than accounted for by developments in Latin America, where devaluations and import compression yielded sharp increases in trade surpluses and a $35 billion change in the region's current-account position—from a deficit of $51 billion to one of

Figure 2.13 Industrial production in select regions, 2000–2002

Percentage change, three-month/three-month, seasonally adjusted annual rate

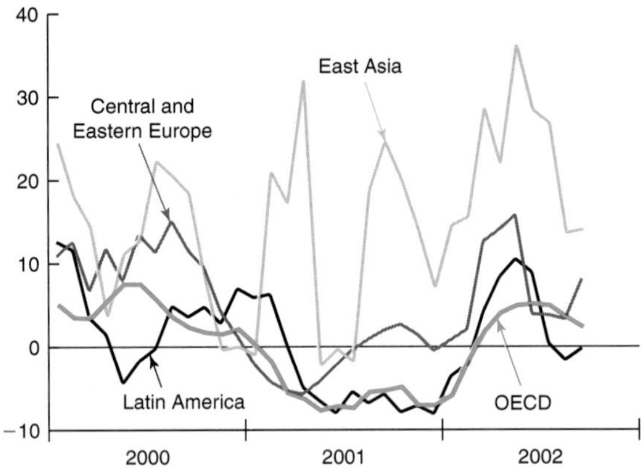

Source: World Bank data.

Figure 2.14 Current-account balances for select regions, 1990–2002

Billions of dollars

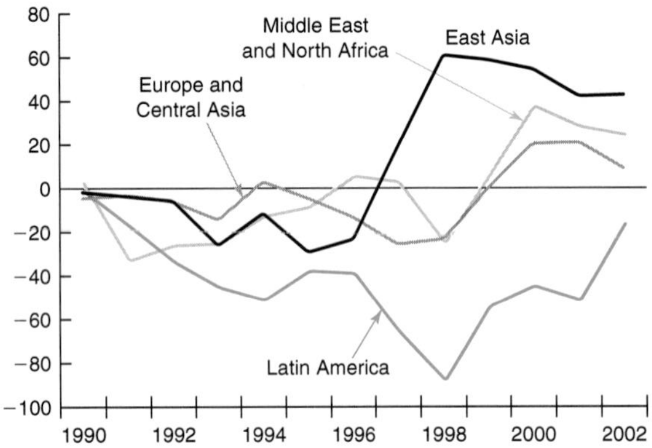

Source: World Bank data.

$16 billion (figure 2.14). East Asian surpluses are being sustained at $40–$45 billion levels, while the increase in oil prices is having divergent effects across Europe and Central Asia and the Middle East and North Africa, where the mix of oil exporters and importers leads to mixed regional results.

Growth in developing countries overall is projected to accelerate to 4 percent in 2003 and to 4.7 percent in 2004. This view of steady improvement partly reflects the end of crisis conditions in several countries where output was severely compressed in 2002. But it is also founded on a number of crucial assumptions about the conditions facing developing countries:

- Some disruptions from possible military actions in Iraq (including a temporary rise in the oil price) are built into the forecasts, but no severe, lasting dislocations are assumed.
- Related to this, the expectation is that world trade will expand by 6.2 percent in 2003, a substantial multiple of the 2.3 percent growth in global GDP, as is normal at early stages of recovery. The strength in trade flows also reflects the gearing up of international production networks, further underpinned by dynamic conditions in China, a new World Trade Organization member, and reinvigoration of regional trade in several areas.
- Financial conditions facing developing countries are expected to be a little less austere in 2003 than in 2001–02. Flows of FDI are projected to rebound slightly, while net debt flows from private sources should be modestly positive, albeit still quite anemic.

China becomes the engine of East Asia

The economies of East Asia and the Pacific grew by 6.7 percent during 2002, impressive in light of the difficult external environment. Despite a rise in volatility, exports contributed solidly to growth, but domestic demand was also strong, thanks to supportive monetary and fiscal policies. Vulnerability to external shocks has been much reduced since 1997 through sustained current-account surpluses, large-scale buildups of reserves, and corporate- and financial-sector restructuring. Notably, there were no major corporate disruptions during the recent turbulence. Regional trade grew, with Chinese imports from other countries in the region up 8 percent in 2002.

Robust growth is set to continue in the medium term. The forecast anticipates average regional growth of more than 6 percent over the next two years, with China increasingly the dominant player in the regional economy (figure 2.15). Exports will continue to play an important role with regional integration and China's admission to the World Trade Organization. Regional investment spending, which has rebounded impressively following

Figure 2.15 Trends in industrial production, 1996–2002

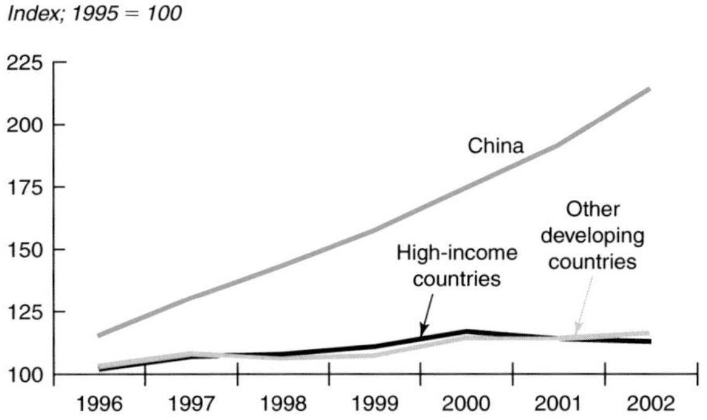

Sources: Datastream; World Bank Development Prospects Group calculations.

the collapses of 1997–98, is also expected to remain strong, contributing to productivity gains and keeping inflation in check. The region's current-account surplus is expected to narrow somewhat over the forecast period, although the region will remain a significant capital exporter. Important exceptions to these relatively rosy near-term prospects are the high-income economies of Hong Kong (China) and Singapore, where performance has recently faltered, and Indonesia, which is still reeling from the Bali bombing.

Four possible tensions hang over this favorable forecast of strong growth, low inflation, and solid external positions:

- The extreme openness of the region leaves it vulnerable to global shocks. While an Iraqi conflict would occur half a world away, any associated sharp, sustained rise in the price of oil would hurt much of the region. For example, a $10 per barrel spike in the price would cost the regions' net energy importers some 0.6 percent of GDP in higher import bills.
- The unpredictability of developments on the Korean peninsula has become a new regional concern, and the memory of the bombing tragedy in Bali is a recent reminder of the problem of terrorism in the region.
- Competition among East Asian exporters for market share in OECD economies will remain fierce, and the question of appropriate exchange-rate levels is likely to emerge as a larger issue, especially given the growing competitiveness and sophistication of Chinese exports.
- There has been a remarkable recovery in the health of much of the region's corporate sector since the dark days of 1998. But levels of corporate leverage in the region remain high, with debts becoming more sustainable now largely because of lower interest rates and a willingness of creditors to roll over debts.[2] It is unlikely in the next couple of years that short-term interest rates in the region will spike up to provoke a new round of corporate distress. Indeed, rates across the region are likely to remain quite low in both nominal and real levels, thus supporting growth. But the corrosive effects of deflation, already painfully evident in Japan, could become more pervasive across the region if measures to promote corporate restructuring are slow.
- Fiscal deficits have risen sharply since 1997 and averaged 3.4 percent of GDP in 2002. The forecast anticipates some narrowing of deficits, as further adjustment is required to ensure longer-term sustainability.

A peace dividend for South Asia

A combination of poor weather, geopolitical insecurity, a subdued external environment, and especially weak European demand put a relative damper on the South Asian economy in 2002. At 4.9 percent, growth was well below the region's potential for a third successive year. On the plus side, there was a reduction of military tensions between India and Pakistan and a ceasefire in the long-running civil war in Sri Lanka. Gains in export momentum during the second half of the year augur well for growth in 2003.

Improving exports and a recovery in agriculture, which accounts for a quarter of the region's output are together expected to boost GDP growth to 5.3 percent over the next years. Increases in export revenue will likely be channeled into higher imports, leading to little overall change in trade positions. Domestic demand should also gather momentum. Private consumption could rise substantially with a recovery in agricultural incomes, especially in India. Investment will remain cautious pending more solid progress in the reform process, while large and persistent fiscal deficits have left little scope for substantial increases in government outlays. Accommodative monetary policies are expected to provide further support for growth, and price pressures should be reasonably well contained over the forecast period.

The outlook for India dominates South Asia's economic prospects. Manufacturing performance in India is showing signs of an incipient upturn, and the burgeoning Bangalore-based international-services sector has experienced much less disruption in demand than high-tech sectors elsewhere.

Further expansion of trade flows would be helped by a reduction of trade barriers in the region. Progress in the Doha round of WTO negotiations will also be important to investment. Key issues for the region are improved access for agricultural goods, textiles, and clothing in high-income markets, and the result of the trade-related intellectual property talks.

Apart from export revenues, workers' remittances have the potential to grow rapidly in coming years as migration pressure is likely to increase and improvements in transportation and communications will complement this trend (see Chapter 7). In the short-run, however, tensions in the Middle East will likely reduce remittances from temporary workers abroad.

Convergence in Eastern Europe and Central Asia

The advance of 4.1 percent in Europe and Central Asia's GDP in 2002 was dominated by a massive 12.8 percentage point turnaround in Turkey's GDP growth as it recovered from a devastating collapse early in 2001. Among the transition countries of the region, growth slowed by a full percentage point to 3.6 percent in 2002. Considering the weakness in Western Europe, and in the capital spending of European companies, much of which is now destined for the East, the transition group weathered the slowdown fairly well. Rising market share in the Euro Area for the countries poised to join the European Union—including the Czech Republic, Hungary, and Poland—tended to offset sharply lower growth in domestic demand. The CIS countries—notably Azerbaijan, Kazakhstan, and the Russian Federation—benefitted from high and rising oil prices.

Growth in the region is expected to hold near present rates—3.5–4 percent—in the near term, although this average hides divergences from country to country:

- The European Union accession process will shape near-term developments in Central Europe even more strongly than it has to date, as the recent Copenhagen Summit established the criteria and schedule of accession for the group of 10 applicant countries. Although there are bound to be some bumps along the way in the process of integration, prospects for the accession countries are now underpinned by expectations of improved performance stemming from growing export demand as the Euro Area recovers, a revival of FDI, and transfers related to the accession process. These circumstances should help growth accelerate from a disappointing 2.4 percent in 2002 to 2.8 percent in 2003 and 4.5 percent by 2005.
- By contrast, the outlook calls for output growth in the CIS countries to moderate in late 2003–04 from growth of 4.4 percent in 2002 as the oil-price boom winds down. Should Middle East tensions escalate on a sustained basis, however, the Russian oil sector could attract additional foreign investment.
- In Turkey, the forecast assumes relative political stability and continued progress on structural reforms, which will permit a slow improvement in performance. The need to run a tight fiscal policy in order to contain the growth of public debt is likely to limit the scope for growth in domestic demand. Turkey could suffer significantly through a collapse of tourism in the case of a military conflict in Iraq.

The fallout from Argentina in Latin America

Latin America and the Caribbean was the one major region where conditions worsened rather than improved during 2002. For the region as a whole, GDP contracted by 0.9 percent, due mainly to the collapse in economic activity in Argentina (from an already low level) in the early months of 2002. Excluding Argentina, growth in the region was 0.8 percent.

The external environment facing the region was difficult in 2002. Tourism suffered badly in the wake of the September 2001 terrorist attacks. But the main negative was the shift in external finance conditions. While overall flows to developing countries were weaker in 2002, they were especially weak to the heavily indebted economies of Latin America:

- Gross market-based financial flows to the region fell by $31 billion, or 40 percent. (Excluding Argentina, the decline was $26 billion, or 38 percent.) As a result, interest rate spreads on the external debt of most borrowers in the region widened appreciably.
- Despite Argentina's default, the region repaid a net amount of $8 billion in net external debt to private creditors, compared to $9 billion in 2002.[3]
- Net inward FDI fell to $42 billion, from $69 billion in 2001, with declines evident across all countries.

The reduced supply of capital to the region forced a remarkably rapid change in the region's current-account position, brought about partly through another round of sharp currency depreciations vis-à-vis other areas of the world. Tighter domestic financial conditions and, in many cases, tighter fiscal policies reduced domestic absorption, while sizeable real devaluations switched domestic supply to exports and domestic demand away from imports. Brazil's export performance was especially impressive in the light of the weakness in Argentina (figure 2.16). For the region overall, the trade

Figure 2.16 Balance-of-trade positions for Argentina and Brazil, 1999–2002

Millions of dollars, three-month moving average, FOB-over-FOB

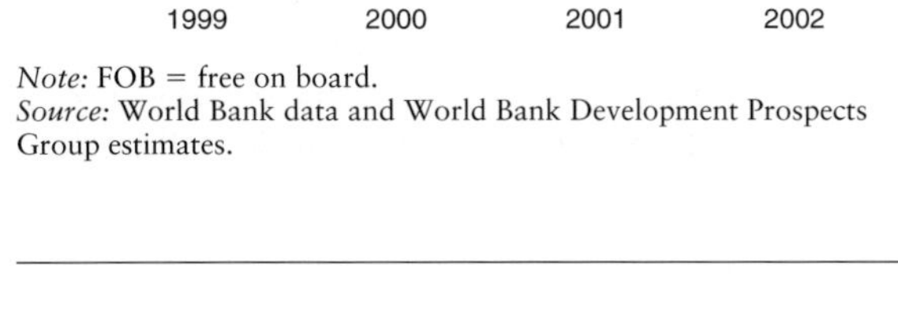

Note: FOB = free on board.
Source: World Bank data and World Bank Development Prospects Group estimates.

position shifted from balance in 2001 to a surplus of $25 billion in 2002. In turn, the region's current-account deficit narrowed by about $35 billion.

Political uncertainty was both a cause and effect of some of Latin America's problems in 2002. Financial markets in Brazil were weak until the election but recovered quickly once newly elected President Lula made clear his commitment to stick with the IMF program. Argentina's economic difficulties led to considerable political uncertainty. New elections are due in April. Early in 2003, political problems flared up again in the República Bolivariana de Venezuela.

Just how these political tensions play out could easily alter the near-term outlook. The challenges seem greatest in the República Bolivariana de Venezuela, where the economy has already contracted sharply in the early months of 2003, thanks to the disruptions from the general strike. Another wild card is how quickly Argentina recovers from the slump of 2001–02. There is now clear evidence that the economy has moved off its lows and that banks have recovered sufficiently for the payments system to be up and running again. What is unknown is how enduring this phase will be. Should the election produce a strong government that is able to reach an early agreement with the IMF and the country's external creditors, then there would be considerable scope for growth. Such upside surprises have often occurred in recent crises (the Republic of Korea, the Russian Federation, and Turkey), even in circumstances where reforms were, at the time, perceived as being incomplete. As it is, the forecast projects a 13.6 percentage point turnaround in Argentina's growth between 2002 and 2003 (−11 percent to +2.6 percent); that it could easily be greater speaks to the extremes the country has suffered in the past 18 months.

The forecast assumes that challenging external financial markets will remain a headwind against the region for the next couple of years, although the worst of the credit cycle is now behind us. The willingness of private-sector debt investors to increase exposure on a net basis is assumed to be limited, with international lending from banks likely to remain the weakest of all the debt components (see chapter 3). With some key economies facing a significant repayment of emergency funding to official creditors in 2003–05, the region will likely have to sustain lower current-account deficits into the recovery. Under these conditions, economic activity will accelerate only gradually toward 4 percent growth by 2004–05.

Cross-currents facing the Middle East and North Africa

Despite high and rising oil prices, growth in the Middle East and North Africa slowed to 2.6 percent in 2002 from 3.2 percent the year earlier. For oil exporters, largely in the Gulf region, lower OPEC quotas were offset by marginally higher prices, and GDP growth was essentially unchanged.

By contrast, diversified exporters of the region (in the Mahgreb and Mashreq) faced lower prices and demand in the European market, plus a substantial negative shock to tourism linked to the attacks of September 11, 2001. Growth for this group was reduced from 4.3 percent in 2001 to 2.5 percent in 2002 (figure 2.17). Across the quite heterogeneous region, private-sector domestic demand slowed, though public consumption increased and budget deficits widened. The apparent failure of oil-dominant countries to capitalize more on recent windfalls highlights the fact that deeper-seated structural problems have yet to be addressed. Even where reforms have been introduced, the pace has been tentative and the response fairly muted. As in the past, the current oil boom appears to have initiated a fiscal spending cycle, with few broader effects.

Figure 2.17 Oil price and GDP growth in the Middle East and North Africa, 1990–2002

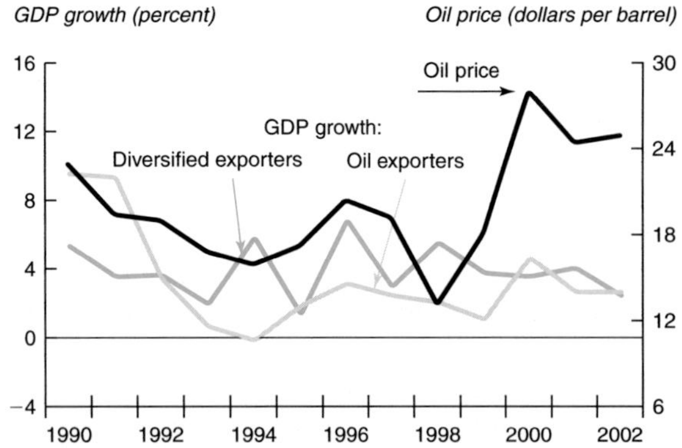

Source: World Bank data and World Bank Development Prospects Group estimates.

For both oil producers and diversified exporters, growth is expected to pick up to 3.5–4 percent over 2003–05 as exports rise and higher incomes stimulate domestic spending. Without structural reforms to raise productivity and promote diversification, however, it will be difficult to sustain growth above that range. Beyond 2003, oil exporters' current-account surpluses will narrow as the oil price slips.

A critical risk is the possibility of military action against Iraq. Neighboring Jordan would be most affected due to its close economic and trade links to Iraq and its proximity, which would affect trade, tourism and investment. Another vulnerable country is the Arab Republic of Egypt, where the balance of payments could deteriorate as tourism and Suez Canal receipts drop.

Sub-Saharan Africa: Steady but subdued growth

The growth performance of Sub-Saharan Africa has been less cyclical than that of other parts of the developing world in recent years, a tendency that is likely to continue in the next few years. The overall pace of per-capita growth remains very low, however, doing little to lift incomes in the region to levels consistent with the achievement of the Millennium Development Goals.

The factors holding back growth have shifted over the past couple of years. In 2001, the main drag was the collapse in world trade and steep decline in prices of non-oil commodities. In 2002, some of these external conditions improved, but few gains were made, as domestic conditions remained unfavorable or worsened in many countries (figure 2.18):

- In Nigeria, GDP contracted as a result of political paralysis, while violent and bloody civil strife prevented Côte d'Ivoire from taking advantage of a 15-year high in cocoa prices. Political strife has also been very damaging in Zimbabwe.
- Unfavorable weather conditions in Eastern and Southern Africa put a damper on agricultural production and left as many as 30 million people at risk of starvation.

Figure 2.18 GDP growth of African non-oil exporters and commodity price index specific to Sub-Saharan Africa, 1990–2002

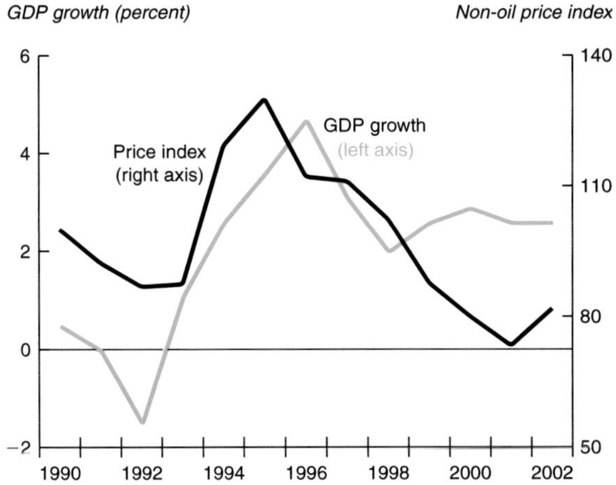

Source: World Bank data and World Bank Development Prospects Group estimates.

- The ongoing problem of HIV/AIDS (human immunodeficiency virus/acquired immune deficiency syndrome) undermines the productive capacity of the region, especially through its debilitating effect on education systems.

Prospects for growth in the region are partly driven by the vagaries of the weather. The forecasted acceleration in growth is conditioned on an assumption of more normal weather patterns, which would give a boost to agricultural output and incomes. Two other important supports to regional growth should be the expected pick-up in external demand, especially once European economies begin to recover in earnest in 2004–05. Nearer term, some gains have already been realized from higher commodity prices—and more are likely in the pipeline. While the level of prices remains low by historic standards, there are indeed signs that the 20-year slide in many commodity prices that has been so painful for much of Sub-Saharan Africa is now coming to an end. The scope for easier policies in the region is limited, but there is a likelihood of some easing in South African monetary policy, especially in the second half of 2003, after a significant tightening in 2002.

Even if commodity markets were to stabilize as expected, the forecast could not call for any significant reversal of recent declines in terms of trade. Furthermore, the region will continue to face deep-seated structural and political problems, including the lack of economic diversification, poor infrastructure and distribution systems, and, most tragically, the HIV/AIDS problem.

The region's ability to finance growth from external sources will remain largely dependent on FDI inflows, and the region's access to international capital markets will remain restricted, except for South Africa. Continued low domestic savings and persistent capital flight will thus hold domestic investment rates to low levels. Accordingly, medium-term prospects for the region are that growth will be limited to around 3.5 percent—somewhat above 1 percent in per-capita terms. Except for a few cases where the policy process is in disarray (Côte d'Ivoire and Zimbabwe), double-digit inflation is rare and should remain so, while moderate fiscal and current-account deficits are projected to narrow.

Outlook for commodity prices

After plummeting to historic lows during the slowdown of 2001, prices for non-oil commodities rose through 2002. Not all these increases have held. As global industrial growth slowed from mid-year, metals prices fell back. Agricultural prices retained more of their gains because of supply problems, especially in coarse grains, aggravated by drought in Australia, Canada, and the United States. The higher price of wheat and close substitutes generated additional export revenue of about $1 billion for Argentina, a large exporter of wheat, maize, and soybeans.

It is common to think of commodity prices in dollar terms. But most commodity prices are determined in world markets, so the price is ultimately set by the balance of global supply and demand.[4] When the dollar weakens, as it has recently, prices tend to rise in dollar terms to stop them falling in yen or euro terms. A moderate decline in the dollar over the next couple of years, as assumed in the forecast, should help boost commodity prices when expressed in dollar terms. Aside from this effect, however, fairly restrained changes in commodity prices (in dollar terms) are expected over the next two years (table 2.1). Prices of nonprecious metals should revive again as global industrial production accelerates through 2003. Higher prices for grains in recent years are apt to stimulate more supply in 2003–05, thus somewhat checking their upward movement. Critically, the overall global outlook for inflation is likely to remain very subdued (see below), suggesting little underlying demand for commodities as an inflation hedge, as there was in the 1970s and early 1980s.

Oil prices have been pushed up to their highest levels since 1991 by war jitters and the strike in the República Bolivariana de Venezuela. Forecasting the oil price over the next year is obviously very hazardous. Further sharp upward movements are plausible in the near term, especially in the event of military intervention in Iraq. The rest of OPEC would have to produce up to capacity, significantly exceeding the current quota, to compensate for the loss of production in Iraq and the earlier shortfalls from the República Bolivariana de Venezuela. Beyond near-term spikes, however, increasing supply and modest growth in demand suggest that current high prices will moderate into 2004, falling to about $21 per barrel.

Is global deflation a threat?

Even with interest rates low and oil prices unexpectedly high, there are few signs of inflationary pressure in industrial countries. Consumer price inflation at the end of 2002 was 1.6 percent, a modest 0.6 percentage point higher than in 2001, the trough of the global slowdown. Given the subdued expansion ahead, there is very little prospect of a general resurgence of price pressures. According to OECD estimates, negative output gaps (the difference between actual and potential GDP) have either opened or widened since 2000; with growth expected to remain below potential for the next two years, these negative gaps are not likely to close (figure 2.19). Slack conditions in labor and product markets will leave little opportunity for raising prices. The result is that domestic factors in the major economies point to continued low inflation in Europe and the United States and sustained *deflation* in Japan.

This message of low inflation is echoed in much of the developing world (figure 2.20). China and some of the newly industrialized economies of East Asia are experiencing deflationary trends. This is helping them to maintain or even improve competitiveness in international markets. In China, deflation is driven by fast productivity growth, the shedding of labor from state-owned enterprises and slack in product markets as capacity expands rapidly while consumer credit is still in its infancy.

Figure 2.19 Output gaps in OECD centers, 2000–2002

Difference between actual and potential GDP percentage points

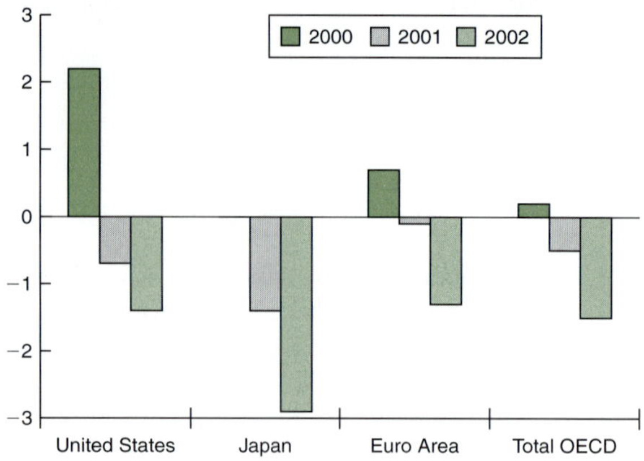

Source: OECD.

Figure 2.20 Inflation rate in OECD and developing regions, 1990–2002

Consumption deflators, local currency (median percentage change)

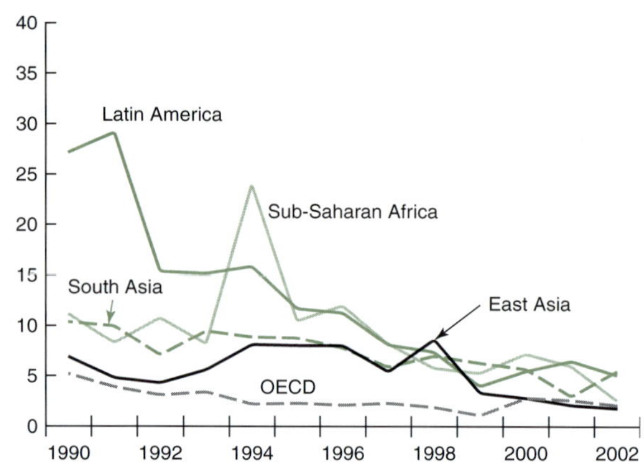

Source: World Bank data and World Bank Development Prospects Group estimates.

Although deflation is beneficial for exporters, sustained deflation must be a concern, however, for heavily indebted enterprises and households, especially in financial systems that do not offer borrowers the opportunity to refinance mortgages at lower interest rates.

The most striking aspect about inflation in Latin America is the failure of significant currency depreciations to spark inflation. Through recent waves of devaluations, the rise in prices has generally been well below the decline in the currency

Box 2.2 Disinflation is a global phenomenon

Inflation has dropped sharply across all high-income countries from its peak in the 1970s following the collapse of the Bretton Woods system of fixed exchange rates and the first global oil crisis. In the 1990s, however, this development became truly global. By the end of the decade, very few countries (at all income levels) had inflation over 10 percent, as fiscal consolidation and increasing central bank independence limited the creation of inflationary conditions. Monetary authorities developed more sophisticated approaches to monitoring and intervening in financial markets, allowing them to target inflation and interest rates directly rather than attempting to control monetary aggregates. Authorities also learned the value of greater transparency and accountability, communicating their intentions promptly and clearly. Perhaps most important, public support has grown for price stability. Other broad trends that promoted noninflationary adjustment were the growth of more open and competitive output markets and the de-indexing of labor contracts, both of which lowered inflationary expectations. The recent surge in productivity growth has further dampened price pressures.

The result has been markedly lower inflation throughout the world and striking new patterns of price adjustment. Whereas 20 years ago a major devaluation would have triggered an inflationary cycle, real adjustment now takes place quickly. Argentina is a case in point. After the currency board was abandoned at the beginning of January 2002, the peso went into free fall, eventually settling at around 3.6 to the dollar, a decline of around 70 percent (it has since strengthened somewhat). However, prices rose only 35 percent. This occurred in Argentina's extreme deflationary environment, with domestic production collapsing, but a similar story could be told about Brazil or South Africa.

Although disinflation has been a broadly beneficial development, it has a dark side if it leads to deflation or unexpectedly low inflation. These make for a dangerous mix with high debt levels.

Deflation increases debt problems through several channels:

- As deflation suppresses future profits, lower equity prices and higher spreads on corporate debt raise financing costs, deter investment, and make debt problems persistent.
- Households faced with higher costs of debt service curtail discretionary spending, exacerbating the deflationary spiral.
- The financial sector may also be affected, since a decline in equity prices erodes the value of collateral. In countries such as Germany and Japan, where banks take direct equity positions, the fall in equity values also shrinks the banks' capital base.

(box 2.2). Moreover, second-round effects have generally been quite short-lived. For example, inflation rose to no more than 9 percent in Brazil in 2002, despite the 24-percent drop in the real versus the dollar. Consumer price hikes in Argentina were only 35 percent in 2002, despite the currency collapse, government default, and restrictions on bank deposits. Dire warnings of a return to hyperinflation proved too pessimistic (just as they had in Indonesia in 1998 and the Russian Federation in 1999), despite a high degree of policy disorder. In explaining why inflation was less than it was feared to be in Latin America and beyond, two factors stand out:

- The devaluations occurred against a backdrop of weak domestic demand and, in most cases, relatively high levels of unemployment and low levels of capacity utilization. Unlike in the 1980s, Latin American economies have generally devalued at the trough rather than the peak of the cycle.[5]
- Long-standing structural reforms, notably measures to open the economy to trade and competition, have provided strength.

In other parts of the developing world, inflation is also at very low levels—few countries have double-digit inflation rates. Even where this is the case, such as in South Africa, there are clear signs that the condition will be temporary and that a significant decline is in the pipeline.

With inflation low in the OECD and negative output gaps likely to grow in coming quarters, it is reasonable to ask whether widespread deflation is a major risk to the global outlook.

The authorities in Europe and the United States will be able to avoid deflation in the current forecast by sustaining easy monetary policies, which will have the effect of allowing most troubled debtors to manage their burdens down without strains sufficient to jeopardize the health of the domestic banking system. With the key central banks mindful of the risks and dangers of deflation, the chances of avoiding generalized global deflation look good.

By contrast, Japan is already well beyond the danger point. There, the difficulty is finding a policy recipe to break the cycle of declining prices that increases the burden of corporations' liabilities. As burdens rise, commercial banks becoming saddled with yet more nonperforming loans. The resulting contraction in new lending leads to more economic contraction and price declines.

Policy actions designed to break into this circle of debt and deflation have gained new impetus, but much remains to be done. Cumulative nonperforming-loan disposals have amounted to ¥82 trillion (some $680 billion) since 1992. Economic activity may be adversely affected in the near term as more stringent accounting criteria are applied to banks, and remaining lines of credit to financially encumbered corporations are terminated. Alongside these restructurings, it is desirable that the Bank of Japan should maintain a truly stimulative monetary policy.

A bumpy takeoff in world trade

With the lowering of trade barriers, the intensification of global production networks and the integration of financial markets, international trade cycles have become strikingly synchronous. Volume growth of developing countries' exports and imports over recent years followed closely the pattern of trade flows in high-income countries. After record growth in 2000, trade volumes fell in the first half of 2001 but started rising again from the fourth quarter of 2001. Although the pattern was similar, average trade growth in developing countries was significantly stronger than in high-income countries. This mainly reflected gains in market share by Central European and East Asian exporters and a rapid expansion of regional trade in both parts of the world.

Within this broad, synchronous trade cycle were eye-catching differences across developing regions, especially on the import side. At the high end of the spectrum, East Asian imports grew at an annual rate of 20 percent before the downturn in 2001, fell cumulatively less than 1 percent during the downturn, and returned to a pace of 20 percent growth during the rebound (table 2.3). At the low end of the spectrum, Latin American imports fell almost 10 percent during the downturn and, after a short upswing, started to fall again in the second half of 2002, reflecting severe constraints on external finance. For both high-income countries and developing countries, trade is expected to grow at a fairly moderate pace in 2003, after a brief downturn in the first quarter. The downturn follows the temporary dip in global industrial production in the fourth quarter 2002. On an annual basis global trade growth is anticipated to reach 6.2 percent in 2003, up from the 3-percent results of 2002. The low growth rate for 2002 reflects partly the decline in trade within 2001; the higher growth rate for 2003 in turn reflects partly the acceleration that occurred in 2002. Most developing regions should share in the acceleration of trade growth, with the trend of growing South-South trade continuing. China is expected to grow in importance as an export market, especially for other countries in East Asia.

Table 2.3 Growth in volume of manufactured imports
(percentage change at annualized rates)

	Q1, 1999–peak in 2000	Cumulative fall in downturn	Growth since the trough of 2001
High-income	11.4	−6.1	7.9
Developing			
East Asia and Pacific	19.6	−0.8	20.2
Middle East and North Africa	8.7	−4.6	2.9
Europe and Central Asia	15.3	−2.4	7.9
Latin America and the Caribbean	12.1	−9.8	−8.4
South Asia	6.6	−7.6	11.5

Source: World Bank staff.

The relatively uniform rebound in the growth of trade volumes implies little change in trade balances in the near future. There will likely be some price effects on trade balances, especially as the dollar continues to weaken. A weaker dollar should increase dollar-based revenues for exporters of non-oil commodities, with a positive impact on their current-account balances in the short term. At the same time, the depreciation of the dollar—together with fixed-debt servicing on dollar-denominated debt—will appear as a capital gain or a rise in real incomes for indebted developing countries, potentially leading to increased import demand. All these effects would be quite modest, however.

Assessing the global flow of funds

Using the pattern of global current-account balances as a starting point, the global flow of funds can be summarized as follows:

- Developing countries export capital to high-income countries.
- Asia and Europe export capital to the Americas.
- These data need to be treated with some care, as the overall global current-account discrepancy was about $130 billion in 2002, implying that far more payments than receipts are being recorded.

The forecast projects that the U.S. current-account deficit, which widened to nearly 5 percent of GDP during 2002, will remain near that level in the short run. This large deficit began to be accumulated in the late 1990s as U.S. economic growth surged and the dollar firmed. This development was not unanticipated, as current-account deficits are associated to a large extent with business fluctuations and the dynamics of investment. What made the U.S. experience exceptional was that the deficit hardly narrowed during the downturn in 2001 and sharply widened further immediately afterward. By 2000, the peak year of the last business cycle, the U.S. current-account deficit reached 4.2 percent of GDP, or 8 percent of the combined savings of the rest of the world (figure 2.21). By contrast, the peak of the last current-account cycle in the United States during the mid 1980s saw the deficit reach 3.4 percent of GDP, or 6 percent of world savings.

It is difficult to identify the full complement of financiers of the U.S. deficit because the global current-account deficit has ballooned, complicating the picture (table 2.4). In the early phase of the run-up of the U.S. deficit, the main flow of capital came from Asia, where the crisis of 1997–98 led to a sharp turn in capital flows. This flow has fallen from its peak, but not by much. During 2001–02, U.S. shortfalls increasingly came to be financed by higher European inflows to equity and fixed-income markets. More recently, official creditors have been the source of an increasing amount of the funding, as central banks (especially in Asia) have resisted upward pressure in their currencies against the dollar. Japan's international reserve holdings currently stand at around $450 billion and China's at $270 billion. These countries are at the high end of the scale, but the breadth and amount of central bank reserve accumulation over the past couple of years is striking (see chapter 1).[6]

There is, of course, no reason why countries should not maintain current-account deficits or surpluses for an extended period. Since 1980, the

Figure 2.21 U.S. net borrowing as a share of rest-of-world savings, 1980–2004

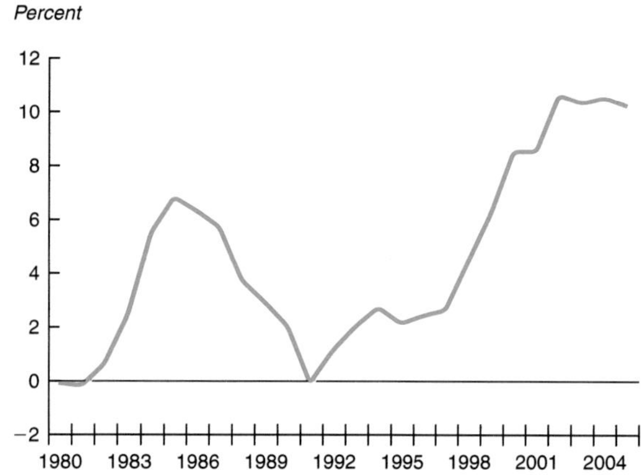

Source: World Bank data.

Table 2.4 Current-account balances
(billions of dollars)

	2001	2002e	2003f
World[a]	−140	−133	−229
High-income	−170	−181	−255
United States	−393	−498	−550
EU (15)	18	80	69
Japan	89	116	115
Developing countries	28	48	26
East Asia and Pacific	43	43	41
Europe and Central Asia	18	9	7
Latin America and the Caribbean	−54	−16	−20
Middle East and North Africa	29	25	10
South Asia	−3	−8	−6
Sab-Saharan Africa	−5	−4	−5

Note: e = estimate, f = forecast.
a. Global current-account discrepancy.
Source: World Bank staff.

Table 2.5 Long-run trends in current account balances, 1980–2002
(percentage of GDP)

	1980–82	1983–85	1986–88	1989–91	1992–94	1995–97	1998–2000	2001	2002	Stan. dev.	Correlation with U.S.
United States	0.0	−2.2	−3.0	−1.0	−1.2	−1.5	−3.2	−3.9	−4.8	1.52	n.a.
Euro Area	−0.9	0.4	0.7	−0.6	−0.3	1.0	0.1	0.5	1.3	0.63	−0.53
Japan	0.0	2.7	3.4	1.8	2.9	1.9	2.7	2.1	2.9	1.00	−0.64
Other OECD	−2.5	−0.5	−1.8	−2.0	−2.1	0.0	−0.3	1.5	1.0	1.44	−0.80
East Asia and Pacific	−1.8	−2.1	0.6	−0.7	−1.2	−1.3	4.7	2.6	2.5	2.39	−0.77
Europe and Central Asia	−0.6	−0.1	0.1	−0.2	−0.6	−0.8	−1.6	1.9	0.8	0.52	0.36
Latin America and the Caribbean	−4.8	−0.6	−1.6	−0.8	−3.0	−2.6	−3.4	−2.9	−1.0	1.34	−0.32
Middle East and North Africa	7.3	−4.6	−3.8	−3.3	−5.2	−0.1	0.7	5.0	4.5	4.57	−0.15
South Asia	−1.9	−1.6	−2.2	−2.3	−1.4	−2.0	−1.0	−0.5	−1.1	0.84	−0.77
Sab-Saharan Africa	−5.1	−2.1	−1.5	−0.7	−1.9	−2.1	−2.1	−1.7	−1.4	1.21	−0.23

Note: n.a. = not applicable, Stan. dev. = standard deviation.
Sources: IMF, *Balance of Payments Yearbook;* World Bank staff.

current-account balances (expressed as a share of GDP) of Japan, the European Union, Europe and Central Asia, and South Asia have been relatively stable (as shown in table 2.5 by the standard deviation in their current-account imbalances). By contrast, the current-account imbalances of East Asia and Pacific and the Middle East and North Africa have been quite volatile. In the latter case, this is no doubt due to the volatility in oil prices.

The significant and negative correlations between the current-account balances of most regions and those of the United States suggest that variations in the U.S. need for savings have been met by much of the rest of the world. In the late 1990s, the rise in the U.S. current-account deficit had a counterpart in increased surpluses in Latin America, East Asia, the Middle East, other OECD countries, and, to a lesser extent, in the European Union.

Several factors were likely at play in the widening of the U.S. deficit—and in its financing. Rapid productivity growth in the United States in the 1990s translated into higher demand for imports, as U.S. consumers spent what they perceived to be permanently higher incomes. This was further reinforced by a rise in the real effective exchange rate, which also encouraged imports. At the same time, sharply higher U.S. investment spending and the run-up in equity prices offered international investors exceptional opportunities. And the United States was perceived as a safe haven during financial turbulence in 1997–98 and 2002.

During a cyclical downturn, such as that in 2001–02, the U.S. current-account deficit would normally be expected to narrow. Although this occurred to some extent, the amount was small. The reason lies partly in the global, synchronized nature of the last downturn, in which U.S. partner demand dropped sharply. Also important was the sharp rise in U.S. public-sector dissaving—a result of fiscal expansion.

At present, there is little evidence to suggest that international investors are unwilling to continue financing the U.S. deficit at close to current levels. A weaker dollar vis-à-vis the euro and the currencies of East Asia (especially the yen and yuan) would restore a better balance. But there are several impediments to engineering such a change. Consistent macroeconomic policies would be required to encourage domestic demand in Europe, Japan, and China to replace net exports as a source of growth. It is unlikely that policymakers will elect to effect such change—and unclear that they would be able to do so even if willing.

The dilemma thus facing policymakers across the global economy, especially those in heavily indebted developing countries, is that a U.S. current-account deficit of about $500 billion is absorbing a very high proportion of global saving. But the means of adjusting this imbalance—reduced U.S. import demand, appreciation against the dollar (and the attendant deflation risks that it might bring), and stepped-up efforts to promote domestic demand—are all either undesirable or unachievable objectives (see box 2.3 for a discussion of the impact of a weaker dollar on developing countries).

But as long as the existing constellation of exchange-rate relationships persists, a constellation that helps foster large U.S. current-account deficits,

Box 2.3 Developing countries and the dollar

Since the summer of 2001, the dollar has lost more than 25 percent of its value against the euro. This erosion affects trade relations and investment positions between the United States and Europe most directly, but it has an important effect on developing countries as well. For developing countries, a change in the value of the dollar may lead to substantial changes in terms of trade, competitiveness, and debt service:

- Exporters of non-oil commodities tend to reap terms-of-trade gains from a weakening dollar. Large segments of supply and demand in many non-oil commodities markets depend on income flows denominated in other currencies. Prices in those markets tend to be determined in currencies other than the dollar. Econometric estimates show that roughly 50 percent of dollar depreciation is translated into a rise in dollar prices of non-oil commodities. And as prices of oil and industrial products are to a larger extent determined in dollars, a weakening of the dollar is likely to generate terms-of-trade gains for non-oil commodity exporters.
- A falling dollar implies a loss of competitiveness for exporters to the United States, or exporters who compete with others whose costs depend on dollar prices. Although fewer developing countries have their exchange rates pegged to the dollar than 10 years ago, different exchange-rate systems still have an impact on competitiveness. An obvious example is the link of the Chinese yuan to the dollar, which gives Chinese exporters a clear advantage vis-à-vis other exporters from the region when the dollar is weak.
- About 60 percent of long-term external debt in developing countries is denominated in dollars. This share may be even higher if one takes into account exchange-rate swaps that developing countries use to limit exposure to fluctuations in the value of other currencies. A weakening of the dollar immediately lowers developing countries' debt service as measured in local currencies.

These mechanisms imply that a weaker dollar is beneficial for non-oil exporters and highly indebted countries—mainly in Latin America and Sub-Saharan Africa—but may adversely affect exporters of industrial and high-tech products in East Asia.

two unfortunate side-effects will develop. First, foreigners will increase their already huge holdings of U.S. assets, many of which are held in liquid form. Second, real resources will continue to be committed to maintaining this pattern of real exchange rates, leading to a possible overinvestment in the tradeable goods sectors in countries and regions where the real exchange rate is being held down by foreign-exchange intervention.

Notes

1. The rate of personal savings from disposable income was 0.8 percent in the fourth quarter of 2001, the lowest level on record. By the fourth quarter of 2002, it had risen to 4.2 percent.

2. See chapter 5. There is also now, if anything, excess demand for dollar-denominated debt issued by East Asian borrowers, leading to the emergence of an "Asia premium" (see chapter 3).

3. This does not include about $8 billion of interest arrears that Argentina built up to private external creditors in 2002. Technically, this should be counted as a short-term net debt inflow.

4. There are a few commodities for which this is not true, since they cannot be easily shipped from one market to another. A good example is natural gas.

5. One exception was Mexico in late 1994. Partly as a result, the inflation pass-through in 1995 was relatively high.

6. Not all of these reserves are held as dollars. Indeed, many central banks are now in the process of diversifying their holdings, especially by acquiring more euros, which may be one factor that has boosted the euro against the dollar over the past year.

3

Coping with Weak Private Debt Flows

Mansoor Dailami, Himmat Kalsi, and William Shaw

Debt flows to developing countries from private-sector creditors were weak again in 2002. For the second year in a row, new loans to, and bond issues by, developing countries were less than the amount of their maturing debt. Developing countries' repayments to private-sector creditors in 2002 exceeded new debt by $9 billion, coming on top of the 2001 figure of $24.8 billion (table 3.1). Gross market-based debt flows fell to $138 billion, from $145 billion in 2001 and $171 billion in 2000 (table 3.2).[1]

But recovering investor confidence in the last quarter of the year brought a narrowing of credit spreads, particularly on investment-grade, emerging-market sovereign debt. Thus it is likely that the third quarter of 2003 was the bottom of the current credit cycle. Any rebound is likely to be very hesitant, however. Net debt flows to developing countries are projected to be slightly positive in 2003 (table 3.3). Gross market-based debt flows are likely to rise somewhat, to about $155 billion. As in 2002, much of this activity will come from European and East Asian borrowers, with Latin America most likely registering another year of weak flows.

Table 3.1 Private-sector debt flows to developing countries, 1991–2002
(billions of dollars)

	1999	2000	2001	2002
Total net flows	0.5	5.1	−24.8	−9.0
By region:				
East Asia and Pacific	−24.1	−25.0	−15.5	−6.0
Europe and Central Asia	16.6	22.2	0.5	7.2
Latin America	10.7	10.0	−8.7	−9.1
Middle East and North Africa	0.5	−3.6	2.9	1.3
South Asia	−2.0	2.9	−2.7	−1.0
Sub-Saharan Africa	−1.2	−1.4	−1.3	−1.4
By component:				
Disbursements	201.7	203.5	195.3	164.3
Amortization	179.9	189.1	203.9	167.2
Change in short term, net	−21.4	−9.4	−16.2	−6.1
Bond financing, net	29.6	17.4	10.1	18.6
Bank and other, net	−29.1	−12.3	−34.9	−27.6

Source: World Bank Debtor Reporting System.

Table 3.2 Gross market-based debt flows to developing countries, 2000–2002
(billions of dollars)

			2002				
	2000	2001	Q1	Q2	Q3	Q4	Year
Total	171	145	35	38	30	35	138
Bonds	58	59	19	17	6	13	55
Banks	113	86	16	21	24	22	83
East Asia	27	17	6	11	5	11	34
Bonds	5	7	4	5	1	3	12
Banks	21	10	3	6	5	8	21
South Asia	4	3	0	1	0	1	2
Bonds	0	0	0	0	0	0	0
Banks	4	3	0	1	0	1	2
Europe and Central Asia	37	27	7	8	8	10	34
Bonds	14	11	5	5	1	5	15
Banks	23	16	3	4	8	5	19
Latin America	83	75	16	9	8	10	44
ex-Argentina	*64*	*69*	*15*	*9*	*8*	*9*	*41*
Bonds	35	34	10	4	3	5	22
Banks	48	41	5	5	6	7	22
Sub-Saharan Africa	12	11	3	2	3	1	9
Bonds	1	2	1	2	0	0	3
Banks	10	9	2	0	3	1	6
Mid. East and North Africa	9	12	3	6	5	1	15
Bonds	2	5	0	1	1	0	3
Banks	6	7	3	5	3	1	12

Source: Dealogic Bondware and Loanware.

Table 3.3 Forecasts of private-sector debt flows, 2001–2004
(billions of dollars)

	2001	2002	2003f	2004f
Total net flows	−24.8	−9.0	5.0	10.0
Bond financing, net	10.1	18.6	20.0	25.0
Bank and other, net	−34.9	−27.6	−15.0	−15.0
Gross market issuance	145	138	155	157

Note: *f* = forecast.
Sources: World Bank Debtor Reporting System and staff estimates; Dealogic Bondware and Loanware.

In the recent history of international credit cycles, the downswing of 2001–02 has been unusual in several respects. It was influenced directly by the market's perception of political risk associated with general elections in Turkey and Brazil, by the impact of Argentina defaulting on its international bond obligations, by the generalized retrenchments of international banks from cross-border exposure to developing countries, and by intense risk aversion. The strength of that aversion revealed deep uncertainty about the global economy, the possibility of military conflict with Iraq, the sharp deterioration in corporate credit in major developed countries, and the emergence of a string of corporate accounting scandals in the United States that undermined investor confidence and induced high volatility in credit markets.

From a longer perspective, 2002 also bore witness to a number of important regulatory and legislative initiatives, market developments, and multilateral measures affecting the pattern of capital flows to developing countries. Two are worth noting.

First, the market has come to make distinctions in the credit quality of emerging market borrowers, both sovereign and corporate, and to price its products accordingly. And it has moved beyond its preoccupation with a single asset class, which grew out of the Brady bonds initiative of the 1980s. An important implication of the new distinctions—and of the divergence between the supply and cost of private debt capital—is the reduced likelihood of financial contagion, as investors should be less prone to sudden, generalized reversals of capital flows. Another implication is the establishment of meaningful yield curves based on particular types of credit issue—sovereign, corporate, or project—and in line with each issue's underlying economic fundamentals and quality. The trend toward greater discrimination has its broader reflection in virtually all segments of international bond markets, where investors' search for quality and safety have resulted in demand for transparent accounting, better corporate governance, and solid protection covenants.

In the second significant development, the restructuring of sovereign debt took center stage in 2002, with new proposals from the official sector generating considerable interest—as well as intense debate. Bond debt has increased significantly as a share of developing countries' total private foreign debt. Because sovereign default will continue to occur occasionally, and given the characteristics of bond instruments—the diversity and anonymity of the investor base, and differences in governing law for internationally issued bonds—consensus is building for new approaches to sovereign bond restructuring that could minimize the costs of debt restructuring and contribute to the efficiency of international debt markets.

The new approaches include a relatively modest *contractual approach,* entailing the use of collective action clauses in the legal documents of bonds issued internationally, and a much more ambitious *statutory approach* that would create a legal foundation for collective action by creditors. The first approach has been favorably received in the marketplace, even though it provides only a partial solution to the collective action problem. In the absence of an international code to facilitate debt restructuring for sovereign borrowers as bankruptcy statutes do for companies, the IMF has proposed a sovereign debt restructuring mechanism, details of which are being worked out. The general idea is to provide a framework that would offer temporary protection to sovereign borrowers against hostile creditor action, to aggregate creditors, and to provide an international forum for dispute resolution—all backed by the force of an international treaty.

Financial innovations often emerge in troubled times, which give rise to novel ideas, new organizational structures, and new ways of doing business. The current global financial turbulence and the credit downswing in developing countries have produced their share of financial innovations, which, if reinforced by appropriate policies and measures, portend well for the stability of capital flows to developing countries. The first innovation discussed in this chapter is the development of significant local bond markets, particularly in Asia. The second is the expansion of markets for the transfer of credit risk, ranging from basic-credit default swaps to sophisticated credit-derivative products such as collateralized debt obligations. The third significant innovation is the movement of the international banking industry from cross-border lending to local financial services. The fourth is the emergence of a nascent market in project bonds designed to finance investments in infrastructure in developing countries.

Taken together, these developments present opportunities for the international financial and policy communities to provide salutary stability to capital flows to developing countries.

Debt-market developments in 2002

The weakness in private debt flows as reported in the World Bank's Debtor Reporting System is corroborated by a wide range of other indicators.

Gross market-based debt-raising activity reported by Dealogic Bondware and Loanware showed a drop in 2002, with total gross debt flows falling to $137 billion from $145 billion in 2001 and $171 billion in 2000 (table 3.2).

The dynamic between the two components of gross lending flows—bank lending and bond issues—shifted as 2002 progressed. Gross bank lending dropped in the first quarter but rebounded by mid-year before fading again at year end. The volume of bank lending was thus almost evenly split between the first and second halves of the year. By contrast, bond issues were strong through the first half of the year but fell sharply at mid-year. Only 34 percent of the year's bonds were issued in the second half of the year, a phenomenon related to Brazil's actions in the run-up to its presidential elections in October.

Also contributing to the drop in overall bond activity was the severe decline in bond issues denominated in euros. Many Argentine bonds had been raised in euros and sold to retail investors in Europe. Losses on these bonds made European investors reluctant to buy new bonds in 2002, leading to a drop in the share of euro-denominated bonds (figure 3.1). Issues denominated in yen virtually disappeared, despite the fact that the currency offers the lowest absolute borrowing costs. The result was a sharp rise in the share of issues denominated in U.S. dollars.

Figure 3.1 Currency composition of new bond issues, 2001 and 2002

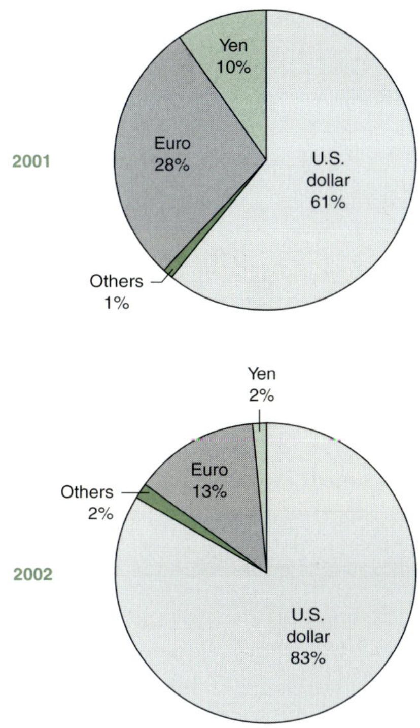

Source: Dealogic Bondware.

The region most dramatically affected by the drop-off in debt flows was the one most heavily dependent on market-based debt financing: Latin America. Gross market-based flows to that region were down by 48 percent in 2002. The weakness in Latin American gross market activity since 2000 in part reflects the virtual disappearance of Argentina from the lending and issuance data. But that occurred mainly in 2001 (when flows to Argentina were down by 68 percent). In 2002, gross flows to Latin America, excluding Argentina, were still down a substantial 40 percent.

Gross debt flows to other parts of the developing world dropped nowhere near as far as they did in Latin America. Flows to the two other regions with sizeable market activity—Europe and Central Asia and East Asia—rose in 2002 over 2001. Flows to East Asia doubled.

Market-based debt flows remain concentrated in upper- and middle-income countries. Low-income countries are not wholly excluded from

Figure 3.2 Debt-market issuance by low-income countries, 2001–2002

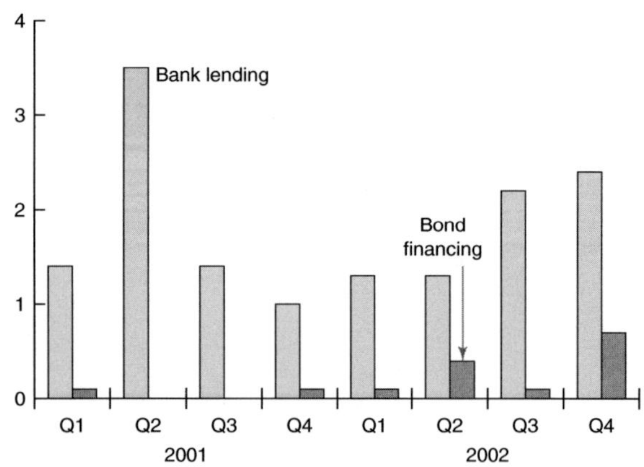

Source: Dealogic Bondware and Loanware.

Figure 3.4 Average regional credit quality, 1997–2003

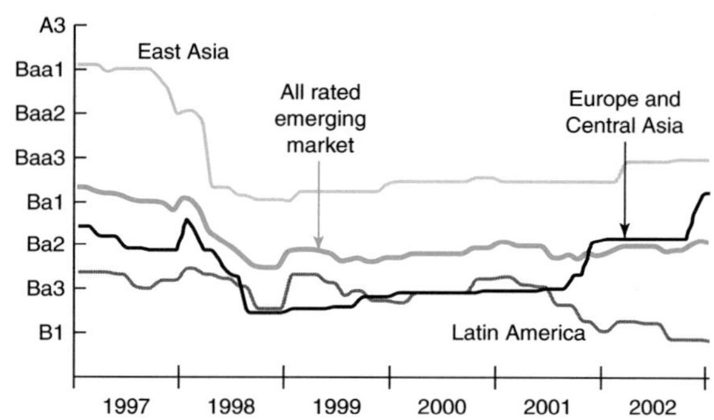

Source: Moody's Investor Service; World Bank staff estimates.

Figure 3.3 Breakdown of bond issuance by credit rating, 2002

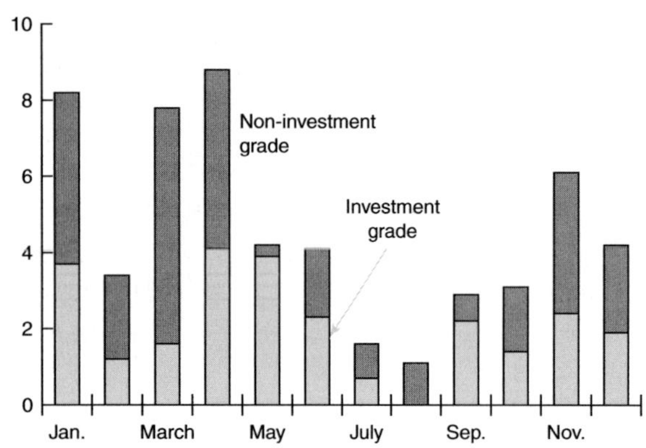

Sources: Dealogic; Moody's Investor Service.

Figure 3.5 Bond issuance and spreads, 2002

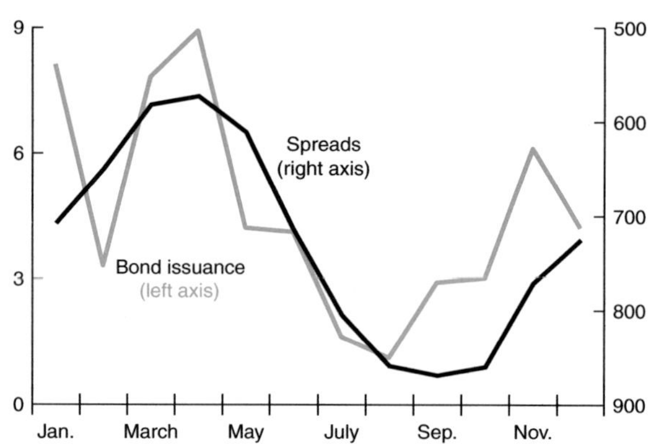

Note: bp = basis points.
Sources: Dealogic Bondware; J.P. Morgan Chase.

the markets, although most of their market-based finance is raised through bank lending (figure 3.2).

Increasingly, market flows are tiered based on credit quality. As the year progressed, flows shifted toward higher-rated borrowers (figure 3.3). In the first half of the year, below-investment-grade issuers accounted for 56 percent of total bond issuance. In the second half of the year, however, these issuers accounted for 44 percent of the total. The tiering in credit quality helps account for the wide variation in the performance of regional flows, as the average credit rating in Latin America is not only well below that in East Asia or Europe and Central Asia, but also has been deteriorating in recent quarters (figure 3.4).

The pattern of a solid first half followed by a weak third quarter is also evident in spreads on emerging market bonds (figure 3.5). Narrowing through April, spreads spiked up to a high point at the end of September. This pattern was driven by developments in Brazil, where spreads widened from a low of 700 basis points in March to a peak of 2,450 basis points in late September. Since then, they have narrowed considerably, signaling an improvement in market conditions that contributed to a revival in bond issuance in the fourth quarter.

Putting the rise in secondary-market spreads into historic context (figure 3.6), the severity of the rise ahead of Argentina's default in 2001 and Brazil's problems in 2002 is notable but pales in comparison with the run-ups experienced at the time of the Mexican crisis in 1995 and the Russian crisis in 1998.

Importantly, the degree of uniformity of movement in spreads continues to decline. For example, the recent difficulties in Argentina and Brazil did spill over to raise Mexican spreads at various points over the past couple of years, but the degree of co-movement was much reduced relative to 1995 and 1998 (figure 3.7).

Figure 3.6 Secondary-market spreads on emerging markets, 1990–2002

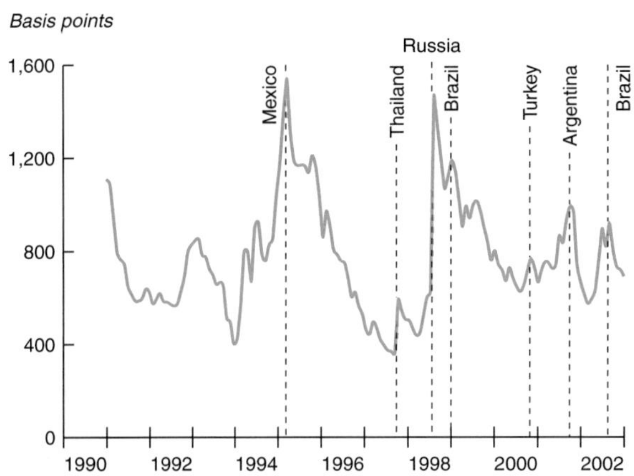

Note: Country names mark date of financial crisis.
Source: J.P. Morgan Chase.

Figure 3.7 Secondary-market spreads on Brazil and Mexico, 1991–2002

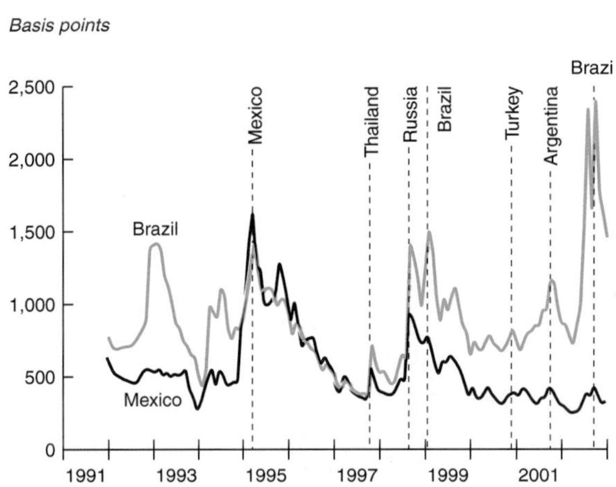

Note: Country names mark date of financial crisis.
Source: J.P. Morgan Chase.

Debt-market prospects for 2003 and beyond

The rally in emerging markets in the fourth quarter of 2002 not only made net debt flows to developing countries less negative for 2002 as a whole than had seemed likely at the end of the third quarter, but also allowed flows in 2003 to begin on a relatively strong note.

It is likely that both gross and net capital market debt flows to developing countries will be higher in 2003 than in 2001–02 (table 3.3):

- Net debt flows are projected to be positive for the first time in three years, although they will remain subdued relative to the peak years of the 1990s. Net issuance of bonds is forecast to be much higher than net bank lending. Indeed, continued bank retrenchment will cause net bank lending to be negative for yet another year in 2003.
- Gross capital market flows to developing countries are expected to rise to $155 billion in 2003 from $137 billion in 2002. By 2005, gross flows of bank lending and portfolio securities together are expected to rise to around $165 billion. This outlook is based on econometric models of capital flows to developing countries that integrate the effects of supply conditions in industrial countries with the demand factors in developing countries. The econometric framework used for generating the forecasts for capital market flows to developing countries is the same as was used in *Global Development Finance 2002* (World Bank 2002).

Debt flows partly reflect lower demand

The drop in debt-related flows to developing countries over recent years is not wholly due to the reluctance of creditors to supply funds. In many cases, reduced *demand* for external debt finance lies behind the diminished flows.

Figure 3.8a Spreads on benchmark bonds, Latin America, 1998–2002

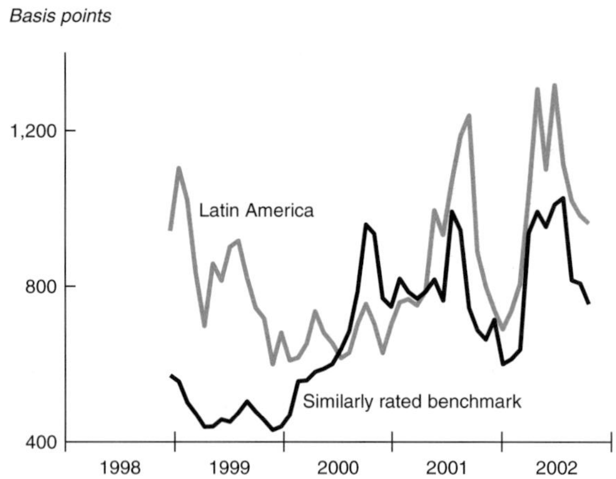

Sources: Bloomberg; J.P. Morgan Chase.

Figure 3.8b Spreads on benchmark bonds, East Asia, 1998–2002

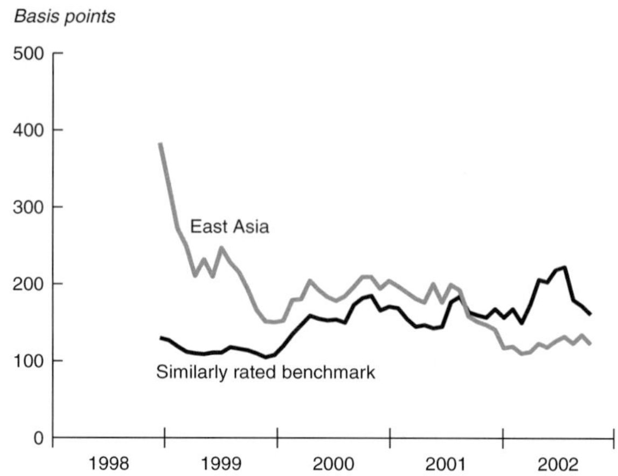

Sources: Bloomberg; J.P. Morgan Chase.

This is especially true for the economies of Asia, which have shifted from being substantial net borrowers in the years leading up to the 1997–98 crisis to a position where they no longer need external debt. Sustained current-account surpluses and steady inflows of FDI mean that many countries in the region have an external financing surplus to deploy. The surplus is being used to pay down external debt and accumulate external assets, either in the form of foreign exchange reserves or privately held assets.

It is hard to determine with precision whether lower flows (and stocks) are a reflection of reduced borrower demand or investor supply. There have been episodes during which identifiable exogenous factors have affected the supply curve, as in the sudden loss of confidence in the Asian crisis of 1997–98, which triggered a considerable fall in domestic investment in all affected countries. In the case of the most recent credit downswing, no major exogenous factor can be identified; hence, the identification problem is not trivial.

Some guide can be provided by pricing, however. In a simple supply-demand framework, a reduction in demand would be associated with a fall in quantity *and* price, while a fall in supply (in this context, reduced availability of debt financing) would be associated with a fall in quantity but a rise in price.

The relevant price in consideration here is not just the interest-rate spread over the risk-free rate (U.S. Treasury securities) offered by the debt in question, but also how that spread has developed in recent quarters relative to similarly rated debt. In the case of Latin America, bond spreads in 2002, on average, rose both absolutely and relative to similarly rated benchmarks (figure 3.8a).

For East Asia, however, the opposite is true: spreads narrowed both absolutely and in relation to similarly rated (investment-grade) benchmarks (figure 3.8b). Evidently, there is a shortage of foreign-currency-denominated bonds issued by East Asian borrowers relative to the demand for such claims—often from bond funds within the region—leading to the emergence of what some market commentators have called an "Asia premium."

Creditors focus on credit risk, not return

Although reduced demand can account for part of the drop-off in debt flows to developing countries, much of the move must be interpreted as a supply shift due to the increased reluctance of investors to hold debt claims on developing countries.

A key ingredient in creditors' willingness to take on debt held by developing countries is the prevailing pattern of interest rates (both short- and long-term) in the major markets. Low returns in the major markets might be expected to promote a flow of funds to higher-yielding developing-country debt,

Figure 3.9 Net debt flows and G3 interest rates, 1984–2002

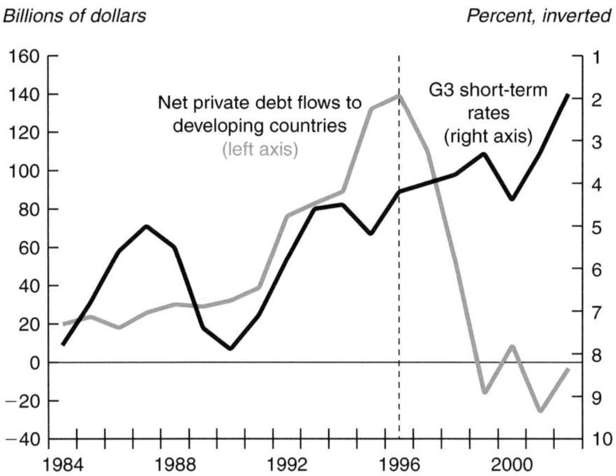

Sources: World Bank Debtor Reporting System; Bloomberg.

while high returns in the major markets would be an attraction to keep this capital at home. Such a "push" factor was commonly identified as a key driver of capital flows to developing countries in the literature of the early 1990s (Calvo, Leiderman, and Reinhart 1993).

From the late 1980s to 1996, this inverse relationship between bond yields in the major industrial countries and net private debt flows to developing countries did indeed hold (figure 3.9). The correlation coefficient between yields and net flows was −0.7. In this framework, it is not difficult to understand what became known as the "Tequila crisis" of 1994–95, when net debt flows to Latin America became anemic. In 1994, G3 bond yields rose by 120 basis points, having fallen steadily from 1990, when the flow of debt finance to developing countries first began to accelerate in earnest.

Since 1996, however, this negative correlation has broken down, and the relationship between net private debt flows and yields has become *positive.* In most years, yields and flows have dropped together. If the pre-1996 relationship between net flows and yields had held in 2002, net debt flows would have been about $160 billion, compared to the drop of $9 billion that was realized.

To make sense of this regime shift, it is important to recognize that investors in developing countries have become more concerned with credit risk than return in their lending attitudes to developing countries. As concerns about overexposure to developing countries mounted in the late 1990s, lower short-term G3 interest rates failed to promote a resumption of capital flows. Indeed, the mass exodus of capital from high-risk developing (and developed) markets to the safety of G3 government bond markets during episodes of severe risk aversion in recent years has helped drive down bond yields in the G3, thus contributing to the positive correlation between flows and yields evident since 1997.

Increased investor wariness about holding lower-rated debt claims can be illustrated by the pattern of investors in the bond market. J.P. Morgan, the investment bank that has typically accounted for the largest share of secondary-market business in developing-country debt, maintains data on the counterparts with which it does business (figure 3.10). These have shifted significantly since the crisis years of 1997–98.[2]

Most important is the notable shrinkage in the share of the market accounted for by institutions with a relatively high tolerance for risk. For example, dedicated emerging-market and macro hedge funds accounted for about 30 percent of this market in December 1998, but only 10 percent in September 2002. By contrast, the share of demand accounted for by "cross-over" high-grade investors has more than tripled, from 9 percent to 32 percent, over the same period. The result has been an increased appetite in the aggregate to hold the debt of higher-rated developing countries, but a reduced appetite to hold the debt of lower-rated borrowers.

A new market in credit derivatives

Investor concern over the risks of investing in developing countries has led to the development of a variety of instruments to manage risk—and new markets in those instruments—just as the intensification of currency and interest rate risk in the 1980s, following the breakdown of the Bretton Woods system of fixed exchange rates, ushered in the development of markets in currency and interest rate derivatives.

Instruments providing insurance against defaults and other credit events have been developing rapidly in global fixed-income markets; with developing-country debt markets at the higher end of the credit-risk spectrum, it is only natural for them to become part of this market.

Figure 3.10 The shifting investor base of emerging-market bond markets

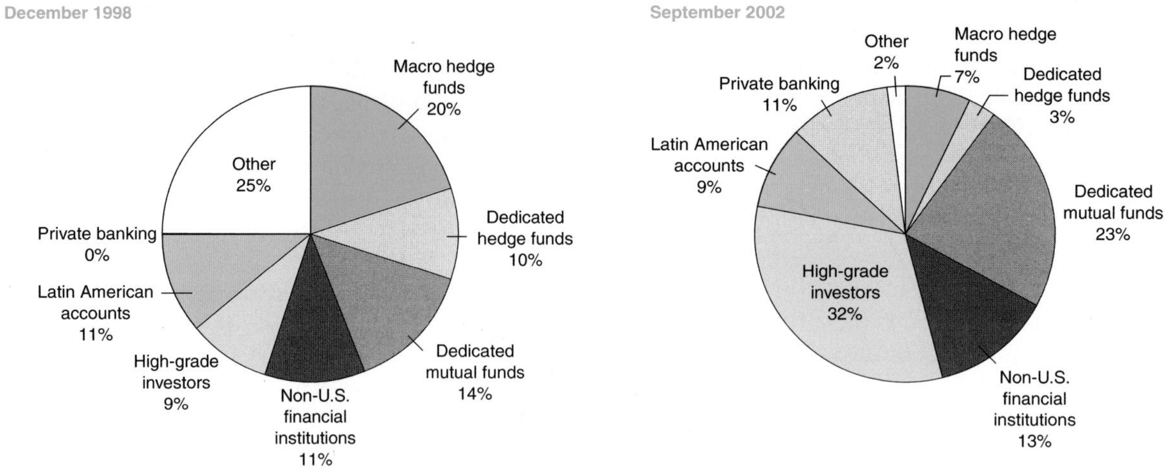

Source: J.P. Morgan Chase.

Markets for credit-risk transfer have registered strong growth in recent years, even though global financial market conditions have been generally subdued. Between 1997 and 2002, the global market expanded more than ten-fold, reaching $2 trillion in outstanding notional amount; it is expected to increase to $4.8 trillion by the end of 2004 (British Bankers Association 2002). As the market has come of age, it has proven resilient to financial turbulence and high-profile corporate and sovereign defaults, gaining confidence as an efficient means of hedging exposure to credit risk embedded in a variety of debt.

For the buyer of default protection, a credit derivative is a type of insurance contract. In the most common arrangement, the credit default swap (CDS), the buyer of credit-default protection pays a periodic premium to the seller. In the event of a default on the underlying credit instrument, the seller pays the buyer an agreed-upon amount.

By providing opportunities to transfer credit risk from banks and other institutions having a comparative advantage in credit relationships and funding to institutions and investors that are prepared to take on risk as part of their diversification and investment strategies, such as insurance companies, credit derivatives have the potential to fundamentally alter the traditional approach to credit-risk management and thereby the lending and borrowing business. Relative to other vehicles of credit protection, such as financial guarantees, credit derivative products offer flexibility, liquidity, and the advantage of standardized trading of credit risk as a separate asset class. Furthermore, as banks enhance their ability to diversify their credit exposure across markets and sectors, they are less likely to be vulnerable to risks (sector- or borrower-specific shocks) emanating from loan concentration—and thus less prone to make sudden changes in their supply of credit.

The natural *buyers of default protection* are institutions with debt exposure against which they prefer to hedge rather than sell. For example, growing concerns about Brazil's ability to service its sovereign debt in 2002 led many financial institutions with illiquid exposures in the country to seek ways to hedge their risk, raising the demand for default insurance. The natural *sellers of default protection* are investors, particularly insurance companies.

A market-based solution to credit risk

Several forces have driven the rapid growth of the credit derivatives market—among them regulatory arbitrage, advances in risk management technology and practice (including the application of value-at-risk methodology), and renewed interest in hedging credit risk as a way of dealing with deteriorating credit quality and rising corporate and sovereign defaults.

Yet the use of credit derivatives to manage credit risk is still only about 2 percent of their use in managing interest rate and currency risks. And the notional amount of credit risk being transferred through credit derivatives is a very small fraction of the debt held by major banks and bondholders.

Credit-derivative deals transacted on emerging-market debt have so far been limited, but the potential for growth seems to be large. Two important characteristics of emerging-market debt flows are likely to make emerging-market debt the new frontier for credit derivatives. First, in times of financial distress, emerging-market debt indexes tend to spike to levels that may not be warranted by a particular country's long-term creditworthiness or underlying economic fundamentals. And, second, the universe of investment-grade emerging-market debt issuers is expanding. Several, including Mexico and Poland, now have investment-grade ratings. Infrastructure project bonds, accompanied by credit enhancements such as political risk insurance (guarantees from multilateral bodies or national export-credit agencies), provide new avenues of emerging-market long-term debt.

Types of investments

Single-name CDSs accounted for about half of the credit-derivatives market at the end of 2001; collateralized debt obligations (CDOs) accounted for 23 percent (British Bankers Association 2002). Other products—total return swaps, credit-linked notes, and credit-spread put options—each accounted for 13 percent or less of the market.

The CDS market offers standardized credit protection on rated corporate and sovereign entities, including emerging-market borrowers. As the CDS market has grown, it has provided valuable price information, supplementing information available in the credit markets and thereby enhancing financial stability and efficiency. In a typical CDS transaction, the maturity is five years and fees or premiums, expressed in basis points on the notional contract amount, are paid quarterly. Trade takes place primarily in the inter-dealer market based on the standard documentation of the International Security Dealers Association (ISDA). The CDS has also provided the building block for the more sophisticated structured products, such as CDOs, which offer investors exposure to a portfolio of reference assets.

In a CDS transaction, the payout to the buyer of credit protection is triggered by a credit event, the precise definition of which is of the utmost importance. ISDA's 1999 credit-derivatives definitions cover six types of events: bankruptcy, obligation acceleration, obligation default, failure to pay, repudiation/moratorium, and restructuring. The definitions have helped market development, but they have not eliminated recourse to courts for dispute resolution.

The 1999 ISDA definitions are under review in response to objections by ratings agencies concerning their liberal language on evidence of a credit event. A fourth draft of the 2002 ISDA credit-derivatives definitions was distributed in November 2002 for consultation.

Bank retrenchment in context

As noted earlier, commercial banks as well as bondholders have become more cautious about extending credit to developing countries. European banks, which led the rapid growth in claims on developing countries through much of the 1990s, are now leading this retrenchment. Even at the end of the decade, when banks of other nationalities began to cut back (especially the Japanese), European banks continued to expand in developing countries, possibly because of the shrinking opportunities offered in the domestic market (due to rapid consolidation of the industry after the successful introduction of the euro). As a result, the share of total claims on developing countries accounted for by European banks has risen to about 77 percent in recent quarters, up from about 64 percent in 1990.

One factor contributing to greater caution on the part of Europe's banks over the near-term will be the path of their stock prices through recent quarters. Europe's banks were hardest hit by the widespread global declines in commercial bank stock prices in 2002 (figure 3.11). The decline reflected growing concerns about credit losses in Argentina and about large corporate losses in North America and Europe.

Beyond the immediate causes of the retrenchment lies a fundamental shift in commercial banks' strategy in recent years away from cross-border lending and toward greater participation in the

Figure 3.11 Performance of bank stocks, January 2002–January 2003

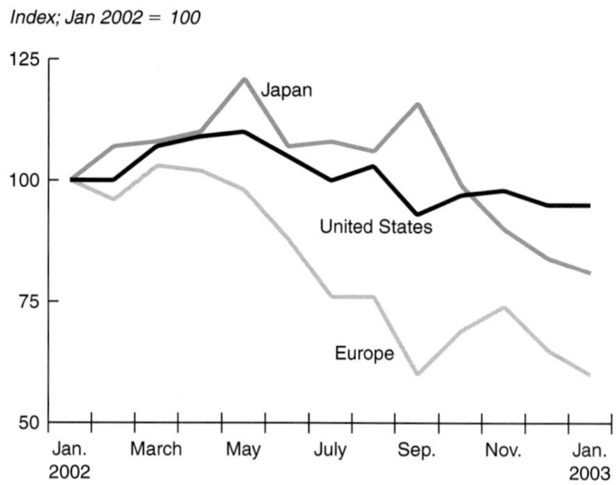

Source: Bloomberg.

local banking market. The shift is best illustrated using data collected by the BIS, which now breaks total claims into local claims, which have been growing rapidly in recent quarters, and cross-border claims, which have been declining (box 3.1).

This trend in bank behavior matches the global shift in external financing from debt to equity. When BIS-area banks focused on cross-border lending, loans invariably were funded in the international market, undertaken in foreign currency, and appeared as a net debt inflow on the capital account of the balance of payments. Local claims, however, are generally denominated in local currency and funded locally, leaving no record of balance-of-payments financing beyond the infusion of equity capital required to establish and capitalize a local banking presence.

In principle, a local banking presence brings with it benefits that extend well beyond the small increase in balance-of-payments financing. It should help improve the efficiency of the local financial intermediation system—thus mobilizing scarce domestic savings more efficiently. These benefits apply to poor countries as well. The significant presence of BIS-area deposit-taking institutions is one of the most important ways in which the poorest developing countries are connected to the global financial system (World Bank 2002).

In recent years, foreign banks invested heavily to create a local market presence in Argentina. The 2001 financial crisis led to severe losses on these investments, raising concern that banks may reconsider their local-market presence in developing countries, especially Latin America. Late in 2002, Spain's Santander bank sold its business in Peru, and Germany's HBV, its business in Brazil. In both cases, the buyer was a local bank.

Basel II

The prospect of international banks' involvement in developing countries will also be significantly shaped by certain global regulatory initiatives, particularly the newly revised Capital Adequacy Accord (Basel II), now under consultation. Scheduled for initial implementation in late 2006 by the member countries of the Basel Committee on Banking Supervision (BCBS), the new accord replaces and in many ways improves the original 1988 accord. The new accord is designed to enhance the safety and soundness of the banking industry worldwide through a better alignment of regulatory capital with banking risks, including credit, market, and operational risks. The minimum capital requirement under the new accord—that is, the ratio of bank assets put aside as a cushion to absorb unexpected losses—would be the same as under the 1988 accord.

The new accord will be based on three pillars: (a) a revised risk-based, minimum-capital requirement rule, (b) a new supervisory review mechanism, and (c) enhanced market discipline. Reflecting the changes that have taken place since 1988 in banking, risk management, and supervisory practices, the new accord emphasizes greater sensitivity to risk, particularly sovereign- and corporate-credit risk, and encourages the development of internal risk-control and management capabilities as an important part of the regulatory approach to the banking industry.

In moving toward a more risk-sensitive approach to credit risk, the accord provides three approaches for assessing capital adequacy: a "standardized" approach and two "internal ratings based" (IRB) approaches that sophisticated banks will be able to use under extensive supervisory review and disclosure requirements. The standardized approach builds essentially on the 1988 methodology of risk-weighted assets and a minimum capital ratio—but with a more refined approach to credit risk. First, risk weights would be set for a bank's exposure to sovereigns, corporations,

Box 3.1 International versus local-currency bank claims

The foreign assets of banks reporting to the BIS can be broken into two components. The first is cross-border claims (or international claims) funded in the international markets. For such claims banks secure deposits (liabilities) in markets other than the country to which the funds are lent (assets). Usually, the funds are raised in the headquarters of the bank. The second component of the bank's foreign assets are its local-currency claims. These are funded by attracting deposits directly in emerging markets.

International claims are the outcome of the traditional business of international banks in developing countries. Local-currency claims, by contrast, are of more recent genesis. They reflect the growing amount of foreign direct investment in the banking and financial sector of emerging markets. Local-currency claims arose from banks' desire to:

- Expand globally into new markets
- Pursue a more equitable growth of assets and liabilities
- Provide protection in the event of exchange-rate and debt crises, such as those of the 1980s and late 1990s.

The local-currency claims of BIS banks operating in emerging markets have risen sharply in relation to international claims (see figure at bottom left)—shooting up from about $130 billion at the end of 1996 to a peak of close to $490 billion at the beginning of 2002. The largest increases were in Latin America, where such claims grew from $66 billion in 1996 to over $290 billion by the beginning of 2002. In Europe and Central Asia local claims went from $12 billion to $87 billion over the same period. The big jump for East Asia came between 1999 and 2000, when claims jumped from $63 billion to $83 billion.

The two asset components pose different risks. International claims expose banks to currency and cross-border-transfer risks, since their claims on borrowers (that is, their assets) are funded in foreign currency (liabilities). Local-currency claims, being funded most often in local markets seldom pose such risks. However, they retain other risks associated with the country—political, legal, and economic.

Local lending is broadly matched by local deposit taking (see table below). By contrast, BIS-area banks have slumped from being net lenders in the cross-border market to being net borrowers (see figure at bottom right). As of March 2002, deposits from emerging markets in BIS-area banks far exceeded their borrowings.

The shift from international claims to local-currency claims, while reducing some risks for both banks and emerging markets, has brought about other risks that are only now beginning to surface. A good example is the case of Argentina, where the disparate treatment of locally funded foreign-currency assets and liabilities, enacted earlier in 2002 in the wake of currency pressures, has prompted some banks to become more cautious about expansion in developing countries in general.

Position of BIS banks for emerging markets, June 2002
(billions of dollars)

	Assets	Liabilities
International claims	793	949
Local currency	472	421

BIS banks' claims on emerging markets, 1983–2002

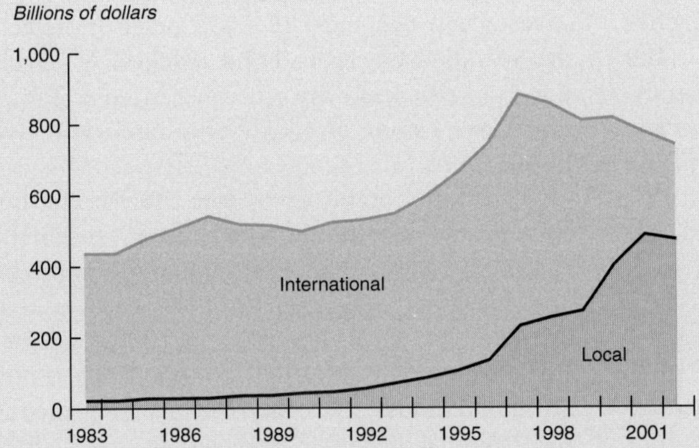

Emerging-market assets minus liabilities, 1983–2002

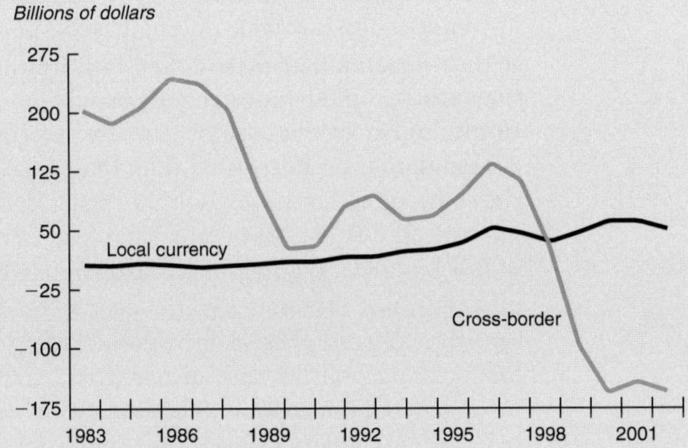

Source: Bank for International Settlements.

and other banks based on ratings from major credit-rating agencies and approved domestic agencies. Second, the system of risk weights for corporate lending would be enlarged to include four weights (20, 50, 100, and 150 percent), replacing the present single weight of 100 percent applied to all corporate exposures regardless of underlying credit quality.

The IRB approaches include a basic (or "foundation") approach and an advanced approach. In both, banks are allowed to use their internal ratings of each borrower's creditworthiness to assess credit risk in their portfolio, subject to certain methodological and disclosure requirements. The advanced version gives banks more discretion; it is expected to be adopted by more sophisticated institutions.

The new method of assessing the minimum-capital requirement is expected to have important implications for emerging-market economies, principally because capital charges for credit risk will be explicitly linked to indicators of credit quality, assessed either externally under the standardized approach or internally under the two ratings-based approaches. The implications include the likelihood of increased costs of capital to emerging-market borrowers, both sovereign and corporate; more limited availability of syndicated project-finance loans to borrowers in infrastructure and related industries; and an "unleveling" of the playing field for domestic banks in favor of international banks active in developing countries.

Concerns over the increased cost of capital under Basel II relate to the cross-border lending of international banks, and the potentially higher capital charges associated with such lending, particularly under the internal, ratings-based approaches that international banks are expected to adopt. The regulatory capital requirements would be significantly higher in the case of non-investment-grade emerging-market borrowers than under Basel I. At the same time, borrowers with a higher credit rating would benefit from a lower cost of capital under Basel II. A quantitative assessment of such effects is not straightforward, as the results are sensitive to a number of factors, including banks' loan pricing policies and, in particular, the extent to which banks' economic capital, which derives loan pricing, may exceed the minimum capital charges under the IRB approach. A recent study by the OECD (Weder and Wedow 2002) estimates the cost in spreads for lower-rated emerging borrowers to be possibly 200 basis points. If, as expected, most domestically owned banks in emerging-market economies adopt the standardized approach to credit risk, they will be at a comparative disadvantage vis-à-vis cross-border lending by international banks when attempting to lend to high-quality domestic borrowers. On the other hand, they will have a comparative advantage in lending to low-quality domestic borrowers (Fischer 2002, Hayes 2002).

Finally, the prospects for capital flows for infrastructure projects from the market in syndicated commercial-bank loans depends on how the BCBS ultimately elects to treat structured credit products, including project finance. The current proposal places project loans in a higher risk category than corporate loans, leading the BCBS to recommend higher capital requirements that could reduce the availability of syndicated project-finance loans and possibly increase their cost to borrowers in infrastructure and other sectors. But according to evidence provided by the private sector in response to the BCBS's recommendation, project-finance loans outperform unsecured corporate loans, both in default rates and recovery performance, thus requiring lower capital charges, not more (Berner and others 2002). The BCBS is reportedly considering this evidence.

The emerging bond market really is emerging

The weakness of international bond issuance by developing countries and the high level of spreads through most of 2002 belie the fact that the so-called emerging bond markets of developing countries really are emerging in several important ways—some of which have important policy implications.

The first notable development is the continued shift from Brady bonds to more conventional eurobond issues in the international market. Buyback and swap activity began in 1996 and peaked in 2000 (figure 3.12). It slowed in 2002, in part because of unfavorable market conditions for new eurobond issues, but also because the outstanding stock of Bradys has fallen by so much that there is not much more of this transformation to complete. Of the $150 billion in Brady bonds

Figure 3.12 Volume of Brady swaps and buybacks, 1996–2002

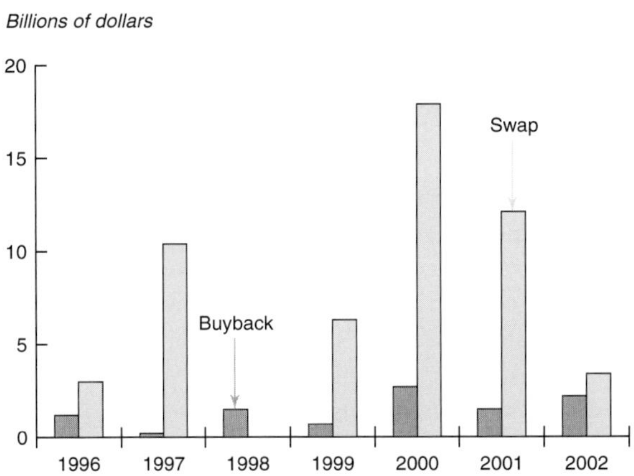

Note. 2002 data are through September.
Source: World Bank staff estimates.

originally issued, only $50 billion are still in circulation. Mexico has reduced its outstanding stock of Bradys from an original issue of $33 billion to just $5 billion. There are two basic reasons for this transformation:

- *Cost.* Brady bonds have consistently traded at a discount to the comparable eurobonds of the same issuer, possibly due to the complexity in the pricing of Bradys (for example, pricing-out collateral). As long as the Brady-eurobond spread differential is positive, sovereign borrowers can realize debt-service savings by exploiting this arbitrage.
- *Reputation enhancement.* Bradys carry with them the stigma of previously rescheduled debt.

The second development is that various features of truly developed markets are now more evident in the markets for developing-country bonds. The emergence in the 1990s of a nascent project bond market to fund long-term infrastructure projects in developing countries—such as electric power plants, roads, ports, airports, telecommunications networks, and water and waste water facilities—which were traditionally the preserve of the public sector, merits attention for several reasons. First, project bonds are a potentially major source of long-term private debt capital linked directly to economic growth and competitiveness. Second, they are a new asset class in the emerging-market debt spectrum, offering asset diversification and investment opportunities particularly to institutional investors, such as insurance companies and pension funds, whose long-term liabilities match the long-term tenor of project bonds. Third, they mirror the shift in the pattern of capital flows from bank loans to publicly issued bonds.

Although the volume of capital raised in the project-bond market remains relatively small, the market has matured, delivering a series of high-profile transactions—among which are the $1.2 billion bond issue by Qatar for the Ras Laffan liquid natural gas project, a $1 billion issue by the República Bolivariana de Venezuela for the Petrozuata oil project, and a $125 million issue by the Philippines for the Quezon power project—and encompassing a broad range of projects, issue sizes, and terms. One important factor contributing to the growth of this market has been the design of creative bond covenants that have provided bondholders contractual protection against certain risks inherent in such projects. An examination of a sample of project bonds issued between January 1993 and March 2002 reveals that project indentures contain the standard covenant provisions aimed at mitigating conflicts of interest arising from asset substitution, dividend policies, claim dilution, and underinvestment. In addition they contain clauses that serve as commitment and incentive devices for host governments and other contracting parties to the project. All sample project bonds were issued under New York Law, under which market practice does not normally include collective action clauses in bond indentures.

The third and most significant development is the shift away from bond issuance in the international markets in favor of issuance in local-currency bond markets. This shift is most important for government issuers, although nascent local-currency bond markets are already an important source of funding for private-sector borrowers in much of Asia. An important rotation from external to domestic debt has already occurred in the pool of public-sector debt in the major emerging economies (figure 3.13). In several countries—among them Brazil, Chile, Hungary, India, the Republic of Korea, Malaysia, Mexico, Poland, South Africa, and Turkey—local-currency fixed-income markets have grown considerably in recent years. In response to several institutional and policy initiatives, they also have undergone

Figure 3.13 Emerging economies: public debt stocks, 1996–2001

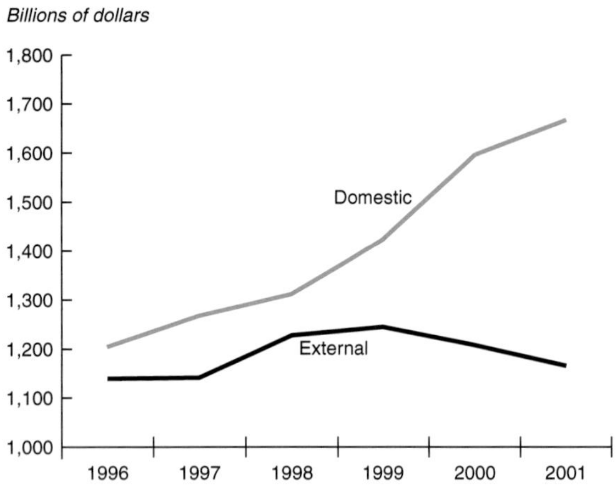

Source: J.P. Morgan Chase.

considerable modernization in terms of trading practice, clearance and settlement mechanisms, and electronic transfer of securities, as well as in market capitalization and pricing procedures. Such markets now offer a range of money market, treasury bill, and longer dated securities. They have adequate liquidity, particularly on the government side, and the depth to respond to the debt issuance needs of the public and corporate sectors. And in countries such as Chile, the Republic of Korea, and Malaysia, which have well-developed local institutional investors (insurance companies, pension funds), local debt markets have developed the capacity to meet needs for long-term infrastructure investment.

A country may choose to develop a local-currency fixed-income market for several reasons. Virtually all developing and transition economies have access to international credit markets only through the use of the hard currencies in which international debt instruments are denominated. But this practice exposes the borrower to the vicissitudes of currency risk—a danger brought home painfully by the East Asian crisis of 1997–98. Local-currency markets provide a natural hedge for domestic borrowers. They may also be attractive as assets that generate returns for foreign investors who seek diversified investment opportunities, particularly in the current environment of subdued returns in more established global financial markets.

The evolution of local fixed-income markets has been helped along by liberalization measures intended to ease or remove barriers to the entry of foreign investors. In India, for instance, foreign institutional investors were allowed as early as 1997 to invest in local fixed-income markets, including government securities. The Republic of Korea took a significant step forward in 2001 when it made the won fully convertible on the capital account. The scope for further reform is great. Although most countries have achieved currency convertibility in their current-account transactions, their currencies are not convertible for capital account transactions. Capital-account transactions in most developing countries are still subject to exchange-rate restrictions and controls.

There are a number of very important features about the movement toward debt denominated in local currency and traded in local markets.

First, the shift toward domestic debt is a natural aspect of the move to floating exchange rates. When governments were choosing to peg their own currencies to another, usually the dollar, borrowing externally in foreign currency was a way of minimizing borrowing costs while signaling to the market the government's commitment to maintain the foreign-exchange peg. The government, of course, was thus vulnerable to considerable exchange-rate risk, one reason why the currency crises in the 1990s often turned quickly into government debt crises. With the move to floating foreign-exchange rates, governments have a greater incentive to borrow in their own currency.

Second, the shift toward domestic debt was fostered by the growing success of macro policy in many developing countries. Developing countries' success in controlling inflation in the new environment of generalized floating foreign-exchange rates has given domestic and foreign investors the confidence to buy locally denominated debt. The key to creating credibility on inflation has been the combination of an operationally independent central bank and a responsible, coherent fiscal policy. Where such necessary conditions have been met, it has proved possible for countries to develop deep and relatively liquid local bond markets and to issue securities with the same long maturities previously seen only in the international market (box 3.2).

Third, locally denominated debt is an important way for countries to overcome "original sin"—the inability of governments to borrow in their own currencies in *international* markets (Eichengreen, Hausmann, and Panizza 2002). Few currencies are

Box 3.2 Local 10-year bond markets

A key step toward stable local-market funding for the public sector is the development of a benchmark 10-year, fixed-rate, coupon bond. To be able to issue such a bond in its own currency, not only must a government achieve an adequate credit rating in the market, but also it must convince market participants, both local and foreign, of its ability to control inflation over the long run. The fact that so many developing countries, including some that suffered severe financial crises in recent years, now have 10-year benchmark issues is an indication of how far their reputation for fiscal soundness has come.

As impressive as the emergence of these long-maturity securities is the convergence in their yields (see figure). For a basket of developing countries, spreads over the core markets of the United States and the Euro Area (Germany) have narrowed to a weighted average of not much more than 250 basis points, down from almost 400 basis points at the start of 2001. Typically, bond-yield convergences such as these have taken much longer to occur, as it takes time to build reputation. The fact that it is happening so quickly for many developing countries is a testament to their policy efforts, to be sure, but it may also reflect the buoyancy of private-sector debt looking for "safe" developing country investments.

Ten-year benchmark government bond yields, 2001–2002

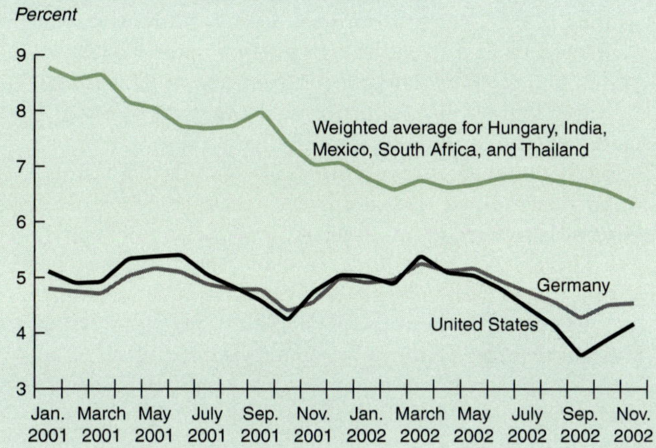

Source: Bloomberg.

used in international markets, and the dollar remains dominant, so it is little surprise that emerging-market governments have made little headway in these markets. Local-market investments in developing countries, by contrast, have become increasingly attractive for bond-market investors in mature markets, partly because yields in the mature markets are so low. Foreign investors are attracted not only by the higher yields offered by developing-country bonds, but also by the prospect of capital gains arising from interest-rate convergence. This phenomenon has been especially visible in recent quarters in the former transition economies of Eastern Europe. To the extent that such cross-border inflows are seen as desirable (which is likely to be the case if they allow developing-country governments to repay foreign-currency debt and thus shift foreign-exchange risks to the investor), then policy measures to develop domestic market infrastructure and regulation will prove as important as the more fundamental policy improvements noted above (IMF and World Bank 2001).

Fourth, there is some risk of crowding-out. If the government borrows in the local market when it could have access to foreign saving through international markets, it might raise the cost of local bond finance to private-sector borrowers. This crowding-out effect might be offset by the boost to the local bond market liquidity that the supply of government benchmarks might provide, however.

Finally, domestic debt shifts the nature of the risks facing borrowers, but it does not remove them. One advantage of borrowing in foreign currency is that the term of the loan is often relatively long. By contrast, most debt issues in emerging local markets are concentrated at the short end of the curve—until the government develops a credible record for good macroeconomic policy. Short maturities leave government borrowers open to considerable rollover risk in the early stages of their transition from international to local markets. Indeed, the interaction of high rollover risk with other adverse macro shocks lies behind many of the crisis episodes of the past 10 years. (For Brazil's experience, see box 3.3.)

The moral of the story is that a government cannot avoid a debt crisis simply by shifting from a pegged to a floating currency. While a floating

Box 3.3 Brazil's experience in 2002

Brazil's experience in 2002 highlights some of the vulnerabilities that can develop even as a government shifts its funding from international to local markets.

Brazil's markets initially responded to the default of neighboring Argentina with remarkable resilience. The currency strengthened during the fourth quarter of 2001 as Argentina plunged into a disorderly default. Moreover, bond-yield spreads narrowed through the first quarter of 2002. Although not immediate, the hit from Argentina was real, however, and led to a reduction of many flows to Brazil, including FDI and trade finance. Partly as a result, markets weakened sharply through the second and third quarters, as bond yields spiked and the currency dropped by almost 40 percent between the end of March and the end of September. This deterioration was eventually halted and partly reversed by the IMF program that began in early September.

Uncertainty about the presidential election in October was another key factor in the country's difficulties. As Lula da Silva, the left-of-center opposition candidate and eventual winner, gained in the polls, markets weakened even though, as a candidate, Lula made a commitment to the strong monetary and fiscal policies that had characterized the Cardoso administration. Once in office, Lula reiterated his commitment to adhere to sound policies and there was a remarkable improvement in Brazilian markets that has lasted through the early months of 2003.

But political uncertainty is by no means the only explanation for Brazil's problems in 2002. Three other factors are important:

- *By objective standards, Brazil has a heavy load of external debt.* Indeed, World Bank classifications put Brazil in the "severely indebted" group of middle-income countries, although well over half of this stock is owed by private-sector borrowers. With investors increasingly unwilling to hold debt from higher-risk developing countries, Brazil suffered.
- *The economy entered 2002 with a relatively high current-account deficit and a declining inward flow of FDI.* With debt investors retrenching, this left little option but to engineer a rapid adjustment in the trade and current-account balances. The real thus came under sharp downward pressure.
- *The domestic public debt structure made the country vulnerable.* The currency was supported at various points in 2001 and 2002 by heavy issuance of dollar-linked government paper. As external adjustment pressures pushed the real lower, the government's debt-to-GDP ratio began to rise sharply, raising concerns in both local and international financial markets. The government was obliged to offer high interest rates and shorter-dated maturities as it rolled over its short-term debt, further raising market worries about debt sustainability. As noted, these concerns faded quickly after both the successful political transition and the announcement by the new government that it would raise the target for the primary budget surplus in 2003, to 4.25 percent of GDP.

foreign-exchange regime may help the country absorb adverse shocks—as well as alleviating the need for the authorities to push interest rates to damagingly high levels to avoid a complete loss of reserves—it does not guarantee government solvency. Only a sustainable long-run fiscal policy can do that.

Until such policies become generalized throughout the developing world, the specter of sovereign debt defaults will haunt financial markets and leave developing countries open to the damage done by frightened creditors hastening to cut their losses. Recently, collective action clauses and a proposed "sovereign debt reduction mechanism" have been developed to keep debt problems from becoming downward spirals of panic and penury. These are discussed in the next section.

Sovereign debt defaults—past, present, and future

The desire of investors to trim their holdings of developing-country debt and shift toward the stronger end of the credit spectrum has put many borrowing countries under severe pressure. For some, this pressure could worsen domestic economic and political problems sufficiently that the outcome is default. According to Beers and Chambers (2002), six sovereign borrowers defaulted in 2002: Argentina (which formally defaulted in January), Gabon, Indonesia (which restructured its syndicated bank credits as required under its Paris Club agreement), Madagascar, Moldova, and Nauru, taking the number of countries in default of their debt to 28 at year end—the highest incidence since 1992. Of these six countries, Indonesia originally reached an agreement for debt restructuring in 1998—thus the country's 2002 bank-debt rescheduling was part of the clean-up begun at that time. Nauru is not classified by the World Bank as a developing country. But it is the magnitude and the potential impact of the Argentine default that have put the issue of sovereign default and bankruptcy back on the international policy agenda. (See the annex to this chapter for a discussion of defaults in 2002, plus a tabulation of commercial-debt restructurings since the 1980s.)

The history of sovereign default

Sovereign borrowers have defaulted on foreign debt since the dawn of international lending (Dammers 1984). In the fourth century B.C., the Attic Maritime Association, to which a majority of Greek city-states belonged, defaulted on loans from the Delos temple. England's King Edward III repudiated his debts to Italian bankers in 1357. France ceased payments on its debt an average of once every 30 years from the 1500s to the 1800s.

Modern lending to emerging markets got under way in the 1820s in the aftermath of the Napoleonic wars (Chancellor 2000). Since that time, sovereign defaults have occurred in four waves (the 1820s, the 1870s, the 1930s, and the 1980s), in part driven by broad cyclical movements in the global economy (figure 3.14). Although the number of countries currently on default in their debt (28) is higher than the peaks of the pre-1980s upturns, the *share* of countries in default is currently much lower (28 out of 202 borrowers).

Figure 3.14 Share of sovereign borrowers in default on debt, 1820–2000

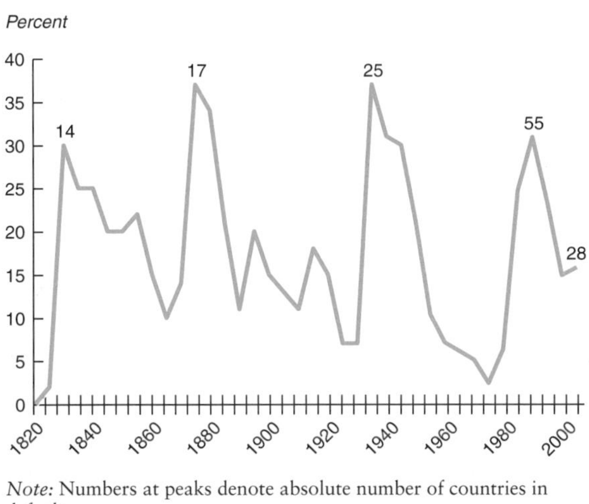

Note: Numbers at peaks denote absolute number of countries in default.
Sources: Suter 1992; Beers and Chambers 2002.

In the 1820s the newly independent countries of Latin America issued bonds in London. The firms arranging these bond issues generally retained at least two years of interest and amortization (Dammers 1984). When these funds were exhausted, all but one of these countries defaulted. Some European countries (e.g., Denmark following the Napoleonic wars; Ramphal 1989) also defaulted. Several states of the United States defaulted in the 1830s and 1840s (Eichengreen 1991).

The second wave of Latin American defaults (accompanied by Turkey and Egypt) came in the 1870s, during a deflationary period for the global economy. Most of these defaults were settled by the 1880s. Lending to emerging markets grew rapidly following World War I and debt difficulties eased. By 1927, only 5 percent of foreign-government obligations were in default, if one excludes pre-revolutionary Russian bonds. The world recession of the 1930s led to widespread and sustained defaults, however, and industrial-country bond markets became effectively closed to developing countries until well after World War II.

There were some notable features to the way that the international capital markets handled sovereign defaults before the First World War.

Defaults during the 19th and early 20th century were often resolved relatively efficiently through private negotiations (Eichengreen and Portes 1995). Bondholders' committees were established to facilitate coordination among investors, and the creation of permanent bondholder committees (without government participation) in the United Kingdom was credited with reducing the cost of negotiations.

Not all defaults were resolved privately, however. In some cases, navies of creditor countries blockaded ports until debt service resumed, seized liquid assets, or took over and ran customs offices of debtor nations (for example, the Arab Republic of Egypt by Britain, Turkey by France). The United States intervened in the Dominican Republic, Haiti, Honduras, and Nicaragua against governments that defaulted on their debt (Dammers 1984). But creditor governments usually viewed defaults as a matter of business rather than politics, and most British governments were reluctant to use their power or influence to support creditor rights in emerging markets.

Creditors demonstrated some flexibility in dealing with default, in part because repayment could rarely be enforced through the seizure of assets (except for the use of gunboat diplomacy) due to a broad interpretation of sovereign immunity. The courts could be contemptuous of attempts to enforce collection of foreign loans. In 1877, an English court characterized Peruvian bonds as essentially unenforceable "engagements of honor" (the equivalent of gambling debts; Kaletsky 1985). Rescheduling agreements and the capitalization of interest into new bonds were common, and often reflected debt relief rather than repayment in full (Ramphal 1989). In general, settlement typically did not involve complete repayment of interest and principle (Cole, Dow, and English 1994).

Default did not necessarily mean exclusion from the capital markets for a lengthy period. Many countries were able to obtain new loans relatively soon after settling their old debts (Cole, Dow, and English 1994). Practice changed in the course of the 19th century. The time from default to the restoration of market access averaged 14 years from 1821 to 1870, a figure that fell to just six years after 1870 (Suter 1992).[3] In general, some settlement was a prerequisite for obtaining new loans. Even after long periods of default, one of more than 50 years, old debts were settled before new loans were made available. Relatively easy access to new loans by defaulted states that agreed to settle their obligations generally reflected changes in regime that indicated more accommodating policies toward foreign creditors. From 1841 to 1843, eight U.S. states and one territory defaulted on obligations that were held largely by residents of other states or Britain. Those states that settled their debts were able to regain access to international credit in the 1850s, while states that refused to settle were for the most part unable to access foreign loans (English 1996). There were even cases of serial defaulters. Guatemala defaulted in 1828, 1864, 1876, 1894, 1900, and 1917, each occasion leading to debt restructuring, followed by successful attempts to raise fresh capital (Ramphal 1989).

By contrast, defaults by a majority of sovereign debtors during the 1930s effectively closed New York, London, and Paris bond markets to foreign sovereign borrowers, particularly less developed countries, until the late 1960s. This likely was due to the breadth and severity of the world recession and the interruption from the war, rather than a change in attitude by lenders. The collapse in commodity prices and rising protectionism cut the export revenues of 41 primary product exporters by about half from 1928–29 to 1932–33, and real interest rates rose to more than 15 percent (Ramphal 1989). In such difficult conditions, countries that did not default (such as Argentina) enjoyed no better capital market access than defaulting countries (Jorgensen and Sachs 1998).

Sovereign default in the 1980s

When sovereign lending from the developed to the developing world began to revive in earnest in the 1970s, the source of lending shifted. The main creditor group was not bondholders, but commercial banks. From 1970 to the late 1980s, banks accounted for about 90 percent of developing countries' public external debt to private creditors (figure 3.15).

Several factors dictated the reemergence of sovereign borrowing in the form of bank loans:

- Banks were flush with liquidity with the recycling of oil wealth and the drop in real interest rates that accompanied rising inflation during the decade. The U.S. long-term bond yield averaged between 6 and 8 percent in every year from 1970 to 1978, while consumer prices increased by almost 7 percent a year.

Figure 3.15 Composition of external debt to private creditors, 1970–2000

Public and publicly guaranteed debt (percent)

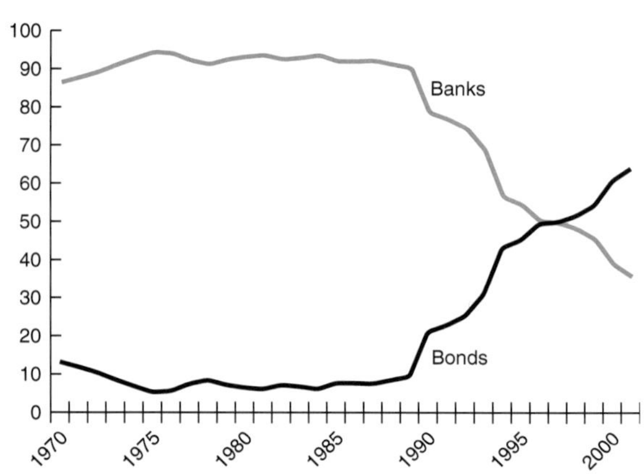

Source: World Bank Debtor Reporting System.

- It was hoped that banks, with their long-term relationships with emerging markets, would be a more savvy source of funds than bond investors.
- Many emerging markets were experiencing respectable growth rates, which bolstered lenders' confidence in repayment prospects. For example, GDP rose by 5.9 percent per year in Latin America in the 1970s (this compares with the average of about 2 percent that prevailed over the subsequent two decades). Moreover, booming commodity prices led to substantial windfall income gains for many developing countries.
- Despite the historical experience, the belief prevailed that major emerging markets would not default, either because "countries do not go out of business"[4] or because the creditor governments would not permit a default, given the vulnerability of their major banks.

The boom in bank lending came to an end with the sharp tightening in U.S. monetary policy at the end of the 1970s. Countries that had borrowed when U.S. real interest rates were close to zero and global growth was buoyant suddenly had to face high real interest rates, depressed global demand, and plunging commodity prices. In the three years following the Mexican payments suspension in August 1982, 24 middle-income countries were forced to renegotiate their debt with commercial banks.

At this point, the concept of a sovereign default became a little murkier. In the end, the defaults and write-downs on bank debts followed a three-stage process in most countries:

Reschedulings. At first, the banks and countries agreed on the rescheduling of principal for the following year—this on the expectation that interest rates would fall, global growth would resume, and countries could quickly return to full payment on their external debts. For example, the agreements reached with Argentina and Brazil in 1983 covered only 12 months; the agreement with the Dominican Republic, 13 months; and the agreement with Mexico, 28 months (reached in August 1983, it consolidated debt over the previous 15 months and the next 12 months) (see annex to this chapter). These agreements involved simply a delay in repayments, with interest accruing on the rescheduled debt, rather than any reduction in the debt burden.

This rescheduling was facilitated by the concentration of holdings of claims. For example, in the United States the top nine banks held more than 60 percent of major U.S. banks' assets in eight of the largest emerging market debtors (Kaletsky 1985). Initially, at least, such rescheduling operations allowed all sides to claim that default had been avoided. For policymakers in the industrial countries, this was a welcome fix, as many important industrial-country banks had very large exposure to developing countries, so that a default could threaten the solvency of industrial-country banking systems. For example, as of March 1984, nine money-center U.S. banks had loans totaling 179 percent of their equity in six developing countries with severe debt difficulties (Kaletsky 1985). Many debtor countries entered into a series of agreements with commercial banks to restructure debt (Mexico had eight in the 1980s; Argentina, Brazil, and the República Bolivariana de Venezuela each had four).

Multiyear restructuring agreements. As the 1980s wore on, the restructuring period grew longer. Multiyear restructuring agreements with commercial banks were introduced in 1984, which economized on time spent in negotiations and reduced the cost of rescheduled debt. But the debt problems remained unresolved, reflecting the failure of simply postponing repayment to address the debt burden, coupled with policy failures by some borrowers and recurrence of external shocks. By 1988, despite significant trade surpluses in many debtors, their nominal level of debt relative to income was as high or higher than it had been in 1982 (figure 3.16).

Moreover, debt continued to trade on secondary markets at a substantial discount to face value, confirming the market's skepticism that debt would ever be repaid in full.[5]

In September 1988, the secondary market price of 13 major debtors traded at an unweighted average of 44 cents on the dollar. The continued debt overhang was believed to constrain growth in the major indebted countries. Expectations that voluntary commercial bank lending would resume to the debtors who rescheduled debt service payments and undertook structural reforms (key elements of the Baker initiative—a U.S. government–led plan to allow countries to grow their way out of debt difficulties along with net new lending) were frustrated. Net commercial bank lending to the 17 countries involved in the Baker initiative averaged less than $3 billion per year from 1985 to 1988.

Figure 3.16 Ratio of debt to gross national income for select countries, 1982 and 1988

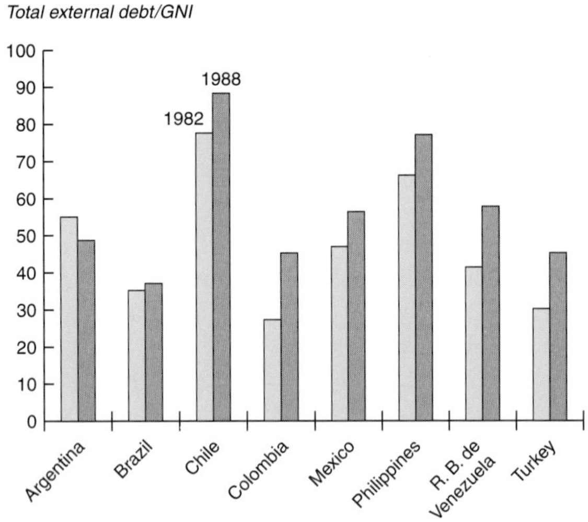

Source: World Bank Debtor Reporting System.

The Brady initiative. The Brady initiative, supported with funds from the World Bank and the IMF, finally provided the framework for a reduction of the debt burden. From 1989 to 1995, 13 countries with $191 billion in commercial bank debt completed debt and debt service reduction (DDSR) operations, which provided for the reduction of nearly 20 percent in the nominal value of commercial bank debt. The DDSR programs included a variety of instruments: buybacks at a discount, exchanges for discount bonds at market rates, par bonds at below-market interest rates, and in some cases, partial payment of arrears and new money bonds. The new obligations were generally securitized, that is, issued in the form of bonds and enhanced by collateral for principal and interest payments. As a result of debt reduction and, in many countries, some rise in growth rates, the average debt to gross national income ratios of the major debtors listed in figure 3.16 fell from 57 percent in 1988 to 43 percent in 1994.

Debt crises in the 1990s

Developing countries' access to bond markets increased as their problems with commercial bank debt declined. Net bond flows to developing countries rose from $11 billion in 1991 to a peak of $40 billion in 1997–98, before dropping with the fallout from the East Asian Crisis.

The rise in bond finance can be attributed to improved prospects and greater stability in many debtor countries; the opening of capital markets, which encouraged greater lending to domestic firms (including state enterprises); market innovations, such as derivatives and securitization, which facilitated greater risk sharing and hence a greater supply of capital; and the reduction of inflation in industrial countries during the 1980s, which made the supply of bond finance more attractive.

As in past episodes, however, the expansion of finance was accompanied by debt crises. Mexico (1994–95), East Asia (1997–98), the Russian Federation (1998), Brazil (1999 and 2002), Turkey (briefly in 1994 and 2000–01), and Argentina (2001–02) all suffered massive economic (and in some cases political and social) dislocations as either the government or the private sector struggled to meet its obligations. The economic cost was huge: output in the eight countries most directly affected by the financial crises of the 1990s fell by almost 3 percent during crisis years, compared with a rise of almost 5 percent in the years before and after the crisis.

Growing official support for countries in crisis. The most striking aspect of the strategy adopted to handle debt crises in the 1990s was a massive increase in official support, despite the fact that the threat posed by emerging-market financial crises to industrial-country banks had eased since the 1980s. Severe debt service problems were often met by financing packages from creditor governments and multilateral institutions, at times (for example, the Republic of Korea) combined with undertakings by commercial banks to roll over short-term credit lines. IMF disbursements jumped beginning in 1995, with the bulk of funds devoted to large rescue packages designed to restore financial stability in major debtors (figure 3.17). Since 1995, 10 major emerging markets have received IMF programs that exceeded 400 percent of quota, whereas 300 percent of quota had been set as a maximum in 1992, with exceptions allowed for extraordinary circumstances (Porzecanski 2002).

Three factors appear to have encouraged this strategy shift to more aggressive official intervention:

- Policymakers became concerned that crises affecting a few borrowers would spill over rapidly to many other securities markets,

Figure 3.17 IMF disbursements, 1984–2002

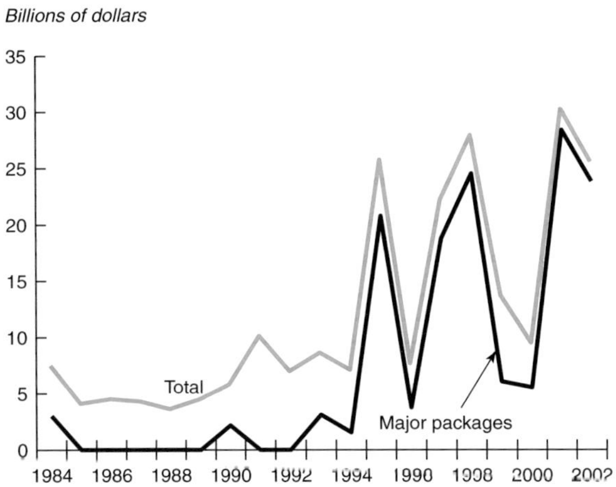

Note: Major packages are defined as those having disbursements in excess of $1 billion.
Source: International Monetary Fund.

including those in both the developing and developed world. Aggressive lending was thus a public good, designed to head off widespread contagion.

- The central role played by bond finance made it difficult to coordinate many diffuse market participants. Adding emergency funding was a way of keeping bond markets liquid at a time of severe selling pressure.
- Political and economic ties between creditor governments and major debtors had strengthened. This was especially important in the U.S.-led support for Mexico in early 1995.

The availability of official resources to refinance debt service has undoubtedly reduced the number of countries forced to declare formal default on their external debt. In this sense, the policy can be viewed as a success.

Legitimate concerns have been expressed about the extent of reliance on official finance during recent crises, however. Most important, the increasing openness of capital account transactions has raised the amount of official resources required to restore confidence.[6] This raises an inherent credibility problem, as a package large enough to reassure creditors completely may have to be so large as to be politically untenable for the major industrial countries. Moreover, such large official financing packages are more likely to increase moral hazard and thus encourage greater risk taking by lenders.[7] Also, as a result of the official support, the country may be even more vulnerable because of the larger amount of inflexible debt on its books.

Market-based approaches to resolving crises. The task of ensuring that private-sector creditors contribute to resolving crises has become more complicated due to the increasing importance of bonds in emerging market debt. During the 1980s debt crisis, holders of 85 percent of a country's debt could be represented by 15 banks with powerful incentives to cooperate, including similar institutional interests, the desire to secure future business with the debtor, a reluctance to oppose their regulators, and the legal obligation to share the proceeds of any litigation with all other creditors (Krueger 2002a).[8] By contrast, bondholders are more numerous and may be anonymous. They generally do not have long-term relationships with debtors or regulators, and their incentive to sue is greater because they often do not have to share the proceeds of litigation. Thus the potential has increased for coordination failures and disorderly debt restructurings, characterized by competition among creditors to collect and legal disputes among creditors and between creditors and the debtor.

A disorderly process can increase the economic disruption suffered by the debtor economy, further impairing the debtors' ability to pay and thus reducing potential payments to creditors (Chari and Kehoe 1998, Miller and Zhang 1998). The potential for an extremely costly default can lead insolvent debtors to delay formal default, for example by increasing the amount of debt at extremely short maturities, forcing domestic institutions subject to regulatory authority to lend to the government, and drawing down reserves to dangerously low levels. Such measures increase the costs to the debtor's economy when default finally occurs. Disorder also can lead to an unpredictable and inequitable allocation of payments to creditors, thus increasing uncertainty and reducing the supply of finance (Cornelli and Felli 1994). Moreover, the likelihood of a disorderly restructuring process can reduce incentives for creditors to participate in necessary restructurings by holding out the promise of higher returns through legal action. Lipworth and Nystedt (2001) argue that the shift from commercial bank lending to Eurobonds following the 1980s debt crisis in part occurred because creditors believed eurobonds would be extremely difficult and costly to restructure.

While the dangers of a disorderly restructuring are real, recent negotiations of bonded debt have been resolved without great difficulty despite the potential for litigation, the requirements of unanimous consent by creditors, and the problems involved in identifying and coordinating the actions of thousands of bondholders. Pakistan (1999), Ukraine (1999 and 2000), and Argentina (2001) undertook voluntary bond exchanges, under which some form of sweetener was included to enhance investor participation, which reached almost 99 percent in Pakistan and Argentina, and 85 percent in the 2000 Ukraine operation. Some observers have cited these examples in claiming that market-based approaches are efficient ways to address sovereign defaults (Roubini 2002).

Despite these successes, there are two reasons why market-based approaches may not deal efficiently with future crises:

- These bond exchanges typically covered just a few bond issues, in a few cases with relatively small amounts of debt (Bolton 2002). The Pakistan issue had a relatively homogeneous investor base that facilitated negotiations. It has not been shown that bond exchanges can be used to deal with a default covering very large amounts of debt and involving multiple instruments.
- Many of these operations did not reduce the present value of the debt (Chuhan 2001), and the Pakistan and Ukraine deals provided significant mark-to-market gains for creditors (substantial upfront cash was included in the Ukraine operation). It is not clear that the operations have restored the solvency of the countries involved (Roubini 2000) (by now the failure of the Argentine operation has become clear). Thus these operations do not demonstrate that private negotiations have achieved an efficient resolution of crises involving bonded debt that restored debt sustainability.

Ecuador and the Russian Federation implemented concerted bond restructurings in August of 2000 that did involve debt reduction—an average of 40 percent in Ecuador and 37 percent in the Russian Federation (see table 3.4). Creditor participation in both operations was high (97 percent in Ecuador). The Ecuador operation was particularly interesting because negotiations took less than a year (much shorter than many of the bank debt restructurings), and the legal advisor was able to cram down the terms on holdouts. While Ecuador's bonds required unanimity to change payment terms, only 51 percent agreement was required to change the nonfinancial terms, so "exit consent" clauses were used to change the terms of the old bond and make them less appealing to potential holdouts. Despite the existence of acceleration and cross-default clauses, creditors did not take legal action to enforce their rights, presumably because litigation is costly and sovereign assets are relatively difficult to attach, despite the increased use of waivers of sovereign immunity for commercial transactions (Roubini 2000). Thus, the Ecuador case does provide some comfort that the restructuring of bonded debt, which involves a write-down of claims, does not have to be disorderly.

Table 3.4 Select bond exchanges, 1999–2001

	Voluntary			Concerted	
	Argentina	Pakistan	Ukraine	Ecuador	Russia
Debt eligible	29.5	0.6	2.7	6.7	31.8
Debt reduction (%)	0.0	0.0	0.0	40.0	37.0
Amounts exchanged	29.5	0.6	2.3	6.6	31.8
Exchange bonds issued	30.4	0.6	2.3	4.0	21.1

Source: Chuhan 2001.

Nevertheless, recent legal cases show that the potential for a more disorderly restructuring process remains. Earlier attempts to buy distressed debt and sue for full payment were generally unsuccessful. Lawsuits were filed during the restructuring of Latin American bonds during the late 1980s and early 1990s, but they achieved little success. Lawsuits also have been filed against Brazil for nonpayment of commercial debt (Priest 2001), with little result.

More recent cases have shown that such a strategy may be profitable. A fund bought some $20 million in Peruvian defaulted debt at a discount of almost 50 percent and obtained court injunctions to prevent the government from repaying other creditors until its claims were settled (ICN 2000). After a New York court ruled in its favor in 2000, Peru faced the potential for a breakdown of the Brady restructuring, which would have further deepened the country's economic difficulties. The government then settled the case, paying the fund a substantial premium over what other creditors received. The same fund has also secured significant payments by suing, or threatening to sue, Panama and Vietnam (Brady Forum 2000). Similar issues arise regarding the restructuring of debt in the Democratic Republic of the Congo (Krueger 2002b). There were reports last year that vulture funds were active in buying Argentine securities (Priest 2001). Some commentators expect "an avalanche of lawsuits against the Argentine government," particularly if foreign bondholders are not provided the same terms as domestic bondholders (Latin American Advisor 2002). Thus, there remains some potential for the disruption of future restructurings of bonded debt.

The search for better crisis management

Reluctance to rely on the provision of large amounts of official finance to resolve debt service difficulties, coupled with potential problems in coordinating bond creditors, have led to increased interest in improving the framework for the restructuring of bonded debt. Two proposals have been the focus of recent debate: the greater use of collective action clauses to facilitate coordination, and international agreement on a legal framework similar to domestic bankruptcy law. In addition, work is continuing on the development of a voluntary code of conduct that would help improve the environment for the resolution of debt difficulties (Krueger 2003).

Collective action clauses

Collective action clauses are provisions of bonds that specify procedures for selecting bondholders' representatives in debt negotiations and provide for the modification of terms on bonds by a substantial majority. They generally prohibit individual bondholders from initiating litigation and require that any funds recovered through litigation be shared with all creditors (Eichengreen 2002). Greater use of collective action clauses could help impose majority-supported debt restructuring agreements on minority creditors, thus reducing the probability of a disorderly default. Bonds issued under U.K. law (which a few years ago accounted for just under 50 percent of the stock of emerging market eurobonds; see Haldane 1999) already have provisions for collective representation, majority, and sharing of repayments. However, bonds issued under U.S. law do not automatically have such provisions.

Empirical research indicates that collective action clauses have either no impact or a positive impact on the terms on lending. Eichengreen and Mody (2000) found that bonds subject to U.K. governing law (which thus include collective action clauses) had lower spreads than bonds subject to U.S. law for more credit-worthy issuers, who appear to benefit from the potential for a more orderly debt restructuring. In contrast, less credit-worthy issuers may pay higher spreads on bonds with collective action clauses. With higher default risk, investors may be more sensitive to the potential for moral hazard implied by making defaults more orderly. However, Becker, Richards, and Thaicharoen (2001) find that neither more nor less creditworthy issuers are charged higher spreads in bonds with collective action clauses.

Collective action clauses could play an important role in facilitating debt negotiations. They provide important protections for the rights of the majority of creditors within a single instrument to achieve agreement with the debtor when a restructuring of debt is necessary. At the same time, greater use of collective action clauses is unlikely to adversely affect the market for sovereign debt. No radical change to existing rules would be required to encourage collective action clauses. Mexico's recent issuance of a bond with a collective action clause is a positive signal that is likely to encourage other investment-grade developing countries to follow suit. And efforts to develop model language for these clauses should facilitate their adoption.

Despite all of these positive aspects, however, two factors suggest collective action clauses are, at best, only part of a solution:

- Collective action clauses played only a marginal role in recent bond restructurings. They were invoked in some of Ukraine's bonds, which may have helped to bind holdout creditors. On the other hand, Pakistan's bonds did have collective action clauses, but they were not used. And bonds issued by Ecuador and the Russian Federation did not have collective action clauses, but holdouts did not disrupt the deal (Roubini 2000). Thus their contribution to resolving future disputes over debt restructurings is uncertain.[9]

- Collective action clauses may not provide sufficient protection against a disorderly restructuring. They only bind acceptance of a debt negotiation by creditors with the same instrument, so they would not help resolve disputes across instruments or classes of creditors. That is, they would not aggregate claims across creditors. Nor would they address the large portion of the existing stock of debt that does not include collective action clauses. And it may be difficult to get some issuers (particularly issuers rated below investment grade) to include such clauses in bond instruments for fear that this would signal the intention to default and erode the issuer's competitive position in the international debt markets.

A sovereign debt restructuring mechanism

The IMF recently proposed a formal bankruptcy procedure (the sovereign debt restructuring mechanism, or SDRM) to enable an insolvent government to seek legal protection from external creditors while negotiating a restructuring of its debt.[10] The proposal is in part modeled on corporate bankruptcy law (see box 3.4), and is still being refined. Only the broad outlines of the proposal are thus discussed here.

The SDRM would be activated at the sovereign's request (Krueger 2002b). The SDRM would provide a legal mechanism for binding a minority of creditors to a debt restructuring agreed upon between a supermajority of creditors and the debtor. New finance would be shielded from restructuring. At the same time, creditor interests would be protected, including the prohibition of payments to nonpriority creditors and sanctions against abuse of the mechanism.[11] It is envisioned that this framework would be invoked rarely and would be applied only to insolvent (as opposed to illiquid) debtors. It would gain force of law through an amendment to the IMF's Articles of Agreement, which requires agreement by three-fifths of the IMF's members holding 85 percent of voting power, and which would be binding on all members.

Approval of the final restructuring would be vested in the debtor and a supermajority of creditors. Disputes could be adjudicated by an independent dispute resolution forum that also would register creditor claims and oversee voting. The role of the IMF, which is both a major creditor and an organization controlled by creditors (Hurlock 1995), would be limited to avoid a conflict of interest. The IMF proposal would not envision the restructuring of multilateral credits, since these are designed to provide a public good rather than to gain commercial advantage.

Potential advantages. The SDRM would address important issues that can impede the resolution of sovereign debt crises. The provision that minority creditors would be bound to a decision by a supermajority of creditors, and for the sharing of proceeds from litigation, would virtually eliminate the incentive for creditors to hold out or undertake legal action that would disrupt a debt restructuring agreement. Thus creditors and debtors would find it easier to reach agreement on a restructuring and ensure that the agreement is implemented. Insolvent debtors would have less incentive to take costly measures to avoid an inevitable default, which could reduce the cost of future defaults. The SDRM would not make default costless, however, nor necessarily reduce the incidence of crises. But it could play a role in encouraging earlier recognition, and thus less costly resolution, of unsustainable debt positions.

To the extent that the SDRM reduces the incentives for insolvent borrowers to delay default, it would also reduce the pressure on international financial institutions to provide emergency finance for insolvent debtors. Thus private lenders would be forced to evaluate the prospects for repayment with a reduced likelihood of official financial support, meaning the costs of borrowing would more accurately reflect actual risks.

The SDRM also could facilitate the attraction of new financing from private sources (referred to as "debtor in possession finance" in domestic bankruptcy procedure) by giving seniority to new loans. Even if the SDRM were rarely invoked, it would encourage negotiations between creditors and debtors and thus facilitate more orderly resolution of debt service difficulties.

Potential disadvantages. The SDRM also has potential drawbacks. An important point is whether radical changes to the international framework for treating sovereign defaults really are necessary to avoid disorderly debt restructuring for insolvent debtors. Recent negotiations over

Box 3.4 Sovereign debt restructuring and domestic bankruptcy law

Facilitating coordination among creditors is an important goal of bankruptcy law. Bankruptcy legislation typically provides for: (a) a stay on legal actions against the debtor to avoid a grab race for assets that lowers the return to creditors as a whole; (b) liquidation or maintenance of the firm as a going concern, depending on which course provides the greatest return to creditors; (c) seniority for new finance, where the firm continues to operate; (d) imposition of a majority-agreed reorganization on potential holdouts, which facilitates a speedy resolution; and (e) monitoring or replacement of management, to safeguard creditor interests against asset stripping and insider payments.

At the same time, these steps to protect creditor interests provide debtors with the potential to undertake strategic defaults: a debtor may seek protection from its creditors through bankruptcy, even though the debtor has the resources to pay.

Balancing the interests of creditors and debtors

A key goal of domestic bankruptcy law is to maintain an appropriate balance between the interests of debtors (becoming free from unpayable debts) and the interests of creditors (maximizing the value of the firm after bankruptcy and ensuring that the incentives to repay debt are maintained).

Considerable differences exist among legal systems in the balance between creditor and debtor interests. Bankruptcy codes have changed over time; no approach to bankruptcy law is clearly superior to all others. In the United States, the treatment of bankrupt railroads in the 19th century evolved from a liquidation procedure to debt reorganization, which preserved the value of the railroad as a going concern. During the 1930s, Chapter 10 of the Chandler Act mandated an administrative model for bankrupt firms, augmenting the power of an independent trustee at the expense of both debtors and creditors, and frequently leading to liquidation. Firms tended to avoid Chapter 10 in favor of Chapter 11, which provided greater potential for maintaining the firm as a going concern. The 1978 Bankruptcy Act, which facilitated the use of the more debtor-friendly provisions of Chapter 11, may have contributed to the boom in the corporate bond market in the 1980s. By contrast, the administrative process under the U.K. bankruptcy law provides more leverage to creditors, who appoint a receiver to take control of the firm. In France and Germany, where the court appoints an administrator to run the firm, bankruptcy institutions tend to be more debtor friendly. In France, maintaining employment is a stated goal.

Sovereign governments are not firms

Differences in the nature of sovereign governments versus firms have important implications for the balance of creditor versus debtor interests. Sovereigns cannot be liquidated and the ability to seize their assets is limited. Thus there is no lower limit to the return to creditors (the liquidation value of the firm in corporate bankruptcy), and creditors' leverage in defining the reorganization agreement and ensuring a speedy resolution is less than in corporate bankruptcies. Moreover, sovereigns cannot be taken over by creditor-imposed management. Thus, creditors cannot ensure that the government's policies are consistent with maximizing their return. The absence of these safeguards for creditor rights is a major reason why many creditors believe that the SDRM would provide excessive leverage to debtors, as compared with the position of firms under domestic bankruptcy legislation.

Other differences between sovereigns and firms provide greater leverage to creditors than in corporate bankruptcy. Sovereigns are ultimately accountable to their people for domestic economic activity. Suspensions of debt service can be met by a flight from domestic assets, resulting in a massive exchange rate devaluation, a banking crisis, and perhaps widespread corporate bankruptcy. Capital controls and bank holidays may be inadequate means of addressing such shocks to the financial system. These economic costs often lead to the replacement of political leadership following a result of a crisis. Thus, sovereigns may face sufficient incentives to repay debt, even if a sovereign bankruptcy system improved their leverage vis-à-vis creditors.

Municipal bankruptcy may provide a closer analogy than corporate bankruptcy to the issues facing the SDRM. Like sovereign nations, municipalities also cannot be liquidated. In the United States the court cannot interfere in a municipality's political or governmental powers. Modeling a sovereign bankruptcy framework on U.S. municipal bankruptcy laws would tend to improve the leverage of debtors. For example, stakeholders such as citizens' groups and labor unions (who are unlikely to have creditor interests at heart) can be represented in bankruptcy procedures, and their interests may be taken into account by the court.

Adopting this approach to sovereign bankruptcy would likely tilt the balance too far in the direction of debtor interests. In the U.S. context, creditor rights can be

Box 3.4 *(continued)*

protected by state oversight, which can limit municipalities' ability to declare bankruptcy or shelter revenues from being used as debt service during bankruptcy. This constraint would not be available in sovereign bankruptcy. Thus relying on the municipal bankruptcy model could lead to arbitrary infringements of creditor rights, as the court would have a larger role in shaping the debt restructuring plan. In contrast, the SDRM is a relatively market-friendly procedure, with the debt restructuring plan the outcome of bargaining between the creditors and debtors.

Sources: Bolton 2002; Kreuger 2002b; Miller and Zhang 1998.

bond restructurings have largely taken place without disruption and with little difficulty in coordinating creditor positions or reaching agreement between debtor and creditors. As noted above, these restructurings often failed to restore solvency and involved relatively few instruments, and recent legal cases have raised concerns regarding the potential for greater disruption in future negotiations. Thus while it is not clear that recent restructurings are useful precedents for a massive default by a major creditor, so far the historical record does not demonstrate that bonded debt restructurings are necessarily more disruptive than commercial-bank debt restructurings.

The availability of orderly bankruptcy through the SDRM could encourage "strategic defaults," suspensions of debt service by countries with the means to repay. If a solvent debtor can choose to default and use the SDRM as a shield against legal redress, then creditors would be less willing to provide funds in the first place (see box 3.5 for views on the sanctions that make sovereign borrowing feasible). However, creditors could refuse to support a restructuring proposal (or a proposal relating to priority financing) by a debtor they considered solvent (IMF 2002). Moreover, the current proposal would enable creditors to terminate the use of the SDRM. Thus, the ability of solvent debtors to use the SDRM as a shield against making debt-service payments is limited.

The SDRM could increase investors' uncertainty regarding their legal rights in case of a crisis. Protection of creditor rights (for example against running down reserves or removal of collateral) may be weak, almost certainly weaker than provided under domestic bankruptcy proceedings. For example, in the United States the court has the power to replace management of firms under Chapter 11 of the bankruptcy code and oversee financial manipulations of municipalities subject to Chapter 9 (Eichengreen 2002).

The SDRM could increase investor uncertainty regarding the outcome and fairness of negotiations. An investor might be willing to agree to a collective action clause that facilitates restructuring of an individual bond by a majority of the bondholders, but be reluctant to commit to a restructuring dictated by a majority of all creditors. The investor might lack knowledge about the composition and interests of all creditors and the terms on other instruments, and be more uncertain about the outcome of a debt negotiation involving all creditors. An investor might be concerned that larger creditors could impose a restructuring that serves their longer-term interests (for example, maintaining relationships with the debtor) rather than gains the maximum from current negotiations. Investors also could worry that parties connected to the sovereign could purchase debt in an attempt to influence the terms of the restructuring (although presumably this practice would be open to challenge under the mechanism envisioned to adjudicate disputes). This potential underlines the importance of increasing the information on the universe of a country's creditors in the context of bond offerings.

Defining the debts potentially covered by the mechanism would be controversial and could distort market valuation of different instruments. Including domestic debt is not envisioned, as the government already has the legal tools required to minimize the collective action problems inherent in restructuring debt subject to the jurisdiction of domestic courts (IMF 2002). However, excluding domestic debt in a world of open capital accounts could lead foreigners to escape the SDRM by

Box 3.5 The cost of default

It is difficult to identify the nature and extent of the costs that are directly attributable to the decision to stop payments on external debt. The declines in output associated with debt crises are typically huge. Hutchison and Neuberger (2001) estimate that currency and balance of payments crises over the 1975–97 period reduced output by about 5–8 percent, even after controlling for other determinants of growth. These costs reflect several factors, including the endogenous macroeconomic responses to the boom/bust cycle that usually characterizes debt crises.

There is indirect evidence that defaults are costly, in that borrowers suffering debt service difficulties and with little hope for voluntary access to additional external loans nevertheless make significant net transfers to their creditors, even during times of severe economic stringency. Thus Latin American debtors that rescheduled during the 1980s paid more than 3 percent of their annual output to private creditors for five years following a rescheduling agreement, and emerging market debtors on average paid more than 2 percent of output for three years after rescheduling, in both the 1980s and 1990s (see figure below). (The net transfer from countries that avoided a crisis and did not enter into a rescheduling agreement was close to zero in both decades.) Presumably these payments reflected the desire to avoid some penalty if debt service payments ceased entirely.

The penalties for default that underpin economists' models of sovereign borrowing include restricted access to future loans (Eaton and Gersowitz 1981), foreign seizure of assets or other interruptions to international trade (Bulow and Rogoff 1998), and a creditor run that precipitates a crisis and severe loss of output (Dooley 2000a):

- Losing access to future loans seems like a weak incentive for maintaining debt service during a crisis. Bulow and Rogoff (1990) find that pure reputation-based debt is not sustainable (that is, the cost of default is too low to provide creditors with adequate assurance that debt will be repaid) under a broad range of assumptions, unless the loss of reputation affects more than simply credit markets. For example, governments are likely to place value on their political ties to other countries, making them reluctant to default (Rogoff 1999).
- The seizure of assets and making it difficult to trade is potentially a severe sanction that could encourage repayment of debt. However, such actions are rarely observed (Dooley 2000b), although cases have been brought to seize sovereign assets (Miller and Zhang 1998). Only a small proportion of a state's assets is usually available to creditors, as most are located on the sovereign's territory, while exports can be transferred to other owners before they leave the debtor country (Miller and Zhang 1998).
- The potential for default to cause severe financial disruption is clear. If debtors and creditors cannot quickly renegotiate contracts, then financial intermediation within the country may break down following a default. Even if governments can discriminate against external creditors in favor of domestic creditors, the former may precipitate a run on the currency, requiring the imposition of capital controls. In turn, capital controls will make it difficult for banks and corporates to service external debts, leading to domestic bankruptcies. Moreover, a default on external debt, particularly one accompanied by limits on access to foreign exchange, is likely to impair overall confidence in the government and the banking system. The growing participation in external borrowing of developing country residents and businesses makes it very difficult to cease payments to foreigners without imposing a considerable cost on the domestic economy. In this view, the output loss from the breakdown of financial arrangements is the cost of default, and it is this threat that makes sovereign borrowers seek to service their debts, and thus makes sovereign borrowing possible.

Net transfers to private creditors

Percentage of GDP, 3, 5, and 10 years after rescheduling

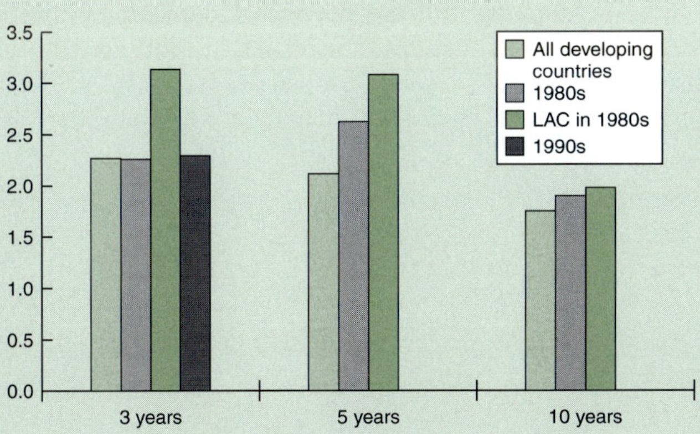

Note: LAC is Latin America and the Caribbean.
Source: World Bank Debtor Reporting System.

lending to the government through domestic residents. Also, governments have felt compelled during some crises to assume the external debt of banks and private corporations, and the treatment of such liabilities may become an important issue. Some flexibility in the treatment of debt would probably be beneficial, but that may not be consistent with a consistent legalistic approach. More broadly, defining what debts are covered in the SDRM is likely to encourage market reactions to lend through other channels. One might expect greater reliance on securitized debt, where the collateral is outside the control of the government (for example, future flow receivables where receipts are paid into an escrow account).

Implementation issues. The SDRM may face challenging implementation problems. The difficulties in reaching agreement on a change in the IMF Articles that would attempt to override domestic law should not be underestimated. Essentially, the SDRM faces considerable opposition, but near-consensus is required for passage. Even if political agreement could be reached, there is some uncertainty whether domestic courts would recognize that the country's treaty obligations (as reflected in the Articles) would override domestic law, particularly in countries that have not approved the change in the Articles. Moreover, the judges appointed to adjudicate disputes would not be accountable to any institution, raising questions about the legitimacy of their decisions (Eichengreen 2002). Thus, the SDRM may not mean the end of litigation, while such disputes could foment greater uncertainty about the ultimate outcome of debt negotiations.

The transition costs of moving toward the SDRM also need to be considered. The current period of reduced flows to emerging markets is likely due to the global economic slowdown and the problems facing some of the major emerging markets. But some creditors may be waiting to see how the controversy over the SDRM is resolved before committing substantial funds. A speedy resolution of this issue is necessary to clearly define the legal framework facing sovereign loans.

Weighing the potential benefits versus the costs of the SDRM is obviously difficult. And this trade-off may vary considerably, depending on the ultimate form of the proposal that will be submitted for approval. One issue worth emphasizing, which is not often addressed in either the academic or official literature on dealing with sovereign bankruptcy, concerns how the implications of financial crises for income distribution and poverty should affect one's view of this trade-off. Debt crises have severe implications for the poor, who had no role in making decisions on borrowing.[12] Whatever the relative cost of crises for different income groups, it is clear that the total cost to the economy is not fully internalized by the borrowers. Thus, institutions concerned about poverty may view the potential costs and benefits of changes in the international financial architecture governing sovereign borrowing very differently from creditors and sovereign borrowers. It may be preferable to undergo considerable expense to reduce the costs of default, even if uncertainty exists concerning whether these steps are necessary and whether they have the potential to reduce the supply of finance by providing too much leverage to sovereign debtors. These concerns are likely one reason for the widespread support for the sovereign bankruptcy proposal among groups concerned about distributional issues.[13]

Annex: Commercial Debt Restructuring

THIS ANNEX PROVIDES A TABULATION OF commercial-debt restructuring activities of developing countries since 1980. It does not include restructuring undertaken voluntarily by sovereigns for the purpose of liability management, such as exchanging existing debt for new fixed-income securities. However, it does include debt buybacks by countries undertaken to preempt formal restructuring of debt or reduce debt hangovers, and aided by official financing.

In 2002, three countries defaulted on their foreign-currency debt. The most prominent default was by Argentina, which formally suspended payments on its public foreign debt of $95 billion—the largest such sovereign default ever. Argentina also defaulted on $2.2 billion of local-currency bonds. While the moratorium on public foreign debt was announced in November 2001, the default was not formalized until January 2002. As of February 2003, formal negotiations to restructure Argentina's foreign-currency debt had not commenced. In April 2002, Gabon defaulted on $30 million worth of bank loans that had been restructured in 1994 under the auspices of the London Club of commercial creditors. The third country to default was Moldova (in June 2002), which for the second time defaulted on a $75 million bond issued in 1998. The outstanding amount on the bond had declined to $40 million and, after the default, was restructured to mature in 2009 instead of 2002. In addition, Madagascar, which remains in default on its foreign-currency debt, defaulted on about $200 million worth of local-currency debt in 2002.

Two countries restructured their previously defaulted debt in 2002. Indonesia completed the restructuring of bank loans worth $1.5 billion, as stipulated under the agreement with the Paris Club of official creditors in April 2001. In August, Seychelles cleared about $70 million in arrears owed to commercial banks.

The International Development Association (IDA) created a Debt Reduction Facility in 1989 to help low-income countries manage their commercial debt burdens. Although there were no IDA-sponsored debt buybacks in 2002, three countries were at an advanced stage of buyback procedures. In April 2001 Tanzania completed a first buyback operation in which $156 million of debt was extinguished. A second and final buyback is expected during 2003. Tanzania's buyback is sponsored by the IDA Debt Reduction Facility and the governments of Germany and Switzerland. Cameroon reached an agreement with the London Club, under the auspices of the IDA Debt Reduction Facility, to buy back about $600 million in eligible debt (including interest arrears) at a price of 14.5 percent of the principal outstanding. The financing proposal for this deal will soon be submitted to the IDA Board for consideration. Negotiations for Mozambique's debt buyback were also in progress.

How to use these tables
The dates shown are those of agreements, not of missed payments. Deferment refers to short-term rollover of current maturities. Rescheduling refers to consolidation of debt into new long-term obligations. It may include arrears as well as future maturities. Interest and short-term debt are included only if indicated in country notes. New money refers to loans arranged for budgetary or balance-of-payments support in conjunction with debt rescheduling, usually in proportion to each creditor bank's exposure. This is sometimes referred to as concerted lending. Short-term credit maintenance refers to understandings by banks to maintain the size of existing trade or other short-term credit facilities, arranged in conjunction with debt rescheduling. The figures for Brady deals include the face value of buybacks and of all debt exchanges. The Brady deals were also known as officially supported debt- and debt-service-reduction agreements.

Albania
Bank debt restructurings
July 1995: Restructuring of $501 million due to commercial banks. Of the total, $371 million was bought back for $96.5 million, funded by grants from IDA Debt Reduction Facility and other donor countries, and $130 million was converted into long-term bonds.

Algeria
Bank debt restructurings
Feb. 1992: 1991–93 Financing Facility, designed to refinance liabilities due between October 1991 and March 1993. Tranche A covered debts with a maturity of 2 years or more and was repayable in 8 years including 3 years grace bearing interest at London Interbank Offered Rate (LIBOR) + 1½ percent. Tranche B covered debts with a maturity of more than 360 days and less than 2 years and was repayable in 5 years including 3 years grace.
June 1995: Rescheduling of $3.2 billion in maturities starting March 1994.

Argentina
Bank debt restructurings
Jan. 1983: Bridge loan ($1.3 billion).
Aug. 1983: New money loan ($0.5 billion).
Aug. 1985: Rescheduling agreement of maturities in January 1982–January 1986 ($9.8 billion); new long-term money ($3.6 billion); maintenance of short-term credit lines ($3.1 billion).
Aug. 1987: Revised restructuring agreement covering amounts under 1983 and 1985 agreements and loans falling due subsequent to those arrangements ($24.3 billion); new long-term money ($1.3 billion); maintenance of short-term credit lines ($3.5 billion).
Brady deal
April 1993: Outstanding stock of $19.3 billion exchanged for either (i) 30-year bonds yielding a market interest rate (LIBOR + 13/16 percent) at a 35 percent discount, or (ii) 30-year par front-loaded interest reduction bonds (FLIRBs)—(first year interest rate 4 percent, rising to 6 percent in year seven and remaining there until maturity. Both bonds were collateralized for principal and contained rolling 12 month interest guarantees. Agreement also included $9.3 billion of past due interest; $0.7 billion was paid in cash at closing; $400 million was written off; the remainder was exchanged for bonds (17-year maturity), repayable in rising installments and yielding LIBOR + 13/16 percent.
Bond market defaults and restructurings
Jan. 2002: Announcement of a moratorium on public foreign debt in December 2001. In January 2002, formalization of default on $95 billion of foreign currency bonds and default on $2.2 billion of local currency bonds. The local currency bonds were exchanged for new debt, which carried covenants less favorable than the original debt. Bonds maturing before 2010 were extended by three years, and the coupon was reduced to 7 percent or less. As of January 2003, the foreign currency bonds were still to be restructured. Stand-by credit facility ($2.98 billion) by the IMF for transitional financial support until August 2003.

Bolivia
Bank debt restructurings
Dec. 1980: Deferment of $200 million of maturities (including short-term debt) in August 1980–March 1981.
April 1981: Rescheduling of $411 million of maturities (including debt deferred in 1980) in April 1981–April 1983.
July 1988: Commercial bank debt retired through a buyback ($272 million) and a local currency bond exchange ($72 million). This was a rolling program and applied only to previously deferred loans.
May 1993: Buyback of $170 million commercial bank debt, funded by grants from IDA Debt Reduction Facility and other donor countries.
Brady deal
July 1992: (i) Cash buyback at 84 percent discount; (ii) Collateralized interest-free 30-year bullet-maturity par bonds; (iii) Short-term discount bonds (84 percent) convertible on maturity into local currency assets at a 1:1.5 ratio, exchangeable into investments for special projects. Past-due interest canceled under all options. Value recovery clause was based on price of tin.

Bosnia and Herzegovina
Bank debt restructurings
Dec. 1997: London Club Agreement to restructure $1.3 billion of principal and past-due interest owed to commercial banks. Past due interest of $700 million was written off. Eligible principal of $600 million was exchanged for $400 million of uncollateralized discount bonds. 37.5 percent of the new bonds carried a 20 year maturity, including 7 years' grace and stepped-up interest rates rising from 2.0 percent in years 1–4 to LIBOR + 13/16 in years 11–20. Servicing on 62.5 percent of the new bonds was linked to economic

performance. The country was not required to make principal or interest payments for the first 10 years. After that the country was required to make debt service payments if per capita income exceeded $2,800 for two consecutive years. Per capita income in 1997 was estimated at $1,079.

Brazil

Bank debt restructurings

Feb. 1983: Rescheduling agreement of $4.8 billion of maturities January 1983–January 1984; new long-term money ($4.2 billion); maintenance of short-term credit lines ($15.7 billion).

Jan. 1984: Rescheduling agreement of $5.9 billion of maturities in January 1984–January 1985; new long-term money ($6.5 billion); maintenance of short-term credit lines ($15.1 billion).

July 1986: Deferment of $9.6 billion and rescheduling agreement of $6.6 billion of maturities in January 1985–January 1986; maintenance of short-term credit lines ($14.7 billion).

Nov. 1988: Rescheduling agreement of $61.5 billion of maturities in January 1987–January 1994; new long-term money ($5.2 billion); maintenance of short-term credit lines ($14.8 billion). Also included a broad package of creditor options.

July 1992: Clearance of interest arrears as of December 31, 1990. Cash payment during 1992: $863 million. When term sheet concluded for long-term debt, the balance was to be converted into 10-year bonds (3 years grace), bearing market interest rates.

Brady deal

April 1994: Four components of debt were restructured totaling $48 billion: (i) debt to foreign banks under the 1988 multiyear deposit facility agreement ($32.5 billion); (ii) debt to Brazilian banks under the multiyear deposit facility agreement; (iii) debt resulting from the 1988 new money facilities ($8.1 billion) and (iv) interest arrears accruing from 1991 to 1994 ($6.0 billion). The first category of debt was restructured following a 6-choice menu: (i) discount bonds, 35 percent discount, 30-year bullet maturity yielding LIBOR + 13/16 percent with principal collateral and a 12-month rolling interest guarantee ($11.2 billion); (ii) par bonds with a reduced fixed-rate interest (yielding 4 percent in the first year and gradually rising to 6 percent in year seven), 30-year bullet maturity, also with principal collateral and a 12-month rolling interest guarantee ($10.5 billion); (iii) front-loaded interest reduction bonds ($1.7 billion), with interest rising from a fixed rate of 4 percent in year one to 6 percent in years five and six and then reverting to LIBOR + 13/16 percent from year seven to maturity, 15 years maturity including 9 years grace, 12-month rolling interest guarantee; (iv) C-bonds, par reduced interest rate bonds with capitalization of interest ($7.1 billion), with repayment terms of 20 years maturity including 10 years grace, interest beginning at 4 percent and the applicable rates in the first 6 years being capitalized, no collateral; (v) conversion bonds ($1.9 billion) combined with new money bonds in a 1:5.5 ratio, interest is LIBOR + 7/8 percent, terms are 18 years maturity including 10 years grace for the conversion bonds and 15 years including 7 years grace for the new money bonds, no collateral; (vi) interest reduction loan with capitalization, maturity of 20 years including 10 years grace, interest rising from 4 percent in year one to 5 percent in year six to LIBOR + 13/16 from year seven to maturity.

Bulgaria

Brady deal

July 1994: Creditors agreed to restructure $8.3 billion in public external debt, including about $2.1 billion in passed-due interest (PDI). The menu for the original debt included: (i) buyback at 0.25 cent per US Dollar ($0.8 billion); (ii) discount bond, 50 percent discount on face value (30 years bullet maturity, market rate, $3.7 billion), the discount bonds were collateralized for principal; (iii) FLIRBs. 18 years maturity, 8 years grace interest beginning at 2 percent, rising to 3 percent in the seventh year and thereafter LIBOR + 13/16 ($1.7 billion). The FLIRBs have one year's interest rolling interest guarantee. Interest arrears were cleared with a cash payment of about 3 percent, a buyback ($0.2 billion), a write-off of $0.2 billion, and the issuance of PDI par bonds ($1.6 billion) with a 17 year maturity, including 7 years grace and a yield of LIBOR + 13/16 percent.

Cameroon

Bank debt restructurings

May 2002: Buyback of $600 million (including interest arrears) of commercial bank debt on which the country has been in arrears since 1985, 14.5 percent of the principal amount due.

Chile

Bank debt restructurings

July 1983: Rescheduling agreement of $2.1 billion of maturities in January 1983–January 1985; new long-term money ($1.3 billion); maintenance of short-term credit lines ($1.7 billion).

Jan. 1984: Consolidation of short-term debt of $1.2 billion.

June 1984: Provision of new long-term money ($0.8 billion).

Nov. 1984: Short-term debt rolled over to June 30, 1985.

Nov. 1985: Short-term trade credit rolled over to 1990. Rescheduling agreement of $3.9 billion of maturities in January 1985–January 1988; new long-term money ($1 billion); maintenance of short-term credit lines ($1.7 billion).

June 1987: Rescheduling agreement of $9.7 billion of maturities in January 1988–January 1992; Maintenance of short-term credit lines ($1.7 billion).

Aug. 1988: Interest spread reduced to 13/16 percent. Also cash buybacks ($439 million).

Dec. 1990: Rescheduling agreement of $4.2 billion of maturities in January 1991–January 1995, including previously rescheduled debt; new long-term money ($0.3 billion). New money bonds not tied to existing banks' exposure.

Congo, Republic of

Bank debt restructurings

Oct. 1986: Agreement in principle, but never concluded, to restructure 1986–88 maturities, repayable in 9 years including 3-year grace, bearing interest at LIBOR + 2⅞ percent. Approximately $200 million of debt would have been restructured. In addition there was a new money provision of $60 million.

Sept. 2002: Debt rescheduling agreement with Paris Club. See the chapter 6 annex for details.

Costa Rica
Bank debt restructurings
Sept. 1983: Rescheduling agreement of $0.7 billion of maturities (including principal arrears) in January 1983–January 1985; new long-term money ($0.2 billion); maintenance of short-term credit lines ($0.2 billion).
May 1985: Rescheduling agreement of $0.5 billion of maturities, including deferment of revolving credit ($2 million) due in January 1985–January 1987; new long-term money ($75 million).
Brady deal
May 1990: Cash buyback at 84 percent discount ($992 million), debt-for-bond-exchange ($579 million), and write-off of $29 million of past-due interest.

Côte d'Ivoire
Bank debt restructurings
Mar. 1985: Rescheduling agreement of $0.5 billion of maturities in December 1983–January 1985; new long-term money ($0.1 billion).
Nov. 1986: Multiyear rescheduling agreement (MYRA) of $0.9 billion of maturities in January 1986–January 1990;
April 1988: Agreement designed to replace the MYRA. Included new money to refinance interest. Interest on the new money portion was LIBOR + 1½ percent. Agreement was not put into effect because interest arrears were not cleared, and current interest payments were suspended in April 1988.
Brady deal
May 1997: Agreement for restructuring $6.5 billion of principal and past-due interest. For eligible principal of $2.3 billion, creditors agreed to (i) exchange $159 million for discount bonds (50 percent discount) subject to stepped-up interest rising from 2.5 percent in years 1–2 to LIBOR + 13/16 in years 11–30; (ii) exchange $1.4 billion for FLIRBs with a maturity of 20 years, including 10 years' grace, and stepped-up interest rising from 2.0 percent in years 1–7 to LIBOR + 13/16 in years 14–20; (iii) buyback $0.7 billion at 24 cents per dollar. Principal was collateralized with 30-year U.S. Treasury zero-coupon bonds for the discount bonds, but not for the FLIRBs. A six-month rolling interest guarantee was required for the FLIRBs, but not for the discount bonds. For past-due interest of $4.2 billion, $30 million was settled in cash at closing, $0.9 billion was exchanged for bonds with a 20-year maturity (half a year of grace period) repayable on a graduated amortization schedule, and $3.3 billion was written off.

Cuba
Bank debt restructurings
Dec. 1983: Rescheduling agreement of $0.1 billion of maturities in September 1982–December 1984; maintenance of short-term credit lines ($0.5 billion).
Dec. 1984: Rescheduling agreement of $0.1 billion of maturities in January 1984–December 1985; maintenance of short-term credit lines ($0.5 billion).
July 1985: Rescheduling agreement of $0.1 billion of maturities in January 1985–December 1986; maintenance of short-term credit lines ($0.5 billion).

Dominican Republic
Bank debt restructurings
Dec. 1983: Rescheduling agreement of $0.5 billion of maturities in December 1982–December 1983 (including short-term debt).
Feb. 1986: Multiyear rescheduling agreement of $0.8 billion of maturities in January 1985–December 2000 (including arrears as of December 31, 1984).
Brady deal
Aug. 1994: Agreement covering principal and interest past-due ($1.2 billion). The agreement had a menu consisting of (i) buybacks ($.4 billion); (ii) discount exchange bonds ($.5 billion) 35 percent discount, to be repaid 30 years bullet maturity, interest rate LIBOR + 13/16 percent; (iii) past-due-interest bonds ($171 million) bearing interest at LIBOR + 13/16 percent, with 3 years grace and 15 years maturity. The accord also included a write-off of $112 million of past-due interest, and $52 million paid in cash at closing.

Ecuador
Bank debt restructurings
Oct. 1983: Rescheduling agreement of $2.8 billion of maturities in November 1982–December 1983; new long-term money ($0.4 billion); maintenance of short-term credit lines ($0.7 billion).
Dec. 1985: Multiyear rescheduling agreement of $4.2 billion of maturities in January 1985–January 2000. New long-term money ($0.2 billion); maintenance of short-term credit lines ($0.7 billion).
Nov. 1987: Replaces the multiyear rescheduling agreement.
Brady deal
Feb. 1995: Agreement restructuring $7.8 billion of principal and part-due interest. For principal, creditors agreed to exchange $2.6 billion for discount bonds (45 percent discount) yielding LIBOR + 13/16 percent and $1.9 billion for par reduced-interest rate bonds. Both bonds had a 30-year bullet maturity, were collateralized for principal, and had a 12-month rolling interest guarantee. The interest rate on the par bonds was 3 percent for the first year, rising to 5 percent in year 11. For past-due interest, $75 billion was to be settled in cash at closing, $2.3 billion was exchanged for bonds with a 20-year maturity (no grace period) repayable on a graduated amortization schedule, $191 million was exchanged for interest equalization bonds, and $582 million was written off.
Bond market defaults and restructurings
Aug. 2000: Agreement to exchange about $5.9 billion in defaulted Brady bonds and eurobonds for $3.9 billion in new 12 and 30-year global bonds. The new 12-year issue was priced to yield 12 percent, and the new 30-year issue carried the multi-coupon with the initial coupon rate of 4 percent. This operation resulted in a 40 percent reduction in principal for the bondholders.

Ethiopia
Bank debt restructurings
Jan. 1996: Debt buyback at 8 cents per U.S. dollar of $226 million owed to commercial banks. Funding for the operation provided by the IDA Debt Reduction facility.

Gabon

Bank debt restructurings

Dec. 1987: Rescheduling agreement of $27 million of maturities in September 1986–December 1987.

Dec. 1991: Rescheduling agreement of $75 million of maturities in January 1989–December 1992.

May 1994: Rescheduling of $187 million of maturities. Principal due through 1994 on debt contracted prior to September 20, 1986 (debt covered by the 1991 agreement, which had not been implemented) was rescheduled. Terms: 10-year maturity including 2½ years grace. Interest: LIBOR + 7/8 percent. Arrears of interest and arrears of post cut-off maturities as of July 1, 1994, were to be repaid between 1994 and 1996.

April 2002: Default on $30 million of bank loans, which had been restructured in 1994.

Gambia, The

Bank debt restructurings

Feb. 1988: Rescheduling of debt outstanding as of 18 December, 1986; new long-term money ($19 million).

Guinea

Bank debt restructurings

April 1988: Rescheduling of short-term debt of $28 million.

Dec. 1998: Buyback of $130 million under the IDA Debt Reduction Facility at 13 cents per US Dollar, financed IDA DRF and other donor countries

Guyana

Bank debt restructurings

Aug. 1982: One-year deferment of $14 million of maturities in March 1982–April 1983.

June 1983: Extension of $12 million due in July 1983–December 1983, previously deferred in 1982.

July 1984: Extension of $11 million due in August 1984–August 1985, previously deferred.

July 1985: Extension of $15 million due in August 1985–December 1986, previously deferred.

July 1988: Deferment of $8 million.

Nov. 1992: Buyback of $69 million under the IDA DRF at 14 cents per US Dollar.

Dec. 1999: Buyback of $55.9 million under the IDA DRF at 9 cents per U.S. dollar, financed IDA DRF and the Switzerland government.

Honduras

Bank debt restructurings

June 1987: Rescheduling agreement of $248 million of maturities due April 1987–December 1989. As two previous agreements (in 1983 and 1984) were not implemented, this agreement incorporated 1981–85 maturities as well, although it too was not signed.

Aug. 1989: Bilateral rescheduling of $101 million, including interest arrears, due to two commercial banks.

Aug. 2001: Buyback of $13 million under the IDA DRF. The buyback price was set at 18 cents per dollar of the principal amount. The IDA and the governments of the Netherlands, Norway, and Switzerland provided funding for the operation.

Indonesia

Bank debt restructurings

June 1998: Agreement on a framework for restructuring $80 billion of the Indonesian private debt. The inter-bank loans were extended into new government-guaranteed loans with maturities of 1 to 4 years, at interest rates of 2.75, 3, 3.25, and 3.5 percent over LIBOR. The corporate debts were to be rescheduled over 8 years, including a 3-year grace period for repayment of principal. Over 8-year rescheduling period, the real interest rate was set to be 5.5 percent, but it would decline to 5 percent for debtors who agree to repay in 5 years. There was also an agreement to pay off trade financing arrears to maintain trade financing from foreign creditor banks.

Sept. 2002: Completion of restructuring of $1.5 billion in syndicated bank credits, as required under the agreement with Paris Club.

Iran, Islamic Republic of

Bank debt restructurings

Mar. 1993: Rescheduling of $2.8 billion of debt outstanding as of March 1993.

Dec. 1994: Rescheduling of $10.9 billion of debt outstanding as of December 1994.

Jamaica

Bank debt restructurings

April 1981: Rescheduling of $126 million of maturities in April 1979–April 1981.

June 1981: Rescheduling of $89 million of maturities in July 1981–March 1983; new long-term money ($89 million).

June 1984: Rescheduling of $164 million of maturities in July 1983–March 1985.

Sept. 1985: Rescheduling of $359 million of maturities in April 1985–March 1987.

May 1987: Rescheduling of $366 million of maturities in January 1987–March 1990; included reduced spreads on earlier rescheduling.

June 1990: Rescheduling of $315 million of maturities in January 1990–December 1991. Also, reduced spreads on earlier rescheduling.

Jordan

Bank debt restructurings

Sept. 1989: Rescheduling agreement in principal of $580 million of maturities in January 1989–June 1991.

Nov. 1989: Provision of new long-term money ($50 million); short-term credit ($50 million) to meet obligations due between January 1989 and June 1990.

Brady deal

Dec. 1993: Agreement restructuring $736 million of principal and $153 million of past-due interest. For restructured principal, a small amount was repurchased at 39 cents per U.S. dollar, $243 was exchanged for discount bonds (35 percent discount); and $493 million was exchanged for par fixed interest bonds. Both bonds had a 30-year bullet maturity with principal collateral and a 6-month rolling interest guarantee. The discount bonds yielded LIBOR + 13/16 percent interest; the yields on par bonds began at 4 percent in the first year, rising to 6 percent in year seven. Regarding past-due interest, $29 million was paid at closing, $91 million was exchanged for non-collateralized bonds with a 12-year maturity including 3-years grace and yielding LIBOR + 13/16 percent, and $33 million was written off. Up-front costs totaled $147 million, all of which was provided from Jordan's own resources.

Korea, Republic of

Bank debt restructurings

Jan. 1998: Agreement to restructure the short-term foreign debts owed to foreign commercial banks. Eligible short-term debt of $21.4 billion was converted into new government-guaranteed loans with maturities of between 1 and 3 years and floating interest rates set between 2.25 and 2.75 percentage points over LIBOR. The commission charged by the government was set between 0.2 and 1.5 percentage points based on the credit rating (Moody's Investors Service or by S&P, and the BIS capital adequacy ratio) of the debtor. Also, the debtor had to meet a reserve requirement of 3 percent of total guaranteed amount in US dollars.

Liberia

Bank debt restructurings

Dec. 1982: Rescheduling of $29 million of maturities in July 1981–June 1982.

June 1983: Consolidation of $26 million of oil facility debt.

Mauritania

Bank debt restructurings

Aug. 1996: Debt buyback of $53.0 million, at a 90 percent discount, owed to commercial banks. Funding for the operation provided by the IDA DRF.

Madagascar

Bank debt restructurings

Nov. 1981: Arrears ($155 million) on overdrafts consolidated into long-term debt.

Oct. 1984: Restructuring of entire stock of debt ($379 million), including arrears.

June 1987: Modification of the terms of the October 1984 restructuring agreement.

May 1990: Rescheduling agreement in principal of $49 million of maturities in April 1990-August 1995.

Jan. 2002: Default on $200 million in local currency debt, in addition to continuing default on foreign currency commercial bank loans.

Malawi

Bank debt restructurings

Mar. 1983: Rescheduling of $59 million of maturities in September 1982–August 1984.

Oct. 1988: Rescheduling of balances as of August 21, 1987 ($36 million).

Mexico

Bank debt restructurings

Aug. 1983: Rescheduling of $23.3 billion of maturities in April 1982–August 1984; new long-term money ($5 billion).

April 1984: New long-term money ($3.8 billion).

Mar. 1985: Multiyear rescheduling agreement of $28 billion, including previously rescheduled debt, maturing in January 1987–December 1991.

Aug. 1985: Multiyear rescheduling agreement of $20.3 billion of maturities (not previously rescheduled) in January 1985–December 1990.

Oct. 1985: Deferent of first payment ($0.9 billion) under the March 1985 agreement.

Mar. 1987: Modification of terms of earlier agreements covering $44.2 billion of maturities; new long-term money ($7.4 billion).

Aug. 1987: Rescheduling of $9.7 billion of private sector debt maturing in January 1988–December 1991.

Mar. 1988: Exchange of debt for 20-year zero-coupon collateralized bonds ($556 million).

Brady deal

Mar. 1990: Agreement restructuring $48.2 billion of debt. In addition to new money of $1 billion, the agreement provided for the exchange of $20.5 billion of debt for bonds at a 35 percent discount, an exchange of $22.4 billion of debt at par for reduced interest rate bonds, and conversion bonds totaling $5.3 billion. The latter were not collateralized and had a tenor of 15 years maturity, including 7 years' grace, and an interest rate of LIBOR + 13/16. The total base also included $693 million not committed to any option.

Moldova

Bond market defaults and restructurings

June 2002: Second default on $75 million foreign currency bond (privately placed) originally issued in 1997. Outstanding amount of the bond reduced to $40 million after the initial default. This time around the maturity of the bond, due in June 2002, was extended until 2009.

Morocco

Bank debt restructurings

Feb. 1986: Agreement in principle (initiated August 1983) rescheduling $531 million maturing in September 1983–December 1984; Short-term credit maintenance ($610 million).

Sept. 1987: Rescheduling of $2.4 billion of maturities in January 1985–December 1988.

Brady deal

June 1990: Rescheduling of $3.2 billion of maturities outstanding as of December 1989. Phase one of this agreement restructured debt; phase two was a Brady deal that would take effect if Morocco had signed an EFF agreement with the IMF by December 31, 1991.

Mozambique

Bank debt restructurings

May 1987: Rescheduling of outstanding stock of debt ($253 million), including interest arrears.

Dec. 1991: Buyback of $124 million of outstanding commercial bank debt at a 90 percent discount, funded by grants from the IDA DRF and from France, the Netherlands, Switzerland, and Sweden.

Nicaragua

Bank debt restructurings

Dec. 1980: Rescheduling of government debt ($582 million), all maturities, including arrears.

Dec. 1981: Rescheduling of nationalized bank debt ($192 million), all maturities, including arrears.

Mar. 1982: Rescheduling of debts of nonfinancial enterprises ($100 million), all maturities, including arrears.

Feb. 1984: Deferment of service on rescheduled debt ($145 million) due between July 1983 and June 1984.

Dec. 1995: Buyback of $1.1 billion of outstanding commercial bank debt at 8 cents per US Dollar.

Niger

Bank debt restructurings

Mar. 1984: Rescheduling of $29 million of maturities in October 1983–March 1986.

April 1986: Rescheduling of $36 million of maturities in October 1985–December 1988.

Mar. 1991: Buyback of all commercial bank debt at 82 percent discount ($107 million). Resources provided by grants from the DRF for IDA-only countries ($10 million), Switzerland ($3 million), and France ($10 million).

Nigeria

Bank debt restructurings

Nov. 1987: Rescheduling of $4.7 billion of maturities, including short-term debt, due between April 1986 and December 1987.

Mar. 1989: Rescheduling of $5.7 billion of short-term debt, including arrears on line of credit.

Brady deal

Jan. 1992: Agreement rescheduling $5.3 billion of debt. The terms provided for a cash-back at 60 percent discount on $3.3 billion, and debt exchanges on $2 billion for collateralized 30-year bullet maturity par bonds with reduced interest rates: 5.5 percent for the first three years, 6.25 percent thereafter. Creditor selections: 62 percent for the buyback; 38 percent for the debt-reduction bond. A third option, new money combined with conversion bonds, was not selected by participating creditor banks.

Panama

Bank debt restructurings

Sept. 1983: Provision of new long-term money ($278 million); short-term credit ($217 million).

Oct. 1985: Rescheduling of $578 million in maturities in January 1985–December 1986; new long-term money ($60 million); maintenance of short-term credit lines ($190 million).

Brady deal

May 1996: Creditors agreed to restructuring of $3.9 billion in public external debt, including $2.0 billion in past due interest. The menu for the principal included: (i) discount bonds at a 45 percent discount of face value (30 years bullet maturity, market rate, $87.8 million); (ii) Par bonds with reduced interest rates and a 30 year bullet repayment ($268.0 million); and (iii) FLIRBs for $1,612.2 million with a tenor of 18 years maturity including 5 years grace period. The discount and the par bonds are collateralized with respect to the principal by U.S. Treasury zero coupon bonds, and with respect to interest in the form of a 9-month rolling interest rate guarantee in the first year rising to 12 months in 2–3 years. The FLIRBs do not require guarantee for the capital, but include a six-month rolling interest guarantee. PDI settlement included progress payments of $30 million, a payment at closing of $100 million, a write-off of $590.4 million arising from the recalculation of penalty interest at a lower interest rate, and PDI par bonds of $1,247.6 million with 20 years' maturity, including 7 years grace, and interest rate of LIBOR + 13/16 percent. Neither principal nor interest was guaranteed. Moreover, Panama could capitalize for the first six, the difference was positive between LIBOR + 13/16 and 4.0 percent p.a.

Peru

Bank debt restructurings

Jan. 1980: Rescheduling of $364 million of maturities in January 1980–December 1980.

July 1983: Rescheduling of $432 million of maturities in March 1983–February 1984; new long-term money ($650 million); maintenance of short-term credit lines ($2 billion).

Brady deal

Nov. 1996: Creditors agreed to restructuring of $8 billion in public external debt, including $3.8 billion in PDI. The menu for the principal included: (i) discount bonds at a 45 percent discount of face value (30 years bullet maturity, market rate, $947 million); (ii) par bonds with reduced interest rates and a 30-year bullet repayment ($189 million); (iii) FLIRBs for $1,779 million with a tenor of 20 years maturity including 8 years grace period; and (iv) a buyback of $1,266 million at 38 cents per US Dollar. The discount and the par bonds were collateralized with respect to the principal by U.S. Treasury zero-coupon bonds, and with respect to interest in the form of a six-month rolling interest rate guarantee secured by cash or permitted investments. The FLIRBs did not require guarantee for the capital, but included a six-month rolling interest guarantee. PDI settlement included progress payments of $83 million, a payment at closing of $225 million—a buyback of $1,217 million at 38 cents per US Dollar, and PDI par bonds of $2,284 million with 20 years' maturity, including 10 years grace, and interest rate of LIBOR + 13/16 percent. Neither principal nor interest was guaranteed. Moreover, Peru could capitalize for the first six, the difference was positive between LIBOR + 13/16 and 4.0 percent p.a.

Philippines

Bank debt restructurings

Jan. 1986: Rescheduling of $5.9 billion in maturities in October 1983–December 1986; new long-term money ($925 million); maintenance of short-term credit lines ($2974 million).

Dec. 1987: Rescheduling of $9 billion in maturities in January 1987–December 1992; maintenance of short-term credit lines ($2,965 million).

Brady deal

Jan. 1990: Agreement provided for $1.3 billion of buybacks at a 50 percent discount.

Dec. 1992: Following implementation of a cash buyback of $1.3 billion on May 14, 1992, banks selected debt exchanges from three options; (i) front-loaded interest-reduction par bonds, yielding LIBOR + 13/16 percent from year seven to maturity (15 years for series A and 15½ year for series B, both including seven years grace); (ii) collateralized step-down/step-up interest reduction bonds yielding 6.5 percent from year six to maturity (25-year bullet maturity for series A and 25½ year for series B); and (iii) new money combined with conversion bonds in a 1 : 4 ratio, with both bonds attaining 17½ (series A) or 17-year (series B) maturity, including five years grace and yielding LIBOR + 13/16 percent. Interest payments on both interest-reduction bonds covered by a rolling 14-month guarantee. Creditor choices (total, $4.4 billion, 96 percent total eligible debt); buybacks, $1.3 billion (27.5 percent): option (a), $0.8 billion (46.3 percent); option (b), $1.9 billion (41.1 percent); option (c), $0.5 billion (11.7 percent).

Poland

Bank debt restructurings

April 1982: Rescheduling of $1.9 billion of maturities in March 1981–December 1981.

Nov. 1982: Rescheduling of $2.2 billion of maturities in January 1982–December 1982.

Nov. 1983: Rescheduling of $1.3 billion of maturities in January 1983–December 1983.

July 1984: Rescheduling of $1.5 billion of maturities, including some short-term trade credits, due in January 1984–December 1987.

Sept. 1986: Rescheduling of $1.9 billion of maturities, including debt rescheduled in 1982, due in January 1986–December 1987.

July 1988: Multiyear rescheduling agreement of $8.3 billion of maturities due in January 1988–December 1993; maintenance of short-term credit lines ($1 billion). Also improved the terms of earlier agreements.

June 1989: Agreement in principal to defer principal due May 1989–December 1990 ($206 million), until December 1991; and in October, the interest due in the fourth quarter of 1989, $145 million, was deferred until the second quarter of 1990.

Brady deal

Oct. 1994: Creditors restructured $14.4 billion. Three categories of debt were affected: (i) long-term debt covered by the 1988 restructuring agreement ($8.9 billion); (ii) debt due under the Revolving Short-Term Arrangement (RSTA) ($1.2 billion); (iii) past-due interest not otherwise restructured ($4.3 billion). The first category was subject to a menu approach: $2.1 billion of long-term debt was repurchased at 41 cents per US Dollar, and $0.3 billion of RSTA debt was repurchased at 38 cents per US Dollar. For the remaining long-term, creditors chose between: (i) discount bonds—45 percent discount ($5.4 billion); (ii), par reduced fixed interest bonds ($0.9 billion); (iii) conversion bonds combined with new money bonds equal to 35 percent of the amount converted ($0.4 billion). The discount bonds and par bonds had 30-year bullet maturities and featured collateralization of principal only. Interest on the discount bonds was LIBOR + 13/16 percent. Interest on the par bonds was 2.75 percent for the first year, rising to 5 percent for year 21. The conversion bonds had a 25-year maturity, including 20-year grace. Their yield in year one was 4.5 percent, rising to 7.5 percent in year 11. The new money bonds had a 15-year maturity, including 10-year grace and yield LIBOR + 13/16 percent. The new money and conversion bonds are not collateralized. The RSTA debt not repurchased ($0.9 billion) was exchanged for 30-year bullet maturity fixed interest bonds, with similar (but slightly different) step/down-step/up arrangements as the par bonds, starting at 2.75 percent in year one and gradually rising to 5 percent in year 21. For past-due interest, $0.8 billion was repurchased with related long-term and RSTA principal. A portion was to be settled with cash payments at closing ($63 million). A portion was written off ($0.8 billion), and the remainder ($2.7 billion), was converted into fixed-interest rate bonds yielding 3.25 percent in year one, rising to 7 percent in year nine. Maturity was 20 years, including 7-years grace. Amortization was graduated.

Romania

Bank debt restructurings

Dec. 1982: Rescheduling of $1.6 billion of maturities in January 1982–December 1982.

June 1983: Rescheduling of $0.6 billion of maturities in January 1983–December 1983.

Sept. 1986: Rescheduling of $0.8 billion in previously rescheduled debt maturing in January 1986–December 1987.

Sept. 1987: Agreement in principal to reschedule $0.8 billion of maturities in January 1986–December 1987.

Russian Federation

Bank debt restructurings

Dec. 1991: Deferment of principal due in December 1991–March 1992 on pre-1991 debt. The deferment was extended for each consecutive quarter until the end of 1993.

July 1993: Rescheduling of the stock of FSU debt contracted prior to January 1, 1991 ($24 billion), to be repaid with 15-year maturity including 5-year grace. In the fourth quarter of 1993, $500 million was to be paid on interest accruing during 1993. At the end of 1993, all remaining unpaid interest (estimated at $3 billion) was then to be consolidated and repaid at a 10-year maturity, including 5 years' grace. The 1993 interest payments were not made; the agreement was not implemented, mainly because Russia refused to accept bankers' requirement that sovereign immunity be waived. However, an understanding was reached on October 5, 1994, that the banks would drop their insistence on a waiver of sovereign immunity and that the Vneshekonombank (or another public entity) would guarantee the debts.

Nov. 1995: Agreement in principle to comprehensively reschedule $33 billion in debt outstanding as of 15 November 1995. Heads of terms were signed for rescheduling debt of the former Soviet Union in the amount of $25.5 billion of principal outstanding and $7.5 billion in accrued interest due. The eligible principal was to be repaid over 25 years, with 7 years of grace, beginning December 15, 1995, in 37 semi-annual payments on a graduated schedule at LIBOR + 13/16 percent per year. It was further agreed that an interest note for $6 billion would be issued with a 20-year maturity and 7 years' grace from December 15, 1995, that would be the same interest rate, listed on the Luxembourg Stock Exchange. The remaining $1.5 billion in interest arrears was paid over 1995–96. By September 1996, the minimum subscribership by commercial banks of $20 billion in outstanding principal was reached which triggered the Russian agreement to the rescheduling package.
Nov. 1998: Outline of an agreement to restructure $13.5 billion of defaulted Treasury bills (GKOs and OFZs). Under the restructuring plan, 10 percent of the defaulted bills was to be redeemed in cash rubles, and 20 percents of the debt was to be exchanged for three-year zero-coupon bonds. The remaining 70 percent of the debt was to be restructured into 4-year and 5-year variable coupon bonds.
Feb. 2000: Agreement to restructure $31.8 billion Soviet-era debts owed to the London Club of commercial banks. The London Club's creditors agreed to write off $11.6 billion of the principal and a 7-year grace period for principal repayments, and swapping the rest of its defaulted debts (PRINs and IANs) for a new 30-year eurobonds. The interest rate on a new eurobond was set at 2.25 percent for the first six months, 2.5 percent for the second six months, and 5 percent for years two and seven—yielding 7.5 percent a year.

São Tomé and Principe
Bank debt restructurings
Aug. 1994: Buyback under the IDA debt-reduction facility at 10 cents per US Dollar. $10.1 million of principal was extinguished (87 percent of eligible debt).

Senegal
Bank debt restructurings
Feb. 1984: Rescheduling of $96 million of maturities in May 1981–June 1984.
May 1985: Rescheduling of $20 million of maturities in July 1984–June 1986.
Jan. 1989: Rescheduling of $37 million.
Dec. 1996: Debt buyback at 8 cents per US Dollar of US$80.0 million owed to commercial banks. Funding for the operation provided by the IDA DRF.

Sierra Leone
Bank debt restructurings
Jan. 1984: Rescheduling of principal arrears ($25 million) outstanding as of December 31, 1983.
Aug. 1995: Buyback, at 13 cents on average per US Dollar, of US$235 million due to commercial banks funded by grants from IDA DRF and other donor countries.

South Africa
Bank debt restructurings
Sept. 1985: Deferment of $13.6 billion maturing in August 1985–Decemebr 1985.
Mar. 1986: Rescheduling of $650 million of maturities in August 1985–June 1987.
Mar. 1987: Rescheduling of $4.5 billion of maturities in July 1987–June 1990.
Oct. 1989: Rescheduling of $7.5 billion of maturities in October 1989–December 1993.
Sept. 1993: Rescheduling of $5 billion, including interest arrears.

Sudan
Bank debt restructurings
Nov. 1981: Rescheduling of $593 million of maturities due in January 1980–March 1982, including principal arrears and some short-term debt.
Mar. 1982: Rescheduling of $3 million of interest arrears and modification of 1981 agreement.
April 1983: Rescheduling of $702 million of interest arrears and modification of 1981 agreement.
Oct. 1985: Rescheduling of $1,037 million (including interest arrears).

Suriname
Bank debt restructurings
Dec. 2001: Clearing of $36 million in principal arrears owed to commercial banks.

Tanzania
Bank debt restructurings
April 2001: Buyback of $76.6 million of eligible principal debt and about $79.2 million of associated interest under the IDA DRF. The buyback price was set at 12 cents per dollar of the principal amount with a 5% of foreign exchange risk margin. The IDA and the governments of Germany and Switzerland provided funding for the operation.

Togo
Bank debt restructurings
Mar. 1980: Rescheduling of $69 million of debts owed to French banks, including arrears of principal. Interest rates varied by currency.
Oct. 1983: Rescheduling of $84 million of debts owed to all commercial bank debt, including previously rescheduled debt.
May 1988: Rescheduling of $48 million restructuring in 1983.
Dec. 1997: Debt buyback at 12.5 cents per dollar of $46.1 million owed to commercial banks. Funding for the operation was provided by the IDA DRF.

Trinidad and Tobago
Bank debt restructurings
Dec. 1989: Rescheduling of $473 million of maturities in September 1988–August 1992.

Turkey
Bank debt restructurings
Mar. 1982: Improvement on the terms of the August 1979 agreement, affecting $2.3 billion of debt.

Uganda
Bank debt restructurings
Feb. 1993: Buyback of $153 million commercial bank debt funded by grants from IDA DRF and other donor countries.

Ukraine
Bond market defaults and restructurings
July 1999: Agreement to restructure a 10-month $163 million eurobond (including principal and interest). Instead of making the $163 million repayment due in June 1999, Ukraine was to repay 20 percent of bond in cash and swap the remaining 80 percent into a D-mark-denominated eurobond with a maturity of 3 years and coupon yield of 16 percent.
Feb. 2000: Agreement to restructure $2.7 billion of the short-term debt obligations. No debt forgiveness or reduction in principal was required from bondholders, and all accrued interest on existing eligible bonds was to be paid in full and in cash; and all accepting investors were to be offered a new 7-year eurobond, denominated either euros or US dollars, at an interest rate of 10 percent for euro-denominated bonds and 11 percent for dollar-denominated bonds.
Mar. 2001: About $21.5 million of the external debt was exchanged for a 6-year eurobond, denominated in either Euro at an interest rate of 10% or U.S. dollar at an interest rate of 11%. Bonds eligible for the exchange were Deutsche Mark 16% eurobond due in February 2001, Euro 10% amortizing notes due in March 2007, U.S. dollar 11% amortizing notes due in March 2007, and U.S. dollar 11% amortizing notes due in March 2007.

Uruguay
Bank debt restructurings
July 1983: Rescheduling of $555 million of maturities in January 1983–December 1984; new long-term money ($240 million).
July 1986: Multiyear rescheduling agreement of $1.7 billion of maturities due in January 1985–December 1989.
Mar. 1988: Rescheduling of $1.5 billion of maturities in January 1990–December 1991, including improvement of terms of the July 1986 agreement.
Brady deal
Feb. 1991: The agreement provided for cash buyback at a 44 percent discount ($628 million), collateralized debt reduction bonds ($535 million), and new money ($89 million) combined with debt conversion notes ($447 million). The repayment terms were: 30-year bullet maturity and 6.75 percent fixed interest for the interest reduction bonds, 16-year maturity including 7 years' grace with LIBOR + 7/8 percent interest for the conversion notes, and 15-year maturity including 7 years' grace with LIBOR + 1 percent interest for the new money notes.

Venezuela, República Bolivariana de
Bank debt restructurings
Feb. 1986: Multiyear rescheduling agreement of $21 billion of maturities due in January 1983–December 1989.
Nov. 1987: Reduction of spread and extension of maturities on the 1986 agreement; new long-term money ($100 million).
Sept. 1988: Interest spread reduced on February 1986 agreement, affecting $20.3 billion in debt.
Dec. 1988: Exchange of debt for bonds outside the framework of the main negotiations.
Brady deal
Dec. 1990: Agreement featured buybacks in the form of 91-day collateralized short-term notes ($1,411 million), exchange for bonds at 30 percent discount ($1,810 million), exchange at par for reduced fixed-rate interest bonds ($7,457 million), exchange for bonds at par with temporary step-down interest rates ($3,027 million), and new money combined with debt conversion bonds ($6,022 million).

Vietnam
Brady deal
Dec. 1997: Agreement restructuring $310.9 million of principal and $486.2 million of past-due interest. For restructured principal, $20.4 million was repurchased at 44 cents per U.S. dollar, $51.6 million was exchanged for discount bonds (50 percent discount); and $238.9 million was exchanged for par fixed interest bonds. Both bonds had 30-year maturity, but the discount bond was repayable in a bullet payment on year 30 while the par bond had a step-up amortization schedule beginning on year 15. Also, 50 percent of the face value due of the par bond was due at maturity. The discount bond was subject to an interest rate of LIBOR plus 13/16 while the par bond was subject to step-up interest rates rising from 3 percent in years 1 and 2 to 5.5 percent in years 21–30. One hundred percent of the discount bonds and 50 percent of the par bonds were guaranteed by U.S. Treasury zero-coupon bonds, and the discount bonds had a 6-month rolling interest guarantee. Regarding past-due interest, $15 million was paid at closing, $294.8 million was exchanged for non-collateralized bonds with an 18-year maturity including 7 years' grace and step-up interest rates, $21.8 million was repurchased at 44 cents per dollar, and $154.6 million was written off.

Yemen, Republic of
Bank debt restructurings
June 2001: Buyback of $362 million of principal and $245 million of associated interest under the IDA DRF. The buyback price was set at 2.94 cents per dollar of the principal amount. The IDA and the governments of the Netherlands, Norway, and Switzerland provided funding for the operation.

Yugoslavia, Federated Republic of

Bank debt restructurings

Oct. 1983: Rescheduling of $1.3 billion of maturities, including a 1-year rollover of short-term bonds, due in January 1983–December 1983; new long-term money ($600 million); maintenance of short-term credit lines ($800 million).

May 1984: Rescheduling of $1.3 billion of maturities due in January 1984–March 1985.

Dec. 1985: Multiyear rescheduling agreement of $4 billion of maturities in January 1985–December 1988.

Sept. 1988: Rescheduling of $7 billion of maturities due in January 1988–December 1989.

Zaire

Bank debt restructurings

April 1980: Rescheduling of $402 million of debt outstanding as of the end of 1979, including arrears.

Jan. 1983: Deferment of principal due in January 1983–December 1983 ($58 million), rescheduled under the April 1980 agreement.

June 1984: Deferment of principal due in January 1984–April 1985 ($64 million), rescheduled under the April 1980 agreement.

May 1985: Deferment of principal due in May 1985–April 1986 ($61 million), rescheduled under the April 1980 agreement.

May 1986: Deferment of principal due in May 1986–April 1987 ($65 million), rescheduled under the April 1980 agreement.

May 1987: Deferment of principal due in May 1987–April 1988 ($61 million), rescheduled under the April 1980 agreement.

June 1989: Deferment of principal to finance monthly payments on outstanding claims, mainly interest on arrears.

Zambia

Bank debt restructurings

Dec. 1984: Rescheduling of $74 million of maturities, including arrears as of February 28, 1983.

Notes

1. We monitor debt flows in two forms. Most meaningful are net flows. These data are hard to trace on a timely basis, however. It is more straightforward to monitor gross market-based actions—publicly announced and completed bond issues and bank loans. These flows are just one influence on net debt flows. The other three—debt repayments, new borrowing not publicly announced, and changes in all short-term debt—cannot be assumed to be static, so it is not possible to map directly from gross market-based flows to net debt. Gross market-based flows are, however, a very helpful indicator of debt-market trends.

2. The pie charts understate the shift from the peak of flows in mid 1997, as the first chart shows the pattern of investors in December 1998, which was well into the retrenchment phase for many of the high-risk investors, especially hedge funds.

3. This improvement may have been due to the development of mechanisms for the orderly restructuring of debts, such as standing bondholders' committees (World Bank 2000a). Also, the speed-up of communications (particularly the laying of the transatlantic cable) may have facilitated negotiations.

4. Walter Wriston wrote this in 1982 (*New York Times,* September 14; quoted in Kaletsky 1985).

5. An active secondary market in developing country loans grew rapidly in the 1980s, reaching an annual volume of $50 billion in 1988. Initially the market was driven by interbank swaps designed to consolidate portfolios and manage risk. The market took off in 1985, however, when Chile and Mexico introduced systematic debt conversion programs (World Bank 1990).

6. In the absence of effective capital controls, the entire monetary base constitutes a claim against the government that might be converted into foreign currency. In practice, governments in crisis can impose capital controls (although these are not 100 percent effective), and presumably the availability of official support would help discourage capital outflows, which limits the likely claim on official resources.

7. Some commentators have also asserted that rescue packages encourage governments to borrow excessively, in anticipation of a bailout. It is doubtful that governments would invite a crisis, however, that almost uniformly culminates in a change of government and loss of power.

8. Roubini (2002) notes that the restructuring of developing countries' bank debt during the 1980s faced considerable difficulties due to the hundreds of banks involved, their different interests (for example, large banks with extensive relationships with debtor countries versus small banks), and the differences in the legal instruments involved. Nevertheless, developing countries' creditors are a much more diverse set today than 20 years ago.

9. Eichengreen (2002) points out that the potential for collective action clauses to be used to invoke bondholders meetings may have facilitated agreement in the Pakistan and Ukraine debt restructurings, even where they were not used.

10. Of course, the International Monetary Fund (IMF) is not the first to consider a legal process for sovereign bankruptcy. Adam Smith mentioned it, and there were extensive discussions of the legal aspects of sovereign debt crises in the first half of the 20th century. More recently, interest in sovereign bankruptcy rose from the late 1970s and gathered steam in the 1990s (Rogoff and Zettelmeyer 2002 provide an extensive discussion).

11. The basic framework is described in Krueger 2002 and IMF 2002.

12. See World Bank 2000b for a discussion of the distributional consequences of financial crises.

13. See, for example, www.attac.org and www.jubilee2000uk.org.

References

Beale, Chris, Michel Chatain, Nathan Fox, Sandra Bell, James Berner, Robert Preminger, and Jan Prins. Fall 2002. "Credit Attributes of Project Finance." *The Journal of Structured and Project Finance:* 5–9.

Becker, Torbjorn, Anthony J. Richards, and Yunyong Thaicharoen. 2001. "Bond Restructuring and Moral Hazard: Are Collective Action Clauses Costly?" International Monetary Fund Seminar Series 44. IMF, Washington, D.C.

Beers, David T., and John Chambers. 2002. "Sovereign Defaults: Moving Higher Again in 2003?" Standard and Poor's Research. New York.

Berner, James, Christopher Beale, Sandra Bell, Michel Chatain, Robert Preminger, and Jan Prins. 2002. "Do Project Finance Loans Outperform Corporate Loans?" *Infrastructure Review 2002*: 20–26.

Bolton, Patrick. 2002. "Towards a Statutory Approach to Sovereign Debt Restructuring: Lessons from Corporate Bankruptcy Practice Around the World." Princeton University. Processed.

Brady Forum. 2000. "Peru-Elliott Case Shifts Balance of Power to Creditors." October 2. www.bradynet.com

British Bankers Association. 2002. *Credit Derivatives Survey 2001/2002.*

Bulow, Jeffrey, and Kenneth Rogoff. 1990. "Cleaning Up Third World Debt Without Getting Taken to the Cleaners." *Journal of Economic Perspectives* 4(1): 31–42.

Calvo, Guillermo, Leonardo Leiderman, and Carmen Reinhart. 1993. "Capital Inflows to Latin America: The Role of External Factors." *IMF Staff Papers* 40 (March).

Chancellor, Edward. 2000. *Devil Take the Hindmost: A History of Financial Speculation.* New York: Plume.

Chari, V. V., and Patrick J. Kehoe. 1998. "Asking the Right Questions about the IMF." *Annual Report.* Minneapolis, Minn.: Federal Reserve Bank of Minneapolis.

Chuhan, Punam. 2001. "Recent External Bond Exchanges." World Bank, Washington, D.C. Processed.

Cole, Harold L., James Dow, and William B. English. 1994. "Default, Settlement, and Signaling: Lending Resumption in a Reputational Model of Sovereign Debt." Research Department Staff Report 180. Federal Reserve Bank of Minneapolis, Minneapolis, Minn.

Cornelli, Francesca, and Leonardo Felli. 1994. "Efficiency of Bankruptcy Procedures." Banca d'Italia Temi di Discussione 245. Rome.

Dammers, Clifford. 1984. "A Brief History of Sovereign Defaults and Reschedulings." In David Suratgar, ed., *Default and Rescheduling: Corporate and Sovereign Borrowers in Difficulty.* London: Euromoney.

Dooley, Michael P. 2000a. "International Financial Architecture and Strategic Default: Can Financial Crises Be Less Painful?" *Carnegie-Rochester Conference Series on Public Policy* 53: 361–77.

———. 2000b. "Debt Management and Crisis in Developing Countries." *Journal of Development Economics* 63: 45–58.

Eaton, Jonathan, and Mark Gersovitz. 1981. "Debt with Potential Repudiation: Theoretical and Empirical Analysis." *Review of Economic Studies* 48(152): 289–309.

Eichengreen, Barry. 1991. "Historical Research on International Lending and Debt." *Journal of Economic Perspectives* 5(2): 149–69.

———. 2002. *Financial Crises and What to Do About Them.* Oxford: Oxford University Press.

Eichengreen, Barry, and Ashoka Mody. 2000. "Would Collective Action Clauses Raise Borrowing Costs?" NBER Working Paper 7458. National Bureau of Economic Research, Cambridge, Mass.

Eichengreen, Barry, and Ricardo Portes. 1995. *Crisis? What Crisis? Orderly Workouts for Sovereign Debtors.* London: Centre for Economic Policy Research.

Eichengreen, Barry, Ricardo Hausmann, and Ugo Panizza. 2002. "Original Sin: The Pain, the Mystery, and the Road to Redemption." Paper prepared for the "Currency and Maturity Matchmaking Conference," Washington, D.C., November 21–22, 2002.

English, William B. 1996. "Understanding the Costs of Sovereign Default: American State Debts in the 1840s." *The American Economic Review* 86(1): 259–75.

Fischer, Stanley. 2002. "Basel II: Risk Management and Implications for Banking in Emerging Market Countries." Paper presented at the International Conference of Banking Supervisors, September 19, Cape Town, South Africa.

Haldane, Andy. 1999. "Private Sector Involvement in Financial Crisis: Analytics and Public Policy Approaches." *Financial Stability Review* 7: 184–202.

Hayes, Simon, Victoria Saporta, and David Lodge. 2002. "The Impact of the New Basel Accord on the Supply of Capital to Emerging Market Economics." *Financial Stability Review* (December): 110–14.

Hurlock, James B. 1995. "Sovereign Debt Default: The Way Ahead for Sovereign Debt." *International Financial Law Review* (U.K.) 14(July): 10–12.

Hutchison, Michael M., and Ilan Neuberger. 2001. "Output Costs of Currency and Balance of Payments Crises in Emerging Markets." University of California at Santa Cruz, Santa Cruz, Calif. Processed.

ICN (Independent Catholic News). 2000. "Vulture Funds Prey on Poorest Countries." November 1. www.indcatholicnews.com

IMF (International Monetary Fund). 2001.

———. 2002. "Sovereign Debt Restructuring Mechanism—Further Considerations." Washington, D.C.

IMF and World Bank. 2001. *Guidelines for Public Debt Management.* Washington, D.C.

Jorgensen, Erika, and Jeffrey Sachs. 1998. "Default and Renegotiation of Latin American Foreign Bonds in the Interwar Period." *NBER Working Paper 2636*: National Bureau of Economic Research, Cambridge, Mass.

Kaletsky, Anatole. 1985. *The Costs of Default.* New York: Priority Press.

Krueger, Anne O. 2002a. "A New Approach to Sovereign Debt Restructuring." International Monetary Fund, Washington, D.C.

———. 2002b. "Sovereign Debt Restructuring Mechanism: One Year Later." Speech given at the Banco de Mexico's Conference on "Macroeconomic Stability, Financial Markets, and Economic Development." November 12, Mexico City. www.imf.org.

———. 2003. Remarks made at the Sovereign Debt Restructuring Mechanism Conference, IMF, Washington, D.C., January 22–23, 2003.

Latin American Advisor. 2002. "Will Argentina's Foreign Creditors Get Equal Treatment?" January 22. www.thedialogue.org

Lipworth, Gabrielle, and Jens Nystedt. 2001. "Crisis Resolution and Private Sector Adaptation." *Finance and Development* 38(2).

Miller, Marcus, and Lei Zhang. 1998. "Sovereign Liquidity Crisis: the Strategic Case for a Payments Standstill." Centre for the Study of Globalization and Regionalization Working Paper no. 35. University of Warwick, Warwick, England.

Porzecanski, Arturo. 2002. "A Critique of Sovereign Bankruptcy Initiatives." ABN-AMRO, New York.

Priest, Andrew. 2001. "Vulture Funds Swoop on Bloodied Argentine Debt." *The Industry Standard.* www.thestandard.com.

Ramphal, Shridath S. 1989. "Sovereign Default: A Backward Glance." *The Washington Quarterly* 11(2): 63–75.

Rogoff, Kenneth. 1999. "International Institutions for Reducing Global Financial Instability." *NBER Working Paper 7265.* National Bureau of Economic Research, Cambridge, Mass.

Rogoff, Kenneth, and Jeromin Zettelmeyer. 2002. "Early Ideas on Sovereign Bankruptcy Reorganization: A Survey." *IMF Working Paper WP/02/57.* International Monetary Fund, Washington, D.C.

Roubini, Nouriel. 2000. "Bail-In, Burden-Sharing, Private Sector Involvement (PSI) in Crisis Resolution and Constructive Engagement of the Private Sector." Stern School of Business. Processed.

———. 2002. "Do We Need a New International Bankruptcy Regime? Comments on Bulow, Sachs, and White." Paper presented at a symposium on "A Bankruptcy Court for Sovereign Debt," April 2, Brookings Institution, Washington, D.C.

Suter, Christian. 1992. *Debt Cycles in the World Economy: Foreign Loans, Financial Crises, and Debt Settlements, 1820–1986.* Boulder, Colo.: Westview Press.

Weder, Beatrice, and Michael Wedow. 2002. "Will Basel II Affect International Capital Flows to Emerging Markets?" Technical Paper 19. OECD Development Center.

Weiss, Wendy. 1997. "Debt and Devaluation: The Burden on Ecuador's Popular Class." *Latin American Perspectives* 24(4): 9–33.

World Bank. 1990. *Global Development Finance 1989/90.* Washington, D.C.

———. 2000a. *Global Development Finance 2000.* Washington, D.C.

———. 2000b. *Global Economic Prospects 2001.* Washington, D.C.

———. 2002. *Global Development Finance 2002.* Washington, D.C.

4

Sustaining and Promoting Equity-Related Finance for Developing Countries

Dilek Aykut, Himmat Kalsi, and Dilip Ratha

THE FLOW OF EQUITY-RELATED FINANCE TO developing countries takes two forms: portfolio investments and direct investments. Combined inflows of both forms totaled a net of about $152 billion in 2002, down from $178 billion in 2001 and from their peak of $196 billion in 1997 (figure 4.1). This decline mirrors the weakness of global equity markets in recent years. However, when viewed against the plunge in debt outstanding to private-sector creditors discussed in chapter 3, the flow of private-sector equity-related capital appears remarkably robust. Indeed, its steadiness is a key part of the significant rotation from debt to equity in the pattern of private financing for developing countries.

Figure 4.1 Net equity flows to developing countries, 1989–2002

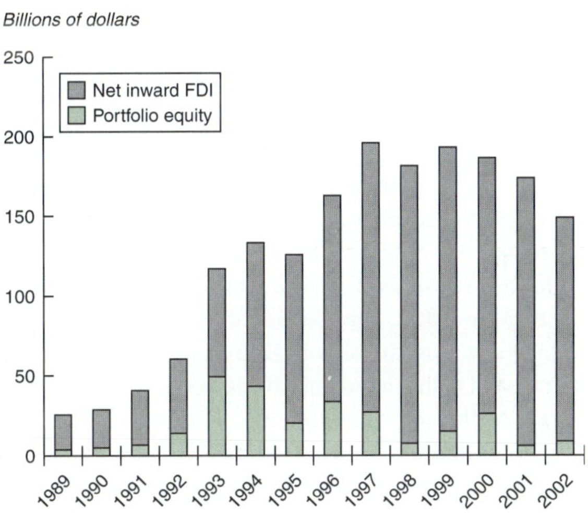

Sources: World Bank, *Global Development Finance: Country Tables* and sources cited therein, various years; UNCTAD, *World Investment Report 2002*; and World Bank staff estimates for 2002.

The first part of this chapter focuses on FDI. After reviewing developments in 2002, the key issue addressed is that of the sustainability of the current, relatively high level of flows. The main message is that although there are several reasons to believe that FDI flows can be sustained at or above current levels in the years ahead, such a result cannot be taken for granted—there are clear vulnerabilities to the current level of FDI. Various factors have reduced returns on FDI in recent years, while the willingness and ability of companies in high-income countries to make long-run, strategic investments in developing countries has been reduced by financial-market pressures.

The second part of the chapter reviews developments in portfolio equity flows in 2002 and early 2003 and puts them in their historic context. It then goes on to ask a basic question about portfolio equity flows: If FDI investors find equity-related investing in developing countries such a good idea, why are portfolio equity flows relatively weak? Why have they failed to rise since the early 1990s? For policymakers faced with weak debt flows, this is an important issue to address. The simple fact is that, due to regular crises and volatile growth, emerging-market equities have offered poor returns over an extended period. Policymakers in developing countries need to maximize the attractiveness of local equity by strengthening domestic institutions, most notably those related to corporate governance, with a view to protecting the rights of minority shareholders.

The chapter closes with a forecast for equity flows for 2003 and beyond. In line with the analysis of the global outlook presented in chapter 2, the forecast is for a gradual rise in flows. For 2003, overall equity inflows are projected to be

$159 billion—$145 billion in FDI and $14 billion in portfolio equity investments.

Direct investment flows in 2002

Net FDI inflows to developing countries fell sharply in 2002 to an estimated $143 billion, or 2.4 percent of GDP, compared to $172 billion (2.9 percent of GDP) in 2001 (table 4.1; figure 4.2). The decline in FDI flows to developing countries was associated with a slowdown in privatization and mergers-and-acquisition (M&A) transactions (figure 4.3).[1] The downturn in FDI flows to developing countries occurred against an even sharper decline (27 percent) in global FDI flows—from $735 billion in 2001 to $534 billion in 2002. As a result, developing countries' share in global FDI actually rose in 2002. Global M&A transactions declined sharply (49 percent) in 2002. The decline was especially steep in the United States, where, in addition to economic slowdown, corporate accounting scandals undermined M&A activity.

Table 4.1 Net inward FDI flows to developing countries, 1999–2002
(billions of dollars)

	1999	2000	2001	2002
Total	179	161	172	143
East Asia and Pacific	49	44	49	57
Europe and Central Asia	28	29	30	29
Latin America and the Caribbean	88	76	69	42
Middle East and North Africa	3	3	6	3
South Asia	3	3	4	5
Sub-Saharan Africa	8	6	14	7

Source: World Bank, *Global Development Finance: Country Tables;* World Bank staff estimates for 2002.

Figure 4.2 Net FDI inflows to developing countries, 1994–2002

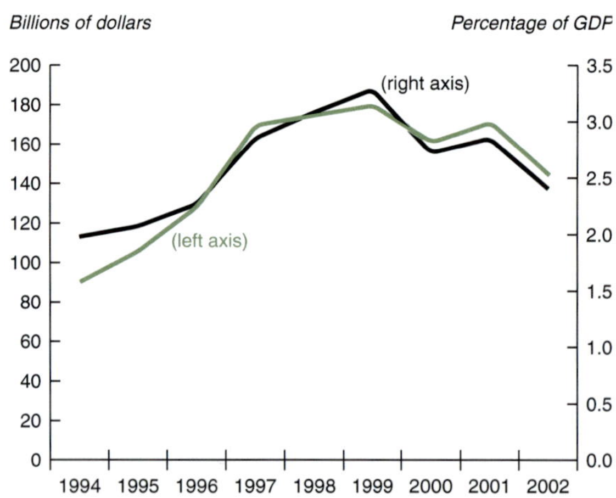

Source: World Bank, *Global Development Finance: Country Tables* and sources cited therein; World Bank, *World Development Indicators*; World Bank staff estimates for 2002.

Figure 4.3 Privatization and M&A in developing countries, 1994–2002

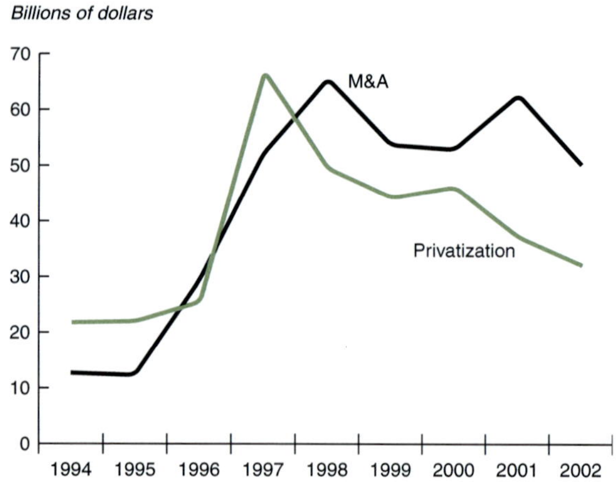

Sources: World Bank, *Global Development Finance*, various years; UNCTAD, *World Investment Report 2002*; OECD, *Financial Market Trends 2002*; EBRD, *Transition Report*, various years; World Bank staff estimates for 2002.

Despite the overall decline in FDI flows to developing countries and another rise in the share of FDI accounted for by China, there was a decline in the overall concentration of FDI. The share of the top 10 recipient countries remains high at 70 percent, but it has declined from about 79 percent in 2000. FDI as a share of GDP in the top 10 recipient countries remains much higher than the average for developing countries—although it has declined since 1999 (figure 4.4). India has joined the top 10 recipients of FDI. Other gainers (compared to 2000) are China, whose share rose to 37 percent of the total in 2002, the Czech Republic, the Russian Federation, and the Slovak Republic. The countries that lost FDI share during this period are Argentina, Brazil, Malaysia, Thailand, and Turkey.

Low-income countries received $7 billion in FDI in 2002, compared to $10 billion the year before. Among the low-income countries, FDI in the 47 least developed countries (as defined by the United Nations) rose slightly to an estimated $4 billion in 2002—due largely to strong performance by Angola.

Figure 4.4 FDI as a share of GDP in developing countries, 1994–2002

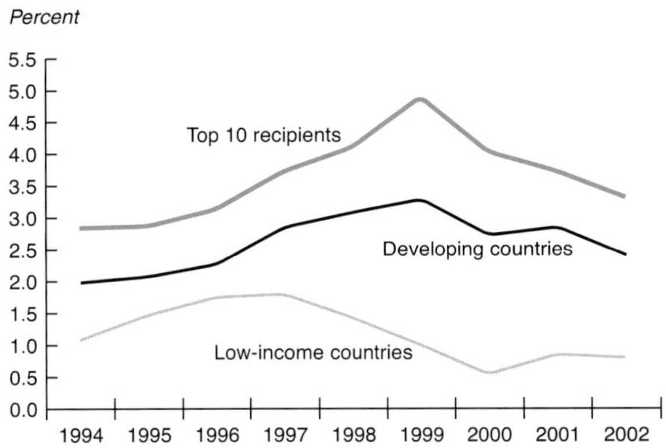

Note: The top 10 recipients of FDI based on the volume of accumulated FDI flows over the period 1992–2001 are (in descending order) China, Brazil, Mexico, Argentina, Poland, Chile, Malaysia, Thailand, the Czech Republic, and the República Bolivariana de Venezuela.
Source: World Bank, *Global Development Finance*: *Country Tables* and sources cited therein, various years; World Bank, *World Development Indicators*, various years; World Bank staff estimates for 2002.

Regional trends in FDI

The dip in FDI flows in 2002 was almost entirely due to the decline in flows to Latin America and the Caribbean (see table 4.1). Three factors accounted for that decline:

- *The regional recession* undermined incentives to invest in the region generally and in Argentina specifically.
- *No large M&A transactions* of the kind that inflated the inflow numbers in recent years occurred in 2002. For example, Mexico's total in 2001 reflected Citibank's acquisition of Banamex, an extraordinarily large transaction. The country's 2002 FDI total was $13.6 billion, about the same as the recent annual average if the Banamex transaction is excluded.
- *The process of privatization is winding down.* Latin American governments have been aggressive sellers of state-owned assets for almost a decade, and many of these assets have been sold to foreign buyers. As the privatization process has moved towards completion, FDI flows related to privatization naturally have declined. For example, FDI flows to Brazil—still the main FDI destination in the region and the second largest in the developing world—fell to an estimated $17 billion, significantly below the more than $30 billion annual average seen in 1999–2000.

The rise in flows to East Asia and Pacific was more than accounted for by another rise in FDI in China, which offset the marginal decline in other countries. China accounted for 92 percent of FDI to the region and for 37 percent of the developing world's total in 2002. Buoyant investment is being driven by the new round of market liberalization, strong optimism about the domestic economy, and the country's accession to the WTO.

FDI flows to Europe and Central Asia held reasonably steady at around $29 billion in 2002, compared to $30 billion in 2001. Flows were strong in the Czech Republic, but weaker to Hungary and Poland, where the tailing off in the privatization process slowed inflows. Flows to Turkey were meager, after being lifted in 2001 by inflows from the sale of mobile phone licenses and a state bank.

FDI flows to South Asia increased moderately in 2002 to an estimated $5 billion. The actual amount may well be higher, given that FDI is significantly understated in India, the largest recipient country in the region (box 4.1).

Adjusting for the sale of Morocco's Maroc-Telecom to Vivendi Universal for $2.2 billion last year, the Middle East and North Africa region experienced a sharp decline in FDI, dropping to about $3 billion from an unusually high level of $6 billion in 2001. The change was due in part to the uncertainty surrounding the region since September 11, 2001. FDI into Sub-Saharan Africa also dropped 49 percent to an estimated $7 billion from the previous year, when FDI inflows were swelled by the sale of South Africa's De Beers.

FDI shifts to services

FDI flows to developing countries' services sectors increased rapidly in the late 1980s and early 1990s. Between 1988 and 1999, service-sector FDI increased at an annual rate of 28 percent and accounted for around 37 percent of total FDI stocks in developing countries in 1999 (World Bank 2002b, chapter 2). The share of infrastructure in total FDI flows nearly doubled during 1990–98. This increase was led by a surge in flows into the telecommunication sector (the increase was around $84 billion, or one-tenth of

Box 4.1 Understated FDI in developing countries

Inflows of FDI may be understated in many developing countries. India's definition of FDI excludes earnings reinvested by foreign investors; other direct investments between direct investors and subsidiaries, branches, and associates; and investments by offshore and domestic venture-capital funds set up by foreigners (Economist Intelligence Unit 2002). If these items are taken into account, India's actual annual level of FDI would rise significantly (from the $2–3 billion reported currently to as much as $8 billion—about 1.7 percent of India's GDP, according to International Finance Corporation 2002). India's government recently proposed to adopt the IMF's definition—as required under the IMF's Special Data Dissemination Standard. Similarly, Indonesia's FDI is also believed to be under-reported. Indonesian balance of payments data indicate that between 1998–2001, total disinvestments in the country reached over $10 billion. While this is consistent with the decline in reported outward investment in Indonesia by high-income OECD countries (which accounted for 70 percent of total investment in Indonesia before 1998), it is not consistent with the fact that their investments stayed at positive levels. One reason for this discrepancy may be that Indonesia does not include reinvested earnings as FDI inflows. Other developing countries that do not include reinvested earnings in FDI inflows are Nigeria, Thailand, and Tunisia (Direct Investment Methodology Survey, IMF 2001).

the change in aggregate FDI stock) as global telecom and utility companies took advantage of their rising stock prices and participated in privatization programs in many developing countries (figure 4.5).[2] Such investment flows peaked in 1998, however, in line with the asset price movements in the information, communication, and technology sector in global markets. Also, privatization efforts began to slow around this period in many developing countries.

Figure 4.5 Private and foreign direct investment into the telecom sector of developing countries, 1990–2000

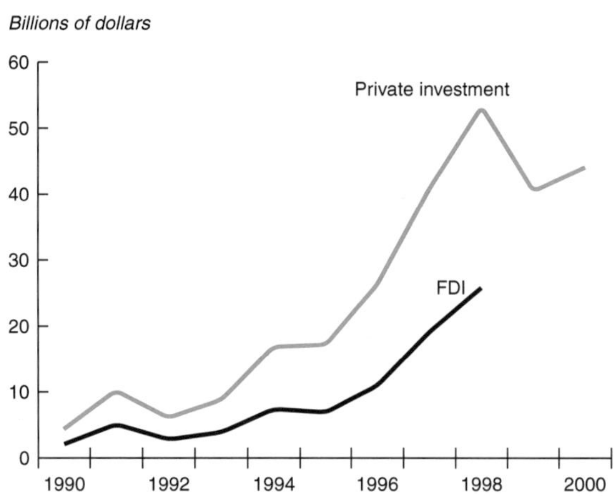

Note: Investments in developing countries. FDI data is not available for recent years.
Sources: Sader 2000; World Bank, *Global Economic Prospects 2003*.

Despite the slump in the global telecommunications sector since 1998, developing countries have continued to receive FDI into this sector. The profile of investors is changing, however. A growing number of new (relatively small) regional firms are now competing with the global players. (The rise in South-South FDI during this period is discussed further below.) The mode of investments is changing, as well, from privatization to licensing and joint ventures.[3] These changes imply that the nominal amount of FDI in telecommunications may continue to remain low even though the number of transactions may increase.

This shift toward services is likely to have increased the benefits of FDI to developing countries. Many services sectors provide important inputs to production, particularly compared with the often limited linkages between extractive industries and the domestic economy. Of course, services comprise a wide variety of economic activities of varying impact on developing economies.[4] For example, the entry of foreign banks has helped improve the efficiency of developing countries' financial sectors, a critical input to growth. Foreign investment in fast-food establishments, on the other hand, is unlikely to generate comparable benefits. Nevertheless, the trend toward greater FDI in service sectors, coupled with extensive examples of FDI in banking and infrastructure, is a positive development that may be missed if only the aggregate trend in FDI is examined.

The extractive industries retain an important share of FDI in developing countries. Oil-exporting countries accounted for about 20 percent of all FDI in developing countries through most of the 1990s.[5] In Sub-Saharan Africa in the second half of the 1990s, FDI stocks in countries where most production occurs in the primary sector—and where FDI is often devoted to oil or mining—increased at about the same rate as in countries with limited primary-sector production.[6]

Despite FDI's overall shift to the service sectors, several of the countries hit by severe economic crises in the late 1990s and the early part of this decade have seen FDI shift out of the service sector and into tradable sectors, particularly manufacturing. Before a crisis, an overvalued exchange rate may encourage rapid growth in service-sector investments, including by foreigners, to serve a domestic market where purchasing power is high—which may partially explain the growth of FDI in the financial sectors of Argentina and Brazil in the late 1990s. But a crisis that cuts domestic incomes and leads to a massive exchange-rate devaluation is likely to shift investment to the export sector and, more broadly, to tradable production. FDI in Thailand's automobile sector increased rapidly after the 1997 crisis, and similar growth can be seen in Turkey over the past two years. The attractiveness of tradable production following devaluation is a major reason why FDI often remains resilient following a crisis (box 4.2).

Box 4.2 The resilience of FDI during a crisis

Foreign direct investment (FDI) tends to be more resilient than portfolio equity or debt flows during a financial crisis in the recipient country (World Bank 1999). This is in part due to the fact that direct investments are long-term strategic decisions that may not be affected by a financial crisis that is perceived to be short-lived.

On the contrary, a fall in asset prices, combined with currency devaluation, may attract more FDI—especially in the tradable sector. FDI flows held up well following crises in Mexico in 1995–96, Korea in 1998–99, Thailand in 1998–99, and Turkey in 2000–01. FDI sagged, however, after the crises in Argentina and Indonesia, both of which present deep-seated social and political risks that currency devaluation cannot address.

FDI and financial crises

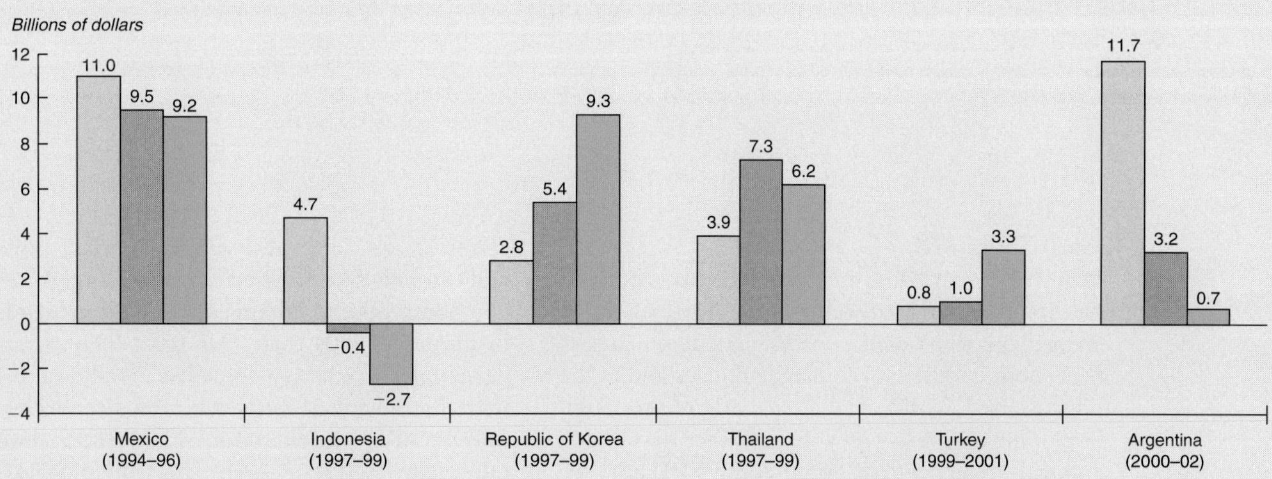

Source: World Bank, *Global Development Finance: Country Tables* and sources cited therein; World Bank staff estimates for 2002.

Box 4.3 Outward flows of FDI from developing countries tend to be underestimated

Under-reporting of outflows of FDI is pervasive, particularly where investors may be attempting to avoid controls on capital and foreign exchange or high taxes on investment income. Some countries—even major emerging markets like Malaysia and Mexico—do not identify FDI outflows in their balance-of-payments statistics. Lax accounting standards, weak tax administration, and differences in the definition of FDI between the source and destination countries introduce further noise in the FDI data.

Evidence of under-reporting can be seen by comparing FDI inflows reported by the United States with outflows to the United States reported by developing countries. Mexico's reported FDI outflows were under $1 billion in 2000 (UNCTAD 2002), whereas the United States reported inward FDI from Mexico of $5.3 billion. Hungary reported a total FDI outflow of $0.3 billion in 1999, while the United States alone reported receiving $5.9 billion from Hungary. Other examples abound. A large investment of $4.4 billion in Telecom Eireann MSA deal in 1999 was not reported by Iran. China's outward FDI numbers are much smaller than those reported as inflows from China in Hong Kong's official statistics. Similarly, according to Hong Kong's Economic and Trade Office, Hong Kong's investments in China surged to $46.4 billion in 2000—yet China's inward FDI numbers show a decline in inflows from Hong Kong.[a]

The inconsistency in data on inflows and outflows is further exacerbated by the activities of offshore financial centers. This is clearly evident from the U.S. data, where an attempt is made to distinguish between the residence of the firm making the investment (usually reported as the source country) and the residence of the owners of the firm, and hence the original source of the funds, referred to in U.S. reports as the "ultimate beneficiary owner." For example, in 2001 FDI to the United States from Switzerland was $56.3 billion. Using the ultimate beneficiary criterion, however, it was close to zero. The bulk of the funds reported as FDI from Switzerland actually originated in a third country. Even this correction, however, cannot completely identify the source of FDI flows in some cases. For example, using the ultimate beneficiary criterion, FDI from Bermuda and Hong Kong totaled $42 billion in 2001. However, it is unlikely that these financial centers were the original source of substantial amounts of foreign investment.

Financial centers may distort the global amount of FDI flows. For example, during 1999–2000, Belgium and Luxembourg reported huge surges in both inward and outward FDI . According to the OECD database, this surge was almost entirely in financial activities (most likely financial intermediation). But these transactions swelled global FDI flows by about $200 billion.

a. "Round-tripping" of flows between China and Hong Kong may have inflated China's inward FDI at the same time it lowered its outward FDI data (see also *Global Development Finance* 2002).

Direct investments in the United States and ultimate beneficiary owners, 2001
(billions of dollars)

	Actual	Ultimate beneficiary
Bermuda	−2.8	19.5
Hong Kong	0.0	22.4
Switzerland	56.3	−0.6

Source: U.S. Department of Commerce.

South-South FDI

With wealth increasing and capital controls lifted in the 1990s, many developing countries have emerged as significant sources of foreign investment, both in other developing countries and in the industrialized world. FDI flows originating from developing countries and going to other developing countries (referred to as South-South FDI) are estimated at $54 billion in 2000, about 36 percent of total FDI inflows to 31 developing countries (table 4.2 on page 91).[7] Outflows of FDI from developing countries are notoriously underreported, however, and can only be estimated indirectly (box 4.3).[8]

South-South FDI appears to have grown faster in the late 1990s than FDI from high-income to developing countries—so-called North-South FDI, with high-income countries now accounting for only about 58 percent of total FDI flows to developing countries (figure 4.6). The United States and Japan account for most of the drop in North-South FDI, investment from Europe having risen in the late 1990s (figure 4.7). The 1990s has seen the

Table 4.2 Estimates of South-South FDI flows, 1995–2000
(billions of dollars)

	1995	1996	1997	1998	1999	2000
FDI flows to developing countries: From all countries (1)	94.0	112.4	148.4	153.7	160.6	148.0
Less: From high-income OECD countries (2)	51.3	58.8	69.8	74.1	93.6	85.5
Less: From high-income non-OECD countries (3)	27.4	28.6	21.2	19.1	17.2	8.6
Equals: Implied South-South FDI (1 – 2 – 3)	15.3	25.0	57.4	60.4	49.7	53.9
As share of total FDI inflows to developing countries	*16.2*	*22.3*	*38.7*	*39.3*	*31.0*	*36.4*

Source: Aykut and Ratha 2002.

Figure 4.6 FDI to developing countries, by source, 1995–2000

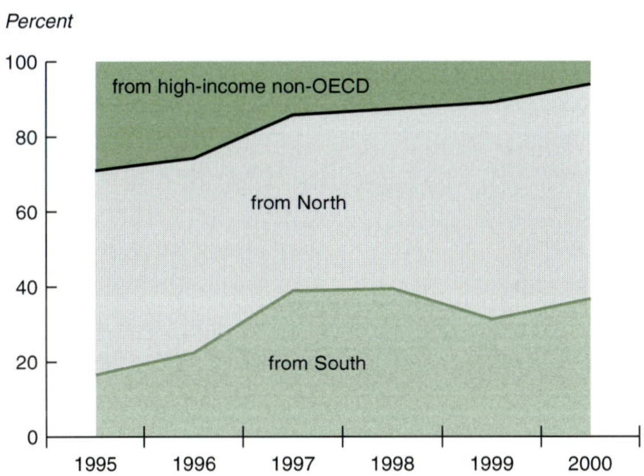

Source: Aykut and Ratha 2002.

Figure 4.7 Major North-South investors

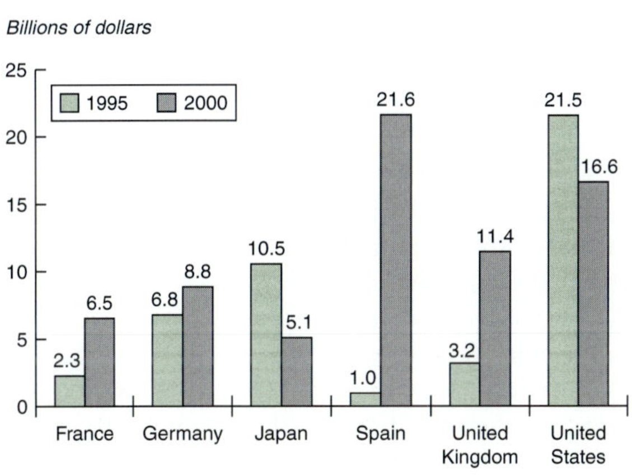

Source: OECD, *Direct Investment Database 2002.*

emergence of several transnational corporations in developing countries—among them Mexico's Cemex (Cementos Mexicanos) and South African Breweries—that have played an important role in FDI outflows (box 4.4).

How sustainable is the current flow of FDI?

The impressive stability of FDI flows to developing countries in the face of weakness in global capital spending, global mergers and acquisitions, and private-sector debt flows to developing countries makes it tempting to assume that the recent level of net inflows can be safely extrapolated well into the future at their current range of about $140–$160 billion (or 2.7 percent of GDP). Would such an extrapolation be valid? Or is FDI apt to suffer a decline similar to that of portfolio equity flows?

Automatic stabilizers for FDI

There are two very important stabilizers to the flow of FDI funds. *First, the stock of existing FDI generates profits that are often retained in the business.* Although plowing profits back into the business does not produce a foreign-exchange flow, it avoids the net foreign-exchange *outflow* that would appear in the current account if the funds were remitted to the parent company. When profits are so retained, this represents an equal and offsetting inflow on the capital account to the outflow from the current account.

Unfortunately, many countries do not provide data on the share of retained profits in FDI (box 4.1).[9] Of the 59 countries that do provide a breakdown of retained earnings in net FDI inflows, retained earnings accounted for slightly less than 20 percent of total net inward FDI in the period 1996–2001 (figure 4.8). If this proportion were applied to developing countries as a whole, then the net inflow due to retained earnings would be on the order of $30 billion.

The region with the highest share of FDI in the form of retained earnings is Sub-Saharan Africa. The nine countries of the region for which data are available show an average share of 31 percent.[10] For China, the largest destination for FDI flows, reinvested earnings accounted for about one-third of net FDI inflows over the 1996–2000 period. For Mexico, the ratio was 21 percent. The countries

Box 4.4 Cemex and South-South FDI

Cementos Mexicanos (Cemex), one of the world's top 100 transnational corporations in terms of foreign assets, is the largest cement company in the Americas and one of the three largest (with Lafarge and Holcim) in the world. It rapidly expanded its global operations in the 1990s both in industrial and developing countries. Approximately two-thirds of its assets and more than 60 percent of its production capacity are in foreign lands, with 40 percent of foreign assets and half of foreign capacity being in developing countries.

The company has focused on acquiring companies in countries with large domestic markets at times when valuations are low. For example, Cemex acquired Vencemos, the largest cement company in República Bolivariana de Venezuela, in 1994, shortly after the currency suffered a 64-percent devaluation. Similarly, Cemex acquired PT Semen Grasik in Indonesia in 1998, soon after the rupiah's three-fold devaluation against the U.S. dollar. Interestingly, Cemex still enjoys a much higher rate of return in its domestic market than in its foreign investments, whether in the North or the South (see table).

Cemex's assets by country as of 2001

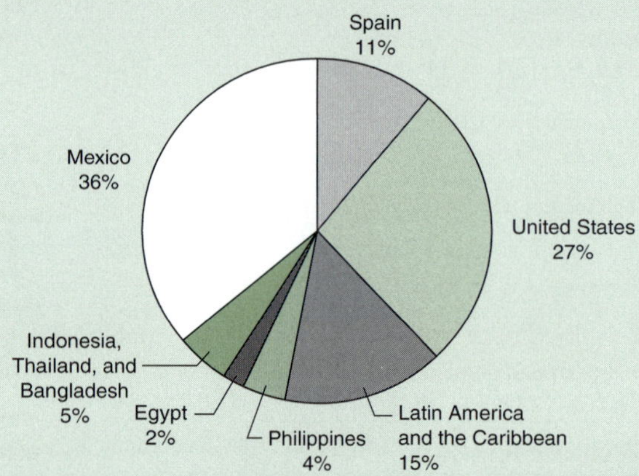

	Percentage rate of return (Operational income/total assets)		
	1999	2000	2001
Mexico	21	24	17
North	15	7	8
South	6	13	7

Note: Excluding unidentified assets classified as "others."
Source: CEMEX Annual Report 2001.

Figure 4.8 Proportion of FDI funded by reinvested earnings, by region, 1996–2001

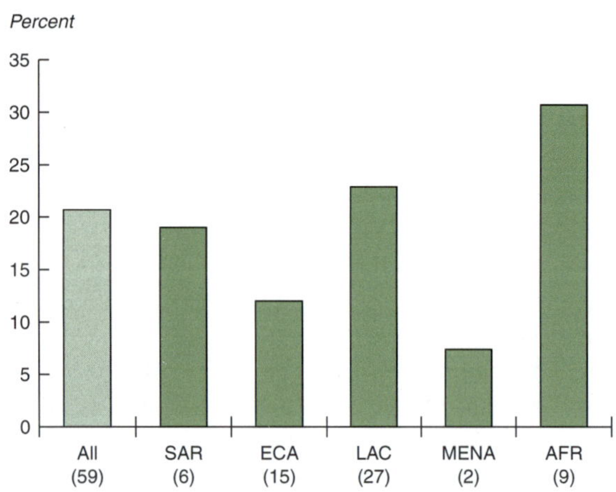

Note: The number of countries is indicated in parentheses. SAR = South Asia, ECA = Europe and Central Asia, LAC = Latin America and the Caribbean, MENA = Middle East and North Africa, AFR = Sub-Saharan Africa.
Source: IMF, *Balance of Payment Statistics 2001.*

with the largest shares of FDI accounted for by retained earnings were: Dominica (65 percent), Swaziland (64 percent), Barbados (59 percent), the Dominican Republic and Namibia (46 percent), Papua New Guinea (45 percent), and Benin (40 percent).

It should not be supposed, of course, that profits earned on FDI in developing countries are automatically reinvested. Whether they are or not will depend on a host of factors, not the least of which is investors' eagerness to build their business in the host country.[11] The balance-of-payments presentations of 56 countries identify the income earned from FDI activities (in the current account) and the component of that income that is plowed back in as an FDI inflow to the capital account. From those presentations it is possible to infer an average propensity to reinvest of just below 40 percent over the period 1996–2001 (figure 4.9).

The countries with the highest average propensity to reinvest earnings are in Eastern Europe and

Figure 4.9 Proportion of FDI earnings reinvested, by region, 1996–2001

Reinvested earnings as a percentage of FDI earnings (balance-of-payments basis)

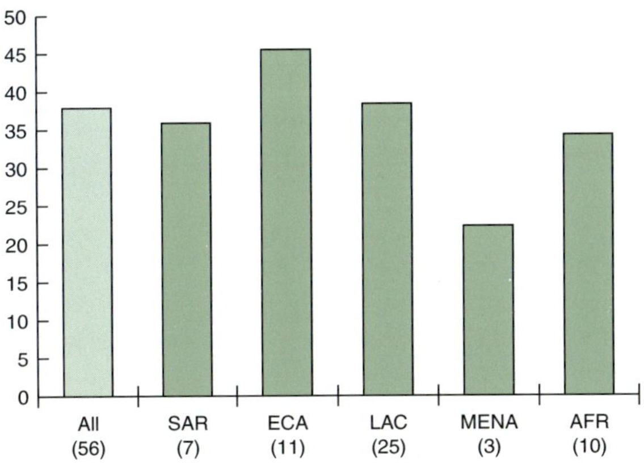

Note: The number of countries is indicated in parentheses. SAR = South Asia, ECA = Europe and Central Asia, LAC = Latin America and the Caribbean, MENA = Middle East and North Africa, AFR = Sub-Saharan Africa.
Source: IMF, *Balance of Payment Statistics 2001.*

Central Asia, where the regional average was 46 percent in 1996–2001. Reinvestment ratios exceeded 50 percent in Lithuania (72 percent), Latvia (69 percent), the Czech Republic (62 percent), the Kyrgyz Republic (61 percent), Croatia (57 percent), Moldova (56 percent), and Estonia (53 percent). Individually, however, the country with the highest reinvestment rate was China (81 percent over the period 1997–2000), which helps to account for the large scale of China's overall net FDI inflows.

The second key stabilizer to FDI flows is depreciation of fixed capital. FDI data reflect gross investment flows. But as soon as a multinational company buys or builds capital equipment or structures in a developing country, those assets begin to depreciate. To maintain the capital stock intact, the investor must add new investment—often through retained earnings. In extractive and manufacturing industries, the need for new investment to offset depreciation is obvious. But in services, too, there is a constant need to upgrade equipment, especially in view of the shortening of the useful life of information technology capital assets.

Estimations of the portion of net inward FDI devoted to maintaining existing capital stock are somewhat arbitrary. UNCTAD (2002) estimates that the stock of inward FDI for the sample of countries covered by this publication was about $1.5 trillion. Our own estimates put that stock at closer to $1.2 trillion. (Both estimates are on a historic cost basis.) Taking the midpoint of the two estimates and assuming a conservative 5-percent rate of depreciation would imply an annual depreciation of about $68 billion. An annual inflow of FDI of $143 billion thus implies about a 6-percent increase in the net capital stock of FDI held in developing countries.

FDI as a stock adjustment process

In assessing the sustainability of the current flow of FDI, it is helpful to bear in mind the implied stocks involved. One way of viewing FDI is as a global adjustment in capital stock—as companies come to recognize the benefits of producing in foreign locations and developing countries offer opportunities to expand and diversify production bases (see World Bank 2002b, chapter 2). Two of the three salient features of this stock adjustment process suggest a sustained flow of FDI; the third implies more caution:

- Foreign investors in developing countries still hold about $2 in debt for every $1 in equity claims (see chapter 1). This gap has been shrinking in recent years as debt claims fall and equity claims rise. While the relative shift from debt to equity could continue simply through the paying down of debt claims, it is most likely that it will also be effected through a rise in equity claims.
- The stock of fixed capital owned by foreigners in developing countries (about $1.2 trillion) is small compared to the overall capital stock of the OECD area and to the share of developing countries in the global capital stock. This would suggest that there is more room for producers and service providers to diversify the physical location of their capital stocks.
- The stock of government-owned assets to be privatized and sold to foreigners is now relatively small. Much of it was sold in the 1990s, which accounts for the recent tailing off in privatization-related FDI. There are important exceptions. In some countries, strategic industries remain under state ownership, such as energy in Mexico. Moreover, the privatization process has barely begun in China (box 4.5).

Box 4.5 Corporatization and FDI in China

Although privatization is slowing in Latin America and Eastern Europe, China still offers significant potential for FDI stemming from corporatization (the process of taking state-owned enterprises and turning them into shareholder-owned enterprises). Between 1997 and 2001, only about $46 billion was raised through corporatization, mergers, and acquisitions in China—compared to about $210 billion raised from new greenfield fixed investments by foreigners. As the process of corporatization accelerates in the years ahead, this is bound to attract more foreign investment.

FDI, M&A, and corporatization in China, 1992–2002

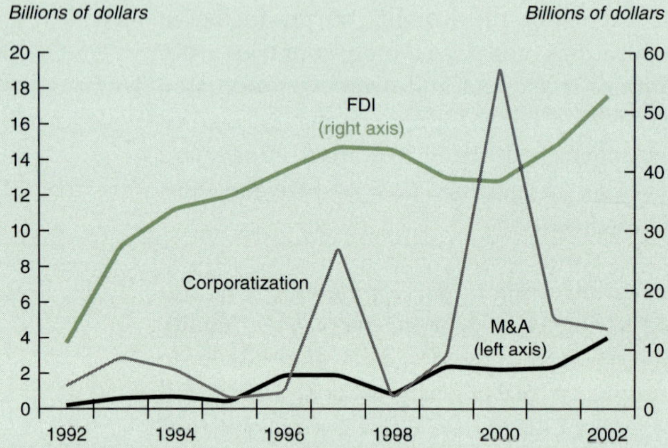

Note: China's corporatization revenues for 2000–02 are World Bank staff estimates based on various sources, including media reports, relevant government reports, and sources cited below.
Sources: World Bank, *Global Development Finance*, various years; UNCTAD, *World Investment Report 2002*; *Economist Intelligence Unit, Country Report*, various issues; Euromoney Bondware; World Bank staff estimates for 2002.

Risk perceptions and rates of return

While the arguments presented above make a solid case that a reasonably high flow of FDI could be sustained into the future, two important considerations warrant caution.

Growing risk perceptions. A key factor in the surge in FDI in the 1990s was the combination of growing investor confidence in the political and regulatory environment in developing countries and the availability of insurance products that allowed investors to hedge against political risks. Events surrounding the Argentine devaluation and default may well lead some investors to raise the degree of risk they attach to foreign investment, especially in Latin America. While such fears may be overblown, policymakers in developing countries would be well advised to focus on creating and maintaining a stable, credible investment climate.

Low returns. An important threat to sustained flows of FDI is doubt over whether such investments can continue to be justified in view of the low returns realized in recent years (figure 4.10). As seen in the case of portfolio equity investments, poor returns have generated low flows. Undoubtedly, FDI investors have stronger stomachs—and fewer mark-to-market requirements—than portfolio investors. But they cannot be wholly indifferent to realized returns on FDI—and the evidence is not wholly encouraging.

Analyzing returns on FDI is hazardous, because the data are limited (Lehmann 2002).[12] But in 25 countries for which meaningful data are available, the average rate of return (in U.S. dollars) on FDI investment was 7.1 percent for the period 1993–2000. Admittedly crude, this estimate was computed by taking balance-of-payment data on FDI income earned and deflating the data using estimates of the stock of FDI. Distinctions can be made among the countries in the sample. Returns from the Arab Republic of Egypt, with an average of 1.3 percent, were very low. By contrast, returns from the Dominican Republic, with an average of 35 percent,

Figure 4.10 Average annual rates of return on inward FDI, by region, 1993–2000

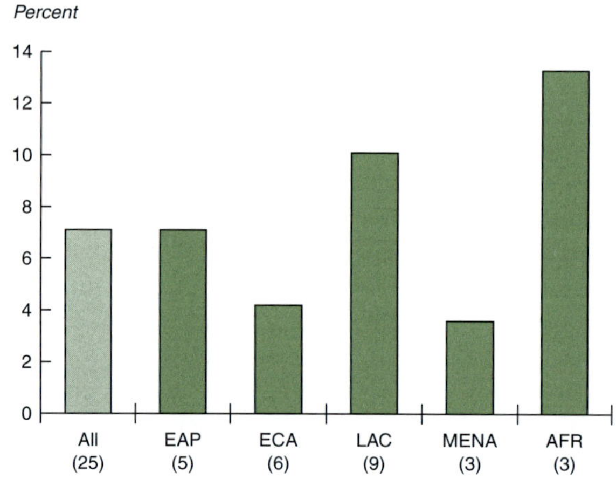

Note: The number of countries is indicated in parentheses. EAP = East Asia and Pacific, ECA = Europe and Central Asia, LAC = Latin America and the Caribbean, MENA = Middle East and North Africa, AFR = Sub-Saharan Africa.
Source: IMF, *Balance of Payment Statistics 2001*.

were extremely high.[13] By region, the highest returns were generated in Sub-Saharan Africa (where the oil sector dominates), and the lowest in the Middle East and North Africa. Countries attracting the largest inflows of FDI—Brazil, China, and Mexico—posted returns that were remarkably close to the average.

At face value, these returns do not look too bad. Although they are not much higher than G-7 bond yields for the same period, investors may well have been happy to receive an average short-run return of 7 percent while waiting for a larger payoff on an investment that most see as having a longer-than-average life. This sanguine interpretation needs to be conditioned by two very important caveats, however:

- *The trend in these measured returns is not favorable.* For most countries in the sample, the trend in rates of return on FDI has been down through the 1990s (figure 4.11). On average, the decline was interrupted in 2000, when the global economy rebounded; the profit fortunes of FDI investors are clearly linked to those of the corporate sector in the economy overall and, ultimately, to overall GDP growth. It is thus highly likely that the data for 2001 and 2002—weak years for developing-country growth—will be disappointing. Broader corporate-sector performance, which is crucial to the evolution of both domestic and foreign investment, is discussed in more detail in chapter 5.

Figure 4.11 Rate of return on FDI and GDP growth, 1995–2000

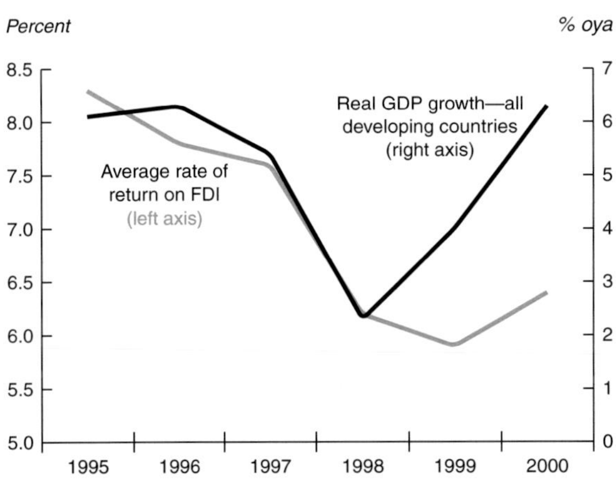

Sources: World Bank, *World Development Indicators, 2002*; IMF, *Balance of Payment Statistics 2001*.

- *These returns measure income flows only and do not reflect capital losses (or gains).* If, for example, a U.S. auto manufacturer invests in a developing country that then suffers a steep currency devaluation and deep recession, the resulting losses would not be reflected in macro-level reports (provided by the IMF) or company-level reports (provided by the U.S. Department of Commerce). Similarly, foreign companies' losses in the past 18 months in Latin America extend far beyond the income statement. Foreign owners of banks in Argentina have seen the value of their investments evaporate. In such extreme circumstances, an explicit write-down of the book value of their assets on the balance sheet is required. Even if this is not done, the stock market will take these capital losses on board when attaching a value to an FDI investing firm.

FDI has been the major source of private-sector equity-related capital in developing countries even during the recent global economic downturn. However, with privatization winding down, the growing risk perceptions attached to these investments, together with their already not very encouraging returns, might adversely affect the stability of flows in the medium term. The same factors would also hamper portfolio equity flows to developing countries, which are already fairly small and quite volatile.

Portfolio equity flows in 2002

Portfolio equity flows to emerging markets are estimated to have increased to around $9 billion in 2002, up from $6 billion in 2001.[14] This rise is best seen as a blip up on a series that has shown a significant decline since peaking in 1993 (figure 4.12; box 4.6 on page 97).

Portfolio investments by region

In 2002, East Asia and Pacific accounted for $5.4 billion, or almost 60 percent, of the total portfolio-equity flows to developing countries, up sharply from $2.9 billion in 2001 (table 4.3). Flows to Latin America slumped to $1 billion from $2.3 billion the year before, due to an outflow of funds from Argentina and foreigners' sales of Brazilian equities

Figure 4.12 Portfolio equity investment in emerging markets, 1989–2002

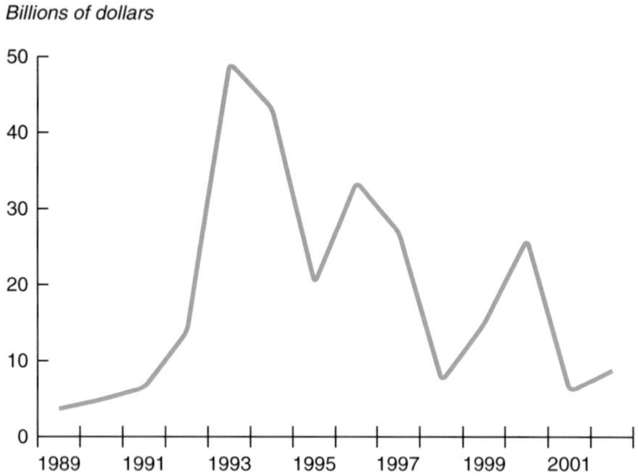

Sources: World Bank, *World Development Indicators, 2002*; IMF, *Balance of Payment Statistics 2001*.

Table 4.3 Net portfolio equity flows to developing countries, 1999–2002
(billions of dollars)

	1999	2000	2001	2002
Total	15.0	26.0	6.0	9.4
East Asia and Pacific	4.6	19.3	2.9	5.4
China	3.8	21.4	3.0	4.0
Europe and Central Asia	2.0	1.2	0.3	1.4
Latin America and the Caribbean	−3.6	−0.4	2.3	1.0
South Asia	2.4	1.7	1.6	0.8
Sub-Saharan Africa	8.9	4.0	−1.0	0.7

Sources: World Bank data based on information from IMF, *Balance of Payment Statistics;* national sources; market sources.

in the secondary market. Increases in investments in the Russian Federation helped boost flows to Europe and Central Asia to $1.4 billion in 2002, up from just $0.3 billion in 2001. A turnaround in South Africa—from net outflows in 2001 to net inflows in 2002—helped bolster Sub-Saharan Africa's share.

Several trends stand out:

- *China dominates,* accounting for more than 40 percent of all developing-country inflows of portfolio equity in 2002 and almost 75 percent of the East Asia region's. China's dominance reflects the concentrated nature of portfolio equity flows (box 4.7 on page 98). This dominance is unlikely to change anytime soon. Until December 2002, most of the Chinese stock market was closed off to foreign investors.[15] Now, however, it is opening. And privatization has yet to occur on a large scale in China (box 4.5).
- *In Asia, portfolio investments included some telecom-related flows.* The Indonesian government—rated B3 by Moody's, the lowest in East Asia—sold some of its stakes in mobile telecommunication companies to foreigners. In October China raised $1.5 billion from the sale of another tranche of China Telecom, although the amount of stock sold and its price were both below initial plans. The collapse in funding for the global telecommunications sector was a key feature of global financial trends in 2001–02. Raising fresh capital in this sector has been impossible for most issuers. That it is being done in parts of developing Asia testifies to the region's ability to insulate itself from some of the negative financial-market trends that have affected the global economy in the past year.
- *Asia and the Russian Federation continue to heal from their crises.* In 1997–98, a substantial amount of portfolio investment (both equity and debt) was withdrawn from Malaysia, and many thought that the subsequent imposition of exchange controls would cut the country off from fresh inflows. Malaysian issuers, however, accounted for about 12 percent of all portfolio-equity inflows to developing countries in 2002, with investors coming from the United States, Europe, and Asia (figure 4.13). In 1998, the Russian Federation

Figure 4.13 Investment profile for equity placement in Malaysia

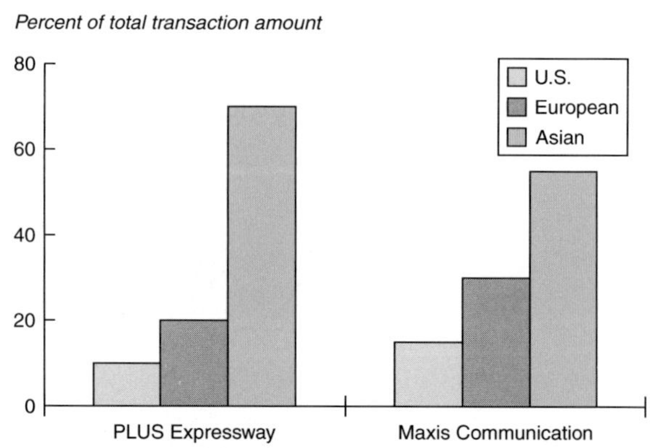

Source: World Bank staff estimates based on information from Dealogic Bondware.

Box 4.6 Revision of the World Bank's data series on portfolio equity investment

The World Bank's data series on portfolio equity investment has been revised historically to include emerging markets that have begun to track and report flows of portfolio equity. The revised series represents the best possible picture of such investments, the measurement of which remains unstandardized across countries and institutions.

What has changed?

The revised series combines balance-of-payments data reported to the IMF, information compiled by the World Bank from official and market sources (supplemented by estimates based on stock market performances), and information reported by the IIF. The previous series (generated since 1993) was based on aggregation of gross international equity placements, investments by country funds, and estimates of foreigners' direct purchases in emerging economies' stock markets.

Why the need for revision?

The old series was dominated by gross international market issues—a good measure of foreigners' initial purchases of equities. Because portfolio equity flows to emerging markets were just beginning to gain momentum at the time, the difference between gross and net was assumed to be minimal—an assumption reinforced by restrictions on capital repatriation in many countries. But foreigners did sell those equities, especially in times of financial-market stress. The new series captures *net* inflows of portfolio equity, since both the IMF and IIF report gross inflows minus outflows.

The old series contributed to the understanding of financial crises. Unlike foreign direct investment, which had been historically tracked by host countries and reported by the IMF and the OECD, there existed at the time the series was created no single source of data on portfolio equity flows. A handful of organizations reported portfolio equity flows data sporadically and with big differences in definitions, country coverage, and degree of detail. Only after the Mexican crisis of 1994–95 did a few countries begin to track such investments. The number of reporting countries has increased slowly over time, with several countries extending their series going back in time to the early 1990s.

Why the combination of various sources?

Limitations in the availability, timeliness, and reliability of data make it necessary to combine several sources.

Comparison of old and revised series, 1989–2001

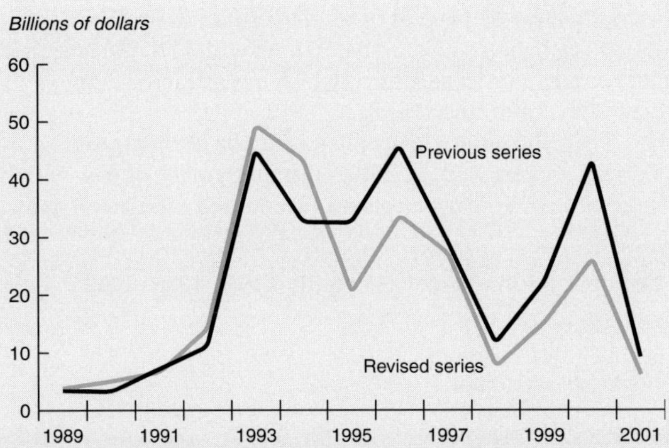

Many countries, including some major ones—China, Indonesia, Malaysia, the Philippines—reported no data until the mid-1990s; Malaysia still reports zero portfolio equity flow in its balance-of-payments series. Data in the balance-of-payments statistics of other countries has not always been consistent with other information, such as data on gross issuance data in international markets.

How does the new series compare?

The previous and revised World Bank series show similar trends in portfolio equity flows to emerging markets (see figure). The old series, however, consistently reported higher volumes, mainly because international equity placements entered the old series on a gross basis. The difference between the series is clearest in the figures for East Asia.

Major divergence from other sources

Both the new and old World Bank series diverge significantly from the IMF's balance-of-payments series in the case of two countries: China and Malaysia. For China, the new World Bank series captures the many equity placements that are attributed by market sources to China but do not appear to be captured by Chinese reporting. For Malaysia, the fact that portfolio equity flows are not reported in the country's balance-of-payments data creates the obvious difference.

Box 4.7 Concentration of portfolio equity flows

Portfolio equity investments, like FDI, tend to be concentrated in a handful of countries. Over the past 13 years, for example, the top eight recipient countries have accounted for 84 percent of total net flows of portfolio equity investment (see figure below). As with FDI, the largest net recipient has been China, which has attracted 22 percent of the total since 1989.

Portfolio equity investments may be concentrated in another way as well. In 2002, a small number of new international equity placements accounted for a significant portion of the overall flow. Of 115 emerging-market deals in the international equity market in 2002, 14 (about 15 percent) accounted for 75 percent of the total raised via international placements (see table below).

Concentration of portfolio equity flows, 1989–2002

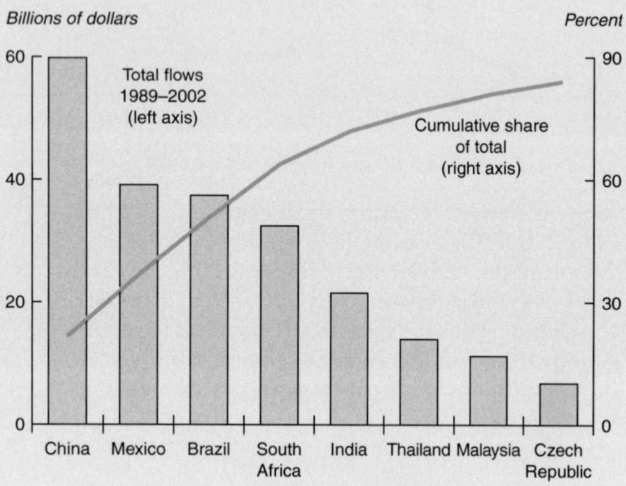

Major international equity placements, 2002

	Millions of Dollars	Sector
Brazil		
Companhia Vale d o Rio Doce	961	Extractive
China		
BOC Hong Kong Ltd	2,204	Banking & Finance
China Telecom Corp Ltd	1,523	Telecom
Indonesia		
PT Telekomunikasi Indonesia	125	Telecom
PT Indonesian Satellite Corp	108	Telecom
Malaysia		
PLUS Expressways Bhd	423	Transport
Maxis Communications Bhd	401	Telecom
Mexico		
Grupo Financiero BBVA	783	Banking & Finance
Russian Federation		
Wimm-Bill-Dann O JSC	238	Agribusiness
NK Yukos OAO	147	Extractive—Oil & Gas
OAO Sibneft	127	Extractive—Oil & Gas
South Africa		
African Rainbow Minerals	149	Extractive
Harmony Gold Mining Co Ltd	111	Extractive
Old Mutual plc	350	Banking & Finance
Percentage of total emerging market placements	76	

Source: Dealogic Bondware.

was the epicenter of the market meltdown. The government's domestic debt default, combined with widespread concern about corporate governance, made it hard to conceive of selling equity securities to foreigners. In 2002, however, Russian issuers raised $1.3 billion.

- *Flows into the mining and extractive sectors were strong.* Globally, issues were concentrated in the primary sectors. Most Russian issues, for example, were in oil and gas. And flows to South Africa were concentrated in the gold-mining sector, where the combination of a depreciated exchange rate and rising gold price appealed to investors. The Brazilian government sold its 35-percent ownership in the mining giant Companhia Vale do Rio Doce (CVRD) via placement of depository receipts. That privatization transaction was oversubscribed five times, even though Argentina had announced shortly before the formal launch that it would default on its debt. Moreover, the performance of the stock subsequent to the sale was strong relative to the local stock market in Brazil, underlining the strength of the sector overall (figures 4.14 and 4.17).

Emerging stock market performance in 2002

Emerging stock markets followed the pattern of the mature markets in 2002—a strong first half, weak third quarter, and some recovery at the end of the year (figure 4.15). Through 2002, however, returns in emerging markets have continued to be higher than in the mature markets, both in absolute terms and adjusted for volatility. By region,

Figure 4.14 Brazilian stock market (Bovespa) versus CVRD, January–November 2002

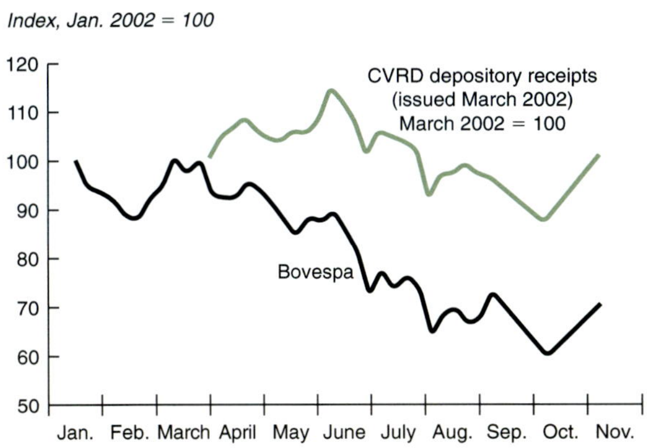

Source: Bloomberg.

Figure 4.16 Emerging stock market performance by region

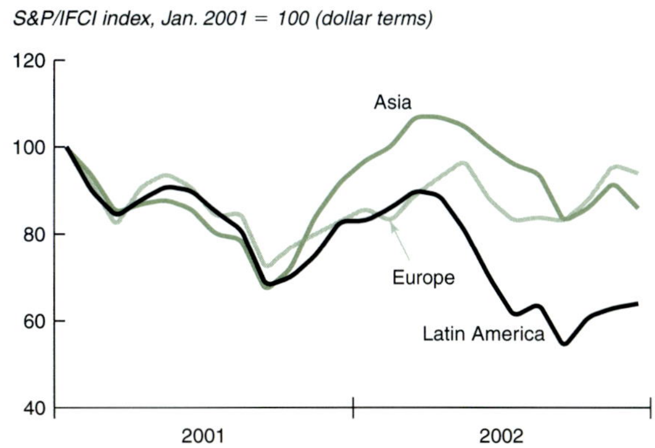

Sources: Standard & Poor's; International Finance Corporation.

Figure 4.15 Performance of equity markets

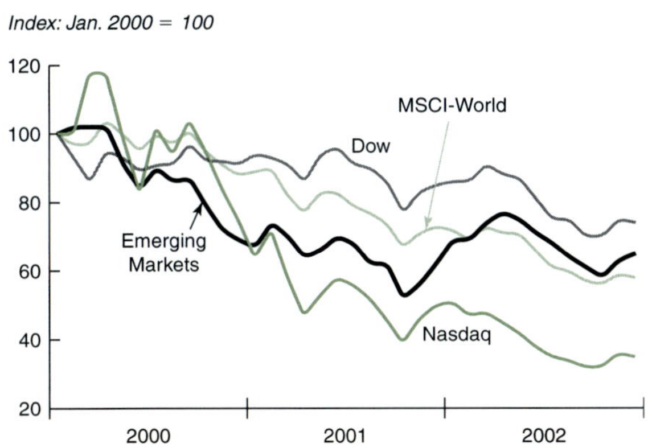

Sources: Bloomberg; Standard & Poor's; International Finance Corporation.

Figure 4.17 Returns in emerging stock market by sector, 2001 and 2002

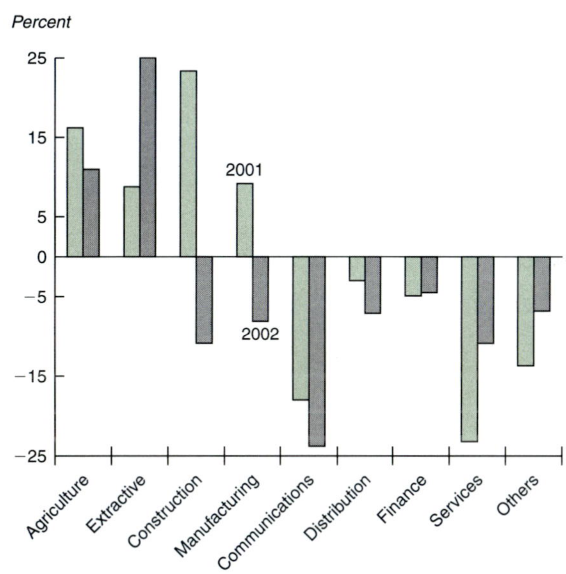

Note: Data for agriculture are from 2001. Other data are from 2002.
Sources: Bloomberg; Standard & Poor's; International Finance Corporation.

the weakest markets were in Latin America, where Argentina was down 60 percent and Brazil 38 percent in dollar terms (figure 4.16). Europe and Central Asia ended the year with an overall increase of 10 percent, again in dollar terms. However, volatility in Asian markets was more extreme, with strong gains through mid-year dissipating in the second half. The region finished with a loss of 7 percent (in dollar terms) for the year.

As in the mature markets, the mediocre results in emerging markets can be attributed to the poor performance of the technology and telecommunications sectors (figure 4.17), which together account for about one-third of stocks traded on emerging markets (the majority being from East Asia). Technology stocks were down by about 15 percent, while communication stocks lost about 25 percent of their value over the year.

The sectors that performed best were agribusiness and extractive industries. Although their average appreciation was about 20 percent in 2002, their contribution to overall performance was limited, as they account for only 14 percent of the overall S&P/IFCI index.

Why are portfolio equity flows so modest?

The early 1990s were the boom phase for portfolio-equity inflows to developing countries. In 1990–94, such flows averaged about $24 billion, nearly half the $52 billion annual average of FDI inflows. With the industrial countries languishing at the time, developing countries were seen by many investors as a source of future growth. Money poured into country funds and individual markets, producing spectacular gains in equity prices. Between December 1990 and December 1993, emerging-market stocks returned an annual average of 34 percent.[16] Between 1997 and 2001, however, portfolio-equity inflows dropped to $16 billion, less than one-tenth of the annual average FDI for the same period. Between December 1993 and October 2002 emerging-market equities returned –4.4 percent annually.

Why was there such a difference in the levels and trends of the two types of equity flows? If portfolio investors have found the purchase of equity in developing countries so unappealing in recent years, why do FDI investors find it so desirable? Three factors probably help account for the differences.

First, investors' perspectives differ. Portfolio flows to developing countries have been weak because the high prices of developing-country stocks in the early 1990s, coupled with subsequent devaluations and sagging growth, have made them a poor investment, on a risk-return basis, over the past decade (figure 4.18). Most FDI investors, too,

Figure 4.18 Risk and return by asset class

Return (percent per annum), monthly data December 1990–August 2002

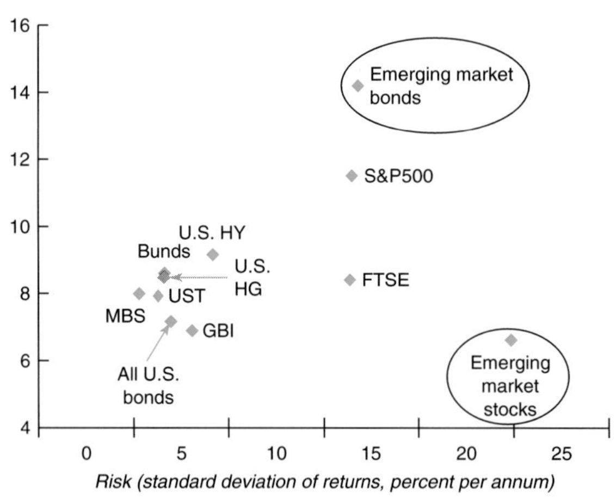

Source: J.P. Morgan, Chase, and Bloomberg.

have seen their returns fall in recent years and have been buffeted by economic crises, but they have persisted in their investments—in part because of their perspective on holding-period returns. FDI investors, who seek to maximize returns over the long run, are not forced continuously to justify their investments. In particular, they do not have to record large capital losses during periods of crisis. By contrast, portfolio investors are mark-to-market investors for whom low short-run returns and high volatility may trigger immediate withdrawals, especially in the case of mutual funds.

Second, investors in developing countries seek control as well as ownership. One reason why FDI investors may fare better in developing countries is that by exercising control they are able to steer the enterprise in a desired direction. By contrast, portfolio investors are, by definition, minority shareholders and may fear that they will find their interests subordinated to those of local owners—a fear that may deter investment even if ill-founded.

A wide and growing literature supports the thesis that stock-market development depends on a good legal system, one that allows for enforcement of the rights of minority shareholders (Demirguc-Kunt and Levine 2001). Weakness in domestic legal structures can be partially overcome if companies list themselves on major exchanges (Claessens, Klingebiel, and Schmukler 2002). By doing so, they may also benefit from cheaper funding than they could find if they remained listed on local markets. For several reasons, however, this solution is not very satisfactory. Migration to a major exchange does not prevent companies from abusing the rights of minority shareholders, but it does reduce liquidity in the local market for the companies that remain, diminishing the effectiveness of this potentially very important vehicle for the promotion of growth of local firms (Levine and Schmukler 2001).

Third, FDI may be rising relative to portfolio equity because it is straightforwardly substituting for it. The companies that FDI investors buy may well be those that portfolio investors hold. Banamex stock was widely held by international investors at the time the Mexican company was bought by Citigroup in 2001. The acquisition thus would have generated a large inflow of FDI but some offset in the form of lower portfolio investment. This effect was even clearer when Spain's Repsol bought Argentina's YPF. Up until the sale,

Box 4.8 FDI can reduce portfolio equity flows: Repsol-YPF

If an investor buys a company in another country by partly acquiring the stock from foreign investors in portfolio equity, the transaction will show up as a portfolio equity outflow that is generally more than offset by a net inflow of FDI.

A good illustration of this phenomenon is provided by the two-stage acquisition of the Argentine oil company, YPF, by the Spanish oil company, Repsol, in 1999. Repsol went into the acquisition already owning 2 percent of YPF's stock. In the first quarter of 1999, it paid the Argentine government $2 billion for the 15 percent of YPF stock that it still held. At this point, YPF's minority foreign portfolio holding, worth $270 million, became an FDI holding. In the second quarter of the year, Repsol bought the remaining 83 percent of the shares, 67 percent of which were owned by foreign portfolio investors. Repsol paid $13.2 billion for the 83 percent stake, of which $10.6 billion was thus a repatriation to foreigners of their portfolio equity investment in Argentina. Added to the conversion of Repsol's own previous portfolio stake, the total outflow of portfolio equity investment related to the YPF sale was $10.9 billion, which partly offset the net FDI inflow of $15.5 billion. The impact of the transaction on Argentina's balance of payments was a net inflow of $4.6 billion.

When adjustment is made for the YPF transaction, Argentina's balance-of-payments figures become much smoother (see table below). FDI shows a steady upward trend through 2000, while underlying portfolio equity investment was close to flat in 1998–99, before turning negative in 2000.

FDI and portfolio equity flows in Argentina, 1998–2000
(billions of dollars)

	1998	1999	2000
FDI recorded	7.3	24.0	11.7
ex-YPF	—	8.5	—
Portfolio equity recorded	−0.2	−10.8	−3.2
ex-YPF	—	0.1	—
Net BoP inflow from YPF	—	4.6	—

Source: IMF, *Balance of Payments Statistics*, 2001; World Bank staff estimates.

YPF had been the main Argentine stock held by foreign portfolio investors (box 4.8).

Forecasts for equity flows in 2003–2005

Portfolio equity flows are projected to show steady gains in 2003–05. New international issuance is projected to rise slightly, and there should be a resumption of net inflows into the secondary market. One uncertainty is how much money might flow to China now that the A-share market is now partly open to foreigners. This is by far the largest component of the Chinese stock market, with a market capitalization of about $300 billion—about three times the size of the markets in mainland equity securities previously open to foreigners.

FDI is expected to continue as the dominant form of capital flow to developing countries over the next three years. After the decline of the last two years, FDI flows are expected to stabilize in 2003 at around $145 billion (or 2.6 percent of GDP), before rising in 2004 and 2005 (table 4.4). Although by 2005 FDI inflows in nominal dollar terms are expected to rise in almost all regions, they are expected to rise faster than GDP only in East Asia and the Pacific (especially China) and in Europe and Central Asia. They are unlikely to keep pace with GDP growth in Latin America and the Caribbean and Sub-Saharan Africa. In Latin America and the Caribbean, FDI flows are expected to decline further in 2003 before recovering in 2004–05.

This outlook is based on an econometric model in which FDI flows to developing countries rise as the prospective rates of return of such investments rise, and as risks decline (see the annex

Table 4.4 Net inward FDI forecasts
(billions of dollars)

	2002	2003	2004	2005
Total	143	145	159	175
East Asia and Pacific	57	61	69	76
Europe and Central Asia	29	30	32	34
Latin America and the Caribbean	42	38	39	42
Middle East and North Africa	3	3	4	4
South Asia	5	6	7	9
Sub-Saharan Africa	7	7	8	9

Box 4.9 Surveys of FDI

The outlook for FDI in developing countries presented in this chapter is consistent with survey evidence. The World Bank's Multilateral Investment Guarantee Agency published a survey of FDI in January 2002. Each year in September A.T. Kearney publishes its "FDI Confidence Index." Both surveys confirm that the two main drivers of FDI in developing countries are the investment climate and relative returns on investment. A third factor that FDI investors considered important was free-trade arrangements—either WTO accession (China) or regional trade arrangements such as the Free Trade Area of the Americas (Brazil). The forward-looking survey by A.T. Kearney (based on interviews with 1,000 company executives worldwide) reported that investors were planning to maintain steady levels of foreign investment in 2003, even though overall they were revising their investment plans downward. This survey reported that China had overtaken the United States as the preferred destination for FDI (see table). The next emerging market in Kearney's ranking was Mexico (in ninth place). Overall the relative ranking of developing countries has generally worsened over the past year, with the exception of Eastern Europe. Three developing countries have dropped out of the top 25: Argentina, Malaysia, and Turkey.

FDI confidence index
(country rankings)

	September 2002	September 2001
China	1	2
Mexico	9	5
Poland	11	11
Brazil	13	3
Czech Republic	14	16
India	15	7
Hungary	16	21
Russian Federation	17	—
Thailand	20	14

—Not available.
Source: A.T. Kearney 2002.

to this chapter). Recent surveys of foreign direct investors suggest similar conclusions (box 4.9).

The most important factors behind the expected recovery in FDI during 2003–05 are an increase in expected rates of return in developing countries *relative to those in developed economies* and a decrease in the volatility of energy prices. Developing economies are expected to grow faster in 2003–05 than in recent years, and also faster than the G-7 economies. Developing-country exports of goods and services are also expected to rise in the medium term, attracting export-oriented FDI.[17]

East Asia and the Pacific overtook Latin America and the Caribbean as the most attractive developing region for FDI in 2002, a trend that is expected to continue in 2003–05. The regional surge is almost entirely caused by China, which is set to continue to be the largest FDI recipient in the developing world over the medium term, according to a September 2002 survey by A.T. Kearney.[18] Its relatively stable political environment, robust economic growth, successful bid for the 2008 Olympics, and recent accession to the WTO are the main drivers behind China's surge. WTO accession will facilitate entry of foreign investors to hitherto forbidden sectors, particularly the nontradable sector, and the consequent increase in FDI is expected to outstrip any decline in FDI that may result from the elimination or reduction of special incentives offered to foreign investors in export-processing zones. China has begun to reduce or abolish preferential treatment for foreign investors (in the form of preferential access to foreign exchange, lower tax rates, cheaper land leases, and other breaks). This is expected to reduce so-called round-tripping of FDI (World Bank 2002a) and, together with the recent decision to allow foreigners to buy Chinese stocks, to raise portfolio equity flows to China. Some of the new flows may come through mergers and acquisitions.

Political and security problems may prevent other developing countries in East Asia—Malaysia, Thailand, the Philippines, Indonesia—from seeing much increase in FDI, according to the September 2002 A.T. Kearney survey, although the picture should vary by sector. The majority of surveyed investors in light manufacturing and the telecommunications and utilities sectors believe that China will not crowd out FDI to other countries; on the contrary, FDI may flow to countries in the region that produce exports for China's domestic markets—now more open after China's WTO entry.

FDI is also expected to increase in Europe and Central Asia in 2003–05. Although most countries in the region, except the Russian Federation, have completed most of their privatization program, the prospect of entry into the European Union is providing an alternative boost to several countries. The Russian Federation is fast reemerging as an attractive destination for foreign investment—A.T. Kearney (2002) lauded it for the year's biggest improvement in investment outlook, citing positive economic prospects and progress in government reforms.

Sluggish growth and a slowdown in economic and political reforms are expected to continue to hold back FDI flows to Latin America. All countries in the region suffered large drops in FDI in 2002, and recovery to precrisis levels is unlikely in the medium term. The region's future, according to investors surveyed by A.T. Kearney, will depend on political and economic reforms as well as the evolution of the Free Trade Area of the Americas.[19]

Even after its recent economic problems, Brazil was the second-largest recipient of FDI among developing countries in 2002. However, the country is not expected to experience any significant revival in FDI inflows in 2003. Foreign investment flows to Mexico should improve modestly, driven by the projected economic recovery in the United States, relatively strong growth of Mexican GDP and exports, and the continued switch from debt to equity. In the rest of the region, Colombia, Peru, and the República Bolivariana de Venezuela are expected to attract modest levels of foreign investment in the primary sector.

FDI flows to South Asia are expected to rise in 2003–05. India is expected to lead this increase if economic reforms and the government's efforts to attract foreign investment continue over the next three years. India's attractiveness to investors in nonfinancial services (telecommunications and utilities) increased significantly following deregulation of the services sector and reductions in tax and tariff rates affecting the wholesale and retail sectors. On the negative side of the ledger, growing security concerns and their associated costs may well hamper investment flows to the region.

Security problems are a major issue in North Africa and the Middle East as well. In addition, the forecasted decline in the oil price may reduce oil-related foreign investment. Foreign investment in Africa is expected to remain unchanged from 2002. Opposition to privatization, high crime rates, and a heavily regulated labor market hinder the outlook for South Africa.

Several downside risks affect the outlook for FDI. First, international travel has become more difficult since September 11, 2001. Second, the recent accounting scandals in the United States have revived concerns about the lack of transparency in the corporate sector in developing countries. The latter consideration is likely to affect all types of capital flows to developing countries, especially those deriving from mergers and acquisitions.

Methodological annex: FDI forecasting model

The forecasts of FDI flows presented in this chapter are based on an econometric model that uses the following explanatory variables:

- The GDP growth rate of the top seven industrial countries (three-year moving average) is used to account for global economic conditions. As the G-7 countries are the major suppliers of FDI, any economic slowdown will adversely affect flows to developed and developing countries.
- The difference between the GDP growth rate of developing countries (three-year moving average) and that of the G-7 countries is a proxy for investors' expectations about excess rates of return in the medium term from investments in a developing country. This variable is especially important for foreign investment directed at supplying domestic markets.
- The growth rate of exports of goods and services (lagged one year) reflects a developing country's attractiveness to export-oriented, efficiency-seeking investors.
- The rating of *Institutional Investor* magazine is a proxy of the investment climate in a developing country—including macroeconomic policies, infrastructure, and institutions.
- An increase in the price of oil should stimulate oil-related foreign investment. It can simultaneously raise the demand for external financing in oil-importing countries and the supply of capital from oil-exporting countries.
- The volatility of oil prices (represented by their one-year rolling standard deviation) is used as a proxy for global economic uncertainty. Increased volatility of energy prices was cited as one of the top five concerns of multinational companies in recent A.T. Kearney surveys (A.T. Kearney 2001 and 2002).
- A lagged dependent variable (FDI/GDP) represents the persistence of FDI flows over time. One reason for such persistence is that FDI includes reinvested earnings and further investments to replenish existing stocks.

The model is similar to the one used in *GDF 2002,* with some important differences. The oil price and its volatility are two new explanatory variables. The growth rates of developing countries and the G-7 countries have been modified. And the investment climate is represented here by the *Institutional Investor* country rating instead of by the World Bank's country performance indicator (World Bank 2002a, p. 50). The model is estimated using panel data for 1991–2001 for 28 developing

Table 4A.1 FDI forecasting model, regression results

Explanatory variable	Coefficient
G7 growth rate, 3-year moving average	0.109*
Growth rate—G7 growth rate (3-year moving average)	0.018*
Growth of exports of goods and services	0.004**
Institutional Investor rating	0.023*
Oil price	0.005*
Volatility of oil price	−0.037*
FDI as percentage of GDP (lagged 1 year)	0.504*
Unweighted adjusted R^2	0.53
Weighted adjusted R^2	0.62
Durbin–Watson statistics	1.97
Number of observations	308

*Indicates significance (computed using White heteroskedasticity-consistent standard errors) at 1 percent level.
**Indicates significance (computed using White heteroskedasticity-consistent standard errors) at 5 percent level.
Note: Dependent variable is FDI as a percentage of GDP.

countries that accounted for more than 80 percent of FDI flows to developing countries in 2001. Regression results are summarized in table 4A.1 on page 104. Predictions of FDI/GDP for the 2003–05 period were obtained by forecasting growth rates of FDI as implied by the model and applying the obtained growth rates to estimated FDI figures for 2002.

Notes

1. Inflows of foreign direct investment (FDI) can be broken into three components: new fixed investments by foreigners (so-called green-field investment) and purchases of existing assets from the private sector (through merger or acquisition) or the public sector (privatization). Assuming the data in figures 4.1 and 4.2 are consistent, implied green-field investment in 2002 amounted to about $60 billion, or about 43 percent of the total.

2. See Sader (2000).

3. In Latin America, for example, WorldCom, AT&T, and France Telecom are now replaced by America Movil (Mexico) and Brasil Telecom. Similarly Vodacom of South Africa is expanding in Sub-Saharan Africa. In 2001, Turkey received more than $1.5 billion in FDI by selling licenses for mobile networks, and India received $1 billion in FDI related to acquisition of local telecom companies. In Brazil, Telecom Americas (Mexico) and Telecom Italia Mobile renewed their licenses in 2002, and Telecom Americas plans to acquire three more licenses to operate in 18 of the country's 26 states. Egyptian Orascom Telecom paid $0.7 billion to Algeria and $0.5 billion to Tunisia for mobile operator licensing. Morocco received $0.9 billion in the sale of mobile licensing to Medi Telecom. Vodacom of South Africa is already active in Nigeria, Cameroon, Rwanda, Uganda, and Swaziland; it is planning to expand in Lesotho, Mozambique, Tanzania, and Congo.

4. Data on the subsectoral distribution of FDI in services are rarely available for developing countries.

5. The share of oil-exporting countries in developing countries' FDI flows is only a proxy for the share of FDI going to extractive industries. It is possible that the sectoral composition of FDI to these countries has also changed over the 1990s.

6. According to UNCTAD (2002), about 55 percent of FDI flows to Africa (Sub-Saharan Africa and North Africa) went to primary sectors during 1995–2000.

7. See World Bank (2002a) and Aykut and Ratha (2002). The estimates are based on 31 developing countries that account for almost 90 percent of total FDI flows to developing countries.

8. Applying the same ratio to all 137 developing countries would imply total South-South FDI flows of almost $60 billion in 2000.

9. Some developing countries such Croatia, Ecuador, Hungary, and Malaysia compile but do not disseminate the data (Direct Investment Methodology Survey, IMF 2001).

10. These countries are Benin, Botswana, Côte d'Ivoire, Namibia, Senegal, Seychelles, Swaziland, Togo, and Uganda. Also note that it is not possible to say, a priori, whether a high or low ratio is better. A high ratio might reflect the fact that FDI is profitable and that investors have a willingness to reinvest profits. But it may also reflect the lack of access to capital from new sources.

11. In this case, it is reasonable to argue that the higher the ratio, the better.

12. There are two basic sources: (a) country data as reported to the IMF through balance-of-payments statistics, and (b) data on returns of U.S. firms as reported to the Department of Commerce (U.S. Department of Commerce 2002). The former are, in principle, more complete, although many analysts express skepticism about their quality. The latter are probably more accurate but relate only to U.S. FDI in developing countries, which was about 21 percent of the global FDI stock at the end of 2001. The data used in this section are mainly those from the IMF.

13. U.S. data corroborate this message on the Dominican Republic but give a completely different picture for the Arab Republic of Egypt (see Lehmann 2002).

14. This total comprises just net inflows of portfolio equity capital (that is, purchases of developing country equities, net of sales). It does not include net outflows (purchases of equities issued in high-income countries, net of sales, by residents in developing countries). Two important data revisions have been made to the portfolio equity inflow estimates for 2001 and previous years since *Global Development Finance 2002*. In that volume, 2001 portfolio equity inflows were estimated at $18.5 billion; in this volume they are just $6 billion. Why? First, the series was refined, which had the effect of reducing the 2001 estimate by $3.2 billion (see box 4.6). Second, the Republic of Korea is now excluded from our estimates, as it has graduated to high-income status. This had the effect of reducing the 2001 estimate by a further $9.3 billion.

15. Since December 2002, foreign investments in this market have been allowed via a Qualified Foreign Institutional Investor scheme. The scheme, however, imposes onerous conditions for the qualification of investors and limits the mobility of funds—it is likely to limit foreign participation, at least initially. The relaxation is another step in the direction of merging the A and B share markets.

16. These returns are calculated using the S&P/IFCI total return index for all emerging economies.

17. In preparing these forecasts, the investment climate variable (represented by IIR) is assumed to remain unchanged during 2002–05.

18. Based on preliminary numbers, China may outstrip the United States as the world's largest FDI recipient in 2002.

19. Brazil's ruling party (PT) organized a referendum in September 2002 opposing Brazil's participation in the Free Trade Area of the Americas. The PT officials have since changed their stance.

References

A.T. Kearney. 2001. "FDI Confidence Index." World Bank, Washington, D.C.

———. 2002. "FDI Confidence Index." World Bank, Washington, D.C.

Aykut, D., and D. Ratha. 2002. "South-South Flows in the 1990s." Background paper for *Global Development Finance 2002*. World Bank, Washington, D.C. Processed.

Claessens, S., D. Klingebiel, and S. Schmukler. 2002. "Explaining the Migration of Stocks from Exchanges in Emerging Economies to International Centers." Discussion Paper Series 3301. Centre for Economic Policy Research (CEPR), London.

Demirguc-Kunt, A., and R. Levine, eds. 2001. *Financial Structure and Economic Development*. Cambridge, Mass.: MIT Press.

Economist Intelligence Unit. 2002. Various reports on developing countries. New York.

IMF (International Monetary Fund). 2001. *Direct Investment Methodology Survey.* Washington, D.C.

Lehmann, A. 2002. "Foreign Direct Investment in Emerging Markets: Income, Repatriations, and Financial Vulnerabilities." IMF Working Paper WP/02/47. International Monetary Fund, Washington, D.C.

Levine, R., and S. Schmukler. 2001. "The Effects of Cross-Listing on Local Equity Markets." World Bank, Washington, D.C. Processed.

Sader, Frank. 2000. "Attracting Foreign Direct Investment into Infrastructure: Why Is It So Difficult?" Foreign Investment Advisory Service Occasional Paper no.12. World Bank, Washington, D.C.

UNCTAD (United Nations Conference on Trade and Development). 2002. *World Investment Report.* New York.

U.S. Department of Commerce. 2002. "U.S. Direct Investment Abroad: Detail of Historical-Cost Position and Related Capital and Income Flows. *Survey of Current Business,* September.

World Bank. 1999. *Global Economic Prospects 1998/99.* Washington, D.C.

———. 2002a. *Global Development Finance 2002.* Washington, D.C.

———. 2002b. *Global Economic Prospects 2003.* Washington D.C.

5

Corporate Financial Structures and Performance in Developing Countries

Dilip Ratha, Sanket Mohapatra, and Philip Suttle

THE SUSTAINABILITY OF FINANCIAL FLOWS to developing countries depends heavily on the health of the corporate sector, which has been at the center of several recent crises. Corporate borrowers now account for more than a fifth of cross-border debt flows, compared with less than 5 percent in 1990, and flows of FDI, the dominant form of external financing for developing countries, are ultimately tied to corporate performance.

Despite efforts to pay down debt since the 1997–98 crisis and the broad shift to flexible exchange rates, the corporate sector in developing countries remains subject to considerable risk. Corporate profitability in developing countries has shown a significant decline in recent years. As is painfully evident from the Asian crisis of 1997–98 and the more recent global high-tech collapse, capital flows that do not produce adequate returns are liable to sudden reversal.

Many Asian corporations remain highly leveraged, in part because they substituted domestic for external debt. Those debt loads are more manageable now than they were in 1997–98, however, because interest rates are lower and creditors are more willing to roll over credits. Companies in Latin America and Eastern Europe, also highly leveraged, have increased their dependence on foreign finance.

Dependence on foreign borrowing brings both risks and benefits. An excessive dependence on external finance hurt many Asian corporations in 1997–98. On the other hand, firms (especially Latin American firms) active in international markets during the 1990s appear to have benefited from a lower cost of capital.

There is a need to improve the quality and timeliness of corporate data in developing countries. Corporate scandals in the major industrial countries have underlined the deficiencies of corporate information in the major markets. As more development finance is channeled through the corporate sector, and with financial markets apt to adjust sharply in response to surprises, it has become important for policy makers and market participants alike to be aware of the scope of the risks that domestic corporates are running. This is not easy to do with the information currently available.

Shifts in corporate-sector debt dependence

It is widely accepted that excess corporate leverage was at the heart of the financial troubles of many East Asian developing countries in 1997–98.[1] Total corporate debt of developing countries of the East Asia and Pacific region grew at a compound annual rate of 16 percent between the end of 1990 and the end of 1997—swelling from $717 billion to $2.4 trillion (or from 80 percent to 105 percent of national income). Their debt-equity ratio, valued at the market price of equity, rose from 3.8 at the end of 1990 to 4.2 at the end of 1997. The foreign debt of the corporate sector (mainly debt owed to banks) grew at a compound annual rate of 27 percent during the same period, far more rapidly than overall debt. As a share of total corporate debt, foreign debt rose from 6 percent at the end of 1990 to 10 percent at the end of 1997.

The corporate collapses in East Asia in 1997–98 produced sharp overall declines in GDP and forced severe and wrenching adjustments in corporate balance sheets, with the severity of the adjustments reflecting the need for a sharp and sustained shift in the private sector's financial balance. That shift has occurred. The aggregate current-account balance of the region shifted from a deficit of 4.8 percent of GDP in 1996 to a surplus of 2.6 percent in 1998. Over the same period, the budget balance of the region moved from a surplus of 0.2 percent of GDP to a deficit of 1.3 percent. The implied swing in the private sector's financial balance—equivalent to 8.9 percentage points of GDP—was carried out largely by a severe compression of spending.

One key result of this shift into financial surplus was that companies in East Asia were able, in the aggregate, to arrest and partly reverse the sustained rise in corporate debt relative to GDP that occurred through the first half of the 1990s (figure 5.1).

The corporate "de-leveraging" process in East Asia had three other important dimensions. First, there was a sharp drop in foreign borrowing. The share of foreign debt in total corporate debt rose steadily between 1990 and 1997 for East Asian economies as a whole, and through 1998 for the four crisis economies, but this ratio has fallen back sharply since then (figure 5.2). Asian companies paid dearly for their brief foray into international borrowing, and the experience has made them far more cautious about foreign-currency borrowing, even as their economies have recovered. Also, the shift to a flexible exchange-rate regime, by reducing implicit guarantees against devaluation risks, has reinforced firms' reluctance to take on foreign debt. The result is that the foreign-currency debt of Asian corporations is now in short supply relative to the demand and trading at relatively tight spreads compared to similarly rated paper from borrowers in other regions (see chapter 3).

Second, some effort has been made to diversify sources of domestic funding. In East Asia, for example, important efforts have been made to strengthen bond markets, helping reduce dependence on bank finance (figure 5.3). However, the

Figure 5.1 Corporate debt relative to GDP in East Asia, 1990–2001

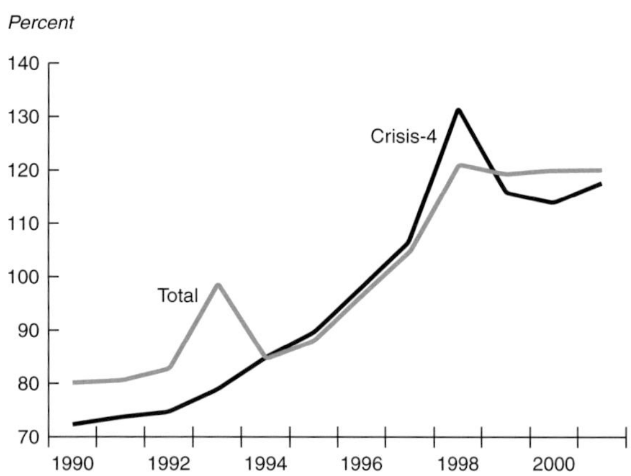

Note: The Crisis-4 countries are Indonesia, the Republic of Korea, Malaysia, and Thailand.
Sources: Bank for International Settlements, International Financial Statistics; World Bank, *World Development Indicators*.

Figure 5.2 Foreign debt relative to total corporate debt in East Asia, 1990–2001

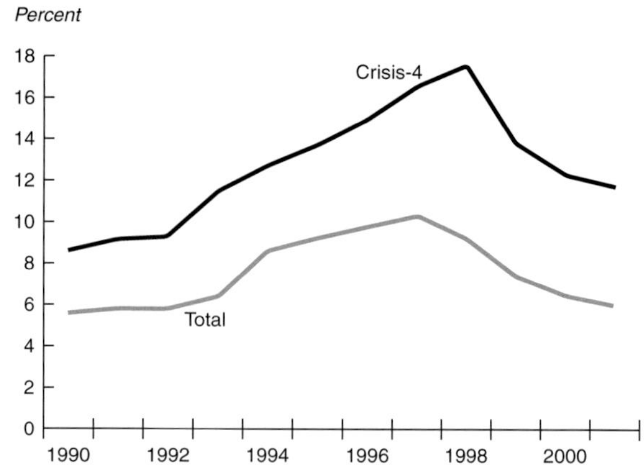

Note: The Crisis-4 countries are Indonesia, the Republic of Korea, Malaysia, and Thailand.
Source: Bank for International Settlements, International Financial Statistics.

Figure 5.3 Dependence on Bank debt in East Asia, 1990–2001

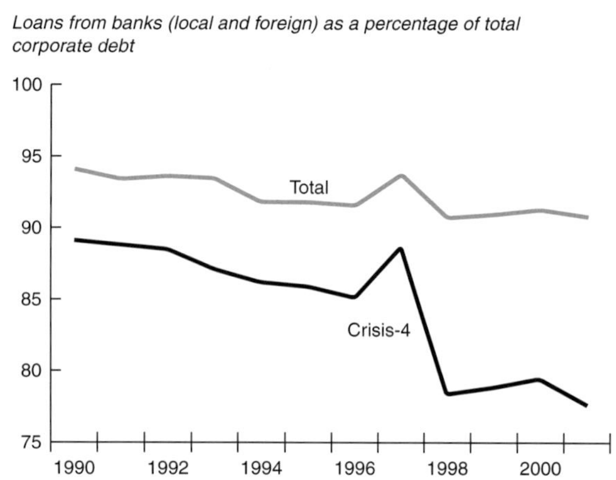

Note: The Crisis-4 countries are Indonesia, the Republic of Korea, Malaysia, and Thailand.
Source: Bank for International Settlements, International Financial Statistics.

range of financing instruments available in emerging markets remains limited when compared with more developed markets such as the United States. One of the strengths of the U.S. financial system is its diversity of funding sources, ranging from commercial banks through a rich array of money and capital markets. Thus when bond-market credit suddenly dried up in the United States in 1998, corporate borrowers were able to turn to banks. Likewise, when the market in short-term commercial paper slumped early in 2002, companies were able to issue longer-term bonds and swap into short-term liabilities.

Third, debt-equity ratios in the region have declined as the result of efforts to pare down debt (especially foreign debt) and raise equity participation in the economy (figure 5.4). FDI in Asia has been relatively high since the crisis years, contributing to a shift in the pattern of foreign liabilities away from debt to equity. The shift has been far from uniform, however. China has been the key beneficiary of stepped-up FDI, while Indonesia has seen a steady exodus of foreign equity capital since 1998 (see chapter 4).

These significant adjustments have helped Asian corporations insulate themselves from global market pressures in recent quarters. In 2001–02, for example, Asian corporations were better insulated from the downturn in the global economy and the deterioration in high-risk debt markets than were their peers in the main industrial economies. In East Asia, with external financing (especially short-term financing) much reduced, there was no significant flight of foreign capital, and domestic lenders remained comfortable with their exposures.

One important difference between 1997–98 and 2001–02 was the trend in local interest rates. In 1997–98, these rose sharply, contributing to a serious deterioration in corporate credit quality and undermining the willingness of both domestic and external creditors to maintain exposures. By contrast, regional interest rates generally fell in 2001–02, giving companies a cushion that allowed them to ride out the downturn far more easily.

Indeed, the low level of regional interest rates is a key ingredient to the sustainability of what remains, after several years of painful adjustment in the region, a very high ratio of corporate leverage. While corporate debt has been trimmed in some economies, it has risen sharply in others—notably China. As a result, debt levels (as a share of GDP) remain very high in East Asia compared to both Latin America and Eastern Europe (figure 5.5).

Similar regional trends (seen from top-down macro data) are also evident from firm-level data (see the methodological annex at the end of the chapter). The average debt-assets ratio for East Asian firms in the sample reached a peak of 68 percent in 1997—it has since fallen (figure 5.6, see also Mako 2001). By contrast, the leverage ratio of Latin American firms dropped during the

Figure 5.4 Corporate debt-equity ratios in East Asia, 1990–2001

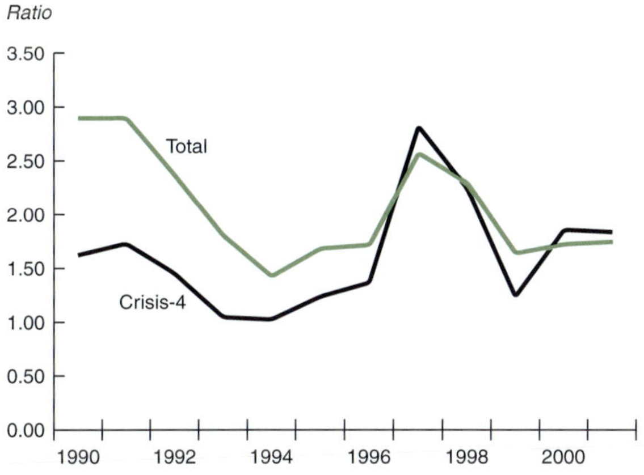

Note: The Crisis-4 countries are Indonesia, the Republic of Korea, Malaysia, and Thailand.
Sources: Bank for International Settlements; S&P Emerging Markets Database.

Figure 5.5 Corporate debt in select regions, 1995, 1997, 2001

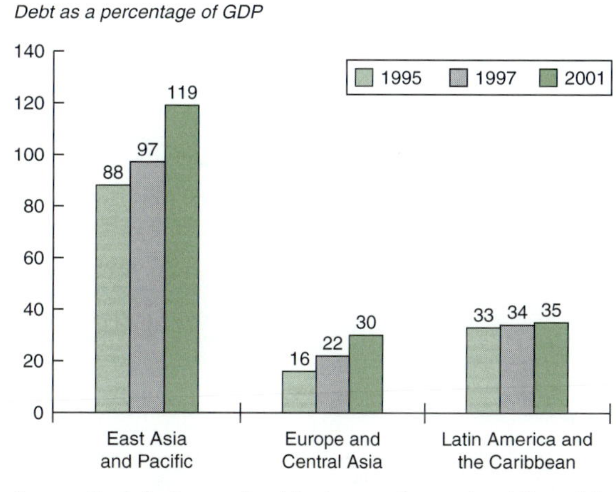

Sources: Bank for International Settlements, International Financial Statistics; World Bank, *World Development Indicators.*

Figure 5.6 Leverage ratios in East Asia and Pacific and Latin America and the Caribbean, 1992–2001

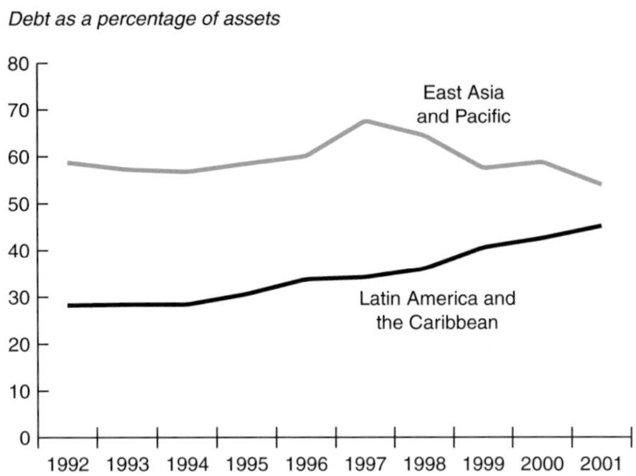

Source: World Bank Staff estimates based on Worldscope data.

Figure 5.8 External borrowing as a share of corporate sector debt in select regions

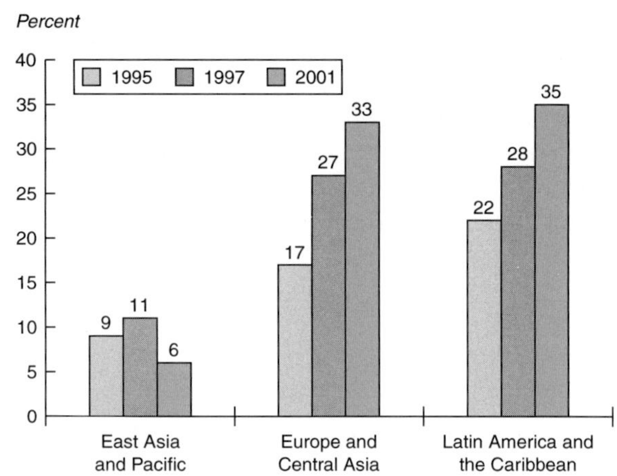

Source: Bank for International Settlements, International Financial Statistics.

Mexican crisis in 1995 but has risen steadily ever since. By 2001 the leverage ratios of East Asia (54 percent) and Latin America (45 percent) had become similar.

While East Asia has been reducing its dependence on foreign-currency debt, however, companies in Latin America and Eastern Europe have been raising their dependence. The share of foreign lending to firms in East Asia has fallen steadily from its peak in 1996, whereas the share of Latin America and Eastern Europe has risen (figure 5.7). The result? As of 2000, the share of total corporate debt accounted for by borrowing from abroad had risen to almost one-third in both Latin America and Eastern Europe (figure 5.8). Expressed as a share of GDP, the foreign debt of the corporate sectors in the two regions was at or above the peak seen in East Asia in 1997 (figure 5.9).

In conclusion, the overall level of corporate leverage remains the main risk facing East Asia; heavy dependence on external debt is the main risk for firms in Eastern Europe and Latin America.

Figure 5.7 Foreign lending to emerging-market corporations, select regions, 1990–2001

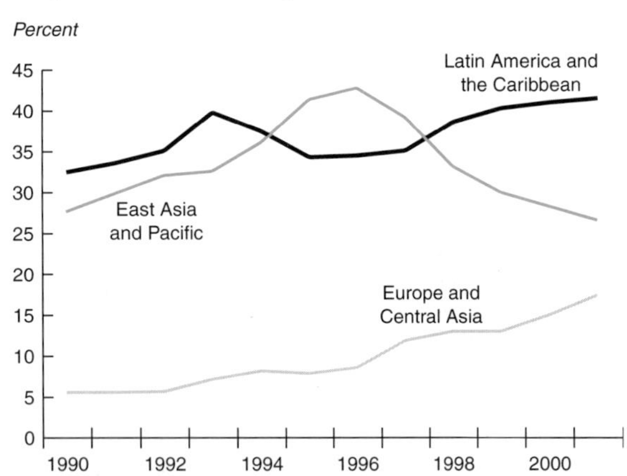

Source: Bank for International Settlements.

Figure 5.9 Corporate foreign debt in select regions, 1990–2001

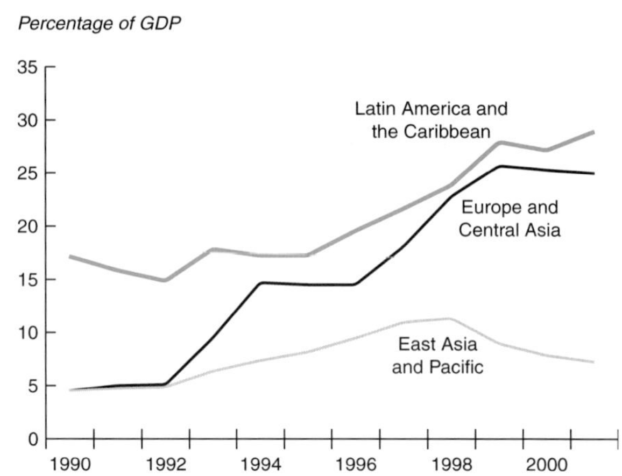

Source: Bank for International Settlements, World Development Indicators.

Short-term corporate debt vulnerability

Companies in developing countries face the challenge of transforming, in a sustainable way, the typically short-term capital they raise from sources outside the firm into fixed, long-term capital suitable for financing the illiquid real assets that make up the physical capital of the firm. For companies in mature economies with deep, well-developed equity markets, this transformation is usually not an insuperable challenge, although the evaporation of market access for several previously high-flying firms in the United States and Europe in 2001–02 illustrates that sudden corporate collapses can occur in even the most sophisticated capital markets.

Firms operating in developing countries, however, often have little choice but to finance fixed-asset accumulation with short-term liabilities. For companies operating in East Asia, such liabilities made up about 62 percent of total corporate debt in 2001. In Eastern Europe, the share was even higher—66 percent (figure 5.10). Latin America had the lowest ratio of short-term debt to total debt: just 50 percent. The dependence on short-term finance in East Asia and Eastern Europe indicates that their primary source of funds remains banks—longer-term markets being either nonexistent or just beginning to reemerge after a period of dormancy.

Figure 5.10 Short-term debt and current liabilities, 1995, 1997, and 2001

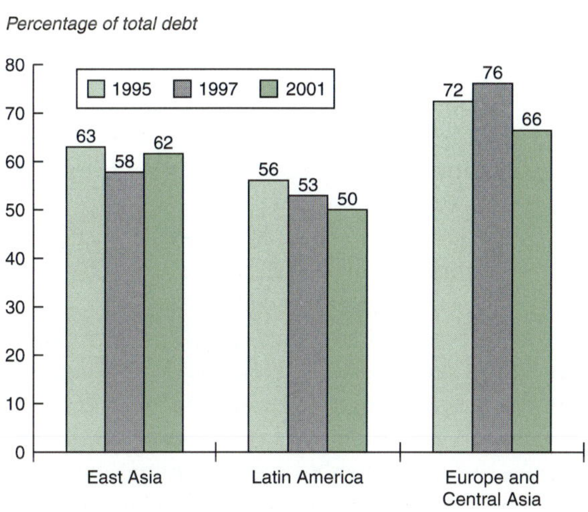

Sources: World Bank Staff estimates; Worldscope.

The low dependence of Latin American firms on short-term finance does not reflect the availability of local long-term financing but rather the *overall* lack of local financing from outside the firm. That lack is a legacy of local instability. While more acute in some countries (Argentina) than others (Chile), the low level for the region as a whole is a sign of poor financial intermediation. Firms in Latin America must depend on internal financing and, as previously noted, funds from abroad.

In Eastern Europe and Central Asia, persistent instability since the collapse of the former Soviet Union, coupled with high and variable inflation, has kept corporate financial structures short. As convergence with the European Union proceeds, however, a lengthening of the maturities of corporate debt should be expected and encouraged.

The downward trend in corporate profits

Profitability is at the heart of corporate health. If the capital employed in an enterprise is not generating an adequate return, the flow of new capital to the firm will dry up. Eventually the holders of the existing stock of capital will seek to exit. The past five years have seen examples of such reversals in large parts of East Asia and in the telecom sectors of the G-7 economies.

To complicate the picture, recent accounting scandals in the United States have reminded us not only that the measurement of profits can be somewhat ambiguous, but also that the quality of corporate accounting sometimes leaves much to be desired.

An examination of the trends in net earnings of the countries in our data sample for the period 1992–2001 (table 5.1 and figure 5.11) yields several important conclusions.[2]

- Profits are low. In 1999–2001, profit margins were about 4.4 percent of sales and 3.0 percent of assets. By way of comparison, the return on assets achieved by the U.S. non-financial corporate sector in 1999–2001 was 4.9 percent.
- Profits do not appear to be rising. The low point in 1998 is understandable in view of the recession that year in many developing countries, but average returns for 1999–2001, the last three years of data, were significantly worse than earlier in the decade. This evidence

Table 5.1 Profitability of nonfinancial firms in emerging markets, 1992–2001
(percent)

	1992–2001											
	Average	Standard deviation	1992	1993	1994	1995	1996	1997	1998	1999	2000	2001
Net income/Assets												
All countries	3.1	0.9	3.9	4.0	3.4	3.7	3.2	2.4	1.1	2.5	3.2	3.2
Emerging Europe and Africa	5.9	2.3	6.1	7.1	7.1	7.7	5.8	4.5	−0.1	6.0	8.3	6.2
(ex-Russian Federation)	6.2	1.2	6.1	7.1	7.1	7.7	7.0	6.4	4.9	6.1	6.3	3.6
Asia	2.2	1.3	2.7	2.9	3.8	3.9	2.5	0.5	−0.3	1.9	1.5	2.2
(ex-China)	1.9	1.4	2.7	2.8	3.8	3.8	2.5	0.4	−0.4	1.6	0.6	1.6
Latin America	3.5	1.0	4.9	4.8	2.6	2.6	3.3	4.3	3.1	2.0	3.8	3.4
Net income/sales												
All countries	4.6	1.2	5.2	5.5	5.8	5.6	5.1	4.2	1.8	4.0	4.6	4.6
Emerging Europe and Africa	6.7	2.8	5.5	6.3	6.6	6.9	7.5	7.5	−0.1	7.6	10.3	9.1
(ex-Russian Federation)	6.0	0.9	5.5	6.3	6.6	6.9	6.7	6.3	5.2	6.1	6.7	3.9
Asia	2.9	1.7	3.6	3.7	5.1	5.1	3.6	0.8	−0.4	2.8	1.9	2.8
(ex-China)	2.6	1.9	3.5	3.6	5.0	4.9	3.5	0.5	−0.5	2.3	0.8	2.0
Latin America	7.5	2.1	10.3	10.2	6.7	6.3	7.8	10.0	6.4	4.2	7.0	6.0

Sources: World Bank staff estimates; Worldscope.

Figure 5.11 Corporate profitability in developing countries, 1992–2001

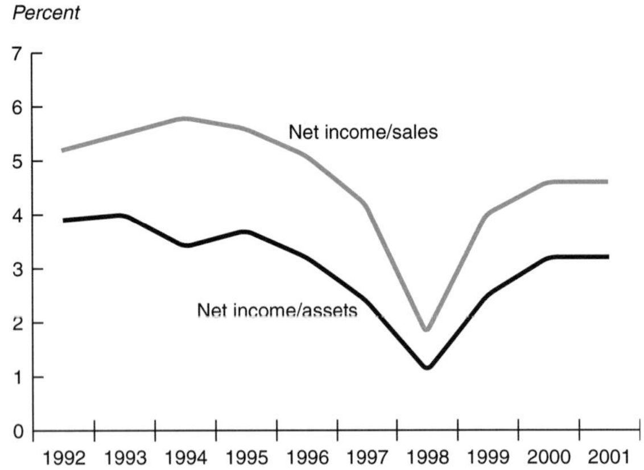

Sources: World Bank staff estimates; Worldscope.

is consistent with the pattern of returns on FDI (see page 95) and on emerging-market equities (see page 100).

- Profit margins and returns on assets are lowest in Asia. Both were negative in 1998; neither has recovered well. In part, the results reflect the higher leverage ratios of the firms in the region; returns on equity are probably not as low as they appear.
- In the past two years, margins and returns have been higher in Europe and Central Asia than elsewhere in the developing world. The Russian Federation has bounced back strongly from collapse in 1998. Elsewhere in the region, profit rates have been relatively more stable than in the Russian Federation, consistent with the pattern of structural improvement in the region after the corporate collapses of the early 1990s.

To get a longer view of the evolution of profits, the data from our sample of 21 countries from 1992 to 2000 have been combined with similar data available for the 1980s (Singh 1995; Glen, Singh, and Matthias 1999). Although there is some discontinuity between the two data sets, their general patterns are similar, allowing a comparison of trends in profit margins since the mid 1980s (figure 5.12). Two trends stand out:

- Margins were generally lower in the 1990s than in the 1980s. Of the six countries pictured in figure 5.12, India is the exception.
- Margins were more volatile in the 1990s. Again, there is one important exception (Brazil), where the relative stability offered by the successful currency program after 1994 stands in contrast with the earlier period of volatility and hyperinflation (1985–93).

Why were profits in many developing countries lower and more volatile in the 1990s, especially as the decade progressed? Because underlying nominal growth of GDP is the key driver of profits, the shocks to GDP brought on by the numerous crises of the 1990s are the main cause of the weakness in profits.

Figure 5.12 Ratios of net income to sales in nonfinancial firms in select countries, 1985–2001

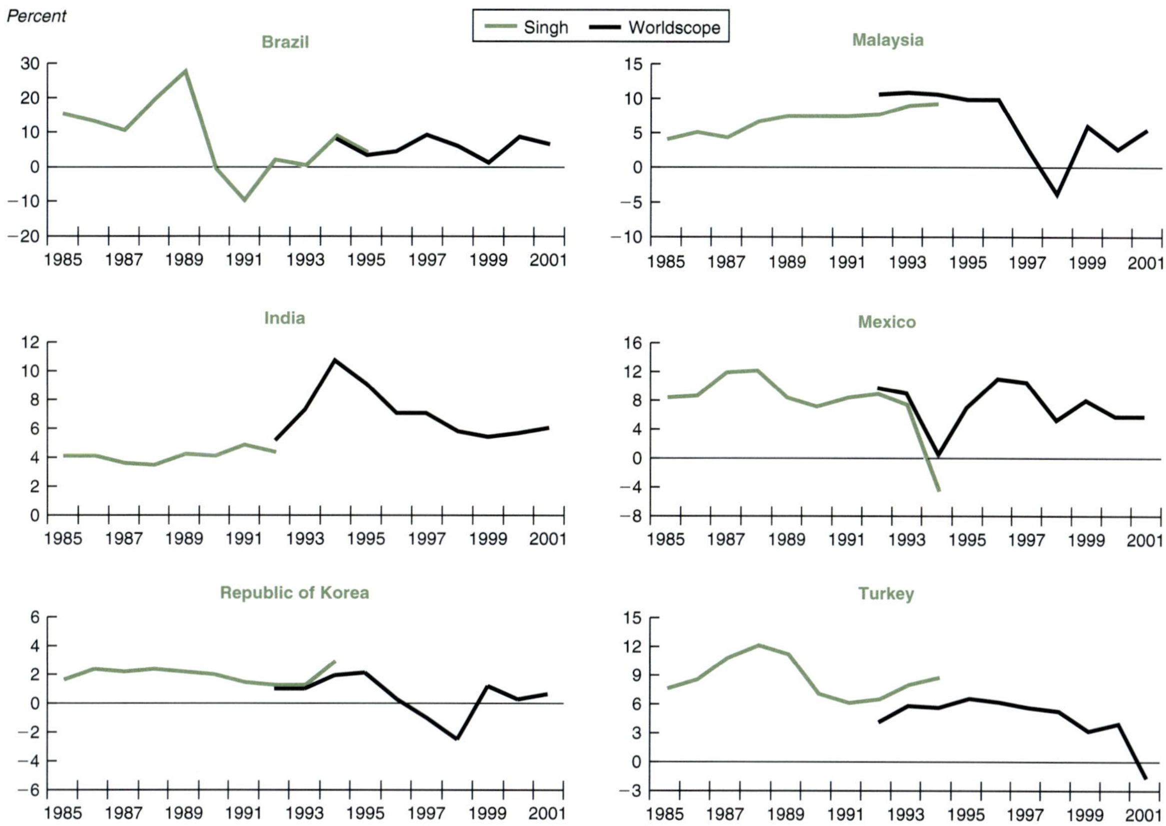

Sources: Worldscope; World Bank Staff estimates; Singh 1995.

Other developments contributed as well. The trend toward lower inflation across the developing world added further downward pressure on nominal GDP growth—and on profits. An otherwise welcome trend toward more open, integrated markets reduced the prices—and profits—of what had been local monopolies. In Brazil, for example, the liberalization of the trade regime in the early 1990s, which helped bring greater competition to domestic-goods industries, also restrained domestic producers' margins (Glen, Lee, and Singh 2001). Similarly, the emphasis on privatization of state-run monopolies, especially in utilities sectors, helped restrain inflation—but also profits.

Finally, the rise in debt costs resulting from significant devaluations—and other events surrounding currency crises, such as sharp drops in real GDP—hit profit margins very hard in Mexico in 1994 and in Malaysia and the Republic of Korea in 1998 (Forbes 2002).

Are profits in developing countries so low as to constitute a problem? Not necessarily. As nominal GDP grows in developing countries, so will profits. But policymakers and analysts would be well advised to pay attention to trends in these variables if, as expected, the primary flow of foreign capital (both debt and equity) to developing countries remains largely oriented to the private business sector. For if profit performance continues to lag as the economy improves, then the sustainability of the current pattern of financing flows dominated by FDI will be very much in question.

Borrowing from abroad and corporate performance

Financing from abroad brings with it both risks and advantages. A firm can reduce its cost of capital by accessing international markets, which have a larger base of investors and are more liquid. And because international markets have better trading and clearance systems, more competition among traders and investment bankers, and better listing and monitoring standards, they are more efficient than local markets. International market access, when successful, may also make a firm more attractive to domestic investors by signaling that the firm is willing to commit to higher standards of corporate governance and disclosure and protection of minority rights.[3]

But international finance also entails risks. A currency devaluation may increase the debt burden of borrowing firms, especially those that have only local currency earnings (Forbes 2002). Unanticipated changes in global interest rates can hurt profitability. And abrupt changes in investor sentiment may make it difficult to roll over debt. The various emerging-market crises of the last decade brought all these risks into sharp focus.

Indeed, an assessment of the relationship between external (international) financing and corporate performance reveals that among nonfinancial firms, market participants (firms that had outstanding foreign debt) tended to show lower profitability than nonparticipants.[4] However, it would be wrong to conclude that borrowing abroad is excessively risky for all firms in developing countries. Indeed, it appears that many companies that participated in the international markets in the 1990s fared better than others that did not. For example, firms that had foreign sales, and firms that were able to roll over debt, were on average more profitable than others that did not (see below).

Not surprisingly, market access over the period 1992–2001 was positively associated with firm size. The average assets of firms that participated in international markets were $2.4 billion during 1998–2001, more than five times the average size ($470 million) of firms that did not have outstanding foreign debt. Within the category of international-market participants, firms that were able to roll over debt (that is, to continue market access) during 1998–2001 were even larger—having average assets of $4.9 billion. Firms that had outstanding debt but did not undertake new borrowing in 1998–2001 were much smaller with assets averaging around $1.8 billion. The association between market access and size is to be expected, given that large firms are less vulnerable than small firms to adverse shocks and are more creditworthy in the eyes of investors.[5]

Firms that borrowed abroad were more highly leveraged than firms that did not. Debt, foreign and domestic, as a share of assets was 53.3 percent during 1998–2001 for market participants—higher than the share of debt to assets (45.8 percent) for firms that did not borrow abroad (figure 5.13).

Even though market participants were more highly indebted, their average cost of credit—or average interest rate, defined as interest expenses as a percentage of debt—was lower than that of nonparticipants through much of the 1990s (figure 5.14).

Figure 5.13 Debt as a percentage of total assets of market participants and nonparticipants, 1998–2001

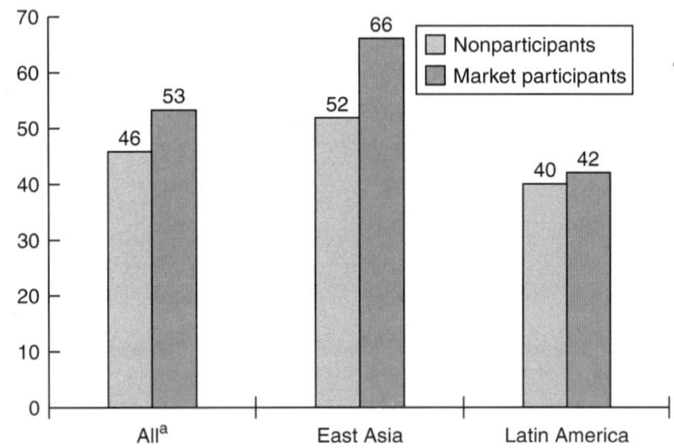

a. All firms in sample described in methodological annex to this chapter.
Sources: World Bank staff estimates; Worldscope; Dealogic.

Figure 5.14 Interest paid relative to debt by market participants and nonparticipants, 1992–2001

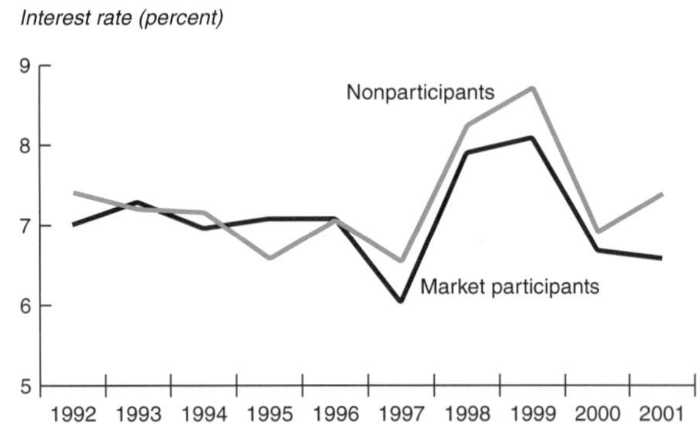

Sources: World Bank Staff estimates; Worldscope; Dealogic.

Prior to the Asian crisis in 1997, average interest costs paid by firms declined as industrial countries cut interest rates during the mid-1990s and emerging market spreads tightened. Following the Asian crisis, interest costs rose for all firms, but firms that had access to the wider international debt markets were able to obtain cheaper credit than those that did not, although they may also have suffered valuation losses as a result of denominating their debt in foreign currency prior to a sharp depreciation. Such mark-to-market debt losses are, however, reflected in the overall profit data analyzed below.[6]

Except for the early 1990s (1992–1994), firms that participated in international debt markets reported lower profits as a share of assets than did nonparticipating firms (figure 5.15). The average profit rate during 1998–2001 for market participants was 2.1 percent, compared to 2.9 percent for nonparticipants (figure 5.16). Evidently, the lower interest costs available from market participation was not sufficient to generate a higher rate of profit for the participating firms, even though many of them were larger in asset size compared to nonparticipating firms.[7] The profit rates between market participants and nonparticipants reached a low in 1998, the year interest rates spiked up and currency-related losses were at their peak.

While this finding does highlight the risks associated with foreign borrowing, it does not necessarily imply that these risks outweigh the benefits (such as low interest rates) that market participation brings. In fact, this finding does not hold true in Latin America where, unlike in East Asia and Europe and Central Asia, market participating firms did report higher profit rates than nonparticipating firms (figure 5.16).[8] Even in East Asia, the lower profit rates reported by market participating firms may be explained in part by the fact that only firms with low profitability (and high investment) may have needed external financing (Lang, Djankov and Claessens 1998). Also the profit performance of firms that were able to maintain access to external credit markets—and so to roll over some of their foreign debt—was better and less affected by cycles than the profit rates of firms that had outstanding foreign debt but could not (or did not) roll it over (figure 5.17). Moreover, the most

Figure 5.15 Corporate profit rates in major emerging markets, 1992–2001

Profits as a percentage of assets

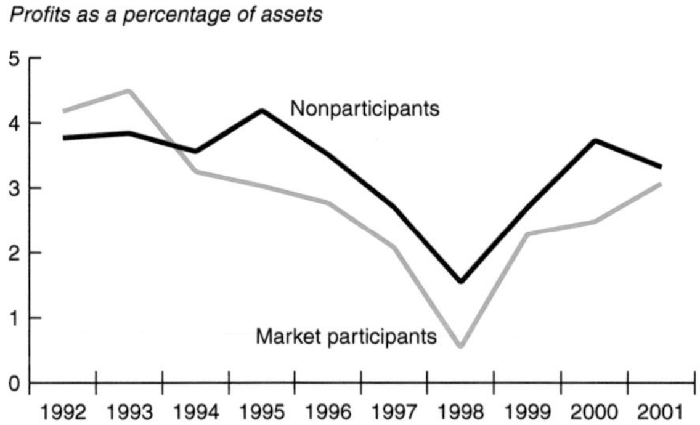

Sources: World Bank Staff estimates; Worldscope; Dealogic.

Figure 5.16 Profit rates by region, 1998–2001

Profits as a percentage of assets

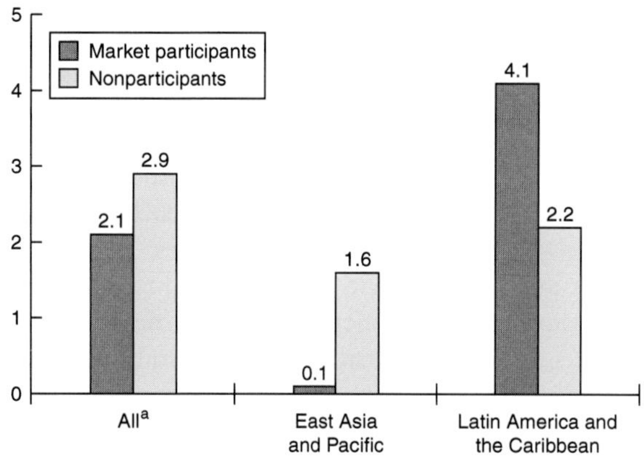

a. All firms in sample described in methodological annex to this chapter.
Sources: World Bank Staff estimates; Worldscope; Dealogic.

Figure 5.17 Profit rates by type of market participant, 1992–2001

Profits as a percentage of assets

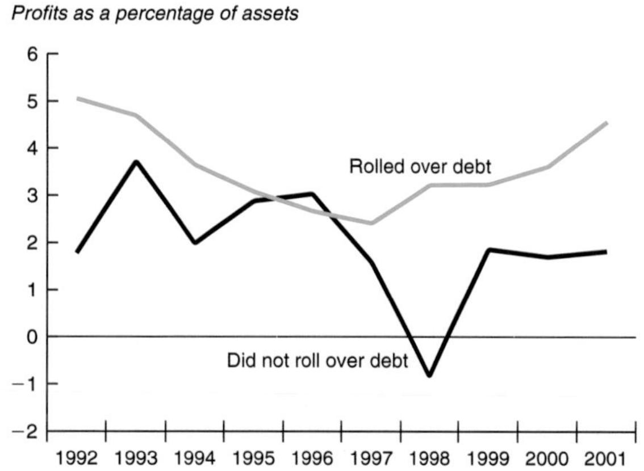

Sources: World Bank staff estimates; Worldscope; Dealogic.

profitable firms in this sample were those that not only participated as borrowers in international markets but also had foreign sales (figure 5.18).[9] For this group, however, profit margins slipped significantly after 1997. This is somewhat surprising, as the more competitive real exchange rate enjoyed by many developing countries since then should have *raised* profit margins in the tradable sector. The exchange-rate benefits must have been eroded by (a) deflationary pressures in global goods markets in recent years and (b) losses resulting from foreign-currency debt, which the existence of foreign-exchange earnings allowed some companies to take on.

A more formal regression analysis of the effect of leverage on corporate profitability (controlling for other factors that also affect profitability) yield two interesting results (see box 5.1). First, both

Figure 5.18 Profit rates of market participants and nonparticipants, 1993–2001

Profits as a percentage of assets

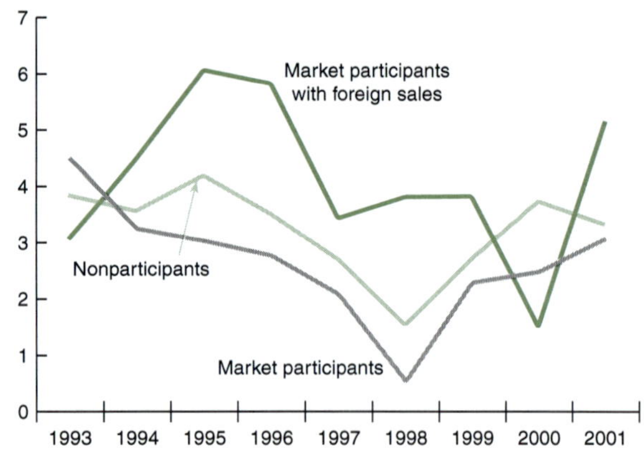

Sources: World Bank Staff estimates; Worldscope; Dealogic.

Box 5.1 The effect of leverage on firm profit rates

We studied the relationship between corporate performance (as measured by its profit rate or earnings before interest and taxes) and corporate finance (debt/assets ratio) using the following model:

Profit rate = a + b∗leverage
+ c∗(leverage)∗(dummy for market participation)
+ d∗(control variables) + error term

where leverage is instrumented by lagged leverage; the dummy for market participation takes the value of 1 for market participants and 0 for others; and control variables are log(sales), square of log(sales), growth of per capita GDP, capital intensity (proxied by capital stock as a ratio of assets), and capital intensity squared, 2-year moving average of profitability (lagged), and 5-year rolling standard deviation of profit rates (these last two variables indicate expected returns and risks). Dummies to account for fixed effects relating to country and sector were added to the regressions. The above specification does not explicitly include variables representing institutions which may affect profit rates and leverage (IMF 2002; p. 99; Klapper and Love 2002); these effects are only indirectly captured through the inclusion of country fixed effects.

This model is estimated using two-stage least squares (instead of ordinary least squares, to control for reverse causality from profitability to leverage). Similar regressions were run using earnings (EBITDA as a percentage of assets) as the dependent variable. The results are summarized in the following table.

Regression results: Effect of leverage on profit rate, 1990–2001

	Profit as a percentage of assets	EBITDA as a percentage of assets
Leverage (debt/assets %)	−0.08**	−0.01
	(−16.4)	(−1.1)
(Leverage)∗(dummy for market participation)	−0.02**	−0.03**
	(−3.9)	(−6.3)
Log(sales)	1.37**	1.94**
	(9.8)	(11.3)
Log(sales), squared	−0.04**	−0.09**
	(−3.1)	(−5.6)
Per capita GDP growth	0.15**	0.04**
	(8.8)	(2.1)
Capital intensity	−0.25	14.76**
	(−0.2)	(9.0)
Capital intensity, squared	−2.58*	−16.31**
	(−1.7)	(−9.2)
Average profitability, 2-year moving average (lagged)	0.43**	0.46**
	(38.6)	(35.4)
Volatility of earnings (5-year rolling standard deviation)	0.01	0.09**
	(0.6)	(4.6)
Adjusted R-squared	0.30	0.31
Number of observations	11,216	10,717

Note: Figures in parentheses indicate t-statistics, ** indicates significance at 5-percent level, and * indicates significance at 10-percent level. All regressions use country and industry fixed-effects using 2-digit SIC codes (not shown in the table). EBITDA is earnings before interest, taxes, depreciation, and amortization.

Source: World Bank staff estimates.

profits and earnings before interest, taxes, depreciation, and amortization decline as a percentage of assets as firms take on more debt relative to their assets. This is similar to the finding of Harvey, Lins, and Roper (2001) that while some debt may improve market discipline in firms, the effect may be overcome by increasing financial risks. Second, the marginal (negative) effect of an increase in leverage on earnings is larger for firms that participate in international debt markets than for other firms.

Why do earnings decline as leverage increases? One reason may be diminishing returns. A firm may take on debt with a view to expanding its operations, but revenue growth is likely to slow as it scales up. Moreover, revenue growth may slow faster in larger firms. This would explain the larger negative effect of leverage on returns for market participants, which are usually significantly larger than nonparticipants. Another reason is that at lower leverage ratios the benefit of the lower cost of foreign borrowing may sufficiently offset losses due to currency depreciation and sudden collapses in investor confidence. As debt levels rise, however, these latter costs become predominant.

Methodological annex

TWO TYPES OF DATA ARE ESPECIALLY USEFUL in tracking trends in corporate finance in developing countries:

- Macroeconomic data, or "top-down" data, from surveys carried out by national and international data collectors.
- Microeconomic data, or "bottom-up" data, compiled from corporate reports.

Each source has strengths and weaknesses. The macro data are, in principle, the most comprehensive and generally quite timely. But they often provide little detail. If too highly aggregated, may make it impossible to distinguish the nonfinancial corporate sector from other parts of the private sector.

The flow-of-funds data compiled for the United States by the Federal Reserve are a model of top-down data. Few developing countries, however, produce such complete accounts.

Firm-level data provide far more detail but suffer from the risk of sample bias. Often only the largest, most sophisticated enterprises are covered, because they are the ones that produce detailed reports. They may also have a time lag arising from the compilers' effort to gather comprehensive, cross-country data.

The absence of comprehensive, timely data is more than a hindrance for researchers; it also is a concern for market participants and policymakers. With financial markets prone to sharp adjustments, and given the easy availability of derivatives and other structuring products that allow corporates to both hedge and increase their risk exposures, it is increasingly important for market participants to be aware of the extent of exposure of the corporate sector as a whole. If the entire sector is overexposed, individual companies are likely to have trouble rolling over their debt in times of market stress.

Four sources of macroeconomic data were used in this study to paint a picture of the liabilities on the aggregate balance sheet of the nonfinancial corporate sector:

(1) Domestic bank credit data from the IMF were used to estimate bank credit, the primary source of credit for most corporate entities in the developing world. The IMF's *International Financial Statistics* (line 32d) includes all credit to the private sector (including households), but the publication does not disaggregate bank credit to consumers. Although this is small in most developing countries, it does bias the debt numbers up.

(2) The *BIS Quarterly Review* provided data on cross-border bank claims, foreign bond issuance, and local bond market issuance.

(3) Domestic equity was estimated based on the market capitalization figures reported in Standard and Poors' Emerging Market Data Base. This source has two drawbacks. First, the use of market values rather than book values makes the equity component (and thus debt-equity ratios) more volatile. Second, the source does not include privately held equity.

(4) Foreign-held equity is estimated using the FDI stock data from chapter 4.

The firm-level data used in this study are from the Worldscope database. We selected only firms for which all the relevant balance sheet items are available. The regional breakdown of the sample is given below.

Table 5A.1 Number of firms in sample

	1992	1993	1994	1995	1996	1997	1998	1999	2000	2001
All	1122	1288	1538	1928	2242	2559	2998	3565	3629	3073
EAP	582	691	774	1032	1181	1245	1347	1618	1840	1695
ECA	17	19	20	68	132	155	177	185	165	117
LAC	141	162	264	308	354	390	533	862	834	706
Others	382	416	480	520	575	769	941	900	790	555

Note: EAP = East Asia and Pacific, ECA = Europe and Central Asia, LAC = Latin America and the Caribbean.

We built a database by matching firm-level balance sheets from Worldscope (December 2002 edition) with issuance data on bonds and syndicated loans from Dealogic Bondware and Loanware. On average about half of annual bond issuance and about 35 percent of annual loan issuance was accounted for by firms matched with Worldscope balance-sheet data.

The resulting database covered firms in 21 emerging markets: Argentina, Brazil, Chile, China, Colombia, the Czech Republic, Hungary, India, Indonesia, Republic of Korea, Malaysia, Mexico, Pakistan, Peru, the Philippines, Poland, the Russian Federation, South Africa, Thailand, Turkey, and República Bolivariana de Venezuela. Because Worldscope data appear quite comprehensive for the period 1992–2001, the analysis in the main text focuses on this period. (Depending on the variable, the number of firms covered in the regression analysis ranged from 1,122 in 1992 to 3,629 in 2000 and 3,073 in 2001.)

The summary statistics presented in the analysis, unless otherwise mentioned, are weighted averages of the financial ratios (with firm assets used as weights). For example, debt-asset ratio is computed as the ratio (expressed as a percentage) of the sum of debt for all firms to that of assets of all firms.

The findings related to foreign market access were derived as follows.

First, firms that had outstanding foreign debt in a given period (called "market participants") were compared with those that had no outstanding foreign debt ("nonparticipants" in the international debt markets, at least for that year). Outstanding foreign debt was calculated by summing all debt issues in international markets (syndicated loans and bonds) during 1990–2001, and subtracting debt that matured during the period. This method ignores outstanding debt issued before 1990, but because private debt flows to emerging markets (and stocks in those markets) were small in the aftermath of the debt crisis of the 1980s, this omission is unlikely to affect the results presented here.

Second, considering all firms with outstanding foreign debt, firms that borrowed from international markets in the current period (that is, firms with rollover) were compared with those that did not (firms without rollover).

Notes

1. See Radelet and Sachs (1998); Dadush, Dasgupta and Ratha (2000); Dasgupta and others (2000).

2. Note that the earnings concept is total earnings, not the narrower and (more arbitrary) concept of operating earnings. In addition to uncertainty over how to measure earnings for a given company, the shifting sample size of our corporate database makes it difficult to compute measures of aggregate profitability that can be compared across time and countries. For example, it does not make sense to add profits, as the number of firms in our sample size varies each year. The alternative—to add together just the earnings of companies for which data are available for the full sample period—involves a huge loss of information, and a considerable risk of bias, as it would reflect (by definition) the selection of firms that were survivors through the whole period. As survivors, these firms might well be expected to have a higher-than-average rate of profitability. Given these constraints, the most meaningful measures of profitability that are available across regions and across time are net earnings of the sample companies as a percentage of sales (profit margins) and net earnings as a percentage of total assets.

3. The growth of international market access in the 1990s was driven by improvements in the macroeconomic environment in emerging-market economies, lifting of capital controls allowing firms to raise financing abroad, and establishment or improvement of legal systems that protected minority shareholder rights. See Levine (1997) for a review.

4. International market participants among banks and other financial companies showed much higher profit rates than nonparticipants. When financial and nonfinancial companies are combined together, again market participants reported higher profit rates.

5. Besides, large firms tend to attract government support, especially during cyclical downturns ("too big to fail"), which further improves their ability to raise debt. Also, larger firms can negotiate better terms with creditors.

6. For firms in developing countries, these valuation losses are one of the biggest components of the difference between operating earnings and overall earnings. We use the latter in this study.

7. This is similar to the view that smaller firms generate higher returns, a well-known result from small capitalized firms in the United States from Fama and French (1992). Some studies, however, have found evidence to the

contrary, that larger emerging-market firms tended to have larger returns on assets (see IMF 2002).

8. The profit rates computed for nonparticipating firms may be underestimated due to the sample selection bias, as firms that underperform drop out of the sample and only relatively better-performing survivors are included in the calculation. Another factor that may affect the comparison of market participants and nonparticipants (especially in East Asia) is that commercial banks were borrowing internationally and on-lending the proceeds in local currency terms to domestic corporations (Dasgupta and others 2000, p. 332). As a result, foreign currency borrowing by nonbank financial corporations would be underreported, reducing the number of market participating firms. When both financial and nonfinancial firms are included, market participants are found to report higher profits than nonparticipants.

9. Firms are not required to report foreign sales in their balance sheets. Thus, the database used here underestimates the number of firms with foreign sales.

References

Dadush, Uri, Dipak Dasgupta, and Dilip Ratha. 2000. "The Role of Short-Term Debt in Recent Crises," *Finance and Development,* December.

Dasgupta, Dipak, Dilip Ratha, Dennis Botman, and Ashish Narain. 2000. "Short-Term Debt and Financial Crises." In Charles Adams, Robert E. Litan and Michael Pomerleano, eds. *Managing Financial and Corporate Distress: Lessons from Asia.* Washington, D.C.: Brookings Institution Press.

Fama, E., and K. French. 1992. "The Cross Section of Expected Stock Returns." *Journal of Finance,* 47(2): 427–65.

Forbes, Kristin J. 2002. "How Do Large Depreciations Affect Firm Performance?" NBER Working Paper 9095. National Bureau of Economic Research, Cambridge, Mass. www.nber.org./papers/w9095.

Glen, Jack, Ajit Singh, and Rudolf Matthias. 1999. "How Intensive Is Competition in the Emerging Markets: An Analysis of Corporates Rates of Return in Nine Emerging Makrets." IMF Working Paper 99/32. International Monetary Fund, Washington, D.C.

Glen, J., K. Lee, and A. Singh. 2001. "Persistence of Profitability and Competition in Emerging Markets." *Economic Letters* 72: 247–53.

Harvey, Campbell R., Karl V. Lins, and Andrew H. Roper. 2001. "The Effect of Capital Structure When Expected Agency Costs Are Extreme." NBER Working Paper 8452. National Bureau of Economic Research, Cambridge, Mass.

IMF (International Monetary Fund). 2002. "Essays on Trade and Finance." Chapter 2 of *World Economic Outlook.* Washington, D.C. www.imf.org.

Klapper, Leora, and Inessa Love. 2002. "Corporate Governance, Investor Protection, and Performance in Emerging Markets." Policy Research Working Paper 2818. World Bank, Washington, D.C.

Lang, Larry, Simeon Djankov, and Stijn Claessens. 1998. "Corporate Growth, Financing, and Risks in the Decade before East Asia's Financial Crisis." Policy Research Working Paper 2017. World Bank, Washington, D.C.

Levine, Ross. 1997. "Financial Development and Economic Growth: Views and Agenda." *Journal of Economic Literature* 35(2): 688–726.

Mako, William P. 2001. "Corporate Restructuring in East Asia: Promoting Best Practices." *Finance and Development* 38(1).

Radelet, S., and J. Sachs. 1998. "The East Asian Financial Crisis: Diagnosis, Remedies, Prospects." *Brookings Papers on Economic Activity* 1: 1–74.

Singh, Ajit. 1995. "Corporate Financial Patterns in Industrializing Economies: A Comparative International Study." Technical Paper 14328. International Finance Corporation, Washington, D.C.

6

Living Up to the Monterrey Commitments: Raising Aid—and Ensuring Its Effectiveness

William Shaw and Eung Ju Kim

THE INTERNATIONAL COMMUNITY FACES significant challenges in assisting developing countries. Aid continues to decline, and many heavily indebted poor countries face daunting problems in achieving sustainable debt levels. Net nonconcessional lending to developing countries is negative—that means developing countries are paying back more nonconcessional funds than they are borrowing. Questions about the effectiveness of aid, particularly to countries that receive large amounts of it, remain a central concern of development policy.

The past year has seen some signs of progress. Initial estimates indicate some rise in concessional flows. In the context of discussions surrounding the United Nations meeting in Monterrey, Mexico, the United States and the European Union agreed to expand their aid programs. If the increases promised in Monterrey are achieved, aid-to-income ratios for the industrial countries should rise over the next three years. Nevertheless, aid will remain below the levels required to meet the Millennium Development Goals, underlining the importance of efforts to increase aid resources. It must be emphasized that the effectiveness of aid depends critically on the quality of recipients' institutions and policies. Both increased resources and strong reform programs are necessary to meet the Millennium Development Goals.

The enhanced Heavily Indebted Poor Countries (HIPC) Initiative made further progress in providing debt relief. Debt relief committed under the HIPC Initiative and other mechanisms have reduced the outstanding debt stock of HIPCs by about $40 billion in net-present-value (NPV) terms—a two-thirds reduction for the 26 countries that have reached decision points. However, the deterioration in the economic environment and accompanying decline in commodity prices mean that several countries may require additional resources to reach sustainable debt levels.

Net disbursements of nonconcessional flows have been negative for the past five years, largely reflecting payments to bilateral export guarantee agencies under debt-restructuring agreements—disbursements of new nonconcessional loans from bilateral agencies have fallen only moderately. But as some countries will continue to owe substantial amortization payments on restructured debt, and several bilateral creditors have reduced their direct-lending operations with the rise in private finance to middle income countries, it is likely that net nonconcessional lending from official sources will continue to be negative over the next few years. In the same period, net nonconcessional flows from multilaterals are unlikely to expand greatly.

Aid helps foster growth and reduce poverty in a strong policy environment. However, the contribution to growth of additional aid does tend to decline as aid rises, in part due to administrative difficulties involved in absorbing large amounts of aid. While the decline in aid over the 1990s has reduced the number of countries receiving very large amounts of aid, some countries face an important challenge in absorbing large aid programs while maintaining aid effectiveness. Nevertheless, most countries that receive a lot of aid have not performed poorly (except for countries suffering from civil or external conflicts), and thus there is no reason to reduce aid flows to good performers to avoid their receiving "too much" aid. Recipients and donors can take steps to improve aid effectiveness, among them devoting more resources to budgetary support (where financial management is adequate), limiting the use of separate institutional arrangements to administer aid projects, and ensuring that civil society is involved in the design of aid programs.

The decline in official financing in 2002

Net disbursements from official sources (including grants) fell to an estimated $46 billion in 2002, down from $57 billion in 2001 (table 6.1). The drop reflects the sharp swings in multilateral lending resulting from the provision of rescue packages to crisis countries, rather than any retreat of official sources from lending to developing countries. The importance of the rescue packages can be seen in the breakdown of net lending from multilateral sources (table 6.2). IMF net disbursements were $19.5 billion in 2001 (compared with negative net lending over the previous two years) but fell to $14 billion in 2002. World Bank lending also fell sharply in 2002. While net lending by IDA rose by $0.6 billion, International Bank for Reconstruction and Development (IBRD) net lending turned negative, as a few countries pre-paid a portion of their IBRD loans.

In contrast to the early 1990s, when the World Bank was the largest source of multilateral finance for developing countries, the major regional development banks (the Inter-American Development Bank, the Asian Development Bank, the European Bank for Reconstruction and Development, and the African Development Bank) together provide about the same level of resources as the World Bank.

Further trends in aid and in nonconcessional official loans are detailed below.

Trends in official development assistance

Official development assistance (ODA) from countries belonging to the Development Assistance Committee (DAC) of the OECD fell to $52 billion in 2001, down $1 billion from the previous year (see table in box 6.1). This decline in part reflected the ap-

Table 6.1 Net official financing of developing countries, 1995–2002
(billions of dollars)

	1995	1996	1997	1998	1999	2000	2001	2002
Total	71.6	31.6	39.7	62.3	42.9	23.4	57.5	49.1
Grants	32.8	27.8	26.7	28.2	29.4	29.6	29.5	32.9
Net lending	38.8	3.8	13.0	34.1	13.5	−6.2	28.0	16.2
Multilateral[a]	28.2	14.0	19.9	37.4	15.7	0.9	35.7	21.3
Concessional	8.8	8.5	7.6	7.4	7.0	5.6	7.2	9.3
Nonconcessional	19.4	5.5	12.3	30.0	8.8	−4.7	28.5	12.0
Bilateral	10.5	−10.2	−6.9	−3.3	−2.3	−7.1	−7.7	−5.1
Concessional	5.5	2.7	0.0	2.5	5.1	1.3	1.5	1.8
Nonconcessional	5.0	−12.9	−6.9	−5.9	−7.3	−8.4	−9.3	−6.9

Note: Data on concessional resources differs from data on ODA due to differences in definitions and country coverage (see box 6.1).
a. Includes IMF.
Source: World Bank Debtor Reporting System.

Table 6.2 Net lending from multilateral sources, 1995–2002
(billions of dollars)

	1995	1996	1997	1998	1999	2000	2001	2002
Total	28.2	14.0	19.9	37.4	15.7	0.9	35.7	21.3
World Bank Group	6.3	7.3	9.2	8.7	8.8	7.8	7.5	1.5
IBRD	1.4	1.5	3.9	3.9	4.2	3.6	2.5	–4.1
IDA	4.9	5.7	5.3	4.8	4.5	4.3	5.0	5.6
Major regional development banks[a]	5.1	4.6	6.3	8.6	9.0	6.2	6.5	1.9
IMF	16.8	1.0	3.4	14.1	−2.2	−10.6	19.5	14.5
Other	0.0	1.1	0.9	5.9	0.1	−2.5	2.2	3.4

a. Inter-American Development Bank, Asian Development Bank, European Bank for Reconstruction and Development, and African Development Bank.
Source: World Bank Debtor Reporting System.

Box 6.1 Defining aid

The international forum for defining aid is the DAC of the OECD.[a] DAC members provided more than 95 percent of international aid in 2000. DAC compiles statistics on aid and other official flows on the basis of information provided to it by bilateral and multilateral agencies.[b]

DAC donors provide two categories of aid—official development assistance (ODA) and official aid (OA). The two forms are similar, except that only developing countries listed on Part I of the DAC "List of Aid Recipients" are eligible to receive ODA. Only ODA may be counted by DAC countries as part of their "aid effort," defined as the donor country's aid budget relative to its GNI.

ODA comprises loans or grants to developing countries and territories provided by donor governments and their agencies for the purpose of promoting economic development and welfare. If the assistance is provided in the form of a loan it must be extended on concessional financial terms, that is, with a grant element of 25 percent or more, calculated as the net present value of the future payment stream discounted at 10 percent.

Countries on Part II of the DAC list (which includes countries in Eastern and Central Europe, the Russian Federation, other independent republics of the former Soviet Union, and a number of high-income countries like French Polynesia, Israel, and New Caledonia) receive OA.

Aid flows to developing countries can be presented from two perspectives, the donors' or the recipients'. Aid *provided by* DAC donors, including ODA and OA, is reported in the table below, which shows bilateral disbursements of concessional financing to developing countries, plus concessional financing from bilateral donors to multilateral institutions (for example, the World Bank's International Development Association).

By contrast, table 6.1 reports disbursements of concessional finance *received by* developing countries from both bilateral and multilateral sources.

The two measures will not be the same mostly because data on concessional flows received do not include technical cooperation grants. Other differences arise because some high-income countries receive OA, and funds from bilateral donors to multilateral institutions do not match those institutions' disbursements to developing countries in any given year.

a. The members of DAC are Australia, Austria, Belgium, Canada, Denmark, Finland, France, Germany, Greece, Ireland, Italy, Japan, Luxembourg, the Netherlands, New Zealand, Norway, Portugal, Spain, Sweden, Switzerland, United Kingdom, and United States.
b. These data are available on the OECD Web site, www.oecd.org.

OA and ODA reported by DAC donors, 1995–2001
(billions of dollars)

	1995	1996	1997	1998	1999	2000	2001
Total aid flows from DAC donors	68.1	61.3	53.8	58.1	62.9	60.6	57.9
Official aid	9.2	5.7	5.3	6.0	6.5	6.9	5.6
Official development assistance	58.9	55.6	48.5	52.1	56.4	53.7	52.3
Bilateral grants	36.2	36.5	31.3	32.5	33.9	33.0	33.4
of which: Technical cooperation	14.3	14.1	12.9	13.1	13.0	12.8	13.6
Debt forgiveness	3.7	3.4	3.1	3.0	2.3	2.0	2.3
Administrative costs	2.9	2.9	2.7	2.8	3.0	3.1	3.0
Net bilateral loans	4.4	2.6	1.1	2.7	4.0	3.0	1.6
Contributions to multilateral institutions	18.3	16.5	16.1	16.9	18.6	17.7	17.3
ODA as a percent of donors' GNI	0.27	0.25	0.22	0.23	0.24	0.22	0.22

Note: Official aid includes DAC aid to high-income countries, the Russian Federation, and Eastern Europe.
Source: OECD Development Assistance Committee.

preciation of the dollar, which reduces the dollar value of ODA recorded in other currencies. In constant prices, net ODA fell by about one percent in 2001. By any measure, aid levels have fallen over the past decade, from 0.34 percent of DAC members' GNI to 0.22 percent (figure 6.1). Note that these aid numbers are prepared on a different basis than the data on official flows shown in table 6.1.

Aid has fallen relative to economic activity in developing countries: the average ratio of aid to

Figure 6.1 Official development assistance, 1990–2001

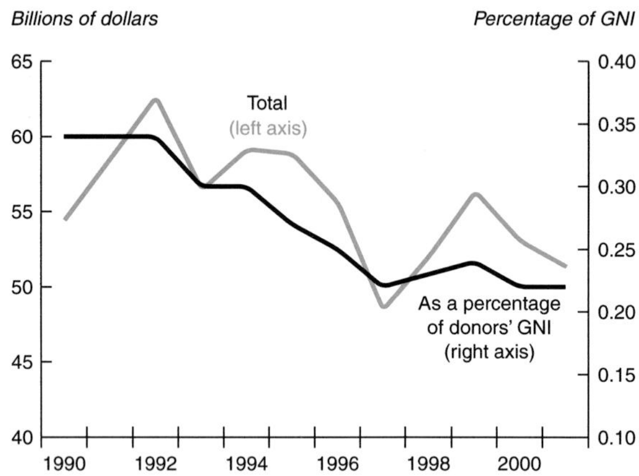

Source: OECD Development Assistance Committee.

recipients' gross national income fell from more than 5 percent in the early 1990s to 3.4 percent in 2000. The early 1990s data reflected the peak in aid receipts, but average aid/income ratios in the years following those peaks were substantially lower than in the early 1980s. These trends in the average level of aid do not just reflect changes in outliers, or developments in middle-income countries that receive little aid. Looking at the median levels, aid has fallen relative to developing countries' expenditures, income, and investment since the late 1980s to early 1990s; similar (although less pronounced) trends can be seen if only low-income countries are considered (figures 6.2a and 6.2b).

It is useful to note that not all of the $52 billion in ODA in 2001 is recorded in developing countries' balance of payments. Of this amount, $14 billion was in the form of technical cooperation grants, for example the payment of consultants to advise developing country governments. While such grants can make an important contribution to development, these funds may be disbursed in the form of payments to industrial country residents, and thus not recorded in developing countries' statistics. Similarly, the DAC includes administrative costs related to managing their development agencies in net ODA. While aid could hardly be provided without such costs, again these funds are not used to finance imports to developing countries.[1] Finally, a portion of bilateral grants is devoted to debt forgiveness. While these funds do contribute to the balance of payments, they do so only by financing debt service payments, which may or may not have been paid in the absence of debt relief. Of course, debt relief provides a valuable long-term benefit by reducing the debt overhang, which can be an important constraint on growth. All in all, net ODA in the form of technical cooperation grants, administrative costs, and debt relief totaled $18.9 billion in 2001, or more than a third of the total.

Grants from nongovernmental organizations (NGOs) show an opposite trend to the official aid data. Grants rose from more than $6 billion in 1995 to about $10 billion in 2001—an amount equal to more than one-sixth the size of official aid.[2] More than half of total grants came from NGOs in the United States, their contributions (to countries on the Part I DAC list) representing about 0.04 percent of GNI, or one-fourth the size of concessional aid flows from the United States, a greater share than any other DAC country (the DAC average is 12 percent). Only four DAC donors provide larger amounts of NGO grants in relation to GNI than does the United States. However, even including NGO grants, most DAC countries still provide a larger amount of aid relative to GNI than does the United States.

Signs of progress

Despite the decline in the dollar value of ODA, the past year saw some progress toward increasing aid. The agreement reached at the International Conference on Financing for Development in Monterrey in March 2002 (the "Monterrey Consensus") reaffirmed the international community's commitment to increasing aid and making progress toward the Millennium Development Goals (see World Bank 2002a for an explanation of the Goals). The European Union (EU) announced plans that would increase its assistance to an average of 0.39 percent of national income by 2006, and some EU members envision further increases in aid. The U.S. administration announced that it would propose increases in its annual contribution by $5 billion for the Millennium Challenge Account and just below $2 billion for an AIDS initiative by 2006. And other DAC members announced plans to raise aid levels. If these pledges are realized, aid would rise to 0.26 percent of industrial countries' GNI, still well below the peak of 0.34 percent of GNI achieved during the 1990s.

Donors underlined the importance of addressing the particular difficulties facing Sub-Saharan Africa. The G-8 summit held later in the year con-

Figure 6.2a Aid flows relative to scale of all developing economies, 1960–2000

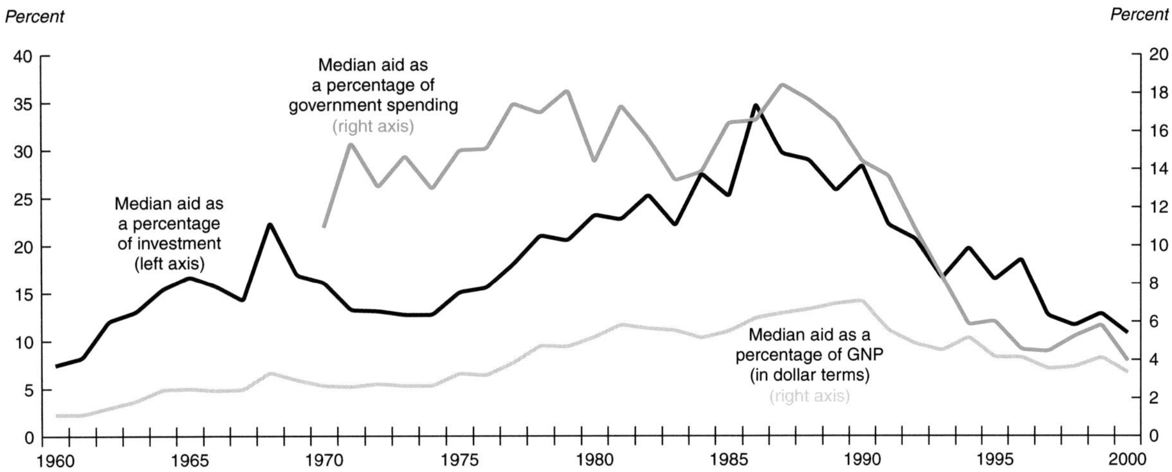

Sources: OECD Development Assistance Committee; World Bank.

Figure 6.2b Aid flows relative to scale of all low-income economies, 1960–2000

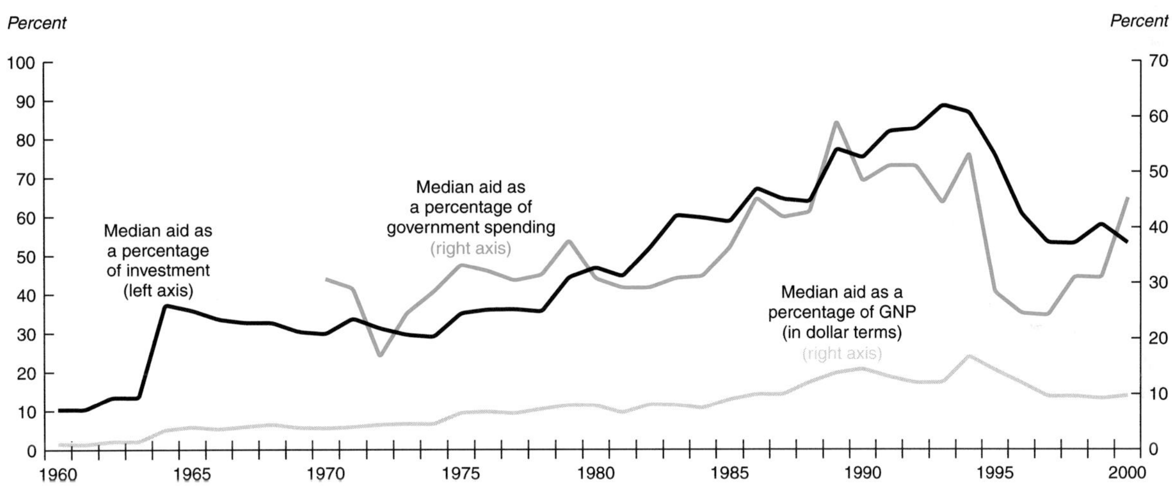

Sources: OECD Development Assistance Committee; World Bank.

cluded with an agreement that up to 50 percent of the additional funds announced at Monterrey would be targeted to Africa (G-8 Summit 2002). The United Kingdom plans to allocate £1 billion of its planned £4.6 billion foreign assistance budget for 2005–06 to Africa (DFID 2002).

The planned rise in aid expenditures should not place a severe financial burden on donors. The proposed increase in U.S. aid would raise U.S. aid flows in 2006 by just 0.06 percent of GNI and 0.2 percent of general government expenditures.[3] The European Union has said that each member will strive to attain ODA expenditures of a minimum of 0.33 percent of GNI by 2006; members already above that level will maintain or improve their aid levels so that the average aid-to-GNI ratio would equal 0.39 percent (OECD 2002). Of the 9 EU countries with aid levels less than 0.33 percent of GNI, the average increase would be 0.07 percent of GNI (figure 6.3). Each person in EU countries that would increase their ODA ratios would have to set aside about $30 of their average annual income of more than $19 thousand. The rise in ODA would average 0.2 percent of general government expenditures; in no country would it require an allocation of more than 0.5 percent of general government expenditures.

Several European countries are experiencing increased budget deficits with the slowdown in

Figure 6.3 Proposed aid increases by nine EU countries

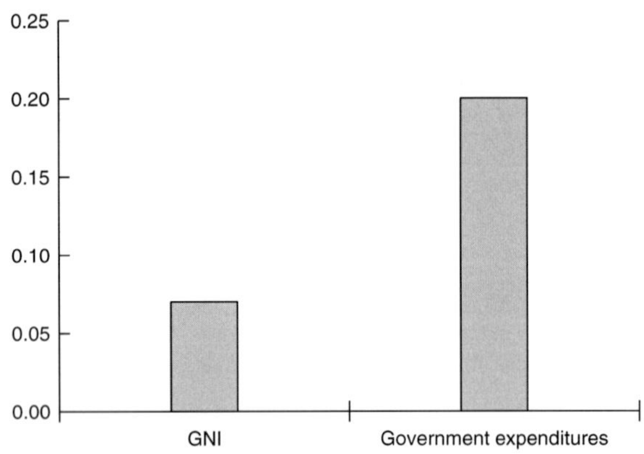

Note: Proposed increases in aid by nine EU countries with aid levels less than 0.33 percent of GNI.
Sources: OECD; World Bank.

growth, and worries are surfacing over the need to contain fiscal pressures at some point. However, of the four EU countries with general government deficits in excess of 1 percent of GDP in 2001, France is already close to the ODA target (and had planned to expand ODA to 0.36 percent of GDP in 2002). In Germany, Italy, and Portugal, the rise in ODA would account for only 0.1 percent, 0.4 percent, and 0.2 percent of outlays. Moreover, the rise in ODA is committed for 2006, at which time cyclical conditions may well have improved.

In committing to an increase in resources, donors also have signaled the need for increased scrutiny of the effectiveness of aid. In the context of the thirteenth replenishment of the International Development Association (IDA13), they have asked IDA management to put in place a system for monitoring progress in development outcomes (see next section). Improving policies and strengthening institutions in developing countries are fundamental steps to increasing aid effectiveness.

One sign of progress is new ideas aimed at raising aid effectiveness and leveraging more resources for aid. The United Kingdom has proposed an International Financing Facility designed to provide additional financing to help meet the Millennium Development Goals. Donors would make commitments to provide a flow of payments over time to the Facility. In turn, the Facility would issue bonds on the strength of these commitments, and allocate these funds through existing bilateral and multilateral institutions to countries pursuing strong policy programs. The goal is to raise aid levels immediately based on future commitments, and ensure that the increased aid is allocated to countries with strong policy programs.

The United States will channel increased assistance into a new Millennium Challenge Account to be managed by a new federal agency. Funds will be allocated—initially only to IDA-eligible countries—on the basis of several indicators, including judgments concerning governance, social sector expenditures and outcomes, and economic policy. Adjustments will be made to a country's rating to take account of other factors, but countries can qualify as better performers only if they demonstrate commitment in all three areas and score better than average on the corruption indicator.

Another positive step was the completion of negotiations over the replenishment of resources for the IDA in July 2002.[4] About SDR 18 billion in resources will be made available during the three year period, primarily from new donor contributions of SDR 10 billion, commitments against IDA's internal resources of SDR 7.3 billion, and transfers from IBRD net income (if available) of about SDR 0.7 billion (figure 6.4).

An expanded use of IDA grants was adopted to address the special difficulties facing some of the poorest and most vulnerable IDA-eligible countries. Grant funding will be expanded to fund HIV/AIDS

Figure 6.4 Sources of IDA resources

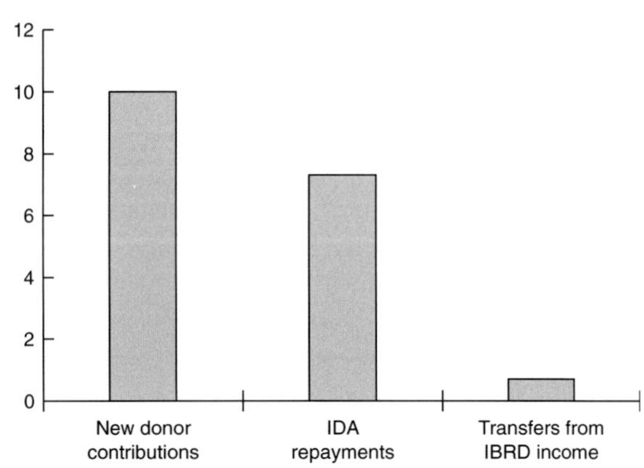

Source: World Bank 2002e.

programs, to assist with recovery from conflict and natural disasters, and to help countries threatened by extreme poverty and debt vulnerability.

The extent of reliance on grants (as opposed to low interest credits) was a major focus of the IDA13 negotiations. Grant funding provided to the poorest countries will increase the concessionality of IDA resources and reduce the risk of adding to the high debt burdens of many IDA borrowers. However, there is a potential for reduced effectiveness if access to grants, as opposed to loans that have to be repaid, erodes fiscal discipline. To mitigate this risk, grants will be subject to the same policies and procedures as IDA credits. The complementarity of the IDA grant program with the efforts of other donors that provide grant funding will need to be assured, and efforts will be required to support the future financing of IDA, which is largely dependent on repayments of earlier credits.[5]

Another key theme of the IDA negotiations was the importance of effective monitoring and evaluation systems, by both recipient countries and the World Bank, to assess progress in meeting poverty reduction targets and promoting development effectiveness. Donors asked IDA management to put in place a system to monitor progress in reaching development outcomes, as set out in the Poverty Reduction Strategy Papers, and to provide a clear indication of how IDA's programs promote the achievement of these outcomes. The Millennium Development Goals will provide a basic point of reference for measuring country progress. Donors also requested that over the course of IDA13, management report on selected input and output indicators in the areas of education, health, and private sector development.

Trade reform and agricultural subsidies

Pushing forward with trade reform in both industrial and developing countries would have a larger impact on improving welfare in developing countries than any of the proposed increases in aid contemplated by the major donors. Some progress has been made in ensuring greater coherence in industrial-country policies toward development. Recent initiatives by the European Union and the United States have increased the openness of their economies to exports from the poorest developing countries. The ministerial meeting of the WTO in November 2001 set the stage for a "development round" of trade talks to address the particular difficulties facing developing countries in the global trading system.

But greater progress is needed in the reform of the EU's Common Agricultural Policy and in U.S. agricultural subsidies, which have serious implications for the ability of the poorest developing countries to raise exports—and for the credibility of U.S. and European policies on trade and aid. High agricultural subsidies and the protection of labor-intensive manufactures continue to depress the potential for developing countries—especially their poorest citizens—to increase their incomes through trade. Industrial countries spend more than $300 billion a year in agricultural subsidies, more than six times the amount they spend on foreign aid. Gaining unrestricted access to industrial countries' markets could boost developing countries' incomes by up to 5 percent, calculated relative to the baseline income forecast in 2015 (World Bank 2002b). Recent proposals to substantially reduce agricultural subsidies provide hope for progress in this area.

The benefit to food importers among the poorest countries would be eroded by the rise in food prices induced by a fall in subsidies. Nevertheless, liberalization in sectors important to the poorer countries could have a significant impact. For example, removing subsidies in the cotton sector alone could lead in the short term to a 50 percent rise in price, boosting African cotton exporters' revenues by some $500 million. This rise would moderate over time, as production rose in response to high prices. Nevertheless, cotton prices would remain about 10 percent over current levels for the foreseeable future.

A strengthening of domestic policies and institutions in developing countries is required to take greater advantage of current trade arrangements, and to reap the maximum benefit of future reforms. Policy barriers to competition, weak infrastructure, and limited government services continue to act as severe impediments to growth in many developing economies (World Bank 2002b). Trade reform can only provide the opportunity for countries to prosper. Developing country governments have to establish the investment climate that enables private-sector firms to capitalize on these opportunities.

The HIPC Initiative

The HIPC Initiative[6] has made substantial progress in reducing the debt burden of the poorest developing countries. As of September 2002, six countries have received irrevocable debt relief under the Enhanced HIPC Initiative.[7] An additional 20 countries have begun to receive interim debt relief.[8] The relief committed so far, together with debt relief provided under traditional mechanisms (such as the Paris Club and additional bilateral debt forgiveness), has reduced the outstanding debt stock of HIPCs by about $40 billion in NPV terms. This amounts to a two-thirds reduction in the debt stock of the 26 countries that have reached decision points under the Enhanced framework. The 26 countries' average ratio of debt service to exports fell from 16.5 percent in 1998–99 to 10 percent in 2001, and debt service as a percentage of government revenues fell from 24 percent in 1998–99 to 15 percent in 2001. Social expenditures in these countries are expected to rise to 9 percent of GDP in 2002, up from 6 percent in 1999, in part financed by resources freed up by HIPC relief.

The HIPC Initiative process

The HIPC Initiative was launched in 1996 to reduce the debt burden of the world's poorest and most heavily indebted countries, in the context of economic and social reform aimed at reducing poverty. The Initiative marked the first time that debt relief was provided to poor countries on a comprehensive basis, including multilateral creditors. Assistance under the Initiative is provided in the context of a policy program aimed at increasing growth and reducing poverty.

Eligible countries are those who can receive highly concessional assistance from the multilateral institutions and face an unsustainable debt situation even after the full application of traditional debt relief mechanisms (such as Naples terms under the Paris Club). Forty-two countries, primarily from Sub-Saharan Africa, are potentially eligible to receive debt relief under the Initiative. The current framework, called the Enhanced HIPC Initiative, reflects a deepening and broadening of the debt relief provided following a major review of the program in 1999.

If a country's debt is found to be unsustainable according to the HIPC criteria—and if other conditions are met—the boards of the World Bank and IMF review and approve a commitment for HIPC relief. At that time, all creditors (multilateral, bilateral, and commercial) are expected to make commitments concerning the relief to be delivered when the HIPC process is completed. The country applying for relief and the World Bank and IMF also agree on a policy framework that includes specific actions (called completion-point triggers) to be completed before irrevocable debt relief is provided. In the interim, the World Bank, IMF, African Development Bank, and other multilateral and bilateral creditors and donors provide debt relief at their discretion, provided the country is meeting the conditions (such as maintaining a stable macroeconomic program) to which it agreed. Once a country has implemented the completion-point triggers, had an IMF Poverty Reduction and Growth Facility in place for at least six months, and had a World Bank Poverty Reduction Strategy Paper Program operating for at least one year, World Bank and IMF Boards meet to approve the provision of debt relief.

Obstacles to achieving and protecting debt sustainability

Despite the accomplishments of the HIPC Initiative, the deterioration in the global economic environment and the related decline in commodity prices have raised concerns about the ability of several HIPCs to reduce their debt burdens to sustainable levels. Of the 23 countries that reached a decision point before June 2001, 11 are estimated to have NPV of debt-to-exports ratios that are at least 15 percentage points higher than had been forecast in the debt-sustainability analysis done at the decision point (World Bank 2002c).

The decline in commodity prices has played an important role in the higher-than-expected debt-to-export ratios. The average export price index of countries whose export revenues were lower than forecast fell by just under 5 percent from the decision point to the estimate for 2001.[9] These countries' exports are concentrated heavily in cotton, coffee, cashews, fish, and copper—commodities that fell steeply in price last year. The countries are slightly more dependent on the export of primary commodities, and have much greater volatility of exports, than other HIPCs. Domestic developments, including policy failures, also contributed to poorer-than-expected performance.

The current framework of the Initiative has the flexibility to respond to a deterioration of the outlook for debt sustainability after countries reach a decision point.[10] If a country's economic circumstances at the completion point have been fundamentally changed due to exogenous developments, then the country may benefit from additional debt relief beyond that envisioned at the decision point, which would reduce their debt-to-exports ratio to 150 percent at completion point.[11] This approach has already been applied in the case of Burkina Faso.

Other issues have slowed implementation of the HIPC Initiative. Some countries that have reached a decision point have encountered problems in the implementation of their macroeconomic programs, and some have taken longer than anticipated to prepare their Poverty Reduction Strategy Paper. World Bank and IMF staff continue to work with the authorities in these countries to develop strategies for moving ahead. In the meantime, the process of reaching the decision point for the remaining countries expected to require HIPC relief will be challenging. Most are affected by conflict[12] or have substantial arrears, both of which complicate the task of designing and implementing a viable reform package.

Challenges remain on the creditor side, as well. Overall, debt relief committed to the 26 HIPCs that have reached their decision points remains 12 percent below the total required. Twenty-four creditor countries that do not belong to the Paris Club have not yet expressed their intention to provide debt relief. Many commercial creditors remain unwilling to participate in the initiative. The claims of non-Paris club bilaterals and commercial creditors are less than 10 percent of the total debt burden, although their participation is important for the debt-sustainability prospects of some HIPCs—and key to the principle of equitable burden sharing. Some recent improvements are notable, however, including commitments to provide debt relief by Bulgaria, India, the Republic of Korea, and Libya.

There also remains the potential for disruption of the HIPC process by creditors bringing legal action for the collection of debts. In a survey of 28 HIPCs, 10 responded that they were facing litigation on credits.

Once they have benefited from debt relief, will HIPCs be able to maintain sustainable debt levels over the medium term? The forecasts done for debt-sustainability analyses generally show that HIPCs can achieve reasonable rates of growth while maintaining sustainable debt levels, assuming strong policy performance and the availability of sufficient resources on highly concessional terms.[13]

How reasonable are these export forecasts? A review of the export projections embodied in decision-point documents of early participants in the HIPC Initiative reveals that those projections turned out to be optimistic in two-third of the countries reviewed, but *pessimistic* in the other third. The countries whose exports were better than expected were those less affected by external shocks (World Bank 2002c).

The review also confirms an earlier finding that projected growth for decision-point HIPCs was significantly higher than would be expected on the basis of past export performance alone.[14] Average annual export growth for 26 HIPCs was projected at 7.5 percent in the decision-point documents, compared with the 4.7 percent achieved over the previous 30 years. However, HIPCs' growth may well accelerate after the decision point because of stronger policy performance and the liberating effects of eliminating debt overhang. In light of these uncertainties, countries are encouraged to develop alternative macroeconomic scenarios: an optimistic scenario based on effective implementation of policy reforms and a conservative scenario that would reflect the country's vulnerabilities and the uncertainties of the external environment. The staffs of the Bank and the Fund will be expected to base their own growth projections on a thorough analysis of the likely sources of growth, and to present their analyses explicitly in discussions with the authorities as well as in staff documents.

The importance of new financing

Key to the long-term debt sustainability of HIPCs is the availability of enough external financing on sufficiently concessional terms to support the countries' poverty reduction and growth strategies. Increases in grants from both bilateral and multilateral development partners will be required. The agreement under IDA13 to provide a proportion of IDA resources in the form of grants to particularly vulnerable low-income countries will be an important step forward in this regard. Although the effect on debt ratios of substituting grants for part of HIPCs' new borrowing would be small in the short term, its cumulative impact could be significant over the longer term. More concessional financing from the international community would help ensure that new external financing was consistent with the repayment capacity of vulnerable countries.

Several proposals have been made to modify the structure of the enhanced HIPC Initiative to increase its effectiveness. Those proposals include:

- Providing debt relief sufficient to finance the social expenditures required to meet the Millennium Development Goals
- Calculating debt relief on the basis of debt service, rather than on the stock of debt (for example, reducing debt service to no more than 2 percent of GDP)
- Extending debt relief to a broader range of poor countries, including Indonesia, Nigeria, Pakistan, and Zimbabwe
- Providing a contingency facility that would protect HIPCs from exogenous shocks for a period of time after the completion point.

These proposals are designed to increase resources to HIPCs and other poor countries, and to address important constraints on development. However, all of these proposals would involve additional costs, calling into question their feasibility when the existing initiatives are not yet fully funded. Some would better be accomplished through new flows—as grants or highly concessional loans—rather than through debt relief. New flows can be more easily tailored to a country's needs than can relief of debt-service payments. Moreover, it would be preferable to avoid continued reliance on debt relief, except where necessary to achieve debt sustainability. Repeated relief can reduce creditors' incentives to lend for good projects and debtors' incentives to repay loans.

One issue that is often lost in the debate over expanding the HIPC Initiative is the source of any new resources provided (box 6.2). Observers who might support the proposals outlined above if they were financed through higher aid allocations by DAC donors might feel very differently if the resources were to be generated by reducing concessional flows to poor countries not in the HIPC group. The HIPC Initiative is necessary to help desperately poor countries establish the sustainable levels of debt required for future economic growth. But once they meet their debt-sustainability targets, their eligibility for aid should be evaluated in tandem with other poor countries that have not built up excessive levels of debt.

The decline in official nonconcessional lending since the 1990s

Net nonconcessional lending from official sources to developing countries dropped sharply over the 1990s, albeit with considerable variability from year to year (figure 6.5). The trend was dominated by the rescue packages provided for countries in crisis in the second half of the 1990s and by repayments under rescheduled export credits.

Bilateral lending

The sharp downward trend in nonconcessional lending through most of the 1990s was due to the dropoff of net lending from bilateral sources. In the early 1990s, developing countries netted between \$3 billion and \$5 billion each year in nonconcessional loans from bilateral sources, while net disbursements turned negative by the middle of the decade (see table 6.1). Some bilateral agencies have scaled down their loans to developing countries. And disbursements and repayments under the U.S. loan to Mexico introduce some volatility in the time series. But the major reason for the substantial negative net disbursements on nonconcessional loans from bilateral sources are repayments of guaranteed export credits. The following discussion reviews all three reasons.

The decline in direct bilateral loans. Net nonconcessional lending from bilateral creditors to developing countries during the 1980s and early 1990s consisted of direct loans from national export credit agencies, along with project lending from other agencies provided at interest rates too high to be counted as concessional. Over the 1990s

Figure 6.5 Net official nonconcessional lending, 1990–2001

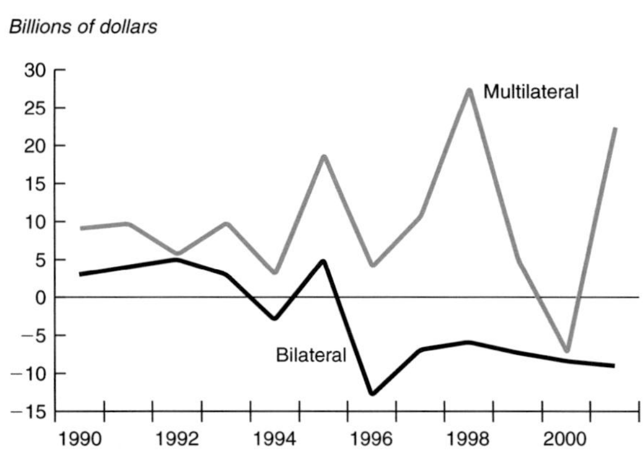

Source: World Bank Debtor Reporting System.

Box 6.2 Is debt relief to HIPCs additional?

One issue in evaluating the impact of the HIPC Initiative is whether the resources devoted to debt relief have been additional to other donor aid. That is, have HIPCs received more resources as a result of the Initiative, or have donors reduced other forms of aid to HIPCs as debt relief rose? It is impossible to answer this question conclusively by looking at the data, as we do not know how much aid HIPCs would have received in the absence of the Initiative.[a] Most countries in the HIPC Initiative reached a decision point in 2000, and it was not until 2001 that they received full interim relief. Hence, it is still too early to evalute additionality with confidence. Also, the data are relatively poor, as different donors account for debt relief in different ways, and the aggregate data may be affected by particular circumstances involving individual countries. Moreover, even in the extreme case that all of the resources devoted to the HIPC Initiative represented no additional net resources to these countries, the Initiative still could have an important impact through allocating more resources to debt relief in heavily indebted countries, and strengthening the link between aid and policy performance. Nevertheless, one important aspect of the Initiative remains the extent to which the HIPCs gain access to additional resources.

Net aid to HIPCs has increased since the start of the HIPC Initiative, from $14.9 billion in 1997 to $15.9 billion in 2001. The rise in aid flows went entirely to countries that had reached a decision or completion point under the Initiative, indicating progress in reform. The total for the other countries was flat over the period. The flow data may not reflect the full amount of resources provided to the HIPCs, as depending on the accounting provision used, the forgiveness of future amortization (for example, in the context of a reduction of the stock of debt) may not show up as aid in the current year. The detailed data on gross disbursements to HIPCs from bilateral donors reveal a leveling off of aid receipts in the late 1990s, after the more than one-third decline in aid to HIPCs during the first half of the 1990s (see figure at right). All in all, the available data indicate a modest rise in total aid resources to HIPCs during the period of the Initiative.

Bilateral flows to HIPC countries, 1990–2000

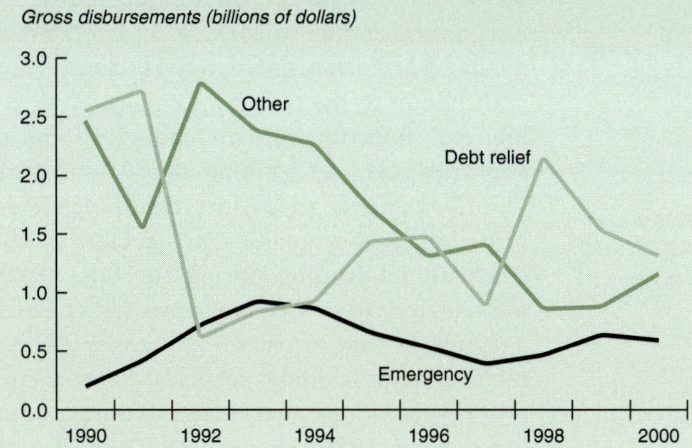

Source: OECD Development Assistance Committee.

Further econometric analysis is required to determine the additionality of HIPC resources and debt relief in general. Birdsall, Claessens, and Diwan (2002) find that in a regression explaining the level of net transfers from donors (a function of the level of debt, policy, poverty, population size, and debt relief), the coefficient on bilateral debt relief is close to zero for high-debt countries. This is consistent with the notion that debt relief provided does not raise the level of net transfers, and is hence not additional. However, their analysis was done before the provision of multilateral debt relief.

There is little reason to expect that the HIPC Initiative should result in a significant increase in aid resources, particularly during a period of aid austerity like the last few years. Nevertheless, the recent increase may indicate that donors are providing more aid to HIPCs as policies improve in the context of the Poverty Reduction Strategy Paper process. But any such reallocation is likely to take considerable time. One would want to see a very substantial shift in aid resources to HIPC countries only if the countries did achieve significant policy improvements, or aid was reallocated from less effective policy environments in countries with fewer poor people.

a. World Bank 2002c, box 1.

governments retreated from providing direct loans to support export activity, partly in recognition of the increasing willingness of private-sector sources to supply this finance and partly out of concern over the increasing debt difficulties of several middle-income countries. For example, the United Kingdom's Commonwealth Development Corporation was privatized, and its activities redirected toward equity financing. At the same time, export credit agencies reduced their activities in the heavily indebted poor countries (which has a numerically small impact on the overall figures, given the dominance of middle-income countries).

The U.S. loan to Mexico. A single operation, the U.S. loan to Mexico during the peso crisis of 1995, introduces some noise into the series under scrutiny here. Net nonconcessional loans from bilateral sources jump from −$2.7 billion in 1994 to $5.2 billion in 1995, before dropping again to −$12.9 billion in 1996. The $8 billion shift from 1994 to 1995 is more than explained by the rise in U.S. net lending to Mexico. In late 1996 repayments by Mexico resulted in net bilateral lending of −$8 billion to the country. Leaving Mexico aside, bilateral nonconcessional lending to developing countries was −$4.5 billion in 1995 and 1996.

Repayments to export credit agencies. The principal reason for the sharp decline in net nonconcessional lending during the late 1990s was the rise in debt service payments under Paris Club agreements that restructured loans guaranteed by bilateral export credit agencies. Several countries restructured their guaranteed export credits during the late 1980s or early 1990s, and payments made under these agreements are recorded as outflows to bilateral creditors. The timing and grace periods on these loans are such that large payments are still being made. For example, Argentina will continue to owe money on its debt restructurings of the 1980s until the middle years of this decade.

What seem to be large negative net disbursements from bilateral creditors misrepresent their contribution to developing countries' financial resources. The disbursement of funds supported by a guarantee is not counted as a bilateral loan (since the identity and often the existence of a guarantee is not reported), whereas once the export credit agency assumes the loan, the repayment is counted as amortization paid to the bilateral agency.

The importance of these three influences can be seen by looking at data on disbursements and amortization payments (figure 6.6). Gross disbursements of nonconcessional loans from bilateral sources exceeded $10 billion per year in the early 1990s, then shot up and fell with the loan to Mexico in 1995–96 before beginning a downwards trend to about $7 billion per year in the last two years. This decline reflects the falloff in direct loans from export credit agencies. However, amortization payments increased sharply beginning in 1994, as the grace periods expired on Paris Club restructurings. Since 1998 amortization payments have averaged about $15 billion per year—twice the level of the early 1990s. It is likely that net nonconcessional lending from bilateral sources will remain negative for several years to come, as

Figure 6.6 Gross flows to and from bilateral creditors, 1990–2001

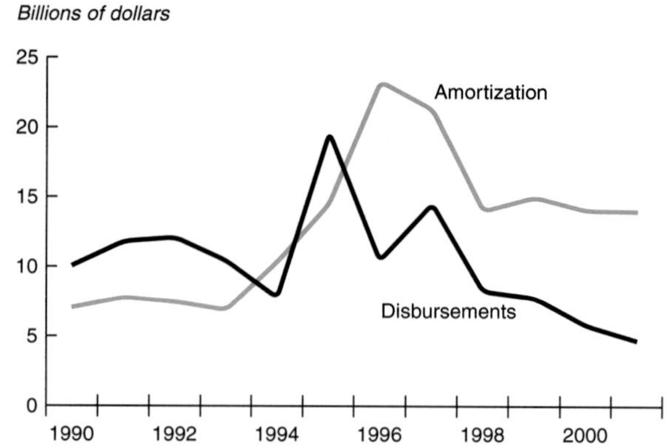

Source: World Bank Debtor Reporting System.

amortization payments are scheduled to remain high until late in this decade.

Multilateral lending

The sharp gyrations in nonconcessional lending from multilaterals in the second half of the 1990s were due largely to the rescue packages extended to countries affected by the crises in East Asia, the Russian Federation, and Latin America. Net nonconcessional lending from multilaterals was constant at about $10 billion per year from 1990 to 1995 and then shot up to a peak of $30 billion in 1998 with the rescue packages. The IMF accounted for the bulk of the increase. Net lending from the regional development banks also increased significantly. Net lending then plummeted in 2000 as rescue package disbursements declined and amortization began to rise, before shooting up again with the emergency financing extended to Argentina in 2001.

Note the rising trend in amortization payments since the early 1990s (figure 6.7). The increase toward the end of the decade reflected in part the short maturities on loans to the crisis countries. But higher amortization also resulted from the substantial gross disbursements of the early 1990s, which averaged $27 billion per year from 1990 to 1994, up from less than $20 billion a year in the last half of the 1980s. As the grace periods on these earlier disbursements expire, net lending will be further reduced unless future disbursements rise substantially. Given the large nonconcessional resources provided to middle-income countries in the early 1990s, and the emergency financing made available

- Limiting the use of separate institutional arrangements to administer aid projects
- Reducing the number of donors operating in individual sectors and improving donor coordination
- Ensuring that civil society is involved in aid programs and policies.

There is no evidence that countries that receive a lot of aid have performed poorly (aside from countries suffering from civil or external conflicts), and the empirical evidence that high aid levels exert an independent, negative impact on governance is unconvincing.

The challenge is for donors to deliver aid—and for recipients to manage their resources—in ways that promote aid effectiveness. The means to be used will depend greatly on the purpose for which the aid is intended and on domestic conditions; there is no "silver bullet" approach to aid management that guarantees effectiveness. Strong governments can ensure that aid is spent according to their own priorities and in ways that are consistent with effective administration. Weak governments can find their policymaking processes and institutional quality disrupted by large aid flows.

Annex: Debt Restructuring with Official Creditors

THIS ANNEX REVIEWS OFFICIAL DEBT rescheduling agreements concluded in 2002.

Rescheduling of intergovernmental loans and officially guaranteed private export credits take place under the aegis of the Paris Club. These agreements are concluded between the debtor government and representatives of creditor countries with export credit facilities. The terms of Paris Club rescheduling are recorded in an agreed minute. To make the debt relief effective, debtor countries must sign bilateral implementing agreements with each creditor. For a description of Paris Club procedures and principles, and details on agreements, see the Paris Club Web site (www.clubdeparis.org).

Developments in 2002

The Paris Club concluded multilateral rescheduling agreements with 10 countries in 2002, covering a total of about $20 billion (table 6A.1). All of these agreements, except the one with Jordan, were concluded with low-income countries. Two agreements (Ghana and Nicaragua) were on Cologne terms, three (Indonesia, Jordan, and Kyrgyz Republic) were on nonconcessional terms, one (the Democratic Republic of Congo) was on Naples terms, one (Côte d'Ivoire) was on Lyon terms, and three (Burkina Faso, Mauritania, and Tanzania) were comprehensive stock-of-debt agreements.

The stock-of-debt operations

Burkina Faso, Mauritania, and Tanzania reached exit stock-of-debt agreements with Paris Club creditors under the Enhanced HIPC Initiative, covering a total of $1.9 billion (table 6A.2). These agreements provided $937 million of NPV reduction in the stock of debt ($22.2 million for Burkina Faso, $188 million for Mauritania, and $737 million for Tanzania). Creditors also committed to grant additional debt relief, on a bilateral basis, to Burkina Faso and Mauritania.

Agreements with other countries

Congo, Democratic Republic

The agreement concluded with the Democratic Republic of Congo in September 2002 consolidated about $9 billion (including an immediate debt cancellation of about $4.6 billion), of which 16 percent relates to ODA loans and 84 percent to commercial credits. The agreement reduced arrears as of June 30, 2002 ($8.5 billion) and debt-service payments falling due from July 1, 2002 to June 30, 2005 ($0.5 billion) on loans contracted prior to June 30, 1983 (the cutoff date) by 67 percent in NPV terms (Naples terms). Creditors also agreed to top up the reduction rate to 90 percent (Cologne terms) when the Democratic Republic of Congo reaches the decision point under the Enhanced HIPC Initiative. On an exceptional basis, creditors agreed to capitalize all moratorium interest falling due until June 30, 2005, on the restructured debt. These amounts will be repaid in 16 semiannual installments beginning March 31, 2006, and ending September 30, 2013. Creditors also deferred all arrears as of June 30, 2002 (arrears will be repaid on a graduated schedule from March 31, 2003, to September 30, 2009) and 100 percent of debt-service payments falling due between July 1, 2002, and December 31, 2002, on post–cutoff date debt (to be repaid in six equal semi-annual installments

Table 6A.1 Paris Club agreements, January 1–December 31, 2002

Country	Signature date (2002)	Cutoff date	Amount (*millions of dollars*)	Concessionality (*percent of NPV*)	Start date of consolidation period	Length (*months*)
Burkina Faso	20 June	1 Jan. 1991	22	90	Debt stock rescheduling	n.a.
Congo, Dem. Rep. of	13 Sept.	30 June 1983	9,000	67	1 July 2002	36
Côte d'Ivoire	10 April	1 July 1983	2,300	80	1 April 2002	33
Ghana	16 May	20 June 1999	160	90	1 Feb. 2002	10
Indonesia	12 April	1 July 1997	5400	n.a.	1 April 2002	21
Jordan	11 July	1 Jan. 1989	1200	n.a.	1 Jan. 2002	72
Kyrgyz Republic	7 March	31 Aug. 2001	99	n.a.	6 Dec. 2001	36
Mauritania	8 July	31 Dec. 1984	188	90	Debt stock rescheduling	n.a.
Nicaragua	13 Dec.	1 Nov. 1988	579	90	1 Oct. 2002	36
Tanzania	17 Jan.	30 June 1986	973	90	Debt stock rescheduling	n.a.

n.a. Not applicable.
Sources: World Bank; Paris Club.

commencing on March 31, 2003, and ending on September 30, 2005).

Côte d'Ivoire

The April 2002 agreement with Côte d'Ivoire restructured an estimated $2.3 billion ($900 million on ODA loans and $1.4 billion of guaranteed commercial credits), of which $1.1 billion comprised principal and interest in arrears (including late interest) and $1.2 billion debt-service payments. The agreement included an immediate cancellation of about $911 million of Côte d'Ivoire's external debt. The agreement reduced arrears at March 31, 2002, and 100 percent of debt-service payments falling due between April 1, 2002, and December 31, 2004, on debts contracted before July 1, 1983 (the cutoff date), by 80 percent in NPV terms (Lyon terms). Creditors also agreed to increase the reduction rate to 90 percent (Cologne terms) after Côte d'Ivoire reaches its Decision Point under the Enhanced HIPC Initiative. In recognition of Côte d'Ivoire's particularly tough economic situation, Paris Club creditors agreed to capitalize 100 percent of moratorium interest falling due from April 1, 2002, to December 31, 2002, on the rescheduled debt. These amounts will be repaid on March 31, 2005. Creditors also deferred 100 percent of arrears on post–cutoff date debt (that is, loans contracted after July 1, 1983). These amounts were to be repaid beginning September 30, 2002, and ending March 31, 2003, but Côte d'Ivoire has not made any payments under its Paris Club agreement since September.

Ghana

The Paris Club creditors concluded an interim debt-relief agreement in May 2002 that provides an immediate cancellation of $90 million of Ghana's external debt. This agreement consolidates a total of $160 million, of which $100 million represents debt-service payments owed to commercial creditors, on debt contracted prior to June 20, 1999 (the cutoff date). It reduced all debt-service payments due to Paris Club creditors falling due between February 1, 2002, and November 30, 2002, by 90 percent in NPV terms (Cologne terms).

Indonesia

In April 2002, the Paris Club creditors restructured about $5.4 billion of Indonesia's debt service ($2.3 billion of ODA loans and $3.1 billion of commercial loans with export credit guarantees). The agreement covered 100 percent of principal falling due between April 1, 2002, and December 31, 2003, and 100 percent of interest payments falling due between April 1, 2002, and December 31, 2002, on all debts contracted before July 1, 1997 (the cutoff date). ODA debt was rescheduled over 20 years, including a 10-year grace period, with 20 equal semi-annual payments beginning on December 1, 2013, and ending on June 1, 2023. A guaranteed commercial loan was rescheduled over 18 years, including a 5-year grace period, with 26 semi-annual payments commencing on December 1, 2008, and ending on June 1, 2021. The progressive repayment schedule for commercial debt will rise from 2 percent of the amount rescheduled at the outset of the repayment period to 6.53 percent by the time of the final installment. Creditors indicated their willingness to consider the rescheduling of an estimated $730 million in interest payments falling due in 2003, depending on the country's need for finance (as identified by the IMF). The agreement also contained a swap clause under which, on a voluntary and bilateral basis, creditors or their appropriate institutions may swap all ODA debts, and up to 20 percent of the amount outstanding on their non-ODA debts as of March 31, 2000, or up to SDR 30 million, whichever is higher.

Jordan

Paris Club creditors reached an exit arrangement with Jordan to restructure approximately $1.2 billion ($270 million in ODA loans and $930 million in commercial loans with export credit guarantee) that addresses graduation from Paris Club rescheduling. The agreement would cover 100 percent of principal and interest falling due between January 1, 2002, and June 30, 2004; 90 percent of principal and interest falling due between July 1, 2004, and December 31, 2005; 80 percent of principal and interest falling due in 2006; and 70 percent of principal and interest falling due in 2007 on all debts contracted before the cutoff date (January 1, 1989), including debt service payments due on all previous agreements concluded with the Paris Club. Repayment of the rescheduled amounts will be made as follows: ODA loans will be repaid in 20 equal semi-annual payments beginning on June 30, 2014, and ending on December 31, 2023, at an interest rate as favorable as the concessional rates applying to those loans. Guaranteed commercial credits will be repaid in 30 semi-annual installments on a graduated schedule rising from 0.53 percent of the total amount rescheduled at the time of the initial payment in June 2007, to 7.65 percent by the time of the final payment in December 31, 2021, at the appropriate market interest rates.

Kyrgyz Republic

The Paris Club signed its first agreement with Kyrgyz Republic in March 2002; the cutoff date was set at August 31, 2001. The agreement restructured $99 million of principal and interest (including $23 million ODA loans) falling due from December 6, 2001 to December 5, 2004. ODA loans are to be repaid within 20 years (including 10 years of grace), at an interest rate as favorable as those applying to concessional loans. Commercial credits were to be repaid in 20 years (including a 5-year grace period), at the appropriate market interest rates. A portion of the moratorium interest on rescheduled debt would be capitalized—up to 50 percent in 2002, 60 percent in 2003, and 70 percent in 2004. These amounts will be repaid in 4 equal semi-annual payments from December 6, 2006, to June 6, 2008. Creditors also committed in principle to consider a stock-of-debt treatment, subject to successful implementation of the IMF program until December 2004.

Nicaragua

In December 2002, Paris Club creditors concluded an interim debt-relief agreement with Nicaragua covering about $579 million (of which $560 million represents pre–cutoff date commercial credits falling due from October 1, 2002, to September 30, 2005), including the immediate cancellation of about $405 million. All debt-service payments falling due between October 1, 2002, and September 30, 2005 will be reduced by 90 percent in NPV terms. The agreement was concluded under Cologne terms: repayment of the rescheduled amount will be made over 40 years, including a 16-year grace period, for ODA credits, and over 23 years, including 6 years of grace, for guaranteed commercial credits.

Other developments in 2002

On March 8, 2002, the Paris Club creditors arranged their second meeting with representatives of the private creditors coordinated by the Institute of International Finance, the Emerging Market Creditors Association, and the Emerging Market Traders Association. They discussed the most important agreements concluded in 2001, and exchanged views on sovereign debt restructuring and the outlook for several countries, including Argentina, Côte d'Ivoire, Ecuador, Indonesia, and Nigeria. Private creditors welcomed the successful launch of the Paris Club Web site, which represents a key step in the Paris Club's program to improve transparency. Both groups of creditors found the exchange of views and information useful and agreed to hold regular meetings at least annually.

Table 6A.2 Multilateral debt-relief agreements with official creditors, January 1980–December 2002

		Consolidation period for current maturities		Consolidation includes				Repayment terms[a]	
Country and date of agreement	Contract cutoff date	Start date	Length *(months)*	Arrears	Previously rescheduled debt	Share of debt consolidated *(percent)*	Amount consolidated *(millions of dollars)*	Maturity *(years/ months)*	Grace *(years/ months)*
Albania*									
1 Dec. 93	30 Sept. 93	Arrears as of 30 Sept. 93		y		100	109	9/3	2/9
Algeria									
1 June 94	30 Sept. 93	1 June 94	12			100	5,345	14/6	3/0
21 July 95	30 Sept. 93	1 July 95	36			100	7,320	13/0	1/6
Angola									
20 July 89	31 Dec. 86	1 July 89	15	y		100	446	9/6	6/0
Argentina									
16 Jan. 85	10 Dec. 83	1 Jan. 85	12	y		90	2,040	9/6	5/0
20 May 87	10 Dec. 83	1 May 87	14	y		100	1,260	9/5	4/11
21 Dec. 89	10 Dec. 83	1 Jan. 90	15	y	y	100	2,400	9/4	5/10
19 Sept. 91	10 Dec. 83	1 Oct. 91	9	y	y	100	1,476	9/9	6/3
21 July 92	10 Dec. 83	1 July 92	33		y	100	2,700	13/8	1/2
Benin									
22 June 89	31 Mar. 89	1 June 89	13	y		100	193	Menu	Menu
18 Dec. 91	31 Mar. 89	1 Jan. 92	19	y		100	152	Menu	Menu
27 June 93	31 Mar. 89	1 Aug. 93	29		y	100	25	Menu	Menu
24 Oct. 96	31 Mar. 89	24 Oct. 96	Stock		y	100	209		Menu
24 Oct. 00	31 Mar. 89	interim relief			y	100	7	Menu	Menu
Bolivia									
18 July 86	31 Dec. 85	1 July 86	12	y		100	449	9/6	5/0
14 Nov. 88	31 Dec. 85	1 Oct. 88	15	y	y	100	226	9/5	5/1
15 Mar. 90	31 Dec. 85	1 Jan. 90	24		y	100	276	Menu	Menu
24 Jan. 92	31 Dec. 85	1 Jan. 92	18		y	100	65	Menu	Menu
24 Mar. 95[b]	31 Dec. 85	1 Jan. 95	36		y	100	482	Menu	Menu
14 Dec. 95	31 Dec. 85	31 Dec. 95	Stock		y	100	881	Menu	Menu
30 Oct. 98	31 Dec. 85	1 Nov. 98	Stock		y	100	561	Menu	Menu
10 July 01	31 Dec. 85	1 Nov. 98	Stock		y	100	685	Menu	Menu
Bosnia and Herzegovina									
30 Oct. 98	2 Dec. 82	1 July 98	10			100	589	Menu	Menu
07 July 00	2 Dec. 82	12 July 00	12			100	9	Menu	Menu
Brazil									
23 Nov. 83	31 Mar. 83	1 Aug. 83	17	y		85	2,337	9/0	5/0
21 Jan. 87	31 Mar. 83	1 Jan. 85	30			100	4,178	5/6	3/0
29 July 88	31 Mar. 83	1 Aug. 88	20	y		100	4,992	9/6	5/0
26 Feb. 92	31 Mar. 83	1 Jan. 92	20	y		100	10,500	13/4	1/10
Bulgaria									
17 Apr. 91	1 Jan. 91	1 Apr. 91	12	y		100	640	10/0	6/6
14 Dec. 92	1 Jan. 91	1 Dec. 92	5	y		100	251	9/10	6/4
13 Apr. 94	1 Jan. 91	1 Apr. 94	13	y		100	200	9/5	5/11
Burkina Faso									
15 Mar. 91	1 Jan. 91	1 Mar. 91	15	y		100	71	Menu	Menu
7 May 93	1 Jan. 91	1 Apr. 93	33	y		100	36	Menu	Menu
20 June 96	1 Jan. 91	20 June 96	Stock		y	100	64	Menu	Menu
24 Oct. 00	1 Jan. 91	interim relief	30		y	100	249	Menu	Menu
20 June 02	1 Jan. 91	1 June 02	Stock		y	100	22	Menu	Menu

(Table continues on next page)

Table 6A.2 Multilateral debt-relief agreements with official creditors, January 1980–December 2002 *(continued)*

Country and date of agreement	Contract cutoff date	Consolidation period for current maturities: Start date	Consolidation period for current maturities: Length *(months)*	Consolidation includes: Arrears	Consolidation includes: Previously rescheduled debt	Share of debt consolidated *(percent)*	Amount consolidated *(millions of dollars)*	Repayment terms[a]: Maturity *(years/ months)*	Repayment terms[a]: Grace *(years/ months)*
Cambodia									
26 Jan. 95	31 Dec. 85	1 Jan. 95	30	y	y	100	249	Menu	Menu
Cameroon									
24 May 89	31 Dec. 88	1 Apr. 89	12	y		100	535	9/6	6/0
23 Jan. 92	31 Dec. 88	1 Jan. 92	9	y		100	1,080	19/5, 14/8	9/11, 8/2
24 Mar. 94	31 Dec. 88	1 Apr. 94	18	y	y	100	1,259	Menu	Menu
16 Nov. 95	31 Dec. 88	1 Oct. 95	12		y	100	1,129	Menu	Menu
24 Oct. 97	31 Dec. 88	1 Oct. 97	36	y		100	1,270	Menu	Menu
24 Jan. 01	31 Dec. 88	1 Jan. 01	35	y		100	1,300	Menu	Menu
Central African Republic									
12 June 81	1 Jan. 81	1 Jan. 81	12	y		85	72	8/6	4/0
9 July 83	1 Jan. 83	1 Jan. 83	12	y		90	13	9/6	5/0
22 Nov. 85	1 Jan. 83	1 July 85	18		y	90	14	9/3	4/9
14 Dec. 88	1 Jan. 83	1 Jan. 89	18		y	100	28	Menu	Menu
15 June 90	1 Jan. 83	1 Jan. 90	12	y	y	100	4	Menu	Menu
12 Apr. 94	1 Jan. 83	1 Apr. 94	12	y	y	100	32	Menu	Menu
25 Sept. 98	1 Jan. 83	1 Sept. 98	34	y	y	100	23	Menu	Menu
Chad									
24 Oct. 89	30 June 89	1 Oct. 89	15	y		100	24	Menu	Menu
28 Feb. 95	30 June 89	1 Apr. 95	12	y		100	24	Menu	Menu
14 June 96	30 June 89	1 Jan. 96	32	y	y	100	12	Menu	Menu
13 June 01	30 June 89	1 May 01	24	y	y	100	15	Menu	Menu
Chile									
17 July 85	1 Jan. 85	1 July 85	18			65	146	6/3	2/9
2 Apr. 87	1 Jan. 85	15 Apr. 87	21			85	157	6/2	2/7
Congo, Democratic Republic of									
9 July 81	1 Jan. 79	1 Jan. 81	24			90	500	9/6	4/0
20 Dec. 83	30 June 83	1 Jan. 84	12	y	y	95	1,497	10/6	5/0
18 Sept. 85	30 June 83	1 Jan. 85	15		y	95	408	9/5	4/11
15 May 86	30 June 83	1 Apr. 86	12		y	100	429	9/6	4/0
18 May 87	30 June 83	1 Apr. 87	13	y	y	100	671	14/6	6/0
23 June 89	30 June 83	1 June 89	13	y	y	100	1,530	Menu	Menu
13 Sept. 02	30 June 83	1 July 02	36	y	y	100	9,000	Menu	Menu
Congo, Republic of									
18 July 86	1 Jan. 86	1 Aug. 86	20	y		95	756	9/2	3/8
13 Sept. 90[c]	1 Jan. 86	1 Sept. 90	21	y	y	100	1,052	14/3	5/9
30 June 94[c]	1 Jan. 86	1 July 94	11	y	y	100	1,175	19/7, 14/7	10/1, 5/1
16 July 96	1 Jan. 86	30 June 96	36	y	y	100	1,758	Menu	Menu
Costa Rica									
11 Jan. 83	1 July 82	1 July 82	18	y		85	136	8/3	3/9
22 Apr. 85	1 July 82	1 Jan. 85	15	y		90	166	9/5	4/11
26 May 89	1 July 82	1 Apr. 89	14	y	y	100	182	9/5	4/11
17 July 91	1 July 82	1 July 91	9	y	y	100	139	9/7	5/1
22 June 93	1 July 82	Arrears as of 31 June 93		y		100	58	6/6	2/0

Table 6A.2 Multilateral debt-relief agreements with official creditors, January 1980–December 2002 *(continued)*

Country and date of agreement	Contract cutoff date	Consolidation period for current maturities: Start date	Consolidation period for current maturities: Length *(months)*	Consolidation includes: Arrears	Consolidation includes: Previously rescheduled debt	Share of debt consolidated *(percent)*	Amount consolidated *(millions of dollars)*	Repayment terms[a]: Maturity *(years/ months)*	Repayment terms[a]: Grace *(years/ months)*
Côte d'Ivoire									
4 May 84	1 July 83	1 Dec. 83	13			100	230	8/6	4/0
25 June 85	1 July 83	1 Jan. 85	12			100	213	8/6	4/0
27 June 86	1 July 83	1 Jan. 86	36			Var.	370	8/7	4/1
18 Dec. 87	1 July 83	1 Jan. 88	16	y	y	100	567	9/4	5/10
18 Dec. 89	1 July 83	1 Jan. 90	16	y	y	100	934	13/4	5/10
20 Nov. 91	1 July 83	1 Oct. 91	12	y	y	100	806	14/6	8/0
22 Mar. 94	1 July 83	1 Mar. 94	37	y	y	100	1,849	Menu	Menu
24 Apr. 98	1 July 83	1 Apr. 98	36	y	y	100	1,402	Menu	Menu
10 Apr. 02	1 July 83	1 Apr. 02	33	y	y	100	2,300	Menu	Menu
Croatia									
21 Mar. 95	2 Dec. 82	1 Jan. 95	12	y	y	100	861	13/7	2/1
Cuba									
1 Mar. 83	1 Sept. 82	1 Sept. 82	16			100	426		
19 July 84	1 Sept. 82	1 Jan. 84	12			100	204	9/0	5/6
18 July 85	1 Sept. 82	1 Jan. 85	12			100	156	9/0	5/6
16 July 86	1 Sept. 82	1 Jan. 86	12		y	100	..	9/6	5/6
Djibouti									
25 May 00		31 Oct. 99	24	y		100	17	10/0	6/0
Dominican Republic									
21 May 85	30 June 84	1 Jan. 85	15	y		90	290	9/5	4/11
22 Nov. 91	30 June 84	1 Oct. 91	18	y	y	100	850	14/3	7/9
Ecuador									
28 July 83	1 Jan. 83	1 June 83	12			85	142	7/6	3/0
24 Apr. 85	1 Jan. 83	1 Jan. 85	36	y		Var.	450	7/6	3/0
20 Jan. 88	1 Jan. 83	1 Jan. 88	14	y		100	438	9/5	4/11
24 Oct. 89	1 Jan. 83	1 Nov. 89	14	y	y	100	397	9/5	5/11
20 Jan. 92	1 Jan. 83	1 Jan. 92	12	y	y	100	339	19/5, 14/6	9/11, 8/0
27 June 94	1 Jan. 83	1 July 94	6	y	y	100	293	19/9, 14/9	10/3, 8/3
15 Sept. 00	1 Jan. 83	1 May 00	12	y	y	100	887	19/9, 17/9	10/3, 8/3
Egypt, Arab Rep. of									
22 May 87	31 Oct. 86	1 Jan. 87	18	y		100	6,350	9/3	4/9
25 May 91	31 Oct. 86	Balances: 30 June 91		y		100	27,864	Menu	Menu
El Salvador									
17 Sept. 90[c]	1 Sept. 90	1 Sept. 90	13	y		100	135	19/6, 14/6	10/0, 8/0
Equatorial Guinea									
22 July 85	1 July 84	1 Jan. 85	18	y		100	38	9/0	4/6
1 Mar. 89	1 July 84	Arrears as of 31 Dec. 88		y	y	100	10	Menu	Menu
2 Apr. 92*	1 July 84	1 Jan. 92	12	y	y	100	32	Menu	Menu
15 Dec. 94*	1 July 84		21	y	y	100	51	Menu	Menu
Ethiopia									
16 Dec. 92	31 Dec. 89	1 Dec. 92	35	y		100	441	Menu	Menu
24 Jan. 97	31 Dec. 89	1 Jan. 97	34	y		100	184	Menu	Menu
5 Apr. 01	31 Dec. 89	1 Mar. 01	36	y	y	100	430	Menu	Menu

(Table continues on next page)

Table 6A.2 Multilateral debt-relief agreements with official creditors, January 1980–December 2002 *(continued)*

Country and date of agreement	Contract cutoff date	Consolidation period for current maturities: Start date	Consolidation period for current maturities: Length *(months)*	Consolidation includes: Arrears	Consolidation includes: Previously rescheduled debt	Share of debt consolidated *(percent)*	Amount consolidated *(millions of dollars)*	Repayment terms[a]: Maturity *(years/months)*	Repayment terms[a]: Grace *(years/months)*
Gabon									
21 Jan. 87	1 July 86	21 Sept. 86	15			100	387	9/5	3/11
21 Mar. 88	1 July 86	1 Jan. 88	12			100	326	9/6	5/0
19 Sept. 89	1 July 86	1 Sept. 89	16	y		100	545	10/0	4/0
24 Oct. 91[d]	1 July 86	1 Oct. 91	15	y	y	100	498	8/0	2/0
15 Apr. 94	1 July 86	1 Apr. 94	12	y	y	100	1,360	14/6	2/0
12 Dec. 95	1 July 86	1 Dec. 95	36	y	y	100	1,030	13/6	1/0
15 Dec. 00	1 July 86	1 Oct. 00	24	y	y	100	687	12/0	3/0
Gambia, The									
19 Sept. 86	1 July 86	1 Oct. 86	12	y		100	17	9/6	5/0
Georgia									
6 Mar. 01	1 Nov. 99	1 Jan. 01	24			100	58	20/0, 20/0	10/0, 3/0
Ghana									
29 Mar. 96	1 Jan. 93	Arrears as of 1 July 95				100	93	4/5	1/0
10 Dec. 01	1 Jan. 93	1 June 01	8	y	y	100	199	Menu	Menu
16 May 02	20 June 99	1 Feb. 02	10			100	160	Menu	Menu
Guatemala									
25 Mar. 93	1 Jan. 91	Arrears as of 31 Mar. 93				100	440	19/6, 14/6	10/0, 8/0
Guinea									
18 Apr. 86	1 Jan. 86	1 Jan. 86	14	y		95	196	9/4	4/11
12 Apr. 89	1 Jan. 86	1 Jan. 89	12	y	y	100	123	Menu	Menu
18 Nov. 92	1 Jan. 86	Arrears as of 31 Dec. 92		y	y	100	203	Menu	Menu
25 Jan. 95	1 Jan. 86	1 Jan. 95	12	y	y	100	156	Menu	Menu
26 Feb. 97	1 Jan. 86	1 Jan. 97	36	y	y	100	123	Menu	Menu
15 May 01	1 Jan. 86	1 Dec. 00	40	y	y	100	151	Menu	Menu
Guinea-Bissau									
27 Oct. 87	31 Dec. 86	1 July 87	18	y		100	25	19/3	9/9
26 Oct. 89	31 Dec. 86	1 Oct. 89	15	y	y	100	21	Menu	Menu
23 Feb. 95	31 Dec. 86	1 Jan. 95	36	y	y	100	195	Menu	Menu
26 Jan. 01	31 Dec. 86	1 Dec. 00	40	y	y	100	141	Menu	Menu
Guyana									
23 May 89	31 Dec. 88	1 Jan. 89	14	y		100	195	19/5	9/11
12 Sept. 90	31 Dec. 88	1 Sept. 90	35	y	y	100	123	Menu	Menu
6 May 93	31 Dec. 88	1 Aug. 93	17	y	y	100	39	Menu	Menu
23 May 96	31 Dec. 88	23 May 96	Stock	y	y	100	793	Menu	Menu
25 June 99	31 Dec. 88	23 May 99	Stock	y	y	100	240	Menu	Menu
Haiti									
30 May 95	1 Oct. 93	31 Mar. 95	12	y		100	117	Menu	Menu
Honduras									
14 Sept. 90[c]	1 June 90	1 Sept. 90	11	y		100	280	19/7, 14/7	8/1, 8/1
26 Oct. 92	1 June 90	1 Oct. 92	34	y	y	100	180	Menu	Menu
29 Feb. 96	1 June 90	30 Jan. 95	12	y	y		112	Menu	Menu
13 Apr. 99	1 June 90	1 Apr. 99	36	y	y	100	411	Menu	Menu
Indonesia*									
28 Sept. 98	1 July 97	1 Aug. 98	20			100	4,176	11/0	3/0
13 April 00	1 July 97	1 Apr. 00	24			100	5,440	14/8	3/3
12 April 02	1 July 97	1 Apr. 02	21			100	5,400	20/0, 18/0	10/0, 5/0

Table 6A.2 Multilateral debt-relief agreements with official creditors, January 1980–December 2002 *(continued)*

Country and date of agreement	Contract cutoff date	Consolidation period for current maturities: Start date	Consolidation period for current maturities: Length *(months)*	Consolidation includes: Arrears	Consolidation includes: Previously rescheduled debt	Share of debt consolidated *(percent)*	Amount consolidated *(millions of dollars)*	Repayment terms[a]: Maturity *(years/months)*	Repayment terms[a]: Grace *(years/months)*
Jamaica									
16 July 84	1 Oct. 83	1 Jan. 84	15	y		100	105	8/5	3/11
19 July 85	1 Oct. 83	1 Apr. 85	12			100	62	9/6	4/0
5 Mar. 87	1 Oct. 83	1 Jan. 87	15	y		100	124	9/5	4/11
24 Oct. 88	1 Oct. 83	1 June 88	18		y	100	147	9/3	4/9
26 Apr. 90	1 Oct. 83	1 Dec. 89	18		y	100	179	9/3	4/9
19 July 91[c]	1 Oct. 83	1 June 91	13		y	100	127	19/6, 14/6	8/9, 6/0
25 Jan. 93[c]	1 Oct. 83	1 Oct. 92	36		y	100	291	18/6, 13/6	9/0, 5/0
Jordan									
19 July 89	1 Jan. 89	1 July 89	18	y		100	587	9/3	4/9
28 Feb. 92	1 Jan. 89	1 Jan. 92	18	y		100	771	19/5, 14/3	9/11, 7/9
28 June 94[c]	1 Jan. 89	1 July 94	35	y	y	100	1,147	18/7, 16/7	9/1, 2/1
23 May 97[c]	1 Jan. 89	1 June 97	21	y	y	100	400	19/2, 14/6	9/8, 2/8
20 May 99	1 Jan. 89	1 Apr. 99	36	y	y	100	821	20/0, 18/0	10/0, 3/0
11 July 02	1 Jan. 89	1 Jan. 02	72		y	100	1,200	9/5, 14/6	
Kenya									
19 Jan. 94	31 Dec. 91	Arrears as of 31 Dec. 93		y		100	535	7/9	1/3
15 Nov. 00	31 Dec. 91	1 July 00	12	y		100	302	20/0, 14/6	10/0, 3/0
Kyrgyz Republic									
7 Mar. 02	31 Aug. 01	6 Dec. 01	36			100	99	20/0, 20/0	10/0, 5/0
Liberia									
19 Dec. 80	1 Jan. 80	1 July 80	18			90	35	7/9	3/3
16 Dec. 81	1 Jan. 80	1 Jan. 82	18			90	25	7/11	3/3
22 Dec. 83	1 Jan. 83	1 July 83	12			90	17	8/6	4/0
17 Dec. 84	1 Jan. 83	1 July 84	12			90	17	9/6	5/0
Macedonia, FYR									
17 July 95	2 Dec. 82	1 July 95	12	y	y	100	288	14/7	3/1
Madagascar									
30 Apr. 81	1 Jan. 81	1 Jan. 81	18	y		85	140	8/3	3/9
13 July 82	1 Jan. 82	1 July 82	12	y		85	107	8/3	3/9
23 Mar. 84	1 July 83	1 July 83	18		y	95	89	10/3	4/9
22 May 85	1 July 83	1 Jan. 85	15		y	100	128	10/5	4/11
23 Oct. 86	1 July 83	1 Apr. 86	21		y	100	212	9/2	4/8
28 Oct. 88	1 July 83	1 Apr. 88	21	y	y	100	254	Menu	Menu
10 July 90	1 July 83	1 June 90	13	y	y	100	139	Menu	Menu
26 Mar. 97	1 July 83	1 Jan. 97	35	y	y	100	1,247	Menu	Menu
4 Sep. 00	1 July 83	1 Jan. 00	12	y	y	100	34	Menu	Menu
7 Mar. 01	1 July 83	1 Dec. 00	38	y	y	100	254	Menu	Menu
Malawi									
22 Sept. 82	1 Jan. 82	1 July 82	12			85	25	8/0	3/6
27 Oct. 83	1 Jan. 82	1 July 83	12			85	26	8/0	3/6
22 Apr. 88	1 Jan. 82	1 Apr. 88	14	y	y	100	27	19/5	9/11
25 Jan. 01	1 Jan. 97	1 Dec. 00	36	y	y	100	68	Menu	Menu
Mali									
27 Oct. 88	1 Jan. 88	1 July 88	16	y		100	63	Menu	Menu
22 Nov. 89	1 Jan. 88	1 Nov. 89	26		y	100	44	Menu	Menu
29 Oct. 92	1 Jan. 88	1 Oct. 92	35	y	y	100	20	Menu	Menu
20 May 96	1 Jan. 88	20 May 96	Stock	y	y	100	33	Menu	Menu
25 Oct. 00	1 Jan. 88	interim relief	12		y	100	4	Menu	Menu

(Table continues on next page)

Table 6A.2 Multilateral debt-relief agreements with official creditors, January 1980–December 2002 *(continued)*

		Consolidation period for current maturities		Consolidation includes				Repayment terms[a]	
Country and date of agreement	Contract cutoff date	Start date	Length *(months)*	Arrears	Previously rescheduled debt	Share of debt consolidated *(percent)*	Amount consolidated *(millions of dollars)*	Maturity *(years/ months)*	Grace *(years/ months)*
Mauritania									
27 Apr. 85	31 Dec. 84	1 Jan. 85	15	y		90	68	8/3	3/9
16 May 86	31 Dec. 84	1 Apr. 86	12			95	27	8/6	4/0
15 June 87	31 Dec. 84	1 Apr. 87	14			95	90	14/5	5/0
19 June 89	31 Dec. 84	1 June 89	12	y	y	100	52	Menu	Menu
25 Jan. 93	31 Dec. 84	1 Jan. 93	24	y	y	100	218	Menu	Menu
28 June 95	31 Dec. 84	1 Jan. 95	36	y	y	100	66	Menu	Menu
16 Mar. 00	31 Dec. 84	1 July 99	36	y	y	100	100	Menu	Menu
8 July 02	31 Dec. 84	1 July 02	Stock		y	100	188	Menu	Menu
Mexico									
22 June 83*	20 Dec. 82	1 July 83	6	y		90	1,199	5/6	3/0
7 Sept. 86	31 Dec. 85	22 Sept. 86	18			100	1,912	8/3	3/9
30 May 89	31 Dec. 85	1 June 89	36			100	2,400	9/7	6/1
Morocco									
25 Oct. 83	1 May 83	1 Sept. 83	16	y		85	1,152	7/3	3/9
17 Sept. 85	1 May 83	1 Sept. 85	18	y		90	1,124	8/3	3/9
6 Mar. 87	1 May 83	1 Mar. 87	16		y	100	1,008	9/3	4/9
26 Oct. 88	1 May 83	1 July 88	18		y	100	969	9/3	4/9
11 Sept. 90[c]	1 May 83	1 Jan. 90	15		y	100	1,390	19/5, 14/5	9/11, 7/11
27 Feb. 92[c]	1 May 83	1 Feb. 92	11	y	y	100	1,303	19/5, 14/7	9/11, 8/1
Mozambique									
25 Oct. 84	1 Feb. 84	1 July 84	12	y		95	283	10/6	5/0
16 June 87	1 Feb. 84	1 June 87	19	y		100	361	19/3	9/9
14 June 90	1 Feb. 84	1 July 90	30	y	y	100	719	Menu	Menu
23 Mar. 93	1 Feb. 84	1 Jan. 94	24		y	100	440	Menu	Menu
21 Nov. 96	1 Feb. 84	1 Nov. 96	36	y	y	100	664	Menu	Menu
9 July 99	1 Feb. 84	1 July 99	Stock	y	y	100	1,860	Menu	Menu
15 Mar. 00	1 Feb. 84	deferral	12	y	y	100	36	Menu	Menu
20 Nov. 00	1 Feb. 84	1 Sept. 01	Stock	y	y	100	2,234	Menu	Menu
Nicaragua									
17 Dec. 91	1 Nov. 88	1 Jan. 92	15	y	y	100	722	Menu	Menu
21 Mar. 95	1 Nov. 88	1 Apr. 95	27	y	y	100	783	Menu	Menu
22 Apr. 98	1 Nov. 88	1 Mar. 98	36	y	y	100	214	Menu	Menu
13 Dec. 02	1 Nov. 88	1 Oct. 02	36		y	100	579	Menu	Menu
Niger									
14 Nov. 83	1 July 83	1 Oct. 83	12			90	36	8/6	4/6
30 Nov. 84	1 July 83	1 Oct. 84	14			90	26	9/5	4/11
21 Nov. 85	1 July 83	1 Dec. 85	12			90	38	9/6	5/0
20 Nov. 86	1 July 83	3 Dec. 86	12			100	34	9/6	5/0
21 Apr. 88	1 July 83	5 Dec. 87	13			100	37	19/6	10/0
16 Dec. 88	1 July 83	1 Jan. 89	12			100	48	Menu	Menu
18 Sept. 90	1 July 83	1 Sept. 90	28	y	y	100	116	Menu	Menu
4 Mar. 94	1 July 83	1 Jan. 94	15	y	y	100	160	Menu	Menu
19 Mar. 96	1 July 83	1 Dec. 96	31	y	y	100	128	Menu	Menu
25 Jan. 01	1 July 83	1 Dec. 00	36	y	y	100	115	Menu	Menu
Nigeria									
16 Dec. 86	1 Oct. 85	1 Oct. 86	15	y		100	6,251	6/6	2/0
3 Mar. 89	1 Oct. 85	1 Jan. 89	16	y		100	5,600	9/4	4/10
18 Jan. 91[c]	1 Oct. 85	1 Jan. 91	15	y		100	3,300	19/5, 14/5	9/11, 7/11
12 Dec. 00	1 Oct. 85	1 Jan. 00	12	y		100	23,100	19/5, 14/5	9/11, 7/11

Table 6A.2 Multilateral debt-relief agreements with official creditors, January 1980–December 2002 *(continued)*

Country and date of agreement	Contract cutoff date	Consolidation period for current maturities: Start date	Consolidation period for current maturities: Length *(months)*	Consolidation includes: Arrears	Consolidation includes: Previously rescheduled debt	Share of debt consolidated *(percent)*	Amount consolidated *(millions of dollars)*	Repayment terms[a]: Maturity *(years/ months)*	Repayment terms[a]: Grace *(years/ months)*
Pakistan									
14 Jan. 81*	1 July 80	15 Jan. 81	18			90	263	Variable	Variable
30 Jan. 99	30 Sept. 97	1 Jan. 99	24	y	y	100	3,250	20/0, 18/0	10/0, 3/0
23 Jan. 01	30 Sept. 97	1 Dec. 00	10	y	y	100	3,250	20/0, 18/0	10/0, 3/0
14 Dec. 01	30 Sept. 97	30 Nov. 01	stock	y	y	100	12,500	38/0, 23/0	15/0, 5/0
Panama									
19 Sept. 85	31 Dec. 84	15 Sept. 85	16			50	19	7/4	2/10
14 Nov. 90[c]	31 Dec. 84	1 Nov. 90	17	y	y	100	200	9/4	4/10
Peru									
26 July 83	1 Jan. 83	1 May 83	12			90	466	7/6	3/0
5 June 84	1 Jan. 83	1 May 84	15			90	704	8/5	4/11
17 Sept. 91[c]	1 Jan. 83	1 Oct. 91	15	y	y	100	5,910	19/5, 14/5	9/11, 7/11
4 May 93[c]	1 Jan. 83	1 Jan. 93	39		y	100	1,527	18/5, 13/5	8/11, 6/11
20 July 96	1 Jan. 83	30 Apr. 96	Stock				6,724	17/0, 19/3	0/6, 2/0
Philippines									
21 Dec. 84	1 Apr. 84	1 Jan. 85	18	y		100	757	9/3	4/9
22 Jan. 87	1 Apr. 84	1 Jan. 87	18			100	862	9/3	4/9
26 May 89	1 Apr. 84	1 June 89	25	y		100	1,850	9/0	5/6
20 June 91[c]	1 Apr. 84	1 July 91	14		y	100	1,096	19/5, 14/5	9/11, 7/11
19 July 94[d]	1 Apr. 84	1 Aug. 94	17	y	y	100	586	19/4, 14/4	9/10, 7/10
Poland									
27 Apr. 81*	1 Jan. 80	1 May 81	8	y		90	2,110	7/6	4/0
15 July 85*	1 Jan. 84	1 Jan. 82	36	y		100	10,930	10/6	5/0
19 Nov. 85*	1 Jan. 84	1 Jan. 86	12			100	1,400	9/2	4/8
16 Dec. 87*	1 Jan. 84	1 Jan. 88	12	y	y	100	9,027	9/0	4/6
16 Feb. 90	1 Jan. 84	1 Jan. 90	15	y	y	100	10,400	13/9	8/3
21 Apr. 91	1 Jan. 84	Balances: 30 Mar. 91		y	y	100	29,871	Menu	Menu
Romania									
9 July 82	1 Jan. 82	1 Jan. 82	12	y		80	234	6/0	3/0
18 May 83	1 Jan. 82	1 Jan. 83	12			60	736	6/0	3/0
Russian Federation									
2 Apr. 93[f]	1 Jan. 91	1 Jan. 93	12	y		100	14,363	10/0	6/0
2 June 94	1 Jan. 91	1 Jan. 94	12			100	7,100	15/2	2/9
3 June 95	1 Jan. 91	1 Jan. 95	12			100	6,400	15/4	2/10
15 Apr. 96	1 Jan. 91	1 Jan. 96	Stock			100	40,200	21/5	2/11
1 Aug. 99	1 Jan. 91	1 July 99	18	y	y	100	8,040	Variable	Variable
Rwanda									
21 July 98	31 Dec. 94	1 July 98	35			100	64	Menu	Menu
São Tomé and Principe									
16 May 00	1 Apr. 99	31 Mar. 00	37	y		100	28	Menu	Menu

(Table continues on next page)

Table 6A.2 Multilateral debt-relief agreements with official creditors, January 1980–December 2002 *(continued)*

Country and date of agreement	Contract cutoff date	Consolidation period for current maturities: Start date	Consolidation period for current maturities: Length *(months)*	Consolidation includes: Arrears	Consolidation includes: Previously rescheduled debt	Share of debt consolidated *(percent)*	Amount consolidated *(millions of dollars)*	Repayment terms[a]: Maturity *(years/ months)*	Repayment terms[a]: Grace *(years/ months)*
Senegal									
13 Oct. 81	1 July 81	1 July 81	12			85	75	8/6	4/0
29 Nov. 82	1 July 81	1 July 82	12			85	74	8/9	4/3
21 Dec. 83	1 Jan. 83	1 July 83	12			90	72	8/6	4/0
18 Jan. 85	1 Jan. 83	1 Jan. 85	18	y		95	122	8/3	3/9
21 Nov. 86	1 Jan. 83	1 July 86	16			100	65	9/4	4/10
17 Nov. 87	1 Jan. 83	1 Nov. 87	12			100	79	15/6	6/0
24 Jan. 89	1 Jan. 83	1 Nov. 88	14		y	100	143	Menu	Menu
12 Feb. 90	1 Jan. 83	1 Jan. 90	12	y	y	100	107	Menu	Menu
21 June 91	1 Jan. 83	1 July 91	12	y	y	100	114	Menu	Menu
3 Mar. 94	1 Jan. 83	1 Jan. 94	15	y	y	100	237	Menu	Menu
20 Apr. 95	1 Jan. 83	1 Apr. 95	29		y	100	169	Menu	Menu
17 June 98	1 Jan. 83	17 June 98	Stock	y	y	100	428	Menu	Menu
24 Oct. 00	1 Jan. 83		interim relief	y	y	100	21	Menu	Menu
Sierra Leone									
8 Nov. 80	1 July 79	1 July 79	30	y		90	37	9/6	4/0
8 Feb. 84	1 July 83	1 Jan. 84	12	y	y	90	25	10/0	5/0
19 Nov. 86	1 July 83	1 July 86	16	y	y	100	86	9/4	4/10
20 Nov. 92	1 July 83	1 Nov. 92	16	y	y	100	164	Menu	Menu
20 July 94	1 July 83	1 Aug. 94	17	y	y	100	42	Menu	Menu
25 Apr. 96	1 July 83	1 Jan. 96	24	y	y	100	39	Menu	Menu
16 Oct. 01	1 July 83	1 Oct. 01	36	y	y	100	180	Menu	Menu
Somalia									
6 Mar. 85	1 Oct. 84	1 Jan. 85	12	y		95	127	9/6	5/0
22 July 87	1 Oct. 84	1 Jan. 87	24	y	y	100	153	19/0	9/6
Sudan									
18 Mar. 82	1 July 81	1 July 81	18	y	y	90	203	9/6	4/6
4 Feb. 83	1 Jan. 83	1 Jan. 83	12		y	100	518	15/0	5/6
2 May 84	1 Jan. 84	1 Jan. 84	12		y	100	249	15/6	6/0
Tanzania									
18 Sept. 86	30 June 86	1 Oct. 86	12	y		100	1,046	9/6	5/0
13 Dec. 88	30 June 86	1 Jan. 89	6	y	y	100	377	Menu	Menu
16 Mar. 90	30 June 86	1 Jan. 90	12	y	y	100	199	Menu	Menu
21 Jan. 92	30 June 86	1 Jan. 92	30	y	y	100	691	Menu	Menu
21 Jan. 97	30 June 86	1 Dec. 96	36	y	y	100	1,608	Menu	Menu
14 Apr. 00	30 June 86	31 Mar. 00	36	y	y	100	714	Menu	Menu
17 Jan. 02	30 June 86	1 Nov. 02	Stock		y	100	973	Menu	Menu
Togo									
20 Feb. 81	1 July 80	1 Jan. 81	24			85	232	8/6	4/0
12 Apr. 83	1 Jan. 83	1 Jan. 83	12	y	y	90	300	9/6	5/0
6 June 84	1 Jan. 83	1 Jan. 84	16		y	95	75	9/4	4/10
24 June 85	1 Jan. 83	1 May 85	12			95	27	10/6	5/0
22 Mar. 88	1 Jan. 83	1 Jan. 88	15	y	y	100	139	15/5	7/11
20 June 89	1 Jan. 83	16 Apr. 89	14		y	100	76	Menu	Menu
9 July 90	1 Jan. 83	1 July 90	24		y	100	88	Menu	Menu
19 June 92[d]	1 Jan. 83	1 July 92	24		y	100	52	Menu	Menu
23 Feb. 95	1 Jan. 83	1 Feb. 95	33	y	y	100	237	Menu	Menu
Trinidad and Tobago									
25 Jan. 89	1 Sept. 88	1 Jan. 89	14	y		100	209	9/5	4/11
27 Apr. 90	1 Sept. 88	1 Mar. 90	13			100	110	8/4	3/10

Table 6A.2 Multilateral debt-relief agreements with official creditors, January 1980–December 2002 *(continued)*

Country and date of agreement	Contract cutoff date	Consolidation period for current maturities: Start date	Consolidation period for current maturities: Length *(months)*	Consolidation includes: Arrears	Consolidation includes: Previously rescheduled debt	Share of debt consolidated *(percent)*	Amount consolidated *(millions of dollars)*	Repayment terms[a]: Maturity *(years/ months)*	Repayment terms[a]: Grace *(years/ months)*
Turkey									
23 July 80*	30 June 80	1 July 80	36	y	y	90	3,000	9/0	4/6
Uganda									
18 Nov. 81	1 July 81	1 July 81	12	y		90	30	9/0	4/6
1 Dec. 82	1 July 81	1 July 82	12			90	19	9/0	4/6
19 June 87	1 July 81	1 July 87	12	y	y	100	170	14/6	6/0
26 Jan. 89	1 July 81	1 Jan. 89	18	y	y	100	89	Menu	Menu
17 June 92	1 July 81	1 July 92	17	y	y	100	39	Menu	Menu
20 Feb. 95	1 July 81	1 Feb. 95	Stock	y	y	100	110	Menu	Menu
24 Apr. 98	1 July 81	1 Apr. 98	Stock		y	100	148	Menu	Menu
12 Sept. 00	1 July 81	1 Sept. 00	Stock		y	100	150	Menu	Menu
Ukraine									
13 July 01	31 Dec. 98	19 Dec. 00	22	y	y	100	580	12/0	3/0
Vietnam									
14 Dec. 93	1 Jan. 90	Arrears as of 31 Dec. 93		y		100	791	Menu	Menu
Yemen, Rep. of									
24 Sept. 96	1 Jan. 93	1 Sept. 96	10	y		100	113	Menu	Menu
20 Nov. 97	1 Jan. 93	1 Nov. 97	36	y		100	1,444	Menu	Menu
14 June 01	1 Jan. 93	31 Dec. 00	Stock	y		100	420	Menu	Menu
Yugoslavia, Fed. Rep. (Serbia/ Montenegro)									
22 May 84*	2 Dec. 82	1 Jan. 84	12			100	500	6/6	4/0
24 May 85*	2 Dec. 82	1 Jan. 85	16			90	812	8/4	3/10
13 May 86*	2 Dec. 82	16 May 86	23			85	901	8/6	4/0
13 July 88*	2 Dec. 82	1 Apr. 88	15		y	100	1,291	9/5	5/11
16 Nov. 01	1 Apr. 88	20 Dec. 00	Stock		y	100	4,500	Menu	Menu
Zambia									
16 May 83	1 Jan. 83	1 Jan. 83	12	y		90	375	9/6	5/0
20 July 84	1 Jan. 83	1 Jan. 84	12	y	y	100	253	9/6	5/0
4 Mar. 86	1 Jan. 83	1 Jan. 86	12	y	y	100	371	9/6	5/0
12 July 90	1 Jan. 83	1 July 90	18	y	y	100	963	Menu	Menu
23 July 92	1 Jan. 83	1 July 92	33	y	y	100	917	Menu	Menu
27 Feb. 96	1 Jan. 83	1 Jan. 96	36	y	y	100	566	Menu	Menu
16 Apr. 99	1 Jan. 83	1 Apr. 99	36	y	y	100	1,060	Menu	Menu

a. Maturity is measured here from the end of the consolidation period to the date of the final amortization payment; the grace period is the time between the end of the consolidation period and the date of the first amortization payment. The secretariat of the Paris Club measures grace and maturity from the midpoint of the consolidation period. "Menu" terms refer to the options agreed to at the 1988 Toronto economic summit meeting.
b. The agreement signed in March 1995 covered a 36-month period, but a new agreement signed in December 1995 covers the stock of debt, starting 12 months after the beginning of the consolidation period of the previous agreement.
c. Agreement with a Paris Club–designated lower-middle-income country with heavy official debt. These agreements also allow for debt conversions, subject to the limit for each creditor country (for non-ODA debt) of US$10 million or 10 percent of the debt outstanding as of the beginning of the consolidation period, whichever is higher. Where two sets of figures for repayment terms (maturity and grace) are given, the first set represents official development assistance (ODA) debt and the second non-ODA debt.
d. Agreement was canceled.
e. Agreement was implemented in 1991 because of the agreement's conditionality on an IMF program, which took place in 1991.
f. Agreement follows the deferral signed in January 1992 by the former Soviet republics.
* The rescheduling was concluded outside of formal Paris Club auspices.
Note: The figures in this table are commitment values (amounts of agreed debt relief). They correspond to the disbursement figures (minus debt forgiveness, when applicable) for debt restructuring shown in the country tables of volume 2. All agreements shown in this table were negotiated through the Paris Club, except those indicated with an asterisk.
Sources: World Bank Debtor Reporting System; IMF data.

Notes

1. Note that a portion of bilaterals' contributions to multilateral agencies (second to the last line in the box table) also is devoted to administrative expenses rather than loans to developing countries.

2. These data cover grants to Part I and Part II countries (excluding an estimate for grants to Israel, which is not a developing country) and include only grants provided from the NGOs' own resources. Funds received from donor governments and channeled through NGOs are included under the statistics on aid.

3. We use general government expenditures to maintain a common definition across OECD countries.

4. This discussion is based on World Bank 2002e.

5. As an initial step, SDR 100 million was set aside to compensate for the loss of future repayments due to the use of grants rather than loans.

6. This section is based on World Bank 2002c.

7. The countries that have reached completion points are Bolivia, Burkina Faso, Mauritania, Mozambique, Tanzania, and Uganda.

8. These countries are Benin, Cameroon, Chad, Ethiopia, the Gambia, Ghana, Guinea, Guinea-Bissau, Guyana, Honduras, Madagascar, Malawi, Mali, Nicaragua, Niger, Rwanda, Sao Tome and Principe, Senegal, Sierra Leone, and Zambia.

9. In contrast, the export price index fell by 1.1 percent in other HIPCs that have reaced a decision point but not yet reached a completion point.

10. See World Bank 2001c. Of the six countries that have already reached their completion points, all except Uganda are in little danger of having their debt-to-export ratios go above the sustainability thresholds defined in the Initiative. Uganda has been adversely affected by the collapse of coffee prices, which has presented considerable challenges to Uganda's ability to achieve sustainable debt levels.

11. The additional assistance, if granted, would be based upon a full account of all debt relief provided by creditors, including additional debt forgiveness beyond HIPC relief provided or committed by official bilateral and commercial creditors. See World Bank 2001c.

12. For an in-depth analysis of the challenges facing postconflict countries, see World Bank 2001a.

13. Note that under the enhanced HIPC Initiative, eligibility for and the amount of debt relief are determined on the basis of actual information. Forecasts play no role.

14. World Bank 2001b.

15. Note that a portion of the IDA commitments included under investment loans is for projects that resemble budget support, as disbursements can be made against a wide variety of expenditures within the sector rather than being limited to specific investments.

16. Islam and Montenegro (2002) find that a higher ratio of primary exports relative to total exports is associated with poorer institutional quality, which they speculate may reflect the association between opportunities for rent seeking and institutional quality. Lane and Tornell (1996) show that resource-rich countries tend to have lower growth rates than resource-poor countries because of competition for rents among powerful elites (although it is hard to demonstrate empirically the link between resource endowments and growth rates).

17. The quality of governance may be influenced by numerous other factors such as religious or legal traditions, or colonial heritage. A convenient implication of using the *change* in the ICRG index from 1982 to 1995 as the dependent variable is that factors such as these, which do not vary over very long periods of time, are unlikely to matter much.

18. The equation is: change in bureaucratic quality = 3.96–0.86 initial bureaucratic quality–1.30 population growth + 1.14 GDP growth − 0.04 aid/GNI. R-squared is 0.53.

19. The equation is: change in bureaucratic quality = 1.4–1.04 initial bureaucratic quality + 0.6 initial GDP per capita − 0.21 population growth + 1.51 GDP growth–0.0 aid/GNI–3.43 aid fragmentation.

20. The first is a Herfindahl index calculated by summing the squared share of aid over all donor agencies. The index is then subtracted from one. The second is from counts of projects and programs provided by the Development Gateway's Accessible Information on Development Activities data base.

References

Alesina, Alberto, and Beatrice Weder. 1999. "Do Corrupt Governments Receive Less Foreign Aid?" NBER Working Paper 7108. National Bureau of Economic Research, Cambridge, Mass.

Birdsall, Nancy, Constantijn Claessens, and Ishac Diwan. 2002. "Will HIPC Matter? The Debt Game and Donor Behavior in Africa." Centre for Economic Policy Research Discussion Paper 3297. London.

Bulir, Ales, and A. Javier Hamann. 2001. "How Volatile and Unpredictable Are Aid Flows and What Are the Policy Implications?" Wider Discussion Paper 2001/143. World Institute for Development Economics Research, United Nations University, Tokyo.

Brautigam, Deborah. 1992. "Governance, Economy, and Foreign Aid." *Studies in Comparative International Development* 27(3): 3–25.

———. 2000. "Aid Dependence and Governance." Almqvist and Wiksell International, Stockholm.

Devarajan, Shantayanan, and Vinaya Swaroop. 1998. "The Implications of Foreign Aid Fungibility for Development Assistance." Policy Research Working Paper 2022, Development Research Group, World Bank, Washington, D.C.

DFID (U.K. Department for International Development). 2002. "Big Boost to UK Budget." *Developments: The International Development Magazine*, Issue 19.

Dollar, David, and Lant Pritchett. 1998. *Assessing Aid: What Works, What Doesn't, and Why*. New York: Oxford University Press.

"G-8 African Action Plan." G-8 Summit, 2002. www.g8.gc.ca/resources/documents-en.asp?#al.

Islam, Roumeen, and Claudio E. Montenegro. 2002. "What Determines the Quality of Institutions?" Background paper for *World Development Report 2002*. World Bank, Washington, D.C.

Kahn, Haider Ali, and Eiichi Hoshino. 1992. "Impact of Foreign Aid on the Fiscal Behavior of LDC Governments." *World Development* 20(4): 1481–88.

Knack, Stephen. 2001. "Aid-Dependence and the Quality of Governance: A Cross-Country Empirical Analysis." *Southern Economic Journal* 68(2): 310–29.

Lane, Philip R., and Aaron Tornell. 1996. "Power, Growth, and the Voracity Effect." *Journal of Economic Growth* 1(June): 213–41.

Lensink, Robert. 1992. "Magnitude and Determinants of Capital Flight: the Case for Six Sub-Saharan African Countries." *De Economist* 140(4): 515–30.

OECD (Organisation for Economic Co-operation and Development). 2002. "A Mixed Picture of Official Development Assistance in 2001." Press release, March 13, Paris.

Pillai, Vel. 1982. "External Economic Dependence and Fiscal Policy Imbalances in Developing Countries: A Case Study of Jordan." *Journal of Development Studies* 19: 5–18.

Stotsky, Janet G., and Asegedech Wolde Mariam. 1997. "Tax Effort in Sub-Saharan Africa." IMF Working Paper 97-107. International Monetary Fund, Washington, D.C.

World Bank. 2001a. "Assistance to Post-Conflict Countries and the HIPC Initiative." Development Committee Paper DC2001-0014. Washington, D.C. Processed. www.worldbank.org/hipc

———. 2001b. "The Challenge of Maintaining Long-Term External Debt Sustainability." Development Committee Paper DC2001-0013. Washington, D.C. Processed. www.worldbank.org/hipc

———. 2001c. "The Enhanced HIPC Initiative—Completion Point Considerations." IDA/SecM2001-0539/1. Washington, D.C. Processed.

———. 2002a. *World Development Indicators.* Washington, D.C.

———. 2002b. *Global Economic Prospects 2003.* Washington, D.C.

———. 2002c. "Heavily Indebted Poor Countries (HIPC) Initiative: Status of Implementation." Development Committee Paper DC2002-0020. World Bank, Washington, D.C.

———. 2002d. *Global Development Finance 2002.* Washington, D.C.

———. 2002e. "Additions to IDA Resources: Thirteenth Replenishment." Report from the Executive Directors of IDA to the Board of Governors of the World Bank. Washington, D.C.

7

Workers' Remittances: An Important and Stable Source of External Development Finance

Dilip Ratha

AS PRIVATE CAPITAL FLOWS HAVE DECLINED, workers' remittances have become an increasingly prominent source of external funding for many developing countries. This chapter examines the relative importance of workers' remittances as a source of development finance and discusses measures that industrial and developing countries could take to increase remittances. The main messages are:

- Remittance flows are the second-largest source, behind FDI, of external funding for developing countries. In 2001, workers' remittance receipts of developing countries stood at $72.3 billion, much higher than total official flows and private non-FDI flows, and 42 percent of total FDI flows to developing countries (table 7.1). Remittances to low-income countries were larger as a share of GDP and imports than were those to middle income countries. Remittances are also more stable than private capital flows, which often move pro-cyclically, thus raising incomes during booms and depressing them during downturns. By contrast, remittances are less volatile—and may even rise—in response to economic cycles in the recipient country. They are expected to rise significantly in the long term, once sluggish labor markets in G-7 economies recover and new procedures for scrutinizing international travelers become routine.
- Remittances are often invested by the recipients, particularly in countries with sound economic policies. Improvements in policies and relaxation of foreign exchange controls in the 1990s may have encouraged the use of remittances for investment.
- By strengthening financial-sector infrastructure and facilitating international travel, countries could increase remittance flows, thereby bringing more funds into formal channels. The transaction costs of fund transfers often exceed

Table 7.1 Remittances received and paid by developing countries in 2001
(billions of dollars)

	All developing	Low-income	Lower middle-income	Upper middle-income
Total remittance receipts	72.3	19.2	35.9	17.3
as % of GDP	1.3	1.9	1.4	0.8
as % of imports	3.9	6.2	5.1	2.7
as % of domestic investment	5.7	9.6	5.0	4.9
as % of FDI inflows	42.4	213.5	43.7	21.7
as % of total private capital inflows	42.9	666.1	44.9	20.2
as % of official flows	260.1	120.6	361.7	867.9
Other current transfers[a]	27.2	6.1	14.0	7.1
Remittances and other current transfers	99.5	25.3	49.9	24.4
Total remittance payments	22.0	1.2	1.7	19.1
excluding Saudi Arabia	6.9	1.2	1.7	4.0

a. Other current transfers include gifts, donations to charities, pensions received by currently retired expatriate workers, and so on. They may also include personal transfers by migrant workers to families back home. See data annex for more details.
Sources: IMF, *Balance of Payments Yearbook 2001;* World Bank, *World Development Indicators 2001.*

20 percent; reducing them by even 5 percentage points could generate annual savings of $3.5 billion for workers sending money home.

- Facilitating international labor mobility is an even more crucial—and controversial—means of increasing remittance flows to developing countries. Greater international migration could generate substantial benefits to the world economy. Developed countries remain wary of relaxing immigration policies, however, as it is feared that immigration would increase competition in local job markets and pose a fiscal burden on local tax payers. Developed countries also fear that large scale immigration may erode cultural values and undermine national security. Developing countries worry about a "brain drain" even though any output losses from emigration of skilled workers may be more than offset by remittances and positive network effects on trade and investment. One positive, though somewhat limited, step in the direction of greater international labor mobility is the so-called Mode-4 proposal for supplying services under consideration in the current round of the General Agreement on Trade in Services.

The first section of the chapter analyzes trends and cycles in workers' remittances in developing countries and compares them to other sources of foreign exchange earnings—among them exports, private capital, and official flows. The next section examines the impact of remittances on growth, investment, and income distribution in recipient economies. The third section discusses means of strengthening the infrastructure for sending remittances. The fourth section deals with international migration—the precondition for remittances. The final section outlines the near- and long-term outlooks for remittances flows to, and migration from, developing countries.

Trends and cycles in workers' remittances in developing countries

In 2001, remittances to developing countries from overseas resident and nonresident workers amounted to $72.3 billion or 1.3 percent of GDP (table 7.1).[1] Remittances were smaller than FDI inflows, but larger than international capital market flows during 1999–2001 (figure 7.1). For most of the 1990s, remittance receipts have exceeded official development assistance.

Figure 7.1 Workers' remittances and other inflows, 1998–2001

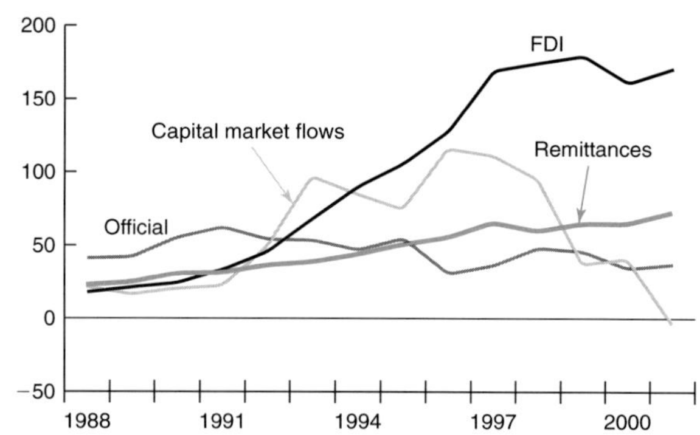

Sources: World Bank, *Global Development Finance*; IMF, *Balance of Payments Yearbook*, various years.

As a share of GDP and other key economic indicators, remittances are significantly higher in low-income countries than in other developing countries. In 2001, remittances to low-income countries were 1.9 percent of GDP and 6.2 percent of imports; in the upper-middle-income countries they were 0.8 percent of GDP and 2.7 percent of imports (figure 7.2). Although in nominal terms the top recipients of remittances included several large countries—India, Mexico, and the Philippines (figure 7.3)—remittances as a share of GDP were larger in low-income countries (see figure 7.4). Latin America and the Caribbean were the largest

Figure 7.2 Remittances as a share of GDP and of imports, 2001

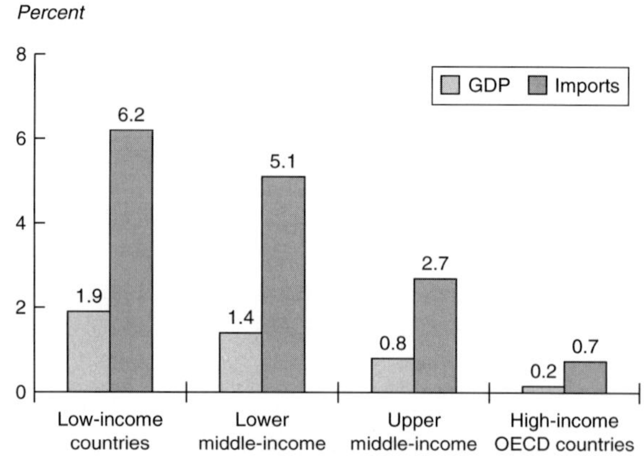

Source: World Bank staff calculations.

Figure 7.3 Top 20 developing-country recipients of workers' remittances, 2001

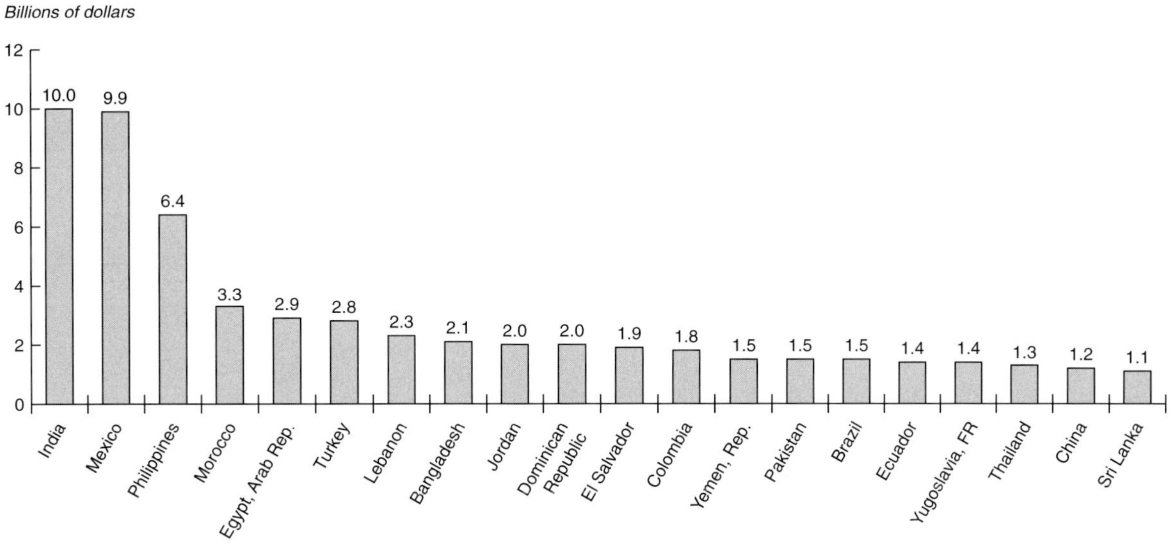

Source: IMF, *Balance of Payments Yearbook.*

Figure 7.4 Top 20 developing-country recipients of workers' remittances, 2001

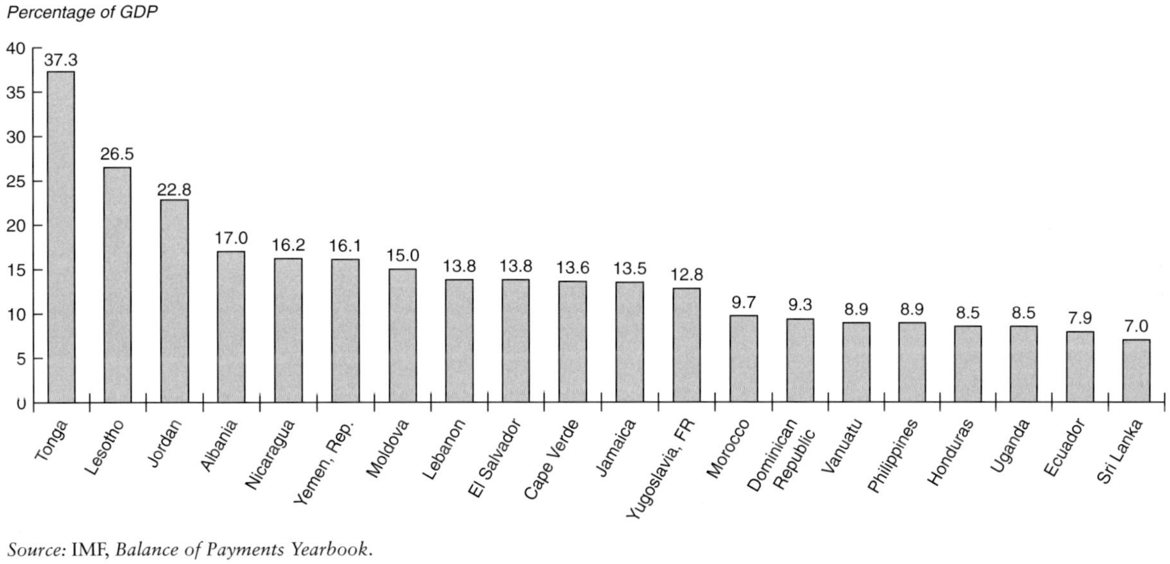

Source: IMF, *Balance of Payments Yearbook.*

recipient of remittances in nominal terms, but relative to the size of GDP, South Asia was the largest recipient, with remittances of nearly 2.5 percent of GDP in 2001 (table 7.2). Remittance flows to Sub-Saharan Africa were also significant.

Workers' remittances are more evenly spread among developing countries than are capital flows: the 10 countries that received the most remittances in 2001 received 60 percent of total remittances to developing countries, significantly below the top 10's share of GDP (68 percent), exports (72 percent), and FDI (74 percent).

The United States and Saudi Arabia are the largest sources of workers' remittances to developing countries. Other top sources are Germany, Belgium, and Switzerland (figure 7.5). Although it is difficult to disaggregate the remittance data, anecdotal evidence suggest that developing countries may have received nearly $18 billion in 2001 from the United States alone.[2] Until the mid-1990s,

Figure 7.5 Top 20 country sources of remittance payments, 2001

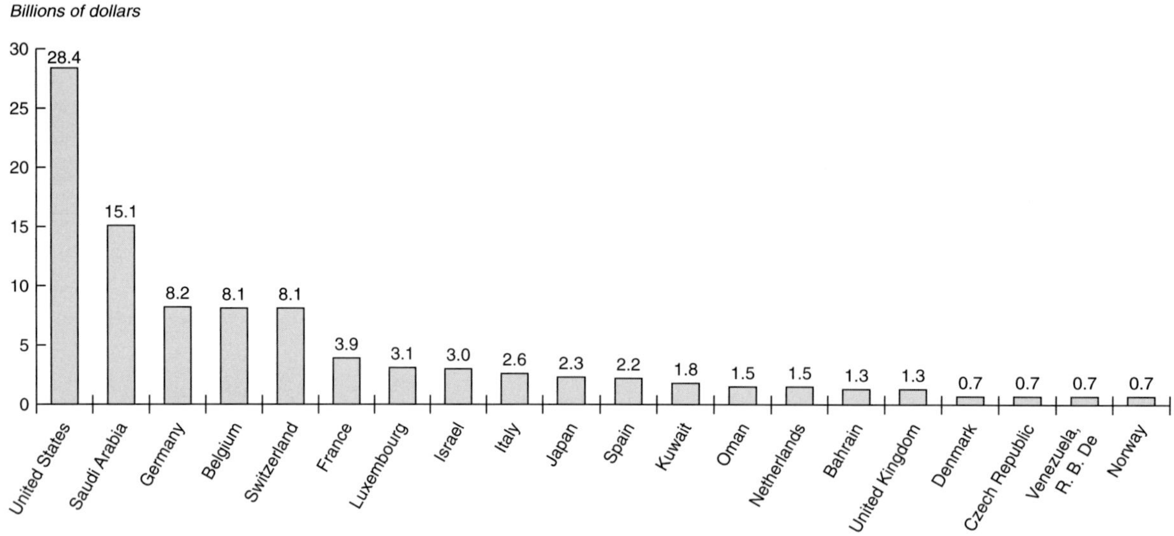

Source: IMF, *Balance of Payments Yearbook.*

Table 7.2 Workers' remittances received by developing countries, by region, 1999–2002

Billions of dollars	1999	2000	2001	2002
Total	67	66	72	80
East Asia and Pacific	11	10	10	11
Europe and Central Asia	8	9	9	10
Latin America and the Caribbean	17	19	23	25
Middle East and North Africa	12	11	14	14
South Asia	15	13	14	16
Sub-Saharan Africa	4	3	3	4
As a percentage GDP	1999	2000	2001	2002
Total	1.2	1.1	1.3	1.3
East Asia and Pacific	0.7	0.7	0.6	0.6
Europe and Central Asia	0.9	0.9	0.9	1.0
Latin America and the Caribbean	1.0	1.0	1.2	1.5
Middle East and North Africa	2.2	1.9	2.3	2.2
South Asia	2.6	2.3	2.3	2.5
Sub-Saharan Africa	1.3	0.8	1.0	1.3

Sources: IMF, *Balance of Payments Yearbook;* World Bank, *World Development Indicators.*

Figure 7.6 The top two sources of remittance payments, 1970–2001

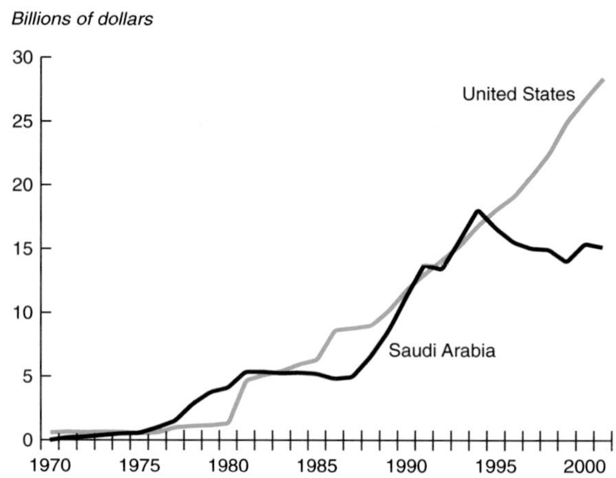

Source: IMF, *Balance of Payments Yearbook.*

when its economic boom (driven by oil exports) subsided, Saudi Arabia was the largest source of remittance payments in the world (figure 7.6), and it still is the largest source on a per capita basis.[3]

A relatively stable source of foreign exchange

Remittances were one of the least volatile sources of foreign exchange earnings for developing countries in the 1990s (see figure 7.1). While capital flows tend to rise during favorable economic cycles and fall in bad times, remittances appear to react less violently and show remarkable stability over time. For example, remittances to developing countries continued to rise steadily in 1998–2001 when private capital flows declined in the wake of the Asian financial crisis. Even the more stable components of capital flows—FDI and official flows—declined in 2000–01, while remittances have continued to rise.

Remittances intended for consumption (by recipient households) should be less volatile than those intended for investment. Migrants may increase remittances in times of economic hardship, especially in low-income countries where their families may depend significantly on remittances as a source of income and may live at close to subsistence levels. Economic downturns may also encourage workers to migrate abroad—and to begin transferring funds to families left behind.

Even when the purpose behind remittances is investment, remittances are less likely to suffer the sharp withdrawal or euphoric surges that characterize portfolio flows to emerging markets. Overseas residents are more likely to continue to invest in their home country despite economic adversity than are foreign investors, an effect that is similar to the home-bias in investment (World Bank 2001). This relative stability has encouraged some emerging market economies to use remittances as collateral against which to borrow on international capital markets on substantially better terms than they otherwise could (box 7.1).

The banking relationships associated with remittance transfers have also attracted some significant FDI deals in developing countries. For banks, intermediating funds transfers from overseas workers to families back home is a high margin business. Some authors estimate that remitters collected about $12 billion in fees in 2001 (Maldonado and Robledo 2002). While the size of this business itself is attractive to banks, new customers who start a relationship with a bank initially for remittance purposes also bring a host of other businesses. The large and fast-growing business opportunities associated with workers' remittances have attracted at least two major FDI deals in Mexico recently. Valued at $12.5 billion, the Citigroup-Banamex deal in 2001 is the single biggest investment south of the border for any U.S. company (*Wall Street Journal*, December 12, 2002). In December 2002, Bank of America paid Santander $1.6 billion for part of Serfin.

Despite greater overall stability, remittances do respond to dramatic changes in economic activity in recipient countries. They rose steadily in the Philippines as the investment climate improved in the early 1990s, becoming more volatile following the financial crisis in the late 1990s (figure 7.7). Similarly, Turkey's remittance receipts increased for most of the 1990s but suffered a decline as the economy slipped into crisis in 1999 and 2000 (figure 7.8). In both cases, however, the decline in remittances, and the volatility, were smaller than those of capital flows.

There is some evidence that remittances have been increasingly used for investment purposes in developing countries, especially in low-income countries. Some studies estimate that remittances from the United States are responsible for almost

Box 7.1 Securitizing future flows of workers' remittances

In recent years, many emerging market issuers have resorted to future-flow securitization to access international markets, often to avoid credit rationing in the face of deteriorating sovereign risks. Workers' remittances have been used quite frequently along with other future-flow receivables such as oil exports or credit card receivables (Ketkar and Ratha 2001). In the hierarchy of future flows that are amenable to international securitization, major international rating agencies rank electronic remittances in the same category as airline ticket receivables, credit card receivables, and telephone receivables, next only to crude oil exports.

For example, in August 2001 Banco do Brasil issued $300 million worth of bonds (with five year maturity) using as collateral future yen remittances from Brazilian workers in Japan. The terms of these bonds were significantly more generous than those available on sovereign issues. Rated BBB+ by Standard and Poors, these securities were several notches higher than Brazil's sovereign foreign currency rating BB– at the time. Other countries, such as El Salvador, Mexico, Panama, and Turkey, have also used future workers' remittance-backed securities to raise external financing. Assuming that about half of all recorded remittances pass through the banking system, and assuming an over-collateralization ratio of 5:1, developing country issuers could potentially raise about $7 billion a year using future remittance-backed securitization. However, developing countries should carefully weigh the trade-off between lower borrowing costs and longer maturities that securitized debt offers and the inflexibility associated with servicing such debt.

Source: Ketkar and Ratha 2001.

Figure 7.7 Remittances and private capital flows to the Philippines, 1978–2001

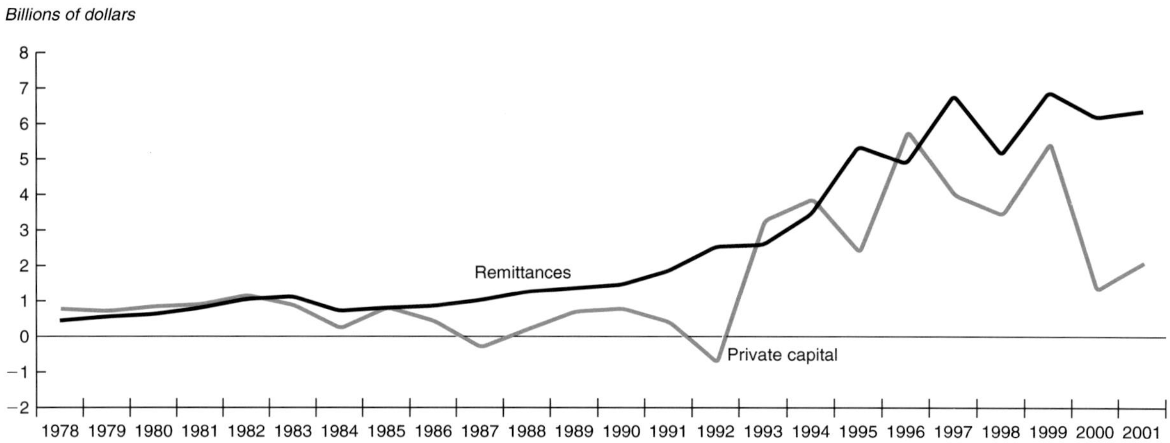

Sources: IMF, *Balance of Payments*; World Bank, *Global Development Finance* database.

Figure 7.8 Remittances and private capital flows to Turkey, 1978–2001

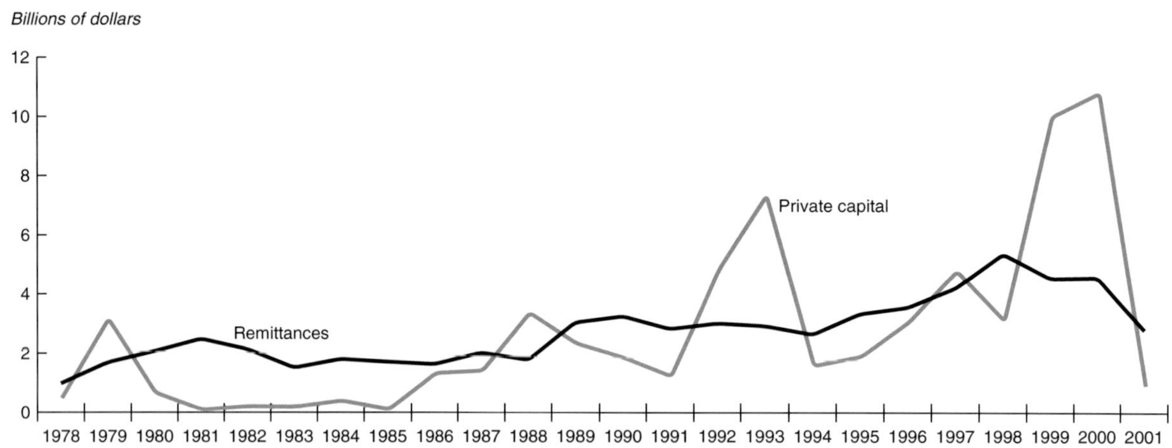

Sources: IMF, *Balance of Payments*; World Bank, *Global Development Finance* database.

one-fifth of the capital invested in microenterprises in urban Mexico (Woodruff and Zenteno 2001).[4] Similarly, in the Arab Republic of Egypt, a large proportion of returning migrants in the late 1980s set up their own enterprises using funds brought back from abroad[5] (McCormick and Wahba 2002). As low-income countries lifted exchange restrictions and liberalized their current and capital accounts in the 1990s, remittance receipts rose sharply, and the volatility of remittances also rose, presumably because these remittances were used for investment purposes (figure 7.9).[6]

Cross-country comparison reveals that remittances are affected by the investment climate in recipient countries in the same manner as capital flows—though to a much lesser degree. During 1996–2000, for example, remittance receipts averaged 0.5 percent of GDP in countries with a higher-than-median level of corruption (as indicated by the index of the International Corruption Research Group) compared to 1.9 percent in countries with lower-than-median corruption (table 7.3). Countries that were more open (in terms of their trade/GDP ratio) or more financially developed (M2/GDP) also received larger remittances.

In contrast to capital flows, however, remittances were significantly higher in countries that were high-risk (as measured by their *Institutional Investor* rating) and had a high level of debt relative to GDP.[7] This is consistent with the finding,

Figure 7.9 Volatility of remittances in the 1990s

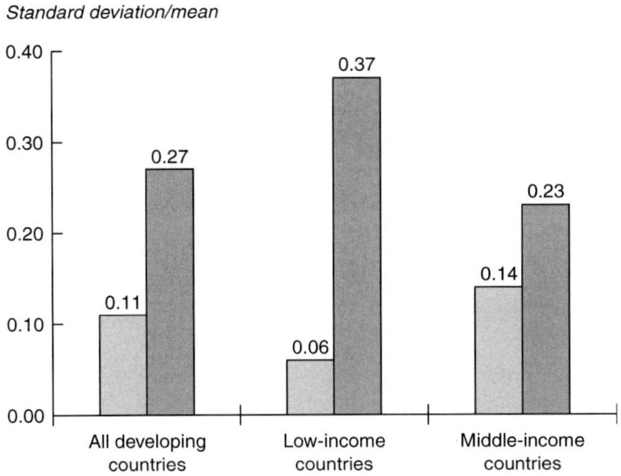

Source: World Bank staff estimates.

Table 7.3 Workers' remittance receipts in developing countries relative to key indicators

(as a percentage of GDP, 1996–2000)

	High	Low
Corruption	0.5	1.9
Inequality (Gini index)	0.9	1.5
M2/GDP	1.2	0.9
Trade/GDP	1.2	1.0
Debt/GDP	2.3	0.8
Country risk (*Institutional Investor* rating)	2.4	1.0

Note: High and low usually refer to above and below the median for the concerned variable. The numbers reported are the sum of remittances of all countries in the group divided by the sum of GDP of the same countries. Average remittances and average GDP during 1996–2000 are used for each country included in these calculations. Lesotho is excluded from these computations.
Sources: World Bank, *World Development Indicators*; World Bank, *Global Development Finance*; IMF balance-of-payments data, World Bank staff estimates.

mentioned earlier, that low-income countries, which are usually high-risk, receive relatively more remittances as a share of GDP than do countries with higher incomes. In fact, in 1996–2000 remittances tended to be higher in poor countries that had lower than median growth rates, probably because most remittances to low-income countries that are performing poorly are for consumption. By contrast, middle-income countries with higher-than-median growth rates had higher remittances, presumably because remittances tend to behave more like investment flows in these countries (table 7.4).

As one would expect, remittance flows are affected by the economic cycle of the source countries. An upturn in the source country increases the income earned by migrant workers. It also attracts more migrants looking for better incomes.[8] For example, remittance payments from the United States surged in tandem with the strong economic growth in the second half of the 1990s. Led by the information-technology sector, the boom caused the United States to revise its immigration policies to enable companies to hire more technology workers from abroad.[9] Remittance payments from Saudi Arabia rose during the oil boom years of the 1970s and early 1980s, but declined in the mid-1980s as oil prices fell, the budget deficit mounted, and the government put limits on hiring foreign workers.[10]

Table 7.4 Remittances relative to growth rate by income group

(remittances as a percentage of GDP, 1996–2000)

	Poor countries	Other
Higher than median growth	3.4	1.0
Lower than median growth	4.2	0.8

Note: Poor countries and other developing countries are defined as in *GDF 2002*.
Source: World Bank, *World Development Indicators*; World Bank, *Global Development Finance*; IMF balance-of-payments data; World Bank staff estimates.

Remittances may remain stable even in economic downturns in source developed countries, however. The source developed countries often have fiscal systems with automatic stabilizers that may offer some income protection to migrant workers during economic downturns. Taylor (2000) found that public income transfer schemes in the United States resulted in increased remittances to Mexico—other things being equal, immigrant households that received Social Security or unemployment insurance were 10 to 15 percent more likely to remit, and their monthly remittances abroad (especially Mexico) were $150 to $200 higher, than immigrant households not receiving public transfers. Another reason for the relative stability of remittances in the face of economic downturns in source countries may be that if migrant workers are forced to return to their home country, they may bring back their entire savings (which shows up as migrants' transfers in the balance of payments). This may have been the case in India during the Gulf War of 1990–91 which forced a large number of Indian workers in the Gulf to return home, but remittances to India did not decline (figure 7.10). (Unlike India, however, remittance flows to Jordan and Yemen from Kuwait and Saudi Arabia declined during the Gulf War.)

Figure 7.10 India's remittance receipts, 1985–2001

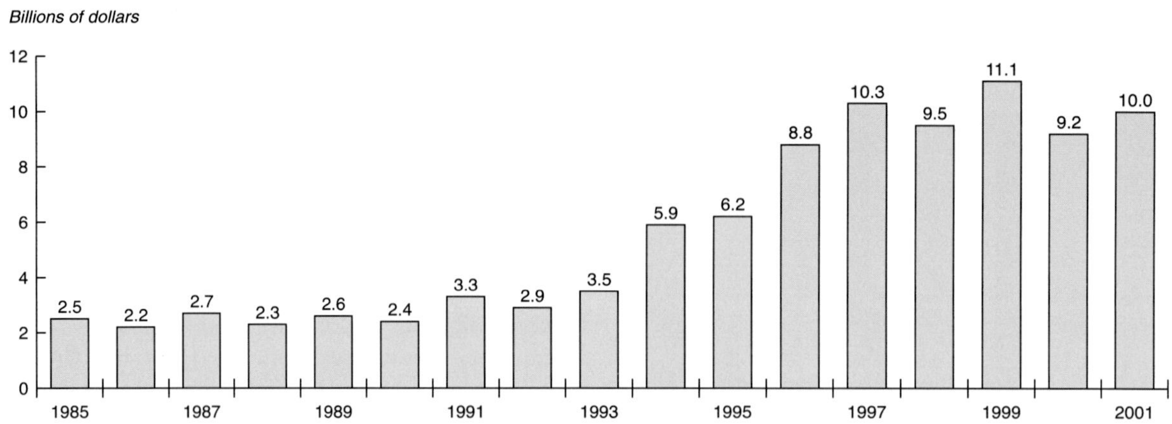

Source: IMF, *Balance of Payments Yearbook.*

Economic effects of remittances

Remittances augment the recipient individuals' incomes and increase the recipient country's foreign exchange reserves. If remittances are invested, they contribute to output growth, and if they are consumed, then also they generate positive multiplier effects (see, for example, Stahl and Arnold 1986). Thus, remittances offset some of the output losses that a developing country may suffer from emigration of its highly skilled workers.[11] Adelman and Taylor (1990) found that for every dollar Mexico received from migrants working abroad, its GNP increased by $2.69 to $3.17, depending on whether remittances were received by urban or rural households.[12] Remittances also more than offset the loss of tax revenue in most developing countries. For example, the net fiscal loss associated with Indian emigration to the United States was estimated at 0.24 to 0.58 percent of Indian GDP in 2001 (Desai, Kapur, and McHale 2001b), but remittances amounted to at least 2.1 percent of GDP in the same year. In the case of unskilled workers who emigrate to escape unemployment, remittances are likely to prove an even clearer net gain to the developing country.

Inward remittances are believed to have a positive impact on savings and investment. Household surveys in Pakistan indicated that in the later 1980s and early 1990s, the marginal propensity to save was higher (0.711) for income from international remittances than from domestic urban-rural remittances (0.49) or rental income (0.085) (Adams 2002 and 1998). Furthermore, such transfers provide the hard currency required for importing scarce inputs that are not available domestically. Remittances may serve as insurance policies against risks associated with new production activities (Taylor 1999). Faini (2001) found that remittances have a positive effect on growth. As mentioned earlier, remittances were a source of investment in Mexico and the Arab Republic of Egypt. Remittances are used in many countries to build schools and clinics (for example, see Martin, Martin, and Weil 2002 for a study of remittances sent to Mali from France; see also Orozco 2000). Lucas (1985) estimated that in five Sub-Saharan African countries, emigration (to work in South African mines) reduced labor supply and crop production in the short run, but enhanced crop productivity and cattle accumulation through invested remittances in the long run.

The evidence on the impact of remittances on income inequality is mixed. Remittances augment incomes and can lift people out of poverty. Some studies argue that remittances may have had an equalizing effect on the distribution of income among socioeconomic groups in Mexico (Taylor 1999; Adelman and Taylor 1990). But remittances may also raise inequality because rich (workers) are better able to pay the high fixed costs associated with international travel.[13] Indeed, household survey data from Pakistan reveal that the share of income originating from external remittances rose with the income groups—the highest income group received the highest share of income from external remittances (table 7.5). Such patterns may be reinforced where remittances are exempted from tax.

Table 7.5 Remittances by income group in Pakistan, 1986–87 to 1990–91

	Average income per capita (1986 rupees, 5-year average)	Percentage of per capita income from external remittances
Lowest 20%	1,176	1.0
Second 20%	1,721	1.7
Third 20%	2,200	4.8
Fourth 20%	2,876	7.2
Highest 20%	5,261	13.8

Source: Adams 1998, based on a survey of 469 Pakistani households during 1986–87 and 1990–91.

Figure 7.11 Average transfer fee and exchange-rate commission for sending $200, February 2000

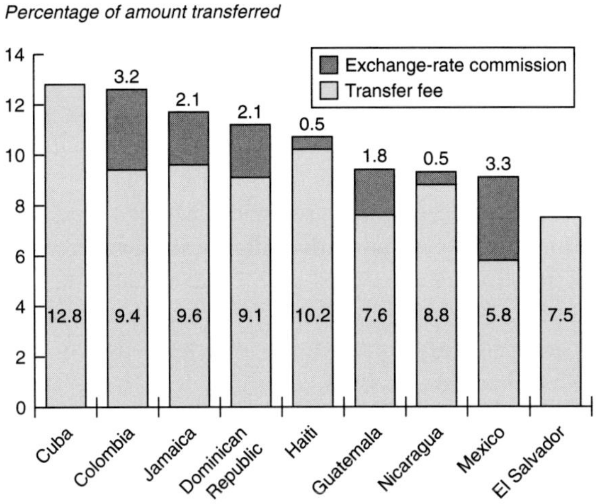

Note: The exchange-rate commission for Cuba and El Salvador is zero.
Sources: Multilateral Investment Fund 2002; Orozco 2002.

Remittances do not necessarily go to countries with poor income distribution, however. During 1996–2000 remittances were nearly twice as high (1.5 percent of GDP) in countries that had relatively even income distribution (represented by Gini index) than in other countries (0.9 percent of GDP). Some studies argue that remittances increase urban-rural inequality as they tend to finance investments in real estate or in enterprises in urban areas. McCormick and Wahba (2002) found that returning migrants in the Arab Republic of Egypt in 1988 tended to set up enterprises in greater Cairo; however, this may have been due to distortions in the economy that discouraged investments in rural areas.

Strengthening the infrastructure supporting remittances

Despite the clear welfare benefits of remittances, weaknesses in the financial sector and in government administration impose substantial transaction costs on migrant workers who send them. Easing these constraints could increase remittance receipts, while bringing a larger share of remittance payments into the formal financial system. Anecdotal evidence suggests that inefficiencies in the banking system—long delays in check clearance, exchange losses, or improper disclosure of transaction costs[14]—deter inward remittances.

The average cost of transferring remittances to Central and South America is in the range of 13 percent, and often exceeds 20 percent (figure 7.11; see also Orozco 2002).[15] These charges, which are astronomical in comparison with the costs of bank transfers among industrial economies, are largely due to the fixed cost of wire transfers combined with the fact that the average remittance transaction tends to be small, usually below $200. Reducing such transactions costs to less than 10 percent would imply an annual savings of $3.5 billion to overseas workers. No doubt a substantial portion of this savings would be remitted.

Improved banking sector technology could substantially reduce transaction costs by expediting check clearance, reducing exchange losses, and improving disclosure, especially in rural areas in developing countries. One promising approach is to establish partnerships between leading banks and the government post office network in countries that do not have banks with extensive branch networks in rural areas. Remittance activities may also be attractive for banks, as margins can be very high.

Banks in many developing countries have not shown much interest in workers' remittances in the past, presumably because of cumbersome paperwork and lack of widespread branch networks. This is beginning to change, however. The efforts to crack down on money laundering and financing terrorism have affected remittances through the informal networks, and a large number of workers are looking for formal banking channels to remit funds. These developments, and the high margins associated with this business, have attracted some new entrants. For example, the International Remittance Network has started offering funds transfer services by linking credit union cooperatives (such as of unionized agricultural workers) with

Citibank branches in the United States and in receiving countries such as El Salvador, Guatemala, and Mexico. Reportedly, the cost of remittance through this new network is only $6.50 per transaction, significantly lower than the costs of using informal networks.

Industrial countries should consider facilitating efforts to reduce the transaction costs of remittances to developing countries. Mexico and the United States are already collaborating to provide better financial services to Mexican migrants (including illegal immigrants), an effort that promises to significantly improve the migrants' access and use of banking services, especially for wiring funds to families back home. Such policies—including measures to improve disclosure[16] in fund transfers—are likely also to benefit the source-country (by generating more tax revenues), as well as banks (by generating fees for fund transfers and other banking services).

Recent surveys of migrants in Los Angeles and New York show that migrants are discouraged from opening bank accounts because of minimum balance requirements—and to a lesser extent, stringent identification requirements. When these obstacles are eased—for example, by accepting Mexican consulates' matrículas or IRS's individual taxpayer identification numbers[17] as valid forms of identification—immigrants can become the source of substantial banking business over and beyond wire transfers (box 7.2). In recent years, "financial fairs" have been held to promote remittances and encourage migrant workers to use the formal banking system (box 7.3).

Facilitating international labor mobility

Facilitating labor mobility between source and destination countries is perhaps the most crucial—and controversial—means of increasing remittance flows to developing countries. Even though world migration pressures have risen, the progress of globalization has been slower in the area of migration (Hatton and Williamson 2002, World Bank 2002) than in trade (Findlay and O'Rourke 2002) and capital flows (Obstfeld and Taylor 2002).

The main concerns of developed countries regarding immigration center on (a) the local jobseekers' fear of competition from migrant workers, (b) the fiscal burden that may result on native taxpayers for providing health and social security to migrants, (c) fears of erosion of cultural identity and problems of assimilation of immigrants, and (d) national security (especially after September 11, 2001).

On the first issue, conceptually increased labor supply due to immigration is expected to depress wages or raise the unemployment rate. Empirical evidence, however, has remained inconclusive as researchers have been unable to isolate the effects of immigration from those of other factors such as differences (between local workers and migrants) in skills, sex, age, and professional education and

Box 7.2 Mexican matrículas consulares boost remittances

For decades, Mexican consulates have been issuing a simple identity card, known as *matrícula consular*, to Mexican citizens living in the United States—legally or illegally. According to a study by the Pew Hispanic Center (2002), 740,000 *matrículas* were issued in the United States during the first nine months of 2002. Designed originally to help police identify persons involved in accidents (or crime), *matrículas* are increasingly accepted as proof of identity when opening accounts at U.S. banks. Some 66 banks (and 801 police departments in 13 states in the United States) now accept the *matrícula* as a valid identification document. (More recently, U.S. banks are showing reluctance in accepting these documents because of concerns about illegal funds tranfers.)

At present, only the Mexican government offers such an identification document to its citizens abroad. Several Central American governments are also considering such cards, which would help their migrant population obtain a bank account and use banks to transfer funds cheaply and transparently.

Source: Pew Hispanic Center.

Box 7.3 Financial fairs to promote remittances and good banking habits among migrants

Developing countries interested in increasing remittance flows from the United States can benefit from the experiences of some innovative "financial fairs" organized in August 2002 in Kansas City and Chicago. Recognizing the multifaceted potential of migrant workers as a source of remittances, tax revenues, and savings, the Community Affairs Office of the Federal Deposit Insurance Corporation staged the fairs in collaboration with the Mexican Consulate, the Internal Revenue Service (IRS), and six private banks. All participants appeared to benefit from the event.

At the fairs, the Mexican consulate issued an identification card (*matrícula*) with photo and U.S. address to undocumented migrant workers from Mexico. The IRS collected back taxes from workers and issued individual taxpayer identification numbers (ITINs) on the spot, sparing everyone the 6–8-week wait. The tax payments entitled workers who were becoming legal residents to claim earned income tax credits—good for an average tax refund of about $1,700 per year—once their papers were processed. The banks accepted the *matrícula* and ITIN as identification from migrants wishing to open bank accounts. Already legalized workers were able to receive earned income tax credits on the spot; some deposited their tax refunds in their newly opened bank accounts.

The documentation requirement for opening new accounts (according to section 326 of the Patriot Act) allows other forms of identification such as passports or even voter registration cards. Some financial institutions (such as U.S. Bank in Kansas City and Second Federal Savings in Chicago) have started accepting voter registration cards as valid identification documents. Following the Mexican model, the Guatemalan consulate has also started issuing identification cards to its citizens in the United States. The cards are accepted by Wells Fargo for opening bank accounts.

Source: Federal Deposit Insurance Corporation.

experience obtained abroad (Coppel, Dumont, and Visco 2001). The dynamic nature of this problem has made it more difficult to assess the effects of migration on labor supply. For example, local workers may move to another location and this may show up as lower employment in their original location, but it would be hard to attribute this fall in employment rate to immigration (see Borjas, Freeman, and Katz 1997; Borjas 1994). Some studies that distinguish between long run and short run impact find that in response to immigration, while unemployment may increase in the short run, in the long run the overall rate of unemployment falls permanently (Gross 1999). The effects of immigration on wages are found to have been negative as expected. Borjas, Freeman, and Katz (1997) found that the 21 percent increase in the number of unskilled migrant workers in the United States from 1975 to 1995 reduced the wage earnings of unskilled local workers by up to 5 percent, not a small amount considering that wages should have increased during this period. (See also World Bank 2002.)

Although the potential adverse effect of immigration on unemployment and wage rates receives a lot of attention, immigration also generates many positive effects. First, migrant workers may relieve the labor shortage in many areas in which native workers do not want to work, and where there were also no substitutes for human labor (e.g., caring for the elderly). Migration may thus increase productivity and moderate inflation as was the case in the United States (especially in the technology sector) in the 1990s. Second, migrant workers tend to be more responsive to labor market conditions than local workers; thus, migration may help soften labor market rigidities and improve productivity (Coppel, Dumont, and Visco 2001). Third, the multiplier effects generated by migrants' spending in the host countries should not be underestimated. Finally, the competition faced by local less skilled workers in developed countries from migrant workers is "neither more nor less than the challenge posed to such workers by imports of labor intensive goods from developing countries" (Winters forthcoming).

On the question of whether immigrants are a fiscal burden on destination industrial countries, again the evidence is mixed. Smith and Edmonston (1997) conclude that immigrants with less than a high school education continue to be a fiscal burden into the next generations, but that skilled immigrants pay more in taxes than what they receive in social security from the state. Other studies have argued that even in the case of unskilled immigrants, the fiscal costs, if any, are limited to the first generation; it is believed that the next generation earns and contributes more in taxes than the corresponding generation of native workers (Borjas 1994). Another contentious point is that the fiscal burden is usually borne by localities, with the federal/national governments getting benefits. Fiscal costs are obviously reduced if migrant workers did not stay in the country until they are eligible to receive social security. Some policy makers have suggested greater use of temporary unskilled workers (as in the Mexican guest workers proposal of U.S. Senator Phil Gramm).[18] However, enforcement of such "revolving door" policies may prove extremely difficult (Mattoo 2002, introduction).

The social costs of immigration, including cultural fears, crime, and national security, are not quantifiable and will continue to act as brakes against attempts to liberalize immigration laws in advanced countries. However, the rising migration trend is unlikely to be reversed as these costs have to be traded off against the benefits of letting in more immigrants at the margin (Winters 2002).

Considering the huge income gap between rich and poor countries, most economists and developing country policy-makers see large benefits in greater international mobility of labor. Winters (forthcoming) estimates that world welfare would increase by more than $150 billion per year if developed countries were to increase their quotas of international temporary workers to 3 percent of their workforce. (See also Rodrik 2001.)

For developing countries, the benefits of migration—and its costs—are more obvious. Countries benefit from workers' remittances and from the rise in real wages (especially for unskilled and unemployed workers) that often occurs as emigration clears the labor market. On the negative side, the emigration of highly skilled workers has been linked to skill shortages, reductions in output, and tax shortfalls in many developing countries. Such burdens appear even heavier for countries where educated workers emigrated in large numbers after receiving highly subsidized technical education. Carrington and Detragiache (1998) estimate that over one-third of individuals with tertiary education from Africa, the Caribbean, and Central America emigrated to the United States and other countries of the OECD. Migration rates are also high in the Islamic Republic of Iran, the Republic of Korea, the Philippines, Taiwan, and Turkey. The International Organization for Migration (1999) estimates that for 40 percent of African countries, more than 35 percent of college graduates reside abroad. Desai, Kapur, and McHale (2001b) discuss the emigration of a significant share of India's information-technology professionals to the United States in the late 1990s. They estimate forgone income-tax revenues associated with that emigration to be one-third of current Indian income-tax receipts.

The negative effects of brain drain are offset to some extent by inward remittances from migrant workers. Source developing countries may also benefit from network effects (business contacts, investments, technological help) from their skilled and successful emigrants abroad (Desai, Kapur, and McHale 2001b). And it is debatable whether the skilled workers, had they not emigrated, would have been used to their full potential given the imperfect work environment in many developing countries.[19] Finally, skilled workers may return to their home country if the investment climate and work environment improve.

From limiting to managing migration

Bhagwati (2003) believes that developed countries should shift the focus of their immigration policies from limiting to managing migration. The goal of such a shift would be to glean the shared benefits of greater international labor mobility and to avoid the undesirable effects of immigration quotas—chief among which are the sufferings of those trying to cross borders illegally and the abuse of illegal immigrants. For their part, developing countries could benefit by adopting a "diaspora approach" in dealing with the emigration of workers, exploiting their potential as a source of capital, remittances and other transfers; building "networks" for trade, tourism, investment promotion, and training youngsters at home; and otherwise harnessing their knowledge, skills, and assets for economic development.[20] At the very least, developing countries could remove the hurdles that their nationals may face in undertaking overseas travel.[21]

Immigration policies in developed countries are so complex that making a direct investment in a developing country is often less cumbersome than bringing in workers to a developed country (Mattoo 2002). To improve transparency in immigration policies Bhagwati (2003) proposes a World Migration Organization that would codify immigration policies and spread best practices. Rodrik (2001) similarly proposes "multilateralizing" immigration rules so that two countries participating in a special arrangement to share workers would not generate adverse spillover effects on other countries.

One positive, albeit limited, step in this direction is the so-called Mode 4 proposal for supplying services under consideration in the current round of the General Agreement on Trade in Services (GATS). The agreement proposes greater freedom for the "temporary movement of individual service suppliers."[22] Although little progress was made when this issue was first negotiated in the Uruguay Round, the member countries of the WTO now seem more willing to negotiate. However, the Mode 4 trade proposal is presently limited in scope to managers, executives, and professionals; thus, countries that are not significant foreign investors and those with unskilled workers are not going to benefit much from progress in the current negotiations.

Prospects for remittance flows to developing countries

Remittance flows have shown remarkable stability over time, and the rising trend evident in recent years is likely to continue in the medium- to long-term. In particular, remittance flows from nonresident or temporary workers are expected to surge in the medium-term. The search for lower costs is driving multinational corporations to hire overseas workers for cross-border jobs. This trend towards more mobility of temporary workers may be reinforced if progress is made on Mode 4 trade in services in the GATS negotiations. Improvements in transportation and communications will complement this trend.

Migration pressure is likely to continue to rise in the foreseeable future (box 7.4).[23] The most important factor in the rise is perhaps the aging of the population—and the implied surge in pension costs—in the developed nations (see, for example, United Nations 2000). Since skilled workers pay more taxes and need less support from state social security systems, future changes to immigration policies are likely to favor permanent-skilled and temporary-unskilled migrants (Desai, Kapur, and McHale 2001a).

In addition to differential changes in dependency ratios, Hatton and Williamson (2002) identified three historical economic determinants of world migration:

- Wide wage gaps between developed and developing countries
- High but falling costs of migration relative to the low incomes in developing countries
- The size of existing migrant stocks in receiving countries (which affects the extent of influx of friends and relatives through family reunification).

Economic growth in some parts of the developing world, for example, East Asia and South Asia, may imply less migration pressure from these regions, but it is unlikely to reduce the migration pressure from Africa. Also South-South migration is likely to increase faster than South-North migration as many fast-growing newly industrialized countries in the South are expected to attract more migration than the industrial countries (Hatton and Williamson 2002). (The only factor that may moderate migration is the casualty from HIV/AIDS.) The possible induction of up to 10 Central and Eastern European countries into the EU is also likely to increase migration from these countries into the EU, but movement of temporary workers is especially likely to surge.[24]

Box 7.4 World migration pressure is high—and rising

In 1994, about 3.6 million persons were on the waiting list for admission to the United States (Hatton and Williamson 2002, Smith and Edmonston 1997). Each year a million people enter the United States legally, 500,000 illegally. The numbers are similar in Europe. Immigration to many Asian countries—among them the Republic of Korea, Malaysia, Taiwan, and Thailand—surged in the 1990s. And the number of asylum seekers remains high. Worldwide asylum applications reached 914,855 in 2001, according to the United Nations High Commissioner for Refugees, with about 940,226 cases awaiting decision.

As demand for migration has risen, so have payments to human traffickers. Fees range from $200–400 along the Mexico-Los Angeles route to $35,000 along the China-New York (see table).

The fees paid to *coyotes,* professional people-smugglers along the U.S.-Mexican border "have doubled, tripled or even quadrupled, depending on the entry corridor and the services offered" (Cornelius 2001). Although this increase is due in part to stricter border enforcement (the total INS budget for the 2002 fiscal year was $5.5 billion, more than triple what it was in 1993; the size of the Border Patrol has more than doubled in size since then), it is also due to rising demand for migration.

Payments to traffickers for selected migration routes
(dollars per person)

Kurdistan-Germany	3,000
China-Europe	10,000–15,000
China-New York	35,000
India/Pakistan-United States	25,000
Arab states-United Arab Emirates	2,000–3,000
North-Africa-Spain	2,000–3,500
Iraq-Europe	4,100–5,000
Middle East-United States	1,000–15,000
Mexico-Los Angeles	200–400
Philippines-Indonesia/Malaysia	3,500

Source: "Migrant Trafficking and Human Smuggling in Europe," International Organization for Migration, 2000 (as reproduced in *The Economist,* Survey of Migration, November 2, 2002).

However, in the near to medium term, this positive outlook for remittance flows to developing countries needs to be moderated in view of the sluggish labor markets in G-7 economies and tighter scrutiny of international travelers following the events of September 1, 2001—factors that are likely to change the geographical composition, as well as the volume, of remittance flows. Given the geopolitical risks of war and conflicts, developing countries in the Middle East and North Africa region and South Asia who supply workers to countries such as Kuwait and Saudi Arabia are likely to experience some declines in remittance flows. Increased migration from central and eastern Europe, after the EU enlargement, may crowd out migration from other countries. These declines are, however, likely to be dominated by positive effects on remittance flows of greater labor mobility, progress in (Mode 4) GATS negotiations, depending on how quickly G-7 economies overcome the economic down cycle.

Annex: Sources of remittance data

IN THIS STUDY, WORKERS' REMITTANCES are defined as the sum of three components: (a) workers' remittances recorded under the heading "current transfers" in the current account of the balance of payments; (b) compensation of employees which includes wages, salaries, and other benefits of border, seasonal, and other non-resident workers (such as local staff of embassies) and which are recorded under the "income" subcategory of the current account; and (c) migrants' transfers which are reported under "capital transfers" in the capital account of the IMF's *Balance of Payments Yearbook* (item codes 2391, 2310, and 2431 respectively).

This broader definition is believed to capture the extent of workers' remittances better than the data reported under the heading of workers' remittances alone. In the Philippines, for example, remittances from overseas Filipino workers through the banking system are largely recorded under compensation of employees (which, strictly speaking, should include only remittances by temporary workers). In the year 2001, compensation of employees amounted to $6.2 billion whereas workers' remittances were just $122 million. In contrast, in India, most remittances reported by authorized dealers are captured under workers' remittances (nearly $10 billion in 2001), and the compensation-of-employees figure ($126 million in 2000) is known to be underestimated. In Turkey, workers' remittances exclude other current transfer credits such as "imports with waiver," that is, imports financed from the earnings of Turkish nationals living abroad; this item needs to be added to remittances.[25]

The above definition does not include transfers through informal channels—such as hand-carries by friends or family members, or in-kind remittances of jewelry, clothes, and other consumer goods, or through hawala. These are believed to be significant in many countries, ranging from 10 to 50 percent of total remittances, but often are not recorded in the official statistics (Puri and Ritzema 2000; El-Qorchi and others 2002). If and when they are recorded, it is not clear to what extent they reflect actual transfers rather than imports. For example, in recent years India has started recording as imports gold brought in by incoming international passengers, previously this was classified as remittances. Thus, data for private transfers in recent years show a slight decline, even though substantially nothing has changed.

The unrecorded portion of remittances may be heading down due to better technology and efforts to crack down on money laundering. These changes make it difficult to interpret current trends. For example, in the first nine months of 2002 remittances to Mexico were up 9.9 percent over the previous year; how much of this rise reflects better reporting and how much a rise in underlying activity is difficult to tell. More extreme is the case of Pakistan which recorded a whopping $2.4 billion in remittance receipts in fiscal year 2002, more than double the $1.1 billion recorded a year earlier (table 7A.1). According to the State Bank of Pakistan (2002), "the turning point was the international crackdown on the Hundi net-

Table 7A.1 Workers' remittance inflows to Pakistan, fiscal 1999–2002
(millions of dollars)

	FY99	FY00	FY01	FY02
Total	1,060	984	1,087	2,389
From U.S.	82	80	135	779
From U.K.	74	73	81	152

Source: State Bank of Pakistan, Annual Report, 2001–02.

work" (especially in the United States and Britain, after September 11, 2001); the other reason might have been the "waning attraction of foreign exchange holdings due to an appreciating Rupee."

Nor does the definition include "other current transfers," which often reflect workers' remittances.

Remittances are supposed to be current transactions that do not involve transfers of ownership of assets. In practice, however, it may be difficult to identify or estimate such transactions. For example, remittances can be masked as capital inflows to take advantage of tax and other incentives. In many countries, nonresident deposits, although classified under the capital account, may in part reflect workers' remittances. For example, the nonresident rupee deposits in India are most likely remittances disguised as deposits—upon maturity, they do not return to the nonresident depositor, because the rupee is not convertible into hard currency.

As with most of the items in the global balance of payments, the estimates of remittances suffer from the fact that inflows and outflows reported by countries do not match. World inflows of remittances totaled $111 billion in 2001—more than 7 percent higher than recorded outward flows ($103 billion).

Notes

1. Remittances are defined as the sum of workers' remittances, compensation of employees and migrants' transfers (see data annex). Remittances are known to be underestimated significantly in the balance-of-payments statistics of the IMF. If other current transfers—which cover food, clothing, consumer goods, medical supplies, gifts, dowries, payments from unfunded pension plans from nongovernmental organizations, and so on—were also to be included, remittance receipts would amount to $99.5 billion or 1.6 percent of GDP in 2001. A frequent practice in the literature is to also include migrants' transfers in remittance receipts. See annex for a discussion of data issues relating to remittances. Remittance payments by developing countries stood at $22 billion in 2001. Most of this amount ($15.1 billion) was paid by Saudi Arabia.

2. One reason why remittance flow data are not disaggregated by source countries or by destination countries is that financial institutions that act as intermediaries often report funds as originating in the most immediate source country. For example, the Philippines tends to attribute a large part of its remittance receipts to the United States because many banks route their fund transfers through the United States. Orozco (2002) suggests that more than 90 percent of remittance flows to Latin American countries originate in the United States.

3. These numbers do not reflect Saudi Arabia's indirect contribution to remittance flows in the form of training unskilled workers, many of whom arrive as unskilled workers in Saudi Arabia and then migrate to other developed countries after acquiring substantial skills.

4. Some governments are trying to encourage the use of remittances for investment purposes. For example, government bodies in Zacatecas, in northern Mexico, give three dollars for every dollar contributed by migrants' associations for investment projects (*The Economist,* February 21, 2002).

5. The funds brought back by return migrants is reported as migrants' transfers in the balance of payments. Unfortunately very few countries report this as a separate item. Presumably a large part of this item is already included in remittance receipts. Among the developing countries, only the Russian Federation reports any sizeable amount of migrants' transfers; but even there, the size has steadily declined, from $4.5 billion in 1994 to $417 million in 2001. The aggregate migrants' transfers to developing countries as reported in the IMF balance-of-payments statistics was only about $1 billion in 2001.

6. For example remittances rose sharply when countries allowed residents to hold onshore foreign currency deposits. Private transfers to Uganda increased from $80 million in 1991 to $415 million in 1996 in response to measures that permitted residents to open foreign currency accounts onshore (Kasekende 2000). In October 2002, Uganda's foreign exchange accounts deposits were 27.8 percent of all deposits.

7. See also Russell (1992, p. 277), Meyers (1998), and Elbadawi and Rocha (1992). Reinforcing this argument, El-Sakka and McNabb (1999) found that inflation had a positive and significant impact on inflow of remittances, probably reflecting the need to boost family support in times of rising prices.

8. Swamy (1981) argues that the economic situation in the host country is the main determinant of the size of remittance flows to developing countries. Straubhaar (1986) similarly argues that "international migration flows are demand-determined by the existence of restrictive immigration control systems."

9. See Clark, Hatton, and Williamson (2002) and World Bank (2002) for a description of changes in U.S. immigration rules and trends. The increase in remittance flows to developing countries coincided with an increase in the migrant population in developed countries. Estimates suggest that migrant stocks in developed countries increased from 3.1 percent in 1965 to 4.5 percent in 1990 (Hatton and Williamson 2002); in all likelihood this trend has continued through the 1990s.

10. The decline in remittances from Gulf countries in the mid-1980s was most likely due to restrictions on hiring new workers from overseas. Birks, Seccombe, and Sinclair (1986) reported that the collapse of oil prices did not result in large-scale exodus of foreign labor from the Arab Gulf states. Remittances intended for investment purposes may decline when the source country's economy is strong and rates of return are high. El-Sakka and McNabb (1999) found that remittance inflows to Egypt were lower when rates of return were higher in Arab source countries during 1967–91.

11. The same skilled workers could be significantly less productive in a developing country (where the unemployment rate is higher and investment climate worse) than in an industrial country. See also Nayyar (1994).

12. Rural households tend to consume more domestically produced goods—and hence generate larger multiplier effects—than urban households.

13. Adams (1993) found from Egyptian household survey data collected in the second half of the 1980s that the relationship between migration and income had an inverted U-shape, suggesting that it is the middle-income types who migrate; the very poor do not migrate because they cannot pay the costs associated with international travel, while the very rich do not want to migrate. After adding land to income, he dismissed this view and concluded that it is the very poor who migrate because they have the most to gain from migrating (and they are able to meet travel costs by presumably selling land).

14. A 2002 survey by the Pew Hispanic Center (sponsored by the Interamerican Development Bank) of 302 Latin American born adults residing in Los Angeles and Miami also found that remitters had significant concerns about the high cost of transferring funds due to flat fees and unfavorable exchange rates. Other concerns include delays in money being delivered to the recipient. This survey revealed that nearly 83 percent of persons interviewed sent money through international money transfer companies such as Western Union or Moneygram, and only 9 percent through banks. The Bank of Mexico (1997) estimated that in 1995, 40 percent of remittances came in through money orders, 24 percent through wire transfers, 27 percent through other electronic means, and 8 percent through cash transfers. Lozano-Ascencio (1998), using surveys of migrants themselves, estimates that 15 percent of remittances entered Mexico as pocket transfers.

15. The cost of transfers through informal channels, such as Hawala, used in other parts of the world is said to be much lower than it is through institutional channels (El-Qorchi 2002).

16. In 2001, the United States amended the Electronic Fund Transfer Act (see the Wire Transfer Fairness and Disclosure Act of 2001), instructing financial institutions or money transmitters initiating an international money transfer to prominently disclose the exchange rate used in the transaction, the exchange rate prevailing at a major financial center of the foreign country as of close of business on the business day immediately preceding the transaction date, all commissions and fees charged, and the exact amount of foreign currency to be received by the customer in the foreign country (see www.ncua.gov, H.R. 1306—Wire Transfer Services).

17. An individual taxpayer identification number (ITIN) is required to open interest-bearing accounts in U.S. banks. Without an ITIN, only checking accounts that do not pay interest can be opened.

18. Senator Gramm has proposed that Mexican "guest workers" be hired on an annual or seasonal basis, and a 15.3 percent payroll tax imposed on their employers would pay for the worker's emergency medical care and an IRA account, which the worker could withdraw at the time of departure back to Mexico. See http://migration.ucdavis.edu/rmn/archive_rmn/oct_2001-10rmn.html.

19. Nayyar (1994) argues that the magnitudes of emigration from India are small compared to the substantial reservoir of unemployed among the educated, and thus the macroeconomic impact is perhaps negligible.

20. Some authors argue that developing countries should also try to tax their rich and successful migrant workers abroad, by changing their tax rules to one based on "nationality" (as in the case of Eritrea, the Philippines, and the United States) from one based on "residence." See Desai, Kapur, and McHale (2001a) and Bhagwati (2003).

21. Such hurdles may include restrictions on or delays in issuance of passports, access to foreign exchange to undertake the initial travel, or simply lack of a communication infrastructure that slows down job search or results in delays in finalizing job contracts. Political instability often disrupts international migration. For example, the number of Mozambican workers in South African mines dropped by half around the period preceding and following Mozambique's independence from the Portuguese in 1975. To some extent, this drop reflected mistrust of "leftist" workers by South African mine owners, but to a large extent, it was also a result of disruption in passport issuance by Mozambique authorities (Lucas 1987).

22. See Mattoo 2002 for a detailed discussion of various aspects of this issue. The other three modes of GATS are: "cross-border supply" (trade in goods), consumption abroad (tourism or study abroad), and commercial presence (supplying services through a branch abroad).

23. The industrial countries may respond to these rising migration pressures by relaxing immigration laws, in particular, by encouraging more temporary migration (akin to the U.S. H-1B visa).

24. A seven-year delay before workers from central and eastern Europe are allowed to work in the EU has been proposed, similar to the "transitional period" arranged for Spain and Portugal when they entered the EU in 1985. Several studies estimate that migration from these countries into the EU would rise to about 2–3 percent of the population of the sending country (see, for example, Boeri and Brucker 2000), but others (Borjas 1999, Drinkwater 2002) estimate smaller numbers. There appears to be a consensus, however, that temporary movement of workers from these countries will increase significantly.

25. One of the techniques devised to cope with the deteriorating external imbalance was a form of foreign borrowing known as the "convertible Turkish Lira deposit" scheme or the Dresdner Bank scheme. The program, dating from the late 1960s, was designed to attract the savings of Turkish nationals working in foreign countries and also the cash deposits that might have been earned in black-market trade, smuggling, or the mis-invoicing of imports and exports. According to the scheme, the Central Bank of Turkey offered interest rates on foreign exchange deposited in Turkish commercial banks 1.75 points above the Euromarket rate while also guaranteeing the foreign exchange value of both principle and interest. Beginning in 1975, the program was broadened to allow nonresidents in general, and not only Turkish nationals working abroad, to hold these deposits. Foreign exchange receipts from this source were transferred from commercial banks to the Turkish central bank and on-lent to government and state enterprises, with expansionary effects on the money supply. Inflation accelerated markedly (still with a fixed exchange rate), worsening

the underlying disequilibrium in the external sector. The Dresdner deposits constituted short-term foreign loans, and therefore the maturity of Turkey's external indebtedness became increasingly short term as the decade progressed, despite earlier rescheduling intended to spread out debt servicing over time. The scheme was withdrawn for a few years, but reintroduced recently. At the end of 2001, such deposits by Turks living in Europe amounted to $10 billion. See Barth and Hemphill (2000).

References

Adams, Richard H., Jr. 1993. "The Economic and Demographic Determinants of International Migration in Rural Egypt." *Journal of Development Studies* 30(1): 146–67.

———. 1998. "Remittances, Investment, and Rural Asset Accumulation in Pakistan." *Economic Development and Cultural Change,* October: 155–73.

———. 2002. "Precautionary Saving from Different Sources of Income: Evidence from Rural Pakistan." Policy Research Working Paper 2761. World Bank, Washington, D.C.

Adelman, Irma, and J. Edward Taylor. 1990. "Is Structural Adjustment with a Human Face Possible? The Case of Mexico." *Journal of Development Studies.* 26: 387–407.

Bank of Mexico. 1997. *The Mexican Economy*. Mexico City.

Barth, Richard, and William Hemphill. 2000. "Financial Programming and Policy: The Case of Turkey." International Monetary Fund Institute, Washington, D.C.

Bhagwati, Jagdish. 2003. "Borders Beyond Control." *Foreign Affairs* 82(1): 98–104.

Birks, J. S., I. J. Seccombe, and C. A. Sinclair. 1986. "Migrant Workers in the Arab Gulf: The Impact of Declining Oil Revenues." *International Migration Review,* 20(4): 799–814.

Boeri, T. and H. Brucker. 2000. "The Impact of Eastern Enlargement on Employment and Wages in the EU Member States." Unpublished report to the European Commission.

Borjas, George J. 1994. "The Economics of Immigration." *Journal of Economic Literature* 32(December): 1667–1717.

———. 1999. "Economic Research on the Determinants of Immigration: Lessons for the European Union." World Bank Technical Paper 438. Washington, D.C.

Borjas, George J., R. B. Freeman, and L. F. Katz. 1997. "How Much Do Immigration and Trade Affect Labor Market Outcomes?" Brookings Papers on Economic Activity 1, Brookings Institution, Washington, D.C.

Carrington, William, and Enrica Detragiache. 1998. "How Big is the Brain Drain." IMF Working Paper WP/98/102. International Monetary Fund, Washington, D.C.

Clark, Ximena, Timothy J. Hatton, and Jeffrey G. Williamson. 2002. "Where Do U.S. Immigrants Come from, and Why?" NBER Working Paper 8998. National Bureau of Economic Research, Cambridge, Mass. www.nber.org/papers/w8998.

Coppel, Jonathan, Jean-Christophe Dumont, and Ignazio Visco. 2001. "Trends in Immigration and Economic Consequences." OECD Economics Department Working Papers 284. Organisation for Economic Co-operation and Development, Paris.

Cornelius. 2001. "Death at the Border: Efficacy and Unintended Consequences of U.S. Immigration Control Policy." *Population and Development Review* 27(4): 661–85.

Desai, Mihir A., Devesh Kapur, and John McHale. 2001a. "Sharing the Spoils: Taxing International Human Capital Flows." Unpublished paper.

———. 2001b. "The Fiscal Impact of the Brain Drain: Indian Emigration to the U.S." Weekly Political Economy Discussion Paper. Harvard University. www.wcfia.harvard.edu/seminars/pegroup.

Drinkwater, Stephen. 2002. "Go West? Assessing the Willingness to Move from Central and Eastern European Countries." Unpublished paper, Department of Economics, University of Surrey, U.K.

Elbadawi, I. A., and R. Rocha. 1992. "Determinants of Expatriate Workers' Remittances in North Africa and Europe." Policy Research Working Paper WPS 1038. World Bank, Washington D.C.

El-Qorchi, Mohammed. 2002. "Hawala." *Finance and Development* 39(4).

El-Qorchi, Mohammed, Samuel M. Maimbo, and John F. Wilson. 2002. "The Hawala Informal Funds Transfer System: An Economic and Regulatory Analysis." Processed.

El-Sakka, M. I. T., and Robert McNabb. 1999. "The Macroeconomic Determinants of Emigrant Remittances." *World Development* 27(8): 1493–1502.

Faini, Ricardo. 2001. "Development, Trade, and Migration." IMF, Washington, D.C. Processed.

Findlay, R., and K. H. O'Rourke. 2002. "Commodity Market Integration 1500–2000." In M. Bordo, A. M. Taylor, and J. G. Williamson, eds., *Globalization in Historical Perspective*. Chicago: University of Chicago Press.

Gross, D. M. 1999. "Three Million Foreigners, Three Million Unemployed? Immigration and the French Labor Market." IMF Working Paper WP/99/124. International Monetary Fund, Washington, D.C.

Hatton, Timothy J., and Jeffrey G. Williamson. 2002. "What Fundamentals Drive World Migration?" NBER Working Paper 9159. National Bureau of Economic Research, Cambridge, Mass.

International Monetary Fund. *Balance of Payments Yearbook*. Washington, D.C. various issues.

International Organization for Migration. 1999. "Return of Qualified African Nationals Programme." Fact Sheet. July.

Kasekende, Louis A. 2000. "Capital Account Liberalization: The Ugandan Experience." Paper presented at the Overseas Development Institute, June 21, London.

Ketkar, Suhas, and Dilip Ratha. 2001. "Development Financing During a Crisis: Securitization of Future Receivables." Policy Research Working Paper 2582. World Bank, Washington, D.C.

Lozano-Ascencio, Fernando. 1998. "Las Remesas de los Migrantes Mexicanos en Estados Unidos: Estimaciones para 1995." In *Migration Between Mexico and the United States: Binational Study, Volume 3, Research Reports and Background Materials.* Mexico City: Mexican Ministry of Foreign Affairs.

Lucas, Robert E. B. 1985. "Mines and Migrants in South Africa." African Studies Center Working Paper 106. Boston University. Reprinted in *American Economic Review* 75(December 1985): 1094–1108.

Lucas, Robert E. B. 1987. "Emigration to South Africa's Mines." *American Economic Review* 77(3): 313–29.

Maldonado, Andrés, and Alejandra Robledo. 2002. "Sending Money Back Home." *The McKinsey Quarterly,* no. 4, 24–26.

Martin, Philip, Susan Martin, and Patrick Weil. 2002. "Best Practice Options: Mali." *International Migration,* 40(3): 87–99.

Mattoo, Aaditya. 2002. "Introduction and Overview." In Aaditya Mattoo and Antonia Carzaniga, eds., *Moving People to Deliver Services: Labor Mobility and the WTO.* Oxford University Press.

McCormick, Barry, and Jackline Wahba. 2002. "Return Migration and Geographical Inequality: The Case of Egypt." Unpublished paper, University of Southampton.

Meyers, Deborah Waller. 1998. "Migrant Remittances to Latin America: Reviewing the Literature." Inter-American Dialogue and The Tomas Rivera Policy Institute, Washington, D.C. May. www.thedialogue.org/publications/meyers.html.

Multilateral Investment Fund. 2002. "Remittances to Latin America and the Caribbean." Inter-American Development Bank. www.iadb.org/mif/website/static/en/study3.doc.

Nayyar, Deepak. 1994. *Migration, Remittances and Capital Flows: The Indian Experience.* Delhi: Oxford University Press.

Obstfeld, M., and A. M. Taylor. 2002. "Globalization and Capital Markets." In M. Bordo, A. M. Taylor, and J. G. Williamson, eds., *Globalization in Historical Perspective.* Chicago: University of Chicago Press.

Orozco, Manuel. 2000. "Latino Hometown Associations as Agents of Development in Latin America." *Inter-American Dialogue.* June.

———. February 28, 2002. Statement to U.S. Senate Committee on Banking, Housing, and Urban Affairs. Oversight Hearing on "Accounting and Investor Protection Issues Raised by Enron and Other Public Companies." http://banking.senate.gov/02_02hrg/022802/orozco.htm.

Pew Hispanic Center. 2002. "Billions in Motion: Latino Immigrants, Remittances and Banking," presentation at a seminar organized by the Multilateral Investment Fund, Inter-American Development Bank, November 22, 2002.

Puri, Shivani, and Tineke Ritzema. 1999. "Migrant Worker Remittances, Micro-Finance and the Informal Economy: Prospects and Issues." Working Paper 21. Social Finance Unit, International Labour Organization, Geneva.

Rodrik, Dani. 2001. "Comments at the Conference on Immigration Policy and the Welfare State." Unpublished paper delivered at the Third European Conference on Immigration Policy and the Welfare State, Trieste, June 23, 2001.

Russell, Sharon Stanton. 1992. "Migrant Remittances and Development." *International Migration: Quarterly Review* 30(3/4): 267–87.

Smith, J. P., and B. Edmonston. 1997. *The New Americans: Economic, Demographic and Fiscal Effects of Immigration.* Washington, D.C.: National Academy Press.

Stahl, Charles W., and Fred Arnold. 1986. "Overseas Workers' Remittances in Asian Development." *International Migration Review* 20(4): 899–925.

State Bank of Pakistan. 2002. *Annual Report.* Karachi.

Straubhaar, Thomas. 1986. "The Causes of International Labor Migrations—A Demand-Determined Approach." *International Migration Review* 20: 835–855.

Swamy, Gurushri. 1981. "International Migrant Workers' Remittances: Issues and Prospects." Staff Working Paper 481. The World Bank, Washington, D.C.

Taylor, J. Edward. 1999. "The New Economics of Labor Migration and the Role of Remittances." *International Migration* 37(1): 63–86.

———. 2000. "Do Government Programs 'Crowd-in' Remittances?" Inter-American Dialogue and the Tomas Rivera Policy Institute, Washington, D.C. January. www.thedialogue.org/publications/taylor.html

United Nations. 2000. "Replacement Migration: Is It a Solution to Declining and Ageing Populations?" Report ESA/P/WP 160, Department of Economic and Social Affairs, Population Division, New York.

World Bank. 2001. *Global Economic Prospects 2002.* Washington, D.C.

———. 2002. *Globalization, Growth, and Poverty.* Policy Research Report. Washington, D.C.

Woodruff, Christopher, and Rene Zenteno. 2001. "Remittances and Microenterprises in Mexico." Unpublished paper, University of California, San Diego.

Winters, Alan. Forthcoming. "The Economic Implications of Liberalising Mode 4 Trade." In Aaditya Mattoo and Antonia Carzaniga, eds., *Moving People to Deliver Services: Labor Mobility and the WTO.* Oxford University Press.

Statistical Appendix

THE SUMMARY STATISTICAL TABLES HAVE been significantly revised for this edition of *Global Development Finance.* The tables in this statistical appendix are now divided into six sections.

- **Summary tables.** These tables provide a snapshot of recent history and the outlook for the global economy and each of the six developing country regions. (For the full World Bank classification of countries by region and income level, see table A.53.)
- **Key macro variables.** These provide detail on growth and inflation indicators by region and (historically) for selected economies. Although detailed country forecasts form the basis for the regional growth and inflation projections, individual developing country forecasts are not shown separately.
- **Current account tables.** These tables combine data from the IMF's balance-of-payments statistics with aid-related data from the OECD's Development Assistance Committee and our own preferred measure of workers' remittances (see the annex to chapter 7).
- **Capital account tables.** New external financing tables have been developed. They combine the IMF's current account, foreign-exchange reserve, and net inward foreign direct investment data with the World Bank's portfolio equity and debtor reporting system (DRS) data to produce an overall tabulation of how regions finance themselves externally.
- **External liabilities and assets.** These are a summary of the DRS debt data that are provided on a country-by-country basis in volume 2. An important variable found in table A43 is the present value of each country's total future debt-service payments (PV). This variable is especially important in the Heavily Indebted Poor Countries (HIPC) Initiative, where countries are classified based on the ratio of the present value of public and publicly guaranteed debt to exports of goods and services, excluding worker remittances.
- **Key debt ratios and country classifications.** These tables provide a summary of indicators typically used by country risk analysts to monitor and classify countries. The World Bank's own debt classifications are defined and tabulated. The precise method used to categorize countries as severely, moderately, or less indebted is shown at the bottom of table A52. The two key ingredients used are the present value of future debt-service streams (PV) to (a) gross national income (GNI) and (b) to exports of goods and services. These variables are averaged over the three years, 1999–2001.

The use of critical values to define the boundaries between indebtedness categories implies that changes in country classifications should be interpreted with caution. If a country has an indicator that is close to the critical value, a small change in the indicator may trigger a change in indebtedness classification even if economic fundamentals have not changed significantly. Moreover, these indicators do not represent an exhaustive set of useful indicators of external debt. They may not, for example, adequately capture the debt-servicing capacity of countries in which government budget constraints are key to debt-service difficulties. Moreover, rising external debt may not necessarily imply payment difficulties, especially if there is a commensurate increase in the country's debt-servicing capacity. Thus, these indicators should be used in the broader context of a country-specific analysis of debt sustainability.

Contents

External liabilities and assets

Key debt ratios and country classifications

Table A.1 The global outlook in summary, 2001–2004
(percent change from previous year, except interest rates and oil price)

						GEP 2003 forecasts	
	2001	2002e	2003f	2004f	2005f	2003	2004
Global conditions							
World trade volume	0.4	3.0	6.2	8.1	8.1	7.0	8.0
Consumer prices							
G-7 countries[a, b]	1.5	1.0	1.4	1.3	1.3	1.2	1.5
United States	2.8	1.6	2.5	2.3	2.1	2.1	2.3
Commodity prices ($ terms)							
Non-oil commodities	−9.1	5.1	8.2	2.3	1.7	5.8	4.4
Oil price (OPEC average)	24.4	24.9	26.0	21.0	20.0	23.0	20.0
Oil price (percent change)	−13.7	2.4	4.3	−19.2	−4.8	−8.0	−13.0
Manufactures unit export value[c]	−2.9	−1.4	5.6	−0.1	1.2	3.0	2.2
Interest rates							
$, 6-month (percent)	3.5	1.8	1.7	3.2	4.2	1.5	3.1
€, 6-month (percent)	4.2	3.3	2.4	2.3	3.1	3.2	3.8
Real GDP growth[d]							
World	**1.2**	**1.7**	**2.3**	**3.2**	**3.1**	**2.5**	**3.1**
Memo item: World (PPP weights)[e]	2.2	2.8	3.2	4.1	4.0	3.4	4.0
High income	**0.8**	**1.4**	**1.9**	**2.9**	**2.6**	**2.1**	**2.7**
OECD countries	0.9	1.4	1.8	2.8	2.6	2.1	2.6
Euro Area	1.5	0.8	1.4	2.6	2.6	1.8	2.6
Japan	0.3	−0.3	0.6	1.6	1.4	0.8	1.3
United States	0.3	2.4	2.5	3.5	3.0	2.6	3.1
Non-OECD countries	−1.1	2.2	3.0	4.3	4.5	3.7	5.3
Developing countries	**2.8**	**3.1**	**4.0**	**4.7**	**4.8**	**3.9**	**4.7**
East Asia and Pacific[f]	5.5	6.7	6.4	6.6	5.9	6.1	6.4
Europe and Central Asia	2.3	4.1	3.7	3.7	4.1	3.4	3.6
Transition Countries	4.5	3.6	3.6	3.5	3.9	3.3	3.5
Latin America and the Caribbean	0.3	−0.9	1.7	3.8	4.5	1.8	3.7
excluding Argentina	1.1	0.8	1.6	3.7	4.7	1.9	3.6
Middle East and North Africa	3.2	2.6	3.7	3.9	3.7	3.5	3.7
Oil exporters	2.2	2.3	3.7	3.6	3.4	3.7	3.6
Diversified economies	4.1	2.5	3.1	4.2	4.2	2.7	3.6
South Asia	4.3	4.9	5.3	5.2	5.3	5.4	5.8
Sub-Saharan Africa	3.2	2.6	3.0	3.6	3.7	3.2	3.9
Memorandum items							
Developing countries							
excluding transition countries	2.6	3.1	4.1	5.0	5.0	4.0	4.9
excluding China and India	1.7	1.7	2.9	3.9	4.3	2.8	3.8

Note: PPP = purchasing power parity, *e* = estimate, and *f* = forecast. GEP 2003 is *Global Economic Prospects and the Developing Countries,* January 2003.

a. Canada, France, Germany, Italy, Japan, the United Kingdom, and the United States.
b. In local currency, aggregated using 1995 GDP weights.
c. Unit value index of manufactured exports from major economies, expressed in U.S. dollars.
d. GDP in 1995 constant dollars; 1995 prices and market exchange rates.
e. GDP measured at 1995 PPP weights.
f. Now excludes the Republic of Korea, which has been reclassified as high income.

Table A.2 East Asia and Pacific outlook in summary, 1981–2003

Real economy *(percent change, unless stated)*	1981–90	1991–00	1997	1998	1999	2000	2001	2002e	2003f
Real GDP growth	7.4	7.7	6.4	0.6	5.6	7.1	5.5	6.7	6.4
Private consumption per capita	5.6	5.7	2.6	−0.5	4.6	6.0	4.1	6.0	6.0
GDP per capita	5.7	6.4	5.2	−0.5	4.5	6.0	4.6	5.7	5.5
Population	1.6	1.2	1.1	1.1	1.1	1.0	0.9	0.9	0.9
Gross domestic investment/GDP[a]	23.2	28.7	30.7	29.2	28.3	29.2	30.5	33.0	34.0
Inflation[b]	5.5	5.6	4.2	9.2	1.8	5.0	6.6	3.1	2.7
Central government budget balance/GDP	−1.3	−1.2	−0.7	−1.5	−2.3	−3.3	−3.3	−3.4	−3.3
Export market growth[c]	6.7	9.6	7.3	−1.2	7.7	14.1	−2.6	3.4	7.3
Export volume[d]	8.2	11.4	13.7	3.6	3.6	21.5	2.6	16.5	13.8
Terms of trade/GDP[e]	−0.3	−0.2	0.1	−0.3	0.4	0.2	−0.3	−0.4	−0.4
Current account/GDP	−1.4	0.5	1.1	4.4	4.2	3.6	2.6	2.5	2.2
Workers remittances (billions of dollars)	—	—	14.2	8.3	10.6	10.3	10.4	11.0	—
Memorandum items									
GDP growth: East Asia excluding China	5.7	4.6	3.3	−9.5	3.1	5.5	2.3	4.2	4.2

External financing and debt *(billions of dollars unless stated)*	1995	1996	1997	1998	1999	2000	2001	2002e	2003f
Net inward FDI	51.3	58.6	62.2	57.6	48.9	44.0	48.9	57.0	61.0
Net inward portfolio equity flows	9.1	10.1	0.0	−2.8	4.6	19.3	2.9	5.4	7.0
Net inward debt flows	54.2	52.0	44.5	−32.5	−11.6	−18.0	−12.0	−8.3	−13.0
From public sources	9.1	3.6	17.3	14.7	12.5	7.0	3.5	−2.3	−8.0
From private sources	45.0	48.4	27.2	−47.2	−24.1	−25.0	−15.5	−6.0	−5.0
Gross market-based capital inflows	60.0	71.5	76.2	27.3	28.2	48.7	20.7	41.0	50.0
Total external debt	462	498	529	535	541	497	504	—	—
Medium- and long-term	352	368	396	449	467	433	411	—	—
Short-term	110	130	133	86	75	64	93	—	—
Owed by public-sector borrowers	263	263	278	295	314	294	289	—	—
Owed by private-sector borrowers	199	235	250	240	227	203	215	—	—
Owed to public-sector creditors	167	160	159	185	206	194	187	—	—
Owed to private-sector creditors	295	338	370	350	335	303	317	—	—
Gross foreign exchange reserves	154.5	199.7	212.5	233.2	262.5	272.6	320.3	377.3	432.3

— Not available.
Note: e = estimate, *f* = forecast.
a. Fixed investment, measured in real terms.
b. Local currency GDP deflator, median.
c. Weighted average growth of import demand in export markets.
d. Goods and non-factor services.
e. Change in terms of trade, measured as a percentage of GDP.

Table A.3 Europe and Central Asia outlook in summary, 1981–2003

Real economy *(percent change, unless stated)*	1981–90	1991–00	1997	1998	1999	2000	2001	2002e	2003f
Real GDP growth	1.6	−1.5	3.1	0.1	1.8	6.5	2.3	4.1	3.7
Private consumption per capita	0.1	0.4	5.3	0.6	−1.2	8.7	5.0	5.6	3.6
GDP per capita	0.7	−1.7	3.0	−0.1	1.6	6.4	2.2	4.0	3.5
Population	0.9	0.2	0.1	0.1	0.2	0.1	0.1	0.1	0.1
Gross domestic investment/GDP[a]	32.1	24.2	22.3	22.3	21.3	22.0	21.5	21.4	21.5
Inflation[b]	1.1	52.5	17.5	11.9	7.6	9.7	7.0	3.8	5.7
Central government budget balance/GDP	−0.5	−4.4	−4.4	−4.5	−5.6	−5.3	−8.4	−7.8	−6.9
Export market growth[c]	3.3	10.2	8.0	4.8	−1.0	11.9	2.6	2.0	6.6
Export volume[d]	0.1	3.1	9.4	4.6	−0.1	13.1	1.7	5.9	7.9
Terms of trade/GDP[e]	0.1	0.2	0.2	−0.6	−0.4	0.8	2.9	−3.0	1.8
Current account/GDP	−0.5	−0.7	−2.5	−2.7	−0.3	2.0	1.9	0.8	0.6
Workers remittances (billions of dollars)	—	—	7.1	9.2	8.1	8.7	8.9	10.0	—
Memorandum items									
GDP growth: Transition countries	1.2	−2.4	2.1	−0.7	3.5	6.3	4.5	3.6	3.6
Central and Eastern Europe	1.1	0.7	3.4	2.8	2.2	3.9	2.8	2.7	3.0
CIS	1.3	−4.4	1.0	−3.6	4.6	8.4	5.8	4.4	4.1

External Financing and Debt *(billions of dollars unless stated)*	1995	1996	1997	1998	1999	2000	2001	2002e	2003f
Net inward FDI	17.0	16.3	21.8	26.0	28.3	29.2	30.1	29.0	30.0
Net inward portfolio equity flows	1.7	4.3	4.0	4.0	2.0	1.2	0.3	1.4	2.0
Net inward debt flows	23.4	22.7	32.6	40.4	15.8	22.0	3.3	11.2	17.0
From public sources	6.8	8.6	6.7	7.4	−0.8	−0.1	2.8	3.9	2.0
From private sources	16.6	14.1	25.9	33.1	16.6	22.2	0.5	7.2	15.0
Gross market-based capital inflows	21.9	26.9	51.2	43.4	31.0	40.7	27.7	35.5	44.0
Total external debt	350	367	387	484	494	504	498	—	—
Medium- and long-term	305	315	331	413	422	423	422	—	—
Short-term	44	52	56	71	72	80	76	—	—
Owed by public-sector borrowers	287	287	289	321	316	305	291	—	—
Owed by private-sector borrowers	63	80	98	163	178	198	207	—	—
Owed to public-sector creditors	157	161	157	173	171	166	159	—	—
Owed to private-sector creditors	193	206	230	312	323	338	339	—	—
Gross foreign exchange reserves	81.1	83.4	90.7	95.6	102.8	119.6	130.0	164.0	189.0

— Not available.
Note: *e* = estimate, *f* = forecast.
a. Fixed investment, measured in real terms.
b. Local currency GDP deflator, median.
c. Weighted average growth of import demand in export markets.
d. Goods and non-factor services.
e. Change in terms of trade, measured as a percentage of GDP.

Table A.4 Latin America and the Caribbean outlook in summary, 1981–2003

Real economy *(percent change, unless stated)*	1981–90	1991–00	1997	1998	1999	2000	2001	2002e	2003f
Real GDP growth	1.1	3.3	5.2	2.0	0.2	3.5	0.3	−0.9	1.7
Private consumption per capita	−1.0	2.3	3.2	−0.2	−1.6	2.1	−0.9	−3.4	0.3
GDP per capita	−0.9	1.6	3.4	0.4	−1.4	1.9	−1.3	−2.4	0.3
Population	2.0	1.7	1.6	1.6	1.6	1.6	1.6	1.5	1.4
Gross domestic investment/GDP[a]	20.1	19.9	21.1	21.3	19.7	19.6	19.1	17.7	17.0
Inflation[b]	17.3	11.9	8.2	6.7	4.2	7.2	6.8	4.6	4.2
Central government budget balance/GDP	−9.1	−3.3	−3.0	−4.0	−3.0	−2.2	−1.8	−2.6	−2.8
Export market growth[c]	4.4	11.3	12.7	7.7	5.0	12.0	−1.2	0.3	6.8
Export volume[d]	5.4	8.6	9.8	7.9	6.3	10.4	0.7	4.0	8.6
Terms of trade/GDP[e]	0.9	0.2	0.4	−0.2	0.2	0.7	−0.3	0.0	−0.4
Current account/GDP	−1.5	−2.8	−3.3	−4.5	−3.2	−2.4	−2.9	−1.0	−1.2
Workers remittances (billions of dollars)	—	—	13.6	14.8	16.9	19.2	22.6	25.0	—
Memorandum items									
GDP growth: Latin America and the Caribbean excluding Argentina	1.6	3.1	4.6	1.7	0.9	4.3	1.1	0.8	1.6
Central America	1.0	4.4	4.7	5.2	4.4	2.9	0.4	1.8	2.8
Caribbean	2.0	4.0	4.8	5.2	5.9	5.9	3.1	2.9	3.9

External Financing and Debt *(billions of dollars unless stated)*	1995	1996	1997	1998	1999	2000	2001	2002e	2003f
Net inward FDI	30.5	44.4	66.1	73.4	87.8	75.8	69.3	42.0	38.0
Net inward portfolio equity flows	4.8	12.2	13.3	−2.1	−3.6	−0.4	2.3	1.0	2.0
Net inward debt flows	61.3	36.0	24.3	37.9	12.3	−1.1	11.4	3.5	0.0
From public sources	22.0	−10.7	−8.6	10.9	1.6	−11.1	20.2	12.6	6.0
From private sources	39.3	46.8	32.9	27.0	10.7	10.0	−8.7	−9.1	−6.0
Gross market-based capital inflows	42.8	84.9	120.6	84.5	75.3	89.9	75.8	45.3	44.0
Total external debt	650	671	702	774	795	783	765	—	—
Medium- and long-term	522	550	575	656	685	677	669	—	—
Short-term	128	121	127	119	109	106	96	—	—
Owed by public-sector borrowers	435	433	413	436	442	433	443	—	—
Owed by private-sector borrowers	215	238	289	338	353	350	322	—	—
Owed to public-sector creditors	217	194	176	180	183	170	181	—	—
Owed to private-sector creditors	432	477	526	594	612	613	584	—	—
Gross foreign exchange reserves	125.1	153.1	166.7	157.5	150.0	152.9	155.9	151.9	161.9

— Not available.
Note: e = estimate, *f* = forecast.
a. Fixed investment, measured in real terms.
b. Local currency GDP deflator, median.
c. Weighted average growth of import demand in export markets.
d. Goods and non-factor services.
e. Change in terms of trade, measured as a percentage of GDP.

Table A.5 Middle East and North Africa outlook in summary, 1981–2003

Real economy *(percent change, unless stated)*	1981–90	1991–00	1997	1998	1999	2000	2001	2002e	2003f
Real GDP growth	2.4	3.2	2.7	3.2	2.0	4.3	3.2	2.6	3.7
Private consumption per capita	1.5	0.2	−0.2	1.2	0.1	1.1	5.1	1.0	1.0
GDP per capita	−0.6	1.0	0.7	1.3	0.1	2.3	1.3	0.7	1.7
Population	3.1	2.2	2.0	2.0	1.9	2.0	1.9	1.9	1.9
Gross domestic investment/GDP[a]	26.7	21.2	21.1	21.5	21.5	21.4	21.5	21.9	22.2
Inflation[b]	8.4	6.4	5.0	0.1	5.7	7.7	3.3	3.8	4.0
Central government budget balance/GDP	−3.9	−0.9	−0.4	−2.5	−1.1	0.5	−0.9	−2.2	−2.2
Export market growth[c]	5.3	10.0	6.9	2.0	8.4	13.2	−1.2	2.3	7.9
Export volume[d]	0.7	5.0	2.6	−1.8	3.4	7.6	3.6	1.4	4.6
Terms of trade/GDP[e]	−0.9	0.5	−0.9	−5.1	5.4	8.7	−1.9	0.0	−2.3
Current account/GDP	−1.7	−2.0	0.5	−5.8	0.8	7.4	5.0	4.5	1.7
Workers remittances (billions of dollars)	—	—	9.4	10.3	10.5	10.9	13.1	14.0	—
Memorandum items									
GDP growth: oil exporters	1.0	2.8	2.4	1.2	−0.2	3.7	2.2	2.3	3.7
Diversified exporters	4.3	3.9	3.0	5.6	3.8	3.6	4.1	2.5	3.1

External Financing and Debt *(billions of dollars unless stated)*	1995	1996	1997	1998	1999	2000	2001	2002e	2003f
Net inward FDI	−0.6	0.7	6.2	7.5	3.2	2.5	5.5	3.0	3.0
Net inward portfolio equity flows	0.1	0.5	0.8	0.3	0.7	0.2	−0.1	0.0	−1.0
Net inward debt flows	2.7	−2.5	−4.4	8.3	−2.2	−6.5	1.7	−0.3	2.5
From public sources	−1.5	−0.8	−4.0	−1.7	−2.7	−2.9	−1.2	−1.6	0.0
From private sources	4.2	−1.7	−0.4	10.0	0.5	−3.6	2.9	1.3	2.5
Gross market-based capital inflows	11.3	4.5	18.7	12.1	13.6	8.9	12.1	14.7	16.0
Total external debt	212	204	195	210	214	202	201	—	—
Medium- and long-term	167	162	154	164	163	156	153	—	—
Short-term	45	42	41	46	50	47	47	—	—
Owed by public-sector borrowers	162	156	147	155	157	149	146	—	—
Owed by private-sector borrowers	50	48	48	55	57	53	55	—	—
Owed to public-sector creditors	118	117	109	112	107	101	98	—	—
Owed to private-sector creditors	94	87	86	98	106	101	102	—	—
Gross foreign exchange reserves	44.9	56.4	63.0	61.6	64.2	76.5	85.2	90.2	90.2

— Not available.
Note: e = estimate, *f* = forecast.
a. Fixed investment, measured in real terms.
b. Local currency GDP deflator, median.
c. Weighted average growth of import demand in export markets.
d. Goods and non-factor services.
e. Change in terms of trade, measured as a percentage of GDP.

Table A.6 South Asia outlook in summary, 1981–2003

Real economy *(percent change, unless stated)*	1981–90	1991–00	1997	1998	1999	2000	2001	2002e	2003f
Real GDP growth	5.8	5.2	4.2	6.0	5.8	4.0	4.3	4.9	5.3
Private consumption per capita	2.3	2.4	1.3	−0.3	−0.1	0.1	3.5	2.0	2.3
GDP per capita	3.5	3.2	2.4	4.1	3.9	2.1	2.6	3.2	3.6
Population	2.2	1.9	1.8	1.8	1.9	1.9	1.7	1.7	1.6
Gross domestic investment/GDP[a]	20.1	21.9	21.8	22.2	22.6	22.8	23.6	23.9	23.9
Inflation[b]	8.9	8.1	7.3	7.5	4.6	5.8	6.1	5.0	5.1
Central government budget balance/GDP	−12.6	−10.3	−9.9	−10.7	−9.8	−9.7	−10.3	−10.3	−9.8
Export market growth[c]	5.0	12.7	8.2	3.7	7.1	12.9	0.2	2.8	6.3
Export volume[d]	6.4	9.3	5.6	8.6	1.8	7.7	3.8	5.3	10.0
Terms of trade/GDP[e]	0.0	−0.1	0.3	0.9	−0.4	−0.8	0.4	0.0	0.2
Current account/GDP	−2.0	−1.5	−1.1	−1.8	−1.0	−1.0	−0.5	−1.1	−0.8
Workers remittances (billions of dollars)	—	—	14.6	13.3	15.1	13.5	14.9	16.0	—
Memorandum items									
GDP growth: South Asia excluding India	5.5	4.3	3.2	3.7	3.6	4.2	3.8	3.9	4.8

External Financing and Debt *(billions of dollars unless stated)*	1995	1996	1997	1998	1999	2000	2001	2002e	2003f
Net inward FDI	2.9	3.5	4.9	3.5	3.1	3.1	4.1	5.0	6.0
Net inward portfolio equity flows	1.6	4.1	2.9	−0.6	2.4	1.7	1.6	0.8	2.0
Net inward debt flows	2.5	2.6	0.6	4.7	0.5	3.4	−0.3	0.9	−1.0
From public sources	−1.2	1.0	0.3	2.3	2.5	0.5	2.5	1.9	−1.0
From private sources	3.7	1.6	0.3	2.4	−2.0	2.9	−2.7	−1.0	0.0
Gross market-based capital inflows	7.4	10.5	12.7	5.1	4.2	4.8	3.3	2.6	3.0
Total external debt	157	155	155	163	167	165	162	—	—
Medium- and long-term	148	145	147	156	160	159	157	—	—
Short-term	9	10	8	7	7	6	5	—	—
Owed by public-sector borrowers	140	135	135	145	150	144	142	—	—
Owed by private-sector borrowers	17	20	20	18	17	21	19	—	—
Owed to public-sector creditors	114	110	104	110	119	108	107	—	—
Owed to private-sector creditors	43	46	51	53	49	57	55	—	—
Gross foreign exchange reserves	24.2	24.8	30.0	32.9	37.9	42.6	52.8	70.8	85.8

— Not available.
Note: *e* = estimate, *f* = forecast.
a. Fixed investment, measured in real terms.
b. Local currency GDP deflator, median.
c. Weighted average growth of import demand in export markets.
d. Goods and non-factor services.
e. Change in terms of trade, measured as a percentage of GDP.

Table A.7 Sub-Saharan Africa outlook in summary, 1981–2003

Real economy *(percent change, unless stated)*	1981–90	1991–00	1997	1998	1999	2000	2001	2002e	2003f
Real GDP growth	1.7	2.2	3.4	2.3	2.5	3.3	3.2	2.6	3.0
Private consumption per capita	−1.0	−0.5	4.0	−1.7	0.0	−2.1	1.0	0.1	0.4
GDP per capita	−1.2	−0.4	0.6	−0.2	0.1	0.8	0.7	0.3	0.6
Population	2.9	2.6	2.8	2.6	2.4	2.5	2.4	2.4	2.3
Gross domestic investment/GDP[a]	18.6	17.0	17.6	18.3	17.8	18.2	18.9	19.4	19.8
Inflation[b]	9.6	9.5	7.2	5.6	5.4	6.8	5.6	4.3	3.9
Central government budget balance/GDP	−4.5	−4.6	−2.8	−3.1	−2.8	−1.4	−1.8	−2.2	−2.4
Export market growth[c]	4.8	14.3	9.1	8.1	6.7	10.7	0.2	2.2	5.6
Export volume[d]	1.5	4.3	5.1	3.1	3.5	5.4	3.8	2.1	7.3
Terms of trade/GDP[e]	0.2	−0.1	−0.3	−2.0	1.3	2.1	−2.0	1.5	−0.6
Current account/GDP	−2.7	−2.0	−2.9	−5.9	−3.6	0.1	−1.7	−1.4	−1.5
Workers remittances (billions of dollars)	—	—	3.8	3.6	3.5	2.0	2.4	4.0	—
Memorandum items									
GDP growth: Sub-Saharan Africa excluding South Africa	2.2	2.7	4.1	3.8	2.9	3.2	3.5	2.4	2.9
Oil exporters	2.0	2.6	4.3	3.6	2.0	4.2	4.3	1.8	3.6
CFA countries	2.1	2.4	5.2	4.8	2.2	2.2	3.1	2.0	2.1

External Financing and Debt *(billions of dollars unless stated)*	1995	1996	1997	1998	1999	2000	2001	2002e	2003f
Net inward FDI	4.3	4.3	8.1	6.5	8.1	6.1	13.8	7.0	7.0
Net inward portfolio equity flows	2.9	2.4	5.6	8.6	8.9	4.0	−1.0	0.7	1.0
Net inward debt flows	7.6	3.2	4.5	−1.4	−0.9	−0.9	−1.0	0.2	−0.5
From public sources	3.5	2.0	1.4	0.5	0.4	0.5	0.3	1.6	1.0
From private sources	4.1	1.2	3.1	−1.9	−1.2	−1.4	−1.3	−1.4	−1.5
Gross market-based capital inflows	7.8	7.8	7.9	6.4	10.0	12.2	11.1	9.9	12.0
Total external debt	235	231	221	228	215	211	203	—	—
Medium- and long-term	195	189	180	186	174	178	171	—	—
Short-term	41	43	41	42	41	33	32	—	—
Owed by public-sector borrowers	183	178	171	178	164	167	158	—	—
Owed by private-sector borrowers	52	53	50	51	51	44	45	—	—
Owed to public-sector creditors	146	144	138	146	135	141	135	—	—
Owed to private-sector creditors	89	87	83	83	80	70	68	—	—
Gross foreign exchange reserves	17.9	20.6	28.1	26.8	28.2	34.0	34.3	34.3	37.3

— Not available.
Note: e = estimate, *f* = forecast.
a. Fixed investment, measured in real terms.
b. Local currency GDP deflator, median.
c. Weighted average growth of import demand in export markets.
d. Goods and non-factor services.
e. Change in terms of trade, measured as a percentage of GDP.

Table A.8 Global real GDP growth, 1981–2003

(GDP in 1995 prices and exchange rates, average annual growth; percent)

	GDP 2001 (1995 dollars)	Average 1981–90	Average 1991–00	1997	1998	1999	2000	2001	Estimate 2002	Forecast 2003
World	33,902	3.0	2.6	3.4	2.1	2.9	3.9	1.2	1.7	2.3
High-income countries	27,679	3.1	2.5	3.2	2.2	2.9	3.7	0.8	1.4	1.9
Industrial countries	26,852	3.1	2.4	3.1	2.2	2.9	3.6	0.9	1.4	1.8
European Union (15)	9,771	2.4	2.0	2.5	2.8	2.7	3.6	1.5	1.0	1.5
Japan	5,701	4.1	1.4	1.8	−1.2	0.2	2.8	0.3	−0.3	0.6
United States	9,040	3.2	3.2	4.4	4.3	4.1	3.8	0.3	2.4	2.5
Other high-income countries	827	4.9	5.4	5.4	1.0	3.7	6.7	−1.1	2.2	3.0
Asian NIEs	623	7.4	6.1	6.3	1.1	5.1	7.8	−1.4	2.8	3.3
Developing countries	6,222	2.6	3.3	4.7	1.8	2.7	5.1	2.8	3.1	4.0
excluding China	5,106	2.2	2.3	4.0	0.7	1.9	4.5	1.9	2.1	3.2
excluding Central Europe and CIS	5,334	3.1	4.6	5.2	2.2	2.6	4.9	2.6	3.1	4.1
Severely indebted	1,602	1.5	3.2	4.4	−0.7	0.2	3.0	0.9	−0.3	2.3
Moderately indebted	1,513	2.6	0.9	3.5	−1.6	1.5	5.8	1.7	3.2	3.1
Less indebted	3,107	3.4	4.7	5.6	5.2	4.8	5.8	4.5	4.9	5.2
Middle-income countries	5,131	2.3	3.3	4.9	2.0	2.5	5.2	2.6	2.9	3.9
Upper middle-income countries	2,306	1.2	3.1	5.1	1.8	0.9	3.9	0.6	−0.4	2.0
Lower middle-income countries	2,825	3.4	3.5	4.7	2.2	3.8	6.4	4.2	5.6	5.4
Low-income countries	1,091	4.2	3.1	3.9	0.7	3.9	4.2	4.3	4.2	4.4
East Asia and Pacific	1,712	7.4	7.7	6.4	0.6	5.6	7.1	5.5	6.7	6.4
China	1,116	9.3	10.1	8.8	7.8	7.1	8.0	7.3	8.0	—
Indonesia	217	6.4	4.2	4.7	−13.0	0.3	5.3	3.3	3.5	—
Europe and Central Asia	1,080	1.6	−1.5	3.1	0.1	1.8	6.5	2.3	4.1	3.7
Russian Federation	378	1.5	−4.0	0.9	−4.9	5.4	9.0	5.0	4.1	—
Turkey	192	5.2	3.6	7.5	3.1	−4.7	7.4	−6.5	6.3	—
Poland	165	−0.3	3.7	6.8	4.8	4.1	4.0	1.0	1.2	—
Latin America and the Caribbean	1,929	1.1	3.3	5.2	2.0	0.2	3.5	0.3	−0.9	1.7
Brazil	797	1.5	2.7	3.3	0.1	1.2	4.0	1.5	1.2	—
Mexico	372	1.8	3.5	6.8	4.9	3.7	6.6	−0.3	1.1	—
Argentina	280	−1.5	4.5	8.1	3.9	−3.4	−0.8	−4.4	−11.0	—
Middle East and North Africa	490	2.4	3.2	2.7	3.2	2.0	4.3	3.2	2.6	3.7
Saudi Arabia	141	0.3	2.3	2.0	1.7	−0.8	4.5	1.2	0.7	—
Iran, Islamic Rep. of	111	2.7	4.2	3.4	2.0	2.5	5.9	4.8	4.9	—
Egypt, Arab Rep. of	80	5.5	4.3	5.5	4.5	6.3	5.1	2.9	2.3	—
South Asia	634	5.8	5.2	4.2	6.0	5.8	4.0	4.3	4.9	5.3
India	488	5.9	5.4	4.6	6.8	6.5	4.0	4.5	5.2	—
Sub-Saharan Africa	378	1.7	2.2	3.4	2.3	2.5	3.3	3.2	2.6	3.0
South Africa	177	1.3	1.7	2.6	0.8	2.0	3.5	2.8	2.9	—
Nigeria	33	1.1	2.6	2.7	1.9	1.1	3.8	4.0	−0.7	—

— Not available.

Table A.9 Global inflation, 1991–2002

(consumer price indices; local currency; percent change[a])

	Weights 1995	Average 1991–2000	1996	1997	1998	1999	2000	2001	Estimate 2002
World	100	3.4	3.3	2.8	2.0	1.9	2.7	1.5	2.1
High-income countries	**85**	**2.2**	**2.2**	**1.9**	**1.2**	**1.3**	**2.1**	**0.9**	**1.5**
Industrial countries	—	2.2	2.2	1.9	1.2	1.4	2.1	1.0	1.6
European Union (15)	—	2.6	2.1	2.1	1.1	1.7	2.5	1.9	2.3
Japan	—	0.7	0.6	1.8	0.6	−1.1	−0.4	−1.2	−0.3
United States	—	2.7	3.3	1.7	1.6	2.7	3.4	1.6	2.4
Other high-income countries	—	3.0	3.6	2.1	0.4	−0.9	0.7	−2.0	−1.1
Asian NIEs	—	3.0	3.6	2.0	0.4	−1.0	0.6	−2.0	−1.2
Developing countries	**15**	**9.7**	**9.2**	**7.3**	**6.6**	**4.8**	**5.9**	**4.6**	**5.5**
excluding China	—	9.7	9.1	7.4	6.7	4.9	5.9	4.6	5.5
excluding Central Europe and CIS	—	9.2	9.1	7.2	6.4	4.5	5.6	4.7	5.6
Severely indebted	—	10.9	9.6	7.3	5.9	4.4	4.9	4.5	5.8
Moderately indebted	—	11.5	11.4	8.9	7.2	6.0	6.6	5.4	5.8
Less indebted	—	7.8	7.1	5.7	6.1	4.2	5.3	4.1	4.7
Middle-income countries	—	9.5	8.0	6.8	6.3	4.5	5.4	4.1	4.9
Upper middle-income countries	—	9.9	8.3	6.7	5.7	5.7	5.8	3.7	5.2
Lower middle-income countries	—	9.3	9.4	7.1	6.5	3.9	5.4	4.8	5.0
Low-income countries	—	10.8	9.8	8.5	8.8	5.5	7.4	6.3	6.2
East Asia and Pacific	—	5.5	5.7	6.1	7.8	2.4	3.1	2.8	4.3
China	—	7.0	7.0	0.4	−1.0	−1.0	0.4	−1.4	−0.1
Indonesia	—	13.4	6.0	10.3	77.6	1.9	9.3	12.5	10.0
Europe and Central Asia	—	27.4	19.2	16.2	10.1	11.1	10.0	6.3	4.2
Russian Federation	—	—	21.8	11.0	84.4	36.5	20.2	18.6	15.1
Turkey	—	74.9	79.8	99.1	69.7	68.8	39.0	68.5	29.7
Poland	—	24.2	18.7	13.2	8.5	9.8	8.6	3.7	0.7
Latin America and the Caribbean	—	12.9	12.6	9.3	7.2	6.1	6.6	5.5	6.8
Brazil	—	180.6	9.6	5.2	1.7	8.9	6.0	7.6	12.5
Mexico	—	17.5	27.7	15.7	18.6	12.3	8.9	4.4	5.7
Argentina	—	9.2	0.1	0.3	0.7	−1.8	−0.7	−1.5	40.9
Middle East and North Africa	—	5.9	4.4	3.8	2.9	3.2	2.4	2.7	1.8
Saudi Arabia	—	0.7	1.2	−0.4	−0.9	−0.6	−1.3	0.0	−1.0
Iran, Islamic Rep. of	—	24.1	20.9	15.8	20.2	19.0	12.8	10.6	16.4
Egypt, Arab Rep. of	—	8.7	5.4	4.3	3.6	3.2	2.3	2.5	3.0
South Asia	—	8.5	12.1	4.7	11.2	1.5	3.7	4.8	4.6
India	—	8.4	10.4	6.3	15.3	0.5	3.5	5.2	4.0
Sub-Saharan Africa	—	8.9	8.1	6.6	5.5	4.9	7.1	4.7	6.1
South Africa	—	8.6	9.3	6.5	8.7	2.5	7.3	4.1	14.5
Nigeria	—	29.0	14.3	10.2	11.9	0.2	14.5	16.5	10.0

— Not available.

a. Developing country aggregates show median rates. Industrial-country aggregates use 1995 US$ GDP weights. World total is GDP weighted average of developing and high income total. Inflation is calculated on a December/December basis.

Table A.10 Commodity prices, 1980–2003
(dollar terms)

	Unit	1980	1990	1997	1998	1999	2000	2001	2002	Forecast 2003
Energy										
Coal, Australia	$/mt	—	39.67	35.10	29.23	25.89	26.25	32.31	27.06	26.00
Crude oil, average	$/bbl	36.87	22.88	19.17	13.07	18.07	28.23	24.35	24.93	24.00
Natural gas, Europe	$/mmbtu	3.40	2.55	2.74	2.42	2.13	3.86	4.06	3.05	3.00
Non-energy commodities										
Agriculture										
Beverages										
Cocoa	¢/kg	260.4	126.7	161.9	167.6	113.5	90.6	106.9	177.8	200.0
Coffee, arabica	¢/kg	346.6	197.2	416.8	298.1	229.1	192.0	137.3	135.7	143.3
Coffee, robusta	¢/kg	324.3	118.2	173.6	182.3	148.9	91.3	60.7	66.2	86.0
Food										
Fats and oils										
Palm oil	$/mt	583.7	289.8	545.8	671.1	436.0	310.3	285.7	390.3	460.0
Soybean meal	$/mt	262.4	200.2	275.8	170.3	152.2	189.2	181.0	175.2	190.0
Soybeans	$/mt	296.2	246.8	295.4	243.3	201.7	211.8	195.8	212.7	240.0
Grains										
Maize	$/mt	125.3	109.3	117.1	102.0	90.2	88.5	89.6	99.3	108.0
Rice, Thailand	$/mt	410.7	270.9	303.5	304.2	248.4	202.4	172.8	191.9	195.0
Wheat, U.S.	$/mt	172.7	135.5	159.5	126.1	112.0	114.1	126.8	148.1	160.0
Other food										
Bananas, U.S.	$/mt	377.3	540.9	517.1	489.5	373.8	424.0	583.3	528.6	529.1
Sugar, world	¢/kg	63.16	27.67	25.06	19.67	13.81	18.04	19.04	15.18	18.0
Raw materials										
Cotton	¢/kg	206.2	181.9	174.8	144.5	117.1	130.2	105.8	101.9	127.9
Rubber, Malaysia	¢/kg	142.5	86.5	101.8	72.2	62.9	69.1	60.0	77.1	86.0
Sawnwood, Malaysia	$/cum	396.0	533.0	664.5	484.2	600.8	594.7	481.4	526.5	570.0
Fertilizers										
Triple superphosphate	$/mt	180.3	131.8	171.9	173.1	154.5	137.7	126.9	133.1	135.0
Metals and minerals										
Aluminum	$/mt	1,456	1,639	1,599	1,357	1,361	1,549	1,444	1,350	1,400
Copper	$/mt	2,182	2,661	2,277	1,654	1,573	1,813	1,578	1,559	1,650
Gold	$/toz	607.9	383.5	331.1	294.2	278.8	279.0	271.0	310.0	335.0
Nickel	$/mt	6,519	8,864	6,927	4,630	6,011	8,638	5,945	6,772	7,500
Memorandum										
Deflator index (MUV 1990 = 100)[a]		78.8	100.0	103.5	99.6	99.3	97.2	94.3	93.0	98.2
Reuters/CRB Commodity Futures index (1967 = 100)		294.2	234.8	242.5	215.2	194.5	218.6	207.3	209.4	—

— Not available.
Note: bbl = barrel, cum = cubic meter, kg = kilogram, mmbtu = million British thermal units, mt = metric ton, toz = troy oz. See http://www.worldbank.org/prospects for details of price series and forecasts.
a. MUV is the unit value index in U.S. dollar terms of manufactures exported from G-5 countries weighted by exports to developing countries.

Table A.11 Commodity price indices, 1980–2003
(real dollar terms, deflated by $ MUV; 1990 = 100)

	Weights[a]	1980	1990	1997	1998	1999	2000	2001	2002	Forecast 2003
Energy										
Coal, Australia		—	100.0	85.5	74.0	65.7	68.1	86.3	73.4	66.7
Crude oil, average		204.5	100.0	80.9	57.3	79.6	127.0	112.8	117.2	115.7
Natural gas, Europe		169.2	100.0	103.8	95.3	84.1	155.8	168.8	128.6	119.8
Non-energy commodities[a]	**100.0**	**159.2**	**100.0**	**113.6**	**99.5**	**88.6**	**89.4**	**83.7**	**89.2**	**91.6**
Agriculture	**69.1**	**175.2**	**100.0**	**124.4**	**108.2**	**93.5**	**90.3**	**84.5**	**93.0**	**96.7**
Beverages	**16.9**	**230.2**	**100.0**	**164.9**	**141.1**	**108.5**	**90.9**	**76.4**	**91.0**	**94.6**
Cocoa	3.9	260.8	100.0	123.4	132.9	90.3	73.6	89.4	150.9	160.8
Coffee, arabica	8.0	223.0	100.0	204.1	151.8	117.0	100.2	73.8	74.0	74.0
Coffee, robusta	2.8	348.2	100.0	141.9	154.8	126.9	79.5	54.5	60.2	74.1
Food	**29.4**	**176.7**	**100.0**	**112.3**	**105.3**	**88.2**	**87.0**	**91.2**	**96.9**	**100.0**
Fats and oils	**10.1**	**188.6**	**100.0**	**142.7**	**133.4**	**105.8**	**99.0**	**94.4**	**108.8**	**117.7**
Palm oil	2.3	255.6	100.0	182.0	232.5	151.6	110.2	104.5	144.8	161.7
Soybean meal	4.1	166.3	100.0	133.1	85.4	76.6	97.3	95.9	94.1	96.7
Soybeans	2.0	152.3	100.0	115.6	99.0	82.3	88.3	84.1	92.7	99.1
Grains	**6.9**	**170.4**	**100.0**	**108.3**	**101.7**	**87.0**	**81.8**	**82.9**	**94.7**	**95.1**
Maize	1.7	145.4	100.0	103.5	93.7	83.2	83.4	87.0	97.7	100.6
Rice, Thailand	2.9	192.4	100.0	108.2	112.7	92.4	76.9	67.6	76.2	73.3
Wheat, U.S.	1.9	161.7	100.0	113.7	93.4	83.3	86.6	99.2	117.5	120.2
Other food	**12.4**	**170.5**	**100.0**	**89.7**	**84.5**	**74.5**	**80.0**	**93.2**	**88.2**	**88.1**
Bananas, U.S.	2.3	88.5	100.0	92.3	90.9	69.6	80.7	114.3	105.1	99.6
Sugar, world	7.5	289.6	100.0	87.5	71.4	50.3	67.1	72.9	59.0	66.2
Raw materials	**22.8**	**132.7**	**100.0**	**109.9**	**87.7**	**89.2**	**94.0**	**82.0**	**89.5**	**94.1**
Cotton	5.9	143.8	100.0	92.8	79.7	64.8	73.7	61.7	60.3	71.6
Rubber, Malaysia	4.8	209.0	100.0	113.7	83.8	73.2	82.3	73.6	95.8	101.3
Sawnwood, Malaysia	2.9	94.3	100.0	120.4	91.2	113.6	114.8	95.7	106.2	108.9
Fertilizers	**2.7**	**163.6**	**100.0**	**115.7**	**122.6**	**114.9**	**108.9**	**104.7**	**108.1**	**102.0**
Triple superphosphate	0.9	173.5	100.0	126.0	131.8	118.1	107.5	102.0	108.6	104.3
Metals and minerals	**28.2**	**119.5**	**100.0**	**87.0**	**75.8**	**74.2**	**85.4**	**79.6**	**78.3**	**77.9**
Aluminum	7.9	112.7	100.0	94.2	83.1	83.6	97.2	93.3	88.5	87.0
Copper	9.3	104.0	100.0	82.6	62.4	59.5	70.1	62.9	63.0	63.1
Gold[a]	—	201.1	100.0	83.4	77.0	73.2	74.9	74.9	86.9	89.0
Nickel	2.2	93.3	100.0	75.5	52.4	68.3	100.3	71.1	82.2	86.2
Memorandum										
Deflator index (MUV 1990 = 100)[b]		78.8	100.0	103.5	99.6	99.4	97.3	96.0	96.5	99.3

— Not available.
a. The World Bank primary commodity price indices are computed from 1988–89 export values in U.S. dollars for low- and middle-income economies, rebased to 1990. Energy and gold prices are not included in the index.
b. MUV is the unit value index in U.S. dollar terms of manufactures exported from the G-5 countries weighted by exports to developing countries.
Source: World Bank Development Prospects Group. See http://www.worldbank.org/prospects for details of price series and forecasts.

Table A.12 Global nominal GDP growth, 1981–2003

(percent change from a year earlier)

	Average								Estimate	Forecast
	1981–90	1991–00	1996	1997	1998	1999	2000	2001	2002	2003
World	9.4	5.9	5.9	6.4	4.6	4.1	5.5	3.2	3.1	3.6
High-income countries	**8.4**	**4.6**	**4.3**	**5.6**	**3.6**	**3.3**	**4.6**	**2.2**	**2.4**	**3.0**
Industrial countries	7.9	4.4	4.1	5.5	3.7	3.3	4.6	2.3	2.4	2.9
European Union (15)	8.6	4.9	3.2	6.7	5.4	3.4	4.9	3.8	3.2	3.2
Japan	6.2	1.5	2.8	2.1	−1.3	−1.3	0.8	−1.2	−1.4	−0.1
United States	7.6	5.4	5.6	6.5	5.6	5.6	5.9	2.6	3.6	4.1
Other high-income countries	25.2	9.2	11.0	8.9	2.0	2.8	6.7	−0.8	1.8	4.2
Asian NIEs	12.2	8.5	9.6	9.4	2.2	1.7	5.6	−1.8	1.1	3.6
Developing countries	**15.2**	**13.5**	**14.9**	**11.4**	**10.1**	**8.8**	**10.6**	**8.9**	**7.2**	**7.6**
excluding China	15.1	13.4	14.7	11.4	10.2	8.8	10.6	8.9	7.1	7.6
excluding Central Europe and CIS	15.2	13.5	14.9	11.4	10.1	8.8	10.6	8.9	7.2	7.6
Severely indebted	15.2	14.8	17.1	10.7	10.2	7.5	10.3	9.7	8.0	7.6
Moderately indebted	14.9	14.7	14.7	11.2	9.8	7.6	8.9	8.8	6.7	7.5
Less indebted	15.6	13.0	13.6	12.1	10.0	10.0	11.5	8.5	8.1	7.8
Middle-income countries	16.4	12.8	14.0	11.1	8.1	8.6	10.6	8.1	6.7	7.4
Upper middle-income countries	16.8	11.8	15.4	11.1	6.6	7.5	10.8	6.6	6.3	7.3
Lower middle-income countries	16.1	13.0	13.4	11.0	8.7	8.6	10.6	8.8	6.7	7.6
Low-income countries	14.3	14.9	16.2	11.9	10.8	9.8	10.5	10.1	8.1	8.0
East Asia and Pacific	13.2	12.0	14.1	11.1	5.2	6.2	11.1	7.3	8.2	8.6
China	15.2	17.0	16.1	9.7	5.2	4.8	9.0	7.3	8.2	—
Indonesia	15.7	19.8	17.2	17.9	57.7	13.1	14.5	16.3	13.7	—
Europe and Central Asia	4.7	59.6	28.2	21.5	13.8	11.9	13.7	12.2	6.0	9.9
Russian Federation	—	277.9	39.3	15.5	10.6	73.9	53.2	23.8	15.3	—
Turkey	54.0	78.7	90.3	95.2	81.1	48.2	60.9	45.6	55.9	—
Poland	71.8	29.1	25.9	21.8	17.2	11.1	11.3	6.4	7.1	—
Latin America and the Caribbean	25.0	16.5	14.9	12.4	12.2	5.6	10.6	7.8	5.9	7.2
Brazil	337.4	214.3	20.5	11.8	5.0	5.4	12.7	10.4	10.0	—
Mexico	66.7	22.2	37.5	25.7	21.0	19.5	19.4	5.1	4.9	—
Argentina	431.4	15.2	5.5	7.6	2.1	−5.2	0.2	−5.5	16.3	—
Middle East and North Africa	12.4	12.1	17.2	7.8	7.0	9.4	10.8	8.1	6.5	7.7
Saudi Arabia	−2.9	5.2	10.6	3.6	−12.3	11.2	21.3	8.3	5.5	—
Iran, Islamic Rep. of	18.6	31.9	31.5	17.3	18.7	26.8	40.1	14.0	10.4	—
Egypt, Arab Rep. of	19.3	13.4	12.5	12.1	8.1	8.6	12.1	6.8	6.4	—
South Asia	14.7	13.2	13.6	12.7	10.8	9.1	9.6	9.9	9.9	10.7
India	14.7	14.3	15.2	11.3	16.3	10.0	11.2	8.0	9.9	—
Sub-Saharan Africa	14.1	14.2	16.3	11.5	11.4	9.7	10.6	10.1	8.1	7.8
South Africa	16.5	11.8	12.7	11.0	7.8	8.6	10.6	9.8	10.4	—
Nigeria	17.9	32.0	42.8	4.1	−3.8	13.5	30.1	10.1	14.2	—

— Not available.

a. Developing countries aggregated using median growth rates. Industrial aggregates use 1995 US$ GDP weights. World total is GDP weighted average of developing and high income total.

Table A.13 Global merchandise export growth, 1981–2003
(merchandise exports [FOB] in dollar terms; average annual growth; percent)

	Exports 2001 (billions of dollars)	Average 1981–90	Average 1991–00	1997	1998	1999	2000	2001	Estimate 2002	Forecast 2003
World	**6,024**	**6.4**	**6.8**	**4.1**	**−2.5**	**3.6**	**12.1**	**−3.8**	**4.3**	**13.7**
High-income countries	**4,541**	**7.4**	**6.0**	**3.2**	**−1.5**	**2.7**	**9.4**	**−4.7**	**3.2**	**14.8**
Industrial countries	4,008	7.1	5.7	3.2	−0.4	2.4	7.8	−3.8	3.0	15.5
European Union (15)	2,246	7.1	5.0	0.8	2.3	0.1	3.0	0.2	6.2	19.0
Japan	384	8.1	5.0	2.4	−8.6	7.6	13.8	−16.1	1.7	7.1
United States	734	6.2	7.2	11.4	−1.1	2.3	12.6	−6.5	−3.9	7.3
Other high-income countries	533	10.7	8.8	3.3	−9.8	5.0	21.6	−10.7	4.2	9.0
Asian NIEs	435	13.2	9.2	3.0	−9.2	4.0	19.0	−11.0	4.9	10.6
Developing countries	**1,500**	**2.7**	**9.6**	**7.4**	**−6.1**	**7.0**	**23.0**	**−0.9**	**6.6**	**10.8**
excluding China	1,234	2.2	8.6	5.3	−7.3	7.2	22.0	−2.4	3.6	8.5
excluding Central Europe and CIS	1,213	3.2	9.7	8.0	−6.4	8.9	22.7	−2.3	6.5	10.4
Severely indebted	215	3.4	6.0	5.9	−9.8	0.3	20.3	−2.0	1.1	10.5
Moderately indebted	481	4.7	9.4	3.7	−7.9	6.9	23.5	−5.6	3.7	9.9
Less indebted	812	1.1	11.1	10.5	−3.7	9.2	24.9	2.2	8.6	11.4
Middle-income countries	1,306	2.5	10.1	8.1	−5.4	7.2	23.5	−0.6	7.1	10.8
Upper middle-income countries	619	1.5	9.9	8.0	−5.0	8.7	23.1	−1.8	3.1	7.3
Lower middle-income countries	688	3.6	10.4	8.1	−5.7	5.9	23.9	0.5	10.7	13.7
Low-income countries	194	3.4	6.9	3.3	−10.4	5.8	24.1	−6.4	2.9	10.9
East Asia and Pacific	509	8.4	14.1	11.9	−2.4	8.3	22.9	−1.9	13.0	16.7
China	266	11.8	17.1	20.9	0.5	6.1	27.9	6.8	20.4	—
Indonesia	56	3.3	9.2	7.5	−8.8	−0.4	27.6	−9.3	0.6	—
Europe and Central Asia	322	1.2	9.0	4.2	−4.8	−1.6	24.7	3.8	6.2	11.4
Russian Federation	102	1.0	9.5	−1.7	−15.9	1.0	39.5	−3.8	6.3	—
Turkey	34	14.8	9.0	0.1	−4.5	−5.9	6.5	11.9	2.8	—
Poland	42	1.9	8.5	11.5	5.6	−7.4	19.4	16.0	4.7	—
Latin America and the Caribbean	351	5.4	10.1	11.1	−1.2	5.7	19.6	−3.6	0.8	5.8
Brazil	58	4.5	5.8	11.0	−3.5	−6.1	14.7	5.7	3.3	—
Mexico	158	11.2	15.8	15.2	6.2	16.0	22.2	−4.8	1.5	—
Argentina	27	4.4	7.9	9.9	0.0	−11.8	13.3	1.0	−5.1	—
Middle East and North Africa	161	−2.8	5.3	−1.4	−28.1	29.9	43.0	−4.6	2.9	−0.5
Saudi Arabia	73	−6.9	5.7	0.0	−36.1	30.7	52.9	−5.9	3.2	—
Iran, Islamic Rep. of	26	−1.6	3.9	−17.9	−28.6	60.3	34.8	−9.9	3.1	—
Egypt, Arab Rep. of	7	4.5	6.1	15.6	−20.3	18.9	34.8	−0.5	3.6	—
South Asia	65	8.4	8.7	6.3	−2.4	6.9	12.6	3.2	3.4	13.2
India	43	8.4	8.9	5.8	−4.6	10.1	14.5	0.7	3.1	—
Sub-Saharan Africa	95	0.7	3.3	0.0	−13.7	7.2	21.1	−3.6	−1.0	9.6
South Africa	31	−0.7	2.7	3.0	−6.1	−2.2	10.5	−3.1	−2.9	—
Nigeria	17	−1.4	3.7	−5.6	−41.0	43.5	51.4	−10.8	−0.6	—

— Not available.

Table A.14 Global merchandise import growth, 1981–2003
(merchandise imports, dollar terms, average annual growth; percent)

	Imports 2001 (billions of dollars)	Average 1981–90	Average 1991–00	1997	1998	1999	2000	2001	Estimate 2002	Forecast 2003
World	**6,021**	**5.9**	**6.9**	**3.8**	**−1.9**	**4.5**	**12.8**	**−3.8**	**3.2**	**15.4**
High-income countries	**4,698**	**6.6**	**6.5**	**3.0**	**−1.1**	**6.2**	**12.3**	**−5.2**	**1.9**	**16.1**
Industrial countries	4,185	6.4	6.1	2.8	0.4	6.3	11.3	−4.5	1.9	16.6
European Union (15)	2,139	5.9	4.8	0.6	3.7	2.3	5.6	−2.1	3.2	19.9
Japan	313	4.9	5.2	−3.2	−18.1	11.4	22.2	−8.6	−5.8	9.5
United States	1,167	7.6	9.5	9.5	5.0	12.4	18.8	−6.1	2.0	10.9
Other high-income countries	513	9.0	9.3	4.3	−11.8	4.9	19.9	−10.9	2.4	12.0
Asian NIEs	415	11.5	9.6	5.3	−13.9	2.6	21.8	−13.0	3.2	13.1
Developing countries	**1,341**	**2.9**	**8.8**	**6.9**	**−4.6**	**−1.7**	**16.6**	**1.6**	**6.2**	**13.2**
excluding China	1,109	2.6	7.7	7.4	−5.2	−4.1	13.5	0.3	3.0	10.5
excluding C.E. Europe/CIS	1,077	3.4	9.4	6.6	−4.7	1.1	18.1	−0.6	5.6	13.1
Severely indebted	171	0.1	6.9	7.7	−7.8	−11.9	8.6	−1.6	−9.7	12.5
Moderately indebted	408	4.4	6.6	4.8	−14.4	−5.5	17.6	−1.7	5.7	12.7
Less indebted	772	2.9	11.1	8.3	4.0	3.8	19.6	4.2	8.6	13.6
Middle-income countries	1,170	3.0	9.6	7.9	−3.5	−1.3	18.4	1.4	6.4	13.5
Upper middle-income countries	559	0.9	11.6	13.7	1.6	−0.8	15.7	−0.8	−0.6	9.5
Lower middle-income countries	612	4.6	8.1	3.2	−8.1	−1.7	21.3	3.5	12.7	16.7
Low-income countries	171	2.9	5.2	1.8	−10.6	−4.2	12.3	−3.6	4.5	11.1
East Asia and Pacific	424	8.9	11.9	0.0	−17.5	11.2	29.1	1.1	14.5	20.7
China	232	9.3	17.6	3.7	0.3	15.9	35.2	8.1	21.5	—
Indonesia	31	6.5	4.6	−2.9	−34.4	−12.2	38.9	−7.1	0.9	—
Europe and Central Asia	303	1.6	7.3	8.5	−4.2	−12.2	16.4	2.2	9.8	12.5
Russian Federation	54	3.8	0.2	5.7	−19.4	−31.9	13.5	19.8	12.3	—
Turkey	39	11.0	8.9	11.3	−5.4	−12.5	35.1	−26.8	17.9	—
Poland	49	−4.1	14.7	16.4	11.7	−0.4	6.8	2.3	5.4	—
Latin America and the Caribbean	352	1.3	12.6	18.4	5.9	−3.8	15.1	−2.0	−6.5	5.6
Brazil	56	−1.0	10.4	12.1	−3.4	−14.6	13.3	−0.5	−15.3	—
Mexico	168	7.8	15.4	22.7	14.0	13.3	22.8	−3.4	0.2	—
Argentina	19	−8.8	20.4	28.1	3.4	−18.4	−1.0	−19.9	−53.4	—
Middle East and North Africa	108	1.2	2.5	0.5	3.5	−2.7	8.1	6.6	6.2	9.7
Saudi Arabia	29	−3.3	2.6	4.0	4.4	−6.6	7.9	3.3	6.1	—
Iran, Islamic Rep. of	19	7.4	−1.9	−5.8	1.2	−6.0	13.2	25.5	7.8	—
Egypt, Arab Rep. of	14	8.9	4.1	7.5	3.3	3.7	1.4	−9.2	3.9	—
South Asia	78	6.0	7.1	2.1	−4.7	3.3	8.7	3.8	7.6	9.6
India	52	7.7	7.8	4.4	−2.0	1.6	9.5	3.5	7.6	—
Sub-Saharan Africa	83	−1.2	3.7	6.6	1.7	−5.1	5.7	−0.2	−5.3	10.1
South Africa	26	−0.9	4.7	4.6	−5.7	−9.8	11.3	−6.0	−1.0	—
Nigeria	9	−7.6	5.9	47.6	−3.1	−6.8	1.6	5.7	2.4	—

— Not available.

Table A.15 Global merchandise trade balances, 1995–2003
(billions of dollars)

	Percent of GDP 2001	1995	1996	1997	1998	1999	2000	2001	Estimate 2002	Forecast 2003
World	**0.0**	**116.2**	**103.9**	**122.9**	**84.8**	**41.2**	**5.0**	**3.4**	**70.0**	**−23.2**
High-income countries	**−0.6**	**117.3**	**91.1**	**104.4**	**86.1**	**−57.8**	**−191.4**	**−157.0**	**−104.7**	**−182.7**
Industrial countries	−0.7	125.4	88.0	106.0	76.9	−68.0	−212.2	−176.4	−134.2	−199.2
European Union (15)	1.4	143.3	170.9	175.6	152.3	107.1	57.1	107.2	179.5	194.1
Japan	1.7	133.6	82.8	102.4	122.9	122.7	116.1	71.7	96.5	96.0
United States	−4.3	−173.8	−189.9	−196.5	−248.8	−348.5	−457.9	−432.5	−483.6	−561.3
Other high-income countries	2.6	−8.0	3.1	−1.6	9.2	10.2	20.8	19.4	29.5	16.4
Asian NIEs	3.7	−7.1	0.5	−9.0	12.7	18.7	11.3	19.4	27.4	19.4
Developing countries	**2.7**	**−1.2**	**12.8**	**18.5**	**−1.3**	**99.0**	**194.0**	**159.3**	**174.7**	**159.5**
excluding China	2.6	−19.2	−6.7	−27.7	−47.9	63.1	159.5	125.3	136.4	125.2
excluding Central Europe and CIS	2.7	−2.1	26.6	40.5	21.8	94.6	158.4	135.9	154.9	140.9
Severely indebted	3.7	−0.4	8.2	5.3	0.9	23.0	46.4	44.7	63.7	67.1
Moderately indebted	5.6	−20.5	−11.8	−16.9	12.8	60.1	94.9	73.2	68.0	63.0
Less indebted	1.2	19.7	16.5	30.1	−14.9	15.9	52.8	39.4	43.1	29.3
Middle-income countries	2.8	12.0	23.9	27.1	6.0	90.2	160.7	136.6	154.1	137.0
Upper middle-income countries	2.6	28.2	34.5	13.2	−19.7	25.2	67.0	60.0	82.5	76.5
Lower middle-income countries	2.9	−16.2	−10.6	13.9	25.7	65.1	92.9	75.7	71.6	60.5
Low-income countries	2.2	−13.1	−11.0	−8.6	−7.3	8.8	29.6	22.7	20.6	22.5
East Asia and Pacific	5.4	0.9	3.5	46.0	98.2	97.6	99.7	84.9	89.3	84.6
China	2.9	18.1	19.5	46.2	46.6	36.0	34.5	34.0	38.4	—
Indonesia	17.5	4.8	6.9	11.9	21.5	24.7	28.8	25.4	25.4	—
Europe and Central Asia	1.9	−12.3	−24.4	−37.4	−37.4	−6.1	13.7	18.8	9.3	6.8
Russian Federation	15.4	20.3	22.5	17.0	16.9	36.1	60.7	47.8	47.6	—
Turkey	−3.1	−13.2	−10.6	−15.4	−14.3	−10.5	−22.4	−4.5	−10.5	—
Poland	−4.4	−1.6	−7.3	−9.8	−12.8	−15.1	−12.3	−7.7	−8.3	—
Latin America and the Caribbean	−0.1	2.3	3.7	−14.6	−36.3	−7.7	4.8	−1.0	24.6	26.6
Brazil	0.5	−3.5	−5.6	−6.8	−6.6	−1.3	−0.8	2.7	13.1	—
Mexico	−1.6	7.1	6.4	0.6	−8.0	−5.7	−8.0	−10.0	−8.0	—
Argentina	2.8	2.4	1.8	−2.1	−3.1	−0.8	2.6	7.6	16.4	—
Middle East and North Africa	9.5	19.4	35.8	33.5	−5.3	24.6	67.8	53.3	51.4	39.4
Saudi Arabia	23.6	24.4	35.4	34.4	11.3	25.0	49.8	44.4	45.0	—
Iran, Islamic Rep. of	5.7	5.6	7.4	4.3	−1.2	7.6	13.1	6.5	5.8	—
Egypt, Arab Rep. of	−7.0	−7.6	−8.4	−8.6	−10.2	−9.9	−8.3	−6.9	−7.2	—
South Asia	−2.0	−13.9	−17.9	−16.1	−14.0	−12.6	−11.5	−12.4	−16.0	−15.2
India	−1.7	−6.7	−10.1	−10.0	−10.8	−8.0	−6.9	−8.4	−10.9	—
Sub-Saharan Africa	4.2	2.3	12.1	7.1	−6.4	3.3	16.1	12.7	16.1	17.3
South Africa	4.7	2.7	2.7	2.3	2.1	4.1	4.3	5.0	4.3	—
Nigeria	19.8	3.5	9.7	5.7	−0.2	4.3	10.8	8.2	7.9	—

— Not available.

Table A.16 Global merchandise trade prices and volumes, 1981–2003

(average annual percent change; prices are in dollar terms unless indicated otherwise)

	Average change								Estimate	Forecast
	1981–90	1991–00	1996	1997	1998	1999	2000	2001	2002	2003
Trade prices										
Manufactured goods prices	2.4	−0.3	−4.9	−7.0	−3.8	−0.3	−2.1	−2.9	−1.4	5.6
(SDR terms)	2.0	0.0	−0.6	−1.9	−2.4	−1.1	1.6	0.3	−3.1	−0.4
Developing countries' export prices	3.2	1.2	6.3	−0.6	−7.3	2.6	7.0	−2.8	−2.2	0.8
Oil price	−4.7	2.1	18.9	−6.1	−31.8	38.3	56.2	−13.7	2.4	−3.7
Non-oil commodity prices	−2.2	−1.4	−5.8	2.2	−15.7	−11.2	−1.3	−9.1	5.1	8.2
Terms of trade										
World	1.5	0.1	0.7	−0.7	0.2	0.6	−1.2	−0.2	0.2	−1.2
High income	1.8	−0.1	0.0	−1.1	1.2	−0.3	−3.1	0.2	1.0	−1.1
Developing countries	0.9	0.3	3.4	0.6	−3.5	2.9	5.4	−1.5	−2.7	−0.8
Severely indebted	7.6	1.0	6.2	1.7	−5.0	3.9	5.9	−1.2	−2.8	−4.5
Moderately indebted	−0.3	1.6	5.2	0.6	−4.3	1.6	6.9	−4.2	−5.5	1.7
Less indebted	−2.4	−0.9	1.2	0.4	−2.3	3.4	4.3	0.2	−1.1	−1.3
Middle-income countries	1.2	0.6	3.5	0.7	−3.2	2.6	5.7	−1.8	−2.6	−0.9
Upper middle-income countries	−1.7	0.6	3.5	0.8	−4.5	4.0	6.9	−1.8	−0.3	−2.6
Lower middle-income countries	3.7	0.7	3.5	0.6	−2.1	1.4	4.7	−1.7	−4.4	0.6
Low-income countries	−1.4	−1.4	2.9	0.0	−4.9	4.2	3.1	0.5	−3.6	−0.7
East Asia and Pacific	−2.4	−1.0	2.7	0.4	−0.9	1.4	0.9	−1.0	−1.4	−1.4
Europe and Central Asia	0.5	1.6	3.3	1.1	−2.5	−1.2	3.2	0.9	−9.5	5.5
Latin America and the Caribbean	8.5	1.6	2.6	3.1	−1.1	1.6	3.9	−1.7	0.2	−1.9
Middle East and North Africa	−6.2	0.9	12.6	−3.6	−21.8	26.5	39.8	−7.5	0.1	−9.0
South Asia	−1.0	−1.6	−3.5	2.6	7.9	−3.6	−7.1	3.4	−0.3	1.7
Sub-Saharan Africa	−0.6	−0.6	1.8	−1.4	−8.4	5.3	9.3	−2.6	−0.2	−2.3
Global merchandise export volumes										
World	**2.9**	**6.9**	**5.3**	**10.0**	**3.8**	**4.8**	**13.0**	**−0.7**	**3.4**	**6.0**
High income	3.8	6.7	5.3	10.5	4.4	4.9	12.8	−1.6	2.0	5.0
Developing countries	**−0.5**	**8.3**	**5.2**	**8.0**	**1.3**	**4.4**	**15.3**	**1.9**	**9.0**	**9.9**
Severely indebted	−6.5	4.4	1.7	6.9	−0.8	−2.1	10.3	5.1	3.5	10.2
Moderately indebted	2.5	7.0	1.7	4.3	−0.1	5.5	15.2	−3.0	7.0	8.2
Less indebted	1.4	10.8	9.2	11.0	2.9	5.8	17.7	3.3	11.7	10.8
Middle-income countries	−0.9	8.5	5.3	8.2	1.5	4.9	15.7	2.1	9.9	10.1
Upper middle-income countries	1.3	8.3	5.5	8.2	2.9	5.1	13.9	−0.8	4.2	8.7
Lower middle-income countries	−2.6	8.6	5.0	8.3	0.2	4.7	17.4	4.7	14.7	11.2
Low-income countries	1.9	7.5	4.9	6.8	0.4	2.0	15.4	−1.4	3.3	8.5
East Asia and Pacific	7.8	13.7	5.5	13.2	2.5	7.6	21.3	2.2	16.3	13.9
Europe and Central Asia	−0.8	6.9	4.7	4.9	2.1	0.8	19.0	−0.2	8.4	6.9
Latin America and the Caribbean	−5.1	7.5	5.8	8.5	3.6	3.9	12.7	−0.3	3.6	8.5
Middle East and North Africa	0.9	3.5	2.3	3.2	−5.8	4.0	2.9	6.0	1.4	4.6
South Asia	6.2	9.0	5.8	5.2	−1.9	6.8	13.0	1.1	3.5	9.3
Sub-Saharan Africa	−1.5	3.0	7.4	2.4	−2.3	1.8	9.5	2.1	1.9	7.1

Table A.17 Global current account balances, 1998–2003
(billions of dollars)

	Percent of GDP (2001)									
	Merchandise balance	Services balance	Income balance	Transfers, net	1998	1999	2000	2001	Estimate 2002	Forecast 2003
World	**−0.4**	**0.1**	**−0.3**	**−0.1**	**−36.2**	**−93.7**	**−156.2**	**−139.7**	**−133.0**	**−228.6**
High-income countries	**−0.7**	**0.2**	**0.1**	**−0.5**	**70.2**	**−84.6**	**−217.4**	**−170.1**	**−181.3**	**−254.8**
Industrial countries	−0.8	0.2	0.1	−0.5	42.6	−114.8	−265.1	−218.1	−240.9	−304.9
European Union (15)	1.0	0.1	−0.6	−0.8	89.0	25.4	−43.1	17.5	79.8	69.0
Japan	1.7	−1.0	1.6	−0.2	119.6	114.9	119.0	88.8	115.7	114.0
United States	−4.2	0.6	0.1	−0.5	−203.8	−292.9	−410.3	−393.4	−498.1	−549.3
Other high-income countries	2.1	5.0	1.3	0.0	27.6	30.3	47.7	48.0	59.6	50.1
Asian NIEs	1.8	9.2	2.1	−1.2	27.0	36.4	33.7	45.0	57.2	53.6
Developing countries	**1.2**	**−0.6**	**−2.1**	**1.6**	**−113.6**	**−10.8**	**61.9**	**27.6**	**48.3**	**26.2**
excluding China	0.7	−0.6	−2.3	1.8	−145.1	−31.9	41.4	10.2	30.0	6.0
excluding C.E. Europe/CIS	1.0	−0.7	−2.3	1.7	−85.0	−9.3	33.8	12.7	38.7	17.8
Severely indebted	0.9	−1.9	−3.8	1.5	−66.7	−40.1	−21.5	−21.7	−0.1	0.8
Moderately indebted	6.0	−0.5	−2.3	1.0	−4.1	42.3	72.9	48.4	47.5	41.4
Less indebted	−0.7	−0.2	−1.5	1.9	−42.8	−13.0	10.5	0.9	0.9	−16.0
Middle-income countries	1.7	−0.4	−2.2	1.2	−85.0	−0.6	56.3	28.2	55.4	35.3
Upper middle-income countries	0.3	−0.6	−2.8	0.7	−103.5	−59.9	−30.2	−34.9	−0.3	−14.6
Lower middle-income countries	2.9	−0.3	−1.8	1.5	18.5	59.2	86.6	63.1	55.7	49.9
Low-income countries	−2.0	−1.6	−1.6	4.3	−28.6	−10.1	5.6	−0.6	−7.1	−9.0
East Asia and Pacific	4.5	−0.9	−1.7	0.5	58.8	60.4	55.7	42.6	42.8	41.0
China	3.0	−0.5	−1.7	0.7	31.5	21.1	20.5	17.4	18.3	—
Indonesia	—	—	—	—	4.1	5.8	8.0	6.9	4.0	—
Europe and Central Asia	1.7	1.0	−1.8	1.3	−26.6	−2.9	18.3	18.3	8.9	6.7
Russian Federation	15.4	−2.7	−1.3	−0.2	0.7	24.7	47.3	34.6	31.2	—
Turkey	−3.1	6.2	−3.4	2.6	2.0	−1.4	−9.8	3.4	−0.7	—
Poland	−4.4	0.5	−0.8	1.7	−6.9	−12.5	−10.0	−5.4	−6.4	—
Latin America and the Caribbean	−0.1	−1.0	−2.9	1.3	−89.5	−55.7	−47.2	−54.1	−16.3	−19.5
Brazil	0.5	−1.5	−3.9	0.3	−33.8	−25.4	−24.6	−23.2	−7.8	—
Mexico	−1.6	−0.7	−2.0	1.5	−16.1	−14.0	−17.8	−17.7	−15.5	—
Argentina	2.8	−1.5	−3.0	0.1	−14.5	−11.9	−8.9	−4.6	8.6	—
Middle East and North Africa	−1.3	1.5	−2.0	5.2	−27.8	4.2	40.8	28.9	24.7	9.5
Saudi Arabia	—	—	—	—	−13.1	0.4	14.3	14.5	13.2	—
Iran, Islamic Rep. of	—	—	—	—	−2.1	6.6	12.6	5.5	4.8	—
Egypt, Arab Rep. of	−7.0	2.0	0.6	4.0	−2.6	−1.6	−1.0	−0.4	−0.4	—
South Asia	−2.2	−0.9	−0.9	4.2	−9.6	−5.5	−6.1	−2.9	−7.6	−6.1
India	−1.9	−0.7	−0.5	3.3	−6.9	−3.2	−4.2	1.1	3.3	—
Sub-Saharan Africa	0.9	−3.2	−4.0	1.7	−19.0	−11.3	0.4	−5.1	−4.3	−5.4
South Africa	4.4	−0.5	−3.4	−0.7	−2.2	−0.6	−0.6	−0.2	−0.7	—
Nigeria	—	—	—	—	−4.2	0.5	7.0	4.9	2.6	—

— Not available.

Table A.18 Global current account balances, 1981–2003
(percent of GDP)

	Average 1981–90	Average 1991–00	1996	1997	1998	1999	2000	2001	Estimate 2002	Forecast 2003
World	**−0.5**	**−0.2**	**−0.1**	**0.1**	**−0.1**	**−0.3**	**−0.5**	**−0.5**	**−0.4**	**−0.7**
High-income countries	**−0.2**	**0.1**	**0.2**	**0.5**	**0.3**	**−0.3**	**−0.9**	**−0.7**	**−0.7**	**−0.9**
Industrial countries	−0.4	−0.1	0.1	0.4	0.2	−0.5	−1.1	−0.9	−1.0	−1.1
European Union (15)	0.1	0.2	1.0	1.5	1.0	0.3	−0.5	0.2	0.9	0.7
Japan	2.3	2.4	1.4	2.2	3.0	2.6	2.5	2.1	2.9	2.8
United States	−1.9	−1.8	−1.5	−1.5	−2.3	−3.2	−4.2	−3.9	−4.8	−5.1
Other high-income countries	10.5	4.0	3.7	4.0	3.8	4.1	5.9	6.3	7.8	6.2
Asian NIEs	6.9	5.2	4.0	3.5	5.3	6.8	5.9	8.5	10.8	9.7
Developing countries	**−1.6**	**−1.6**	**−1.6**	**−1.5**	**−2.0**	**−0.2**	**1.0**	**0.5**	**0.8**	**0.4**
excluding China	−1.8	−2.3	−2.0	−2.5	−3.1	−0.7	0.9	0.2	0.6	0.1
excluding Central Europe and CIS	−1.7	−1.6	−1.7	−1.3	−1.7	−0.2	0.7	0.2	0.8	0.3
Severely indebted	−2.2	−2.5	−2.9	−3.7	−4.5	−3.2	−1.6	−1.8	0.0	0.1
Moderately indebted	−2.0	−1.5	−1.7	−2.1	−0.3	3.4	5.4	3.6	3.5	2.8
Less indebted	−1.1	−1.2	−0.8	0.0	−1.5	−0.4	0.3	0.0	0.0	−0.4
Middle-income countries	−1.3	−1.6	−1.3	−1.3	−1.8	0.0	1.2	0.6	1.1	0.7
Upper middle-income countries	−1.5	−2.9	−2.2	−3.3	−4.5	−2.8	−1.3	−1.5	0.0	−0.7
Lower middle-income countries	−1.2	−0.2	−0.6	0.5	0.8	2.5	3.4	2.4	2.0	1.7
Low-income countries	−2.7	−2.0	−2.8	−2.6	−3.1	−1.0	0.6	−0.1	−0.6	−0.7
East Asia and Pacific	−1.4	0.5	−1.8	1.1	4.4	4.2	3.6	2.6	2.5	2.2
China	0.2	1.6	0.9	4.1	3.3	2.1	1.9	1.5	1.5	1.5
Indonesia	−3.1	−0.4	−3.4	−2.3	4.3	4.1	5.2	4.7	2.2	1.0
Europe and Central Asia	−0.5	−2.5	−1.3	−2.5	−2.7	−0.3	2.0	1.9	0.8	0.6
Russian Federation	—	—	2.8	0.5	0.2	12.8	18.2	11.2	9.5	8.6
Turkey	−1.3	−1.1	−1.3	−1.4	1.0	−0.7	−4.9	2.3	−0.4	−0.9
Poland	−1.4	−3.7	−2.3	−4.0	−4.4	−8.1	−6.3	−3.1	−3.4	−3.6
Latin America and the Caribbean	−1.5	−2.8	−2.2	−3.3	−4.5	−3.2	−2.4	−2.9	−1.0	−1.2
Brazil	−1.1	−2.1	−3.0	−3.8	−4.3	−4.8	−4.1	−4.6	−1.7	−0.9
Mexico	−0.8	−3.7	−0.8	−1.9	−3.8	−2.9	−3.1	−2.9	−2.5	−3.9
Argentina	−2.2	−3.1	−2.5	−4.2	−4.9	−4.2	−3.1	−1.7	8.5	9.0
Middle East and North Africa	−1.7	−2.0	0.6	0.5	−5.8	0.8	7.4	5.0	4.5	1.7
Saudi Arabia	−7.3	−6.6	0.5	0.2	−10.2	0.3	8.3	7.7	6.6	2.4
Iran, Islamic Rep. of	−0.4	1.9	5.0	2.2	−2.1	6.6	12.5	4.7	5.3	2.0
Egypt, Arab Rep. of	−3.4	1.5	−0.3	−0.9	−3.1	1.8	−1.0	−0.4	−0.4	−0.4
South Asia	−2.0	−1.5	−2.5	−1.1	−1.8	−1.0	−1.0	−0.5	−1.1	−0.8
India	−1.7	−1.2	−1.6	−0.7	−1.7	−0.7	−0.9	−0.7	−1.2	−0.9
Sub-Saharan Africa	−2.7	−2.0	−0.5	−2.9	−5.9	−3.6	0.1	−1.7	−1.4	−1.5
South Africa	0.4	−0.2	−1.3	−1.5	−1.6	−0.5	−0.4	−0.1	−0.6	−0.3
Nigeria	−0.7	0.4	9.9	1.5	−13.2	1.5	16.9	11.9	5.8	2.0

Table A.19 Workers' remittances received by developing countries, 1995–2002
(billions of dollars)

	1995	1996	1997	1998	1999	2000	2001	2002e
All developing countries	**48.1**	**52.6**	**62.7**	**59.5**	**64.6**	**64.5**	**72.3**	**80.0**
East Asia and Pacific	8.3	9.5	14.2	8.3	10.6	10.3	10.4	11.0
China	0.4	1.7	4.6	0.3	0.5	0.8	1.2	—
Indonesia	0.7	0.8	0.7	1.0	1.1	1.2	1.0	—
Malaysia	0.1	0.2	0.2	0.2	0.3	0.3	0.3	—
Philippines	5.4	4.9	6.8	5.1	6.9	6.2	6.4	—
Thailand	1.7	1.8	1.7	1.4	1.5	1.7	1.3	—
Europe and Central Asia	5.5	6.2	7.1	9.2	8.1	8.7	8.9	10.0
Albania	0.4	0.6	0.3	0.5	0.4	0.6	0.7	—
Croatia	0.5	0.7	0.6	0.6	0.5	0.6	0.7	—
Poland	0.7	0.8	0.8	1.1	0.8	0.8	1.1	—
Russian Federation	0.2	0.1	0.2	0.3	0.4	0.5	0.6	—
Turkey	3.3	3.5	4.2	5.4	4.5	4.6	2.8	—
Latin America and the Caribbean	12.8	12.8	13.6	14.8	16.9	19.2	22.6	25.0
Brazil	3.0	2.1	1.6	1.2	1.5	1.4	1.5	—
Colombia	0.7	0.6	0.7	0.5	1.3	1.6	1.8	—
Dominican Republic	0.8	1.0	1.1	1.4	1.6	1.8	2.0	—
El Salvador	1.1	1.1	1.2	1.3	1.4	1.8	1.9	—
Mexico	4.4	5.0	5.5	6.5	6.6	7.6	9.9	—
Middle East and North Africa	8.6	9.1	9.4	10.3	10.5	10.9	13.1	14.0
Egypt, Arab Rep. of	3.2	3.1	3.7	3.4	3.2	2.9	2.9	—
Jordan	1.2	1.5	1.7	1.5	1.7	1.8	2.0	—
Lebanon	—	—	—	1.2	1.4	1.6	2.3	—
Morocco	2.0	2.2	1.9	2.0	1.9	2.2	3.3	—
South Asia	10.0	12.3	14.6	13.3	15.1	13.5	14.9	16.0
Bangladesh	1.2	1.3	1.5	1.6	1.8	2.0	2.1	—
India	6.2	8.8	10.3	9.5	11.1	9.2	10.0	—
Pakistan	1.7	1.3	1.7	1.2	1.0	1.1	1.5	—
Sri Lanka	0.8	0.8	0.9	1.0	1.1	1.2	1.1	—
Sub-Saharan Africa	2.7	2.7	3.8	3.6	3.5	2.0	2.4	4.0
Lesotho	0.4	0.4	0.4	0.3	0.3	0.3	0.2	—
Nigeria	0.8	0.9	1.9	1.6	1.3	—	—	—
Senegal	0.1	0.2	0.2	0.1	0.2	0.2	0.2	—
Sudan	0.3	0.2	0.4	0.7	0.7	0.6	0.7	—

— Not available.
Note: e = estimate.

Table A.20 Net official development assistance from DAC countries to developing countries and multilateral organizations, by donor, 1995–2001
(billions of dollars)

	1995	1996	1997	1998	1999	2000	2001
Total ODA	**58.9**	**55.6**	**48.5**	**52.1**	**56.4**	**53.7**	**52.3**
Australia	1.2	1.1	1.1	1.0	1.0	1.0	0.9
Austria	0.8	0.6	0.5	0.5	0.5	0.4	0.5
Belgium	1.0	0.9	0.8	0.9	0.8	0.8	0.9
Canada	2.1	1.8	2.0	1.7	1.7	1.7	1.5
Denmark	1.6	1.8	1.6	1.7	1.7	1.7	1.6
Finland	0.4	0.4	0.4	0.4	0.4	0.4	0.4
France	8.4	7.5	6.3	5.7	5.6	4.1	4.2
Germany	7.5	7.6	5.9	5.6	5.5	5.0	5.0
Greece	—	0.2	0.2	0.2	0.2	0.2	0.2
Ireland	0.2	0.2	0.2	0.2	0.2	0.2	0.3
Italy	1.6	2.4	1.3	2.3	1.8	1.4	1.6
Japan	14.5	9.4	9.4	10.6	15.3	13.5	9.8
Luxembourg	0.1	0.1	0.1	0.1	0.1	0.1	0.1
Netherlands	3.2	3.2	2.9	3.0	3.1	3.1	3.2
New Zealand	0.1	0.1	0.2	0.1	0.1	0.1	0.1
Norway	1.2	1.3	1.3	1.3	1.4	1.3	1.3
Portugal	0.3	0.2	0.3	0.3	0.3	0.3	0.3
Spain	1.3	1.3	1.2	1.4	1.4	1.2	1.7
Sweden	1.7	2.0	1.7	1.6	1.6	1.8	1.7
Switzerland	1.1	1.0	0.9	0.9	1.0	0.9	0.9
United Kingdom	3.2	3.2	3.4	3.9	3.4	4.5	4.6
United States	7.4	9.4	6.9	8.8	9.1	10.0	11.4

— Not available.

Table A.21 Net official development assistance to developing countries, by recipient, 1995–2001
(billions of dollars)

	1995	1996	1997	1998	1999	2000	2001
All developing countries[a]	**61.0**	**51.9**	**46.6**	**50.3**	**52.4**	**50.5**	**52.0**
Unspecified	8.5	6.5	7.6	7.9	7.9	9.0	8.5
East Asia and Pacific	9.5	7.6	6.6	8.0	9.4	8.0	6.8
China	3.5	2.6	2.1	2.4	2.4	1.7	1.5
Indonesia	1.4	1.1	0.8	1.3	2.2	1.7	1.5
Philippines	0.9	0.9	0.7	0.6	0.7	0.6	0.6
Vietnam	0.8	0.9	1.0	1.2	1.4	1.7	1.4
Europe and Central Asia	9.5	6.9	5.6	7.0	9.6	9.6	9.1
Bosnia and Herzegovina	0.9	0.8	0.9	0.9	1.0	0.7	0.6
Poland	3.8	1.2	0.9	0.9	1.2	1.4	1.0
Russian Federation	1.6	1.3	0.8	1.1	1.9	1.6	1.1
Yugoslavia, Fed. Rep. of	0.1	0.1	0.1	0.1	0.7	1.1	1.3
Latin America and the Caribbean	5.7	5.5	4.5	4.5	4.7	3.8	5.2
Bolivia	0.7	0.8	0.7	0.6	0.6	0.5	0.7
Honduras	0.4	0.4	0.3	0.3	0.8	0.4	0.7
Nicaragua	0.7	0.9	0.4	0.6	0.7	0.6	0.9
Middle East and North Africa	4.9	5.3	4.8	4.7	4.3	3.7	3.9
Egypt, Arab Rep. of	2.0	2.2	2.0	2.0	1.6	1.3	1.3
Jordan	0.5	0.5	0.5	0.4	0.4	0.6	0.4
Morocco	0.5	0.7	0.5	0.5	0.7	0.4	0.5
South Asia	5.2	5.2	4.3	4.9	4.3	4.2	5.9
Bangladesh	1.3	1.2	1.0	1.2	1.2	1.2	1.0
India	1.7	1.9	1.6	1.6	1.5	1.5	1.7
Pakistan	0.8	0.9	0.6	1.1	0.7	0.7	1.9
Sub-Saharan Africa	17.8	15.0	13.3	13.3	12.2	12.2	12.7
Côte d'Ivoire	1.2	1.0	0.4	1.0	0.4	0.4	0.2
Ethiopia	0.9	0.8	0.6	0.7	0.6	0.7	1.1
Mozambique	1.1	0.9	0.9	1.0	0.8	0.9	0.9
Tanzania	0.9	0.9	0.9	1.0	1.0	1.0	1.2
Zambia	2.0	0.6	0.6	0.3	0.6	0.8	0.4

Note: Total net ODA flows from DAC countries, multilateral organizations, and non-DAC countries.
a. This total does not include regionally unallocated and unspecified amounts due to the different country grouping used by the OECD.

Table A.22 External financing: all developing countries, 1997–2003
(billions of dollars)

	1997	1998	1999	2000	2001	2002e	2003f
Current account balance	−91.4	−113.6	−10.7	61.9	27.6	48.3	26.2
as a percentage of GDP	−1.5	−2.0	−0.2	1.0	0.5	0.8	0.4
Financed by:							
Net equity flows	196.0	181.9	194.3	186.7	177.6	152.3	158.0
Net FDI inflows	169.3	174.5	179.3	160.6	171.7	143.0	145.0
Net portfolio equity inflows	26.7	7.4	15.0	26.0	6.0	9.3	13.0
Net debt flows	102.1	57.4	13.9	−1.0	3.2	7.2	5.0
Official creditors	13.0	34.1	13.5	−6.2	28.0	16.2	0.0
World Bank	9.2	8.7	8.8	7.8	7.5	1.5	—
IMF	3.4	14.1	−2.2	−10.6	19.5	14.5	—
Others	0.5	11.2	6.9	−3.4	1.0	0.2	—
Private creditors	89.1	23.3	0.5	5.1	−24.8	−9.0	5.0
Net medium- and long-term debt flows	84.0	87.4	21.9	14.5	−8.6	−2.9	—
Bonds	38.4	39.7	29.6	17.4	10.1	18.6	—
Banks	43.1	51.4	−5.9	2.6	−11.8	−16.0	—
Others	2.5	−3.6	−1.8	−5.5	−7.0	−5.5	—
Net short-term debt flows	5.0	−64.2	−21.4	−9.4	−16.2	−6.1	—
Balancing item[a]	−153.8	−109.0	−160.1	−192.5	−128.2	−97.8	−81.2
Change in reserves (− = increase)	−52.9	−16.6	−37.3	−55.1	−80.3	−110.0	−108.0
Memo items:							
Bilateral aid grants (ex. technical cooperation grants)	26.7	28.2	29.4	29.6	29.5	32.9	32.0
Net private flows (debt + equity)	285.1	205.2	194.7	191.8	152.8	143.3	163.0
Net official flows (aid + debt)	39.7	62.3	42.9	23.4	57.5	49.0	32.0
Workers' remittances	62.7	59.5	64.6	64.5	72.3	80.0	—

— Not available.
Note: e = estimate; *f* = forecast.
a. Combination of errors and omissions and net acquisition of foreign assets (including FDI) by developing countries.

Table A.23 External financing: East Asia and Pacific, 1997–2003
(billions of dollars)

	1997	1998	1999	2000	2001	2002e	2003f
Current account balance	16.1	58.8	60.4	55.7	42.6	42.8	41.0
as a percentage of GDP	1.1	4.4	4.2	3.6	2.6	2.5	2.2
Financed by:							
Net equity flows	62.2	54.8	53.5	63.3	51.8	62.4	68.0
Net FDI inflows	62.2	57.6	48.9	44.0	48.9	57.0	61.0
Net portfolio equity inflows	0.0	−2.8	4.6	19.3	2.9	5.4	7.0
Net debt flows	44.5	−32.5	−11.6	−18.0	−12.0	−8.3	−13.0
Official creditors	17.3	14.7	12.5	7.0	3.5	−2.3	−8.0
World Bank	2.0	2.8	2.4	1.8	0.9	−1.9	—
IMF	5.9	7.0	1.9	1.2	−2.5	−2.8	—
Others	9.3	4.8	8.2	3.9	5.1	2.4	—
Private creditors	27.2	−47.2	−24.1	−25.0	−15.5	−6.0	−5.0
Net medium- and long-term debt flows	22.8	−3.3	−10.7	−14.8	−15.0	−6.6	—
Bonds	13.3	0.7	0.9	−1.6	−0.4	6.5	—
Banks	3.9	−4.9	−11.5	−11.8	−12.9	−12.0	—
Others	5.6	0.9	−0.2	−1.3	−1.8	−1.1	—
Net short-term debt flows	4.4	−43.9	−13.4	−10.2	−0.4	0.6	—
Balancing item[a]	−110.1	−60.4	−73.0	−90.9	−34.8	−40.0	−41.0
Change in reserves (− = increase)	−12.8	−20.7	−29.3	−10.1	−47.7	−57.0	−55.0
Memo items:							
Bilateral aid grants (ex. technical cooperation grants)	2.4	2.5	2.7	2.6	2.2	2.1	2.0
Net private flows (debt + equity)	89.5	7.6	29.4	38.3	36.4	56.4	63.0
Net official flows (aid + debt)	19.7	17.2	15.3	9.5	5.7	−0.2	−6.0
Workers' remittances	14.2	8.3	10.6	10.3	10.4	11.0	—

— Not available.
Note: e = estimate; *f* = forecast.
a. Combination of errors and omissions and net acquisition of foreign assets (including FDI) by developing countries.

Table A.24 External financing: Europe and Central Asia, 1997–2003
(billions of dollars)

	1997	1998	1999	2000	2001	2002e	2003f
Current account balance	−27.8	−26.6	−2.9	18.3	18.3	8.9	6.7
as a percentage of GDP	−2.5	−2.7	−0.3	2.0	1.9	0.8	0.6
Financed by:							
Net equity flows	25.9	29.9	30.2	30.4	30.4	30.4	32.0
Net FDI inflows	21.8	26.0	28.3	29.2	30.1	29.0	30.0
Net portfolio equity inflows	4.0	4.0	2.0	1.2	0.3	1.4	2.0
Net debt flows	32.6	40.4	15.8	22.0	3.3	11.2	17.0
Official creditors	6.7	7.4	−0.8	−0.1	2.8	3.9	2.0
World Bank	3.9	1.6	1.9	2.1	2.1	0.9	—
IMF	2.4	5.3	−3.1	−0.7	6.1	4.8	—
Others	0.3	0.5	0.4	−1.5	−5.4	−1.8	—
Private creditors	25.9	33.1	16.6	22.2	0.5	7.2	15.0
Net medium- and long-term debt flows	17.4	28.7	17.6	12.7	5.8	10.8	—
Bonds	9.2	16.0	8.2	6.1	0.7	5.1	—
Banks	8.1	13.8	10.3	8.4	7.2	7.1	—
Others	0.1	−1.1	−1.0	−1.7	−2.1	−1.3	—
Net short-term debt flows	8.5	4.4	−1.0	9.5	−5.3	−3.6	—
Balancing item[a]	−23.5	−38.8	−36.7	−51.6	−41.6	−16.5	−30.7
Change in reserves (− = increase)	−7.3	−4.9	−6.5	−19.1	−10.3	−34.0	−25.0
Memo items:							
Bilateral aid grants (ex. technical cooperation grants)	5.4	5.8	8.0	8.3	7.4	9.6	10.0
Net private flows (debt + equity)	51.8	63.0	46.8	52.6	30.9	37.6	47.0
Net official flows (aid + debt)	12.1	13.2	7.2	8.2	10.2	13.5	12.0
Workers' remittances	7.1	9.2	8.1	8.7	8.9	10.0	—

— Not available.
Note: e = estimate; *f* = forecast.
a. Combination of errors and omissions and net acquisition of foreign assets (including FDI) by developing countries.

Table A.25 External financing: Latin America and the Caribbean, 1997–2003
(billions of dollars)

	1997	1998	1999	2000	2001	2002e	2003f
Current account balance	−66.3	−89.5	−55.7	−47.2	−54.1	−16.3	−19.5
as a percentage of GDP	−3.3	−4.5	−3.2	−2.4	−2.9	−1.0	−1.2
Financed by:							
Net equity flows	79.4	71.3	84.2	75.4	71.6	43.0	40.0
Net FDI inflows	66.1	73.4	87.8	75.8	69.3	42.0	38.0
Net portfolio equity inflows	13.3	−2.1	−3.6	−0.4	2.3	1.0	2.0
Net debt flows	24.3	37.9	12.3	−1.1	11.4	3.5	0.0
Official creditors	−8.6	10.9	1.6	−11.1	20.2	12.6	6.0
World Bank	0.8	2.4	2.1	2.0	1.3	−0.3	—
IMF	−3.9	2.5	−0.9	−10.7	15.6	12.3	—
Others	−5.4	6.0	0.4	−2.4	3.3	0.7	—
Private creditors	32.9	27.0	10.7	10.0	−8.7	−9.1	−6.0
Net medium- and long-term debt flows	41.6	54.4	18.6	12.6	0.5	−5.6	—
Bonds	11.0	17.3	19.1	5.3	3.5	4.5	—
Banks	31.4	39.3	−1.4	8.3	−1.4	−8.3	—
Others	−0.9	−2.3	1.0	−0.9	−1.6	−1.8	—
Net short-term debt flows	−8.6	−27.4	−7.9	−2.6	−9.2	−3.5	—
Balancing item[a]	−23.8	−28.8	−48.2	−24.2	−25.9	−34.3	−10.5
Change in reserves (− = increase)	−13.5	9.2	7.5	−2.9	−2.9	4.0	−10.0
Memo items:							
Bilateral aid grants (ex. technical cooperation grants)	2.8	3.3	3.0	2.5	3.2	3.2	3.0
Net private flows (debt + equity)	112.3	98.3	94.9	85.4	62.8	33.9	34.0
Net official flows (aid + debt)	−5.8	14.2	4.5	−8.6	23.4	15.8	9.0
Workers' remittances	13.6	14.8	16.9	19.2	22.6	25.0	—

— Not available.
Note: e = estimate; *f* = forecast.
a. Combination of errors and omissions and net acquisition of foreign assets (including FDI) by developing countries.

Table A.26 External financing: Middle East and North Africa, 1997–2003
(billions of dollars)

	1997	1998	1999	2000	2001	2002e	2003f
Current account balance	2.3	−27.8	4.2	40.8	28.9	24.7	9.5
as a percentage of GDP	0.5	−5.8	0.8	7.4	5.0	4.5	1.7
Financed by:							
Net equity flows	7.0	7.8	3.9	2.7	5.3	3.0	2.0
Net FDI inflows	6.2	7.5	3.2	2.5	5.5	3.0	3.0
Net portfolio equity inflows	0.8	0.3	0.7	0.2	−0.1	0.0	−1.0
Net debt flows	−4.4	8.3	−2.2	−6.5	1.7	−0.3	2.5
Official creditors	−4.0	−1.7	−2.7	−2.9	−1.2	−1.6	0.0
World Bank	−0.3	−0.2	0.2	−0.3	−0.1	−0.3	—
IMF	0.3	0.0	0.0	−0.2	−0.1	−0.3	—
Others	−4.0	−1.5	−3.0	−2.4	−1.0	−1.0	—
Private creditors	−0.4	10.0	0.5	−3.6	2.9	1.3	2.5
Net medium- and long-term debt flows	0.2	5.4	−0.8	0.4	2.1	1.0	—
Bonds	1.5	1.3	1.4	1.2	4.4	2.3	—
Banks	0.1	3.8	−1.2	0.6	−1.4	−0.6	—
Others	−1.4	0.3	−1.1	−1.5	−0.9	−0.7	—
Net short-term debt flows	−0.6	4.6	1.3	−4.0	0.8	0.3	—
Balancing item[a]	1.7	10.3	−3.3	−24.8	−27.2	−22.4	−14.0
Change in reserves (− = increase)	−6.6	1.5	−2.6	−12.2	−8.8	−5.0	0.0
Memo items:							
Bilateral aid grants (ex. technical cooperation grants)	4.0	4.2	3.3	3.8	3.2	3.4	3.0
Net private flows (debt + equity)	6.9	17.8	4.4	−0.9	8.3	4.3	4.5
Net official flows (aid + debt)	0.0	2.5	0.6	0.9	2.0	1.8	3.0
Workers' remittances	9.4	10.3	10.5	10.9	13.1	14.0	—

— Not available.
Note: e = estimate; *f* = forecast.
a. Combination of errors and omissions and net acquisition of foreign assets (including FDI) by developing countries.

Table A.27 External financing: South Asia, 1997–2003
(billions of dollars)

	1997	1998	1999	2000	2001	2002e	2003f
Current account balance	−5.8	−9.6	−5.5	−6.1	−2.9	−7.6	−6.1
as a percentage of GDP	−1.1	−1.8	−1.0	−1.0	−0.5	−1.1	−0.8
Financed by:							
Net equity flows	7.8	2.9	5.5	4.7	5.7	5.8	8.0
Net FDI inflows	4.9	3.5	3.1	3.1	4.1	5.0	6.0
Net portfolio equity inflows	2.9	−0.6	2.4	1.7	1.6	0.8	2.0
Net debt flows	0.6	4.7	0.5	3.4	−0.3	0.9	−1.0
Official creditors	0.3	2.3	2.5	0.5	2.5	1.9	−1.0
World Bank	1.1	0.8	1.0	0.7	1.5	1.1	—
IMF	−0.8	−0.4	−0.1	−0.3	0.3	0.1	—
Others	0.0	2.0	1.6	0.0	0.7	0.7	—
Private creditors	0.3	2.4	−2.0	2.9	−2.7	−1.0	0.0
Net medium- and long-term debt flows	2.4	3.7	−2.1	3.9	−1.9	−1.6	—
Bonds	2.3	4.2	−1.2	5.4	0.0	−0.4	—
Banks	1.3	0.7	−0.5	−2.0	−1.7	−1.1	—
Others	−1.2	−1.2	−0.4	0.5	−0.1	−0.1	—
Net short-term debt flows	−2.1	−1.3	0.1	−1.0	−0.9	0.6	—
Balancing item[a]	2.6	4.9	4.5	2.6	7.8	19.0	14.1
Change in reserves (− = increase)	−5.2	−3.0	−5.0	−4.7	−10.2	−18.0	−15.0
Memo items:							
Bilateral aid grants (ex. technical cooperation grants)	2.4	2.3	2.4	2.3	3.6	4.2	4.0
Net private flows (debt + equity)	8.2	5.3	3.5	7.7	2.9	4.8	8.0
Net official flows (aid + debt)	2.7	4.6	4.9	2.8	6.0	6.0	3.0
Workers' remittances	14.6	13.3	15.1	13.5	14.9	16.0	—

— Not available.
Note: e = estimate; *f* = forecast.
a. Combination of errors and omissions and net acquisition of foreign assets (including FDI) by developing countries.

Table A.28 External financing: Sub-Saharan Africa, 1997–2003
(billions of dollars)

	1997	1998	1999	2000	2001	2002e	2003f
Current account balance	−9.9	−19.0	−11.3	0.4	−5.1	−4.3	−5.4
as a percentage of GDP	−2.9	−5.9	−3.6	0.1	−1.7	−1.4	−1.5
Financed by:							
Net equity flows	13.7	15.1	17.0	10.1	12.8	7.7	8.0
Net FDI inflows	8.1	6.5	8.1	6.1	13.8	7.0	7.0
Net portfolio equity inflows	5.6	8.6	8.9	4.0	−1.0	0.7	1.0
Net debt flows	4.5	−1.4	−0.9	−0.9	−1.0	0.2	−0.5
Official creditors	1.4	0.5	0.4	0.5	0.3	1.6	1.0
World Bank	1.7	1.3	1.1	1.5	1.8	1.9	—
IMF	−0.5	−0.3	0.0	0.1	0.1	0.5	—
Others	0.3	−0.5	−0.7	−1.0	−1.6	−0.8	—
Private creditors	3.1	−1.9	−1.2	−1.4	−1.3	−1.4	−1.5
Net medium- and long-term debt flows	−0.4	−1.4	−0.7	−0.3	−0.2	−0.9	—
Bonds	1.0	0.3	1.2	1.0	1.9	0.6	—
Banks	−1.6	−1.3	−1.7	−0.8	−1.6	−1.1	—
Others	0.2	−0.4	−0.2	−0.5	−0.5	−0.4	—
Net short-term debt flows	3.5	−0.5	−0.6	−1.1	−1.1	−0.5	—
Balancing item[a]	−0.8	3.9	−3.4	−3.6	−6.4	−3.7	0.9
Change in reserves (− = increase)	−7.6	1.4	−1.5	−6.0	−0.3	0.0	−3.0
Memo items:							
Bilateral aid grants (ex. technical cooperation grants)	9.6	10.1	10.0	10.0	9.9	10.4	10.0
Net private flows (debt + equity)	16.8	13.2	15.8	8.7	11.6	6.3	6.5
Net official flows (aid + debt)	11.1	10.6	10.3	10.6	10.2	12.0	11.0
Workers' remittances	3.8	3.6	3.5	2.0	2.4	4.0	—

— Not available.
Note: e = estimate; *f* = forecast.
a. Combination of errors and omissions and net acquisition of foreign assets (including FDI) by developing countries.

Table A.29 Net inward foreign direct investment in developing countries, 1995–2003
(billions of dollars)

	1995	1996	1997	1998	1999	2000	2001	2002e	2003f
All developing countries	**105.6**	**127.9**	**169.3**	**174.5**	**179.3**	**160.6**	**171.7**	**143.0**	**145.0**
East Asia and Pacific	51.3	58.6	62.2	57.6	48.9	44.0	48.9	57.0	61.0
China	35.8	40.2	44.2	43.8	38.8	38.4	44.2	52.7	—
Malaysia	4.2	5.1	5.1	2.2	3.9	3.8	0.6	2.8	—
Philippines	1.5	1.5	1.2	2.3	0.6	1.2	1.8	1.3	—
Thailand	2.1	2.3	3.9	7.3	6.2	3.4	3.8	0.7	—
Vietnam	2.3	2.4	2.2	1.7	1.4	1.3	1.3	1.5	—
Europe and Central Asia	17.0	16.3	21.8	26.0	28.3	29.2	30.1	29.0	30.0
Czech Republic	2.6	1.4	1.3	3.7	6.3	5.0	4.9	8.1	—
Hungary	4.5	2.3	2.2	2.0	2.0	1.6	2.4	1.0	—
Poland	3.7	4.5	4.9	6.4	7.3	9.3	5.7	4.1	—
Russian Federation	2.1	2.6	4.9	2.8	3.3	2.7	2.5	3.0	—
Slovak Republic	0.2	0.4	0.2	0.6	0.4	2.1	1.5	4.0	—
Latin America and the Caribbean	30.5	44.4	66.1	73.4	87.8	75.8	69.3	42.0	38.0
Argentina	5.6	6.9	9.2	7.3	24.0	11.7	3.2	0.7	—
Brazil	4.9	11.2	19.7	31.9	28.6	32.8	22.6	16.6	—
Chile	3.0	5.0	5.3	4.8	9.0	3.6	4.5	1.7	—
Mexico	9.5	9.2	12.8	11.9	12.5	14.2	24.7	13.6	—
Venezuela, R.B. de	1.0	2.2	5.5	4.5	3.3	4.5	3.4	1.4	—
Middle East and North Africa	−0.6	0.7	6.2	7.5	3.2	2.5	5.5	3.0	3.0
Algeria	0.0	0.3	0.3	0.5	0.5	0.4	1.2	0.7	—
Egypt, Arab Rep. of	0.6	0.6	0.9	1.1	1.1	1.2	0.5	0.6	—
Morocco	0.4	0.4	1.1	0.3	0.8	0.2	2.7	0.4	—
South Asia	2.9	3.5	4.9	3.5	3.1	3.1	4.1	5.0	6.0
India	2.1	2.4	3.6	2.6	2.2	2.3	3.4	3.6	—
Pakistan	0.7	0.9	0.7	0.5	0.5	0.3	0.4	0.8	—
Sri Lanka	0.1	0.1	0.4	0.2	0.2	0.2	0.2	0.2	—
Sub-Saharan Africa	4.3	4.3	8.1	6.5	8.1	6.1	13.8	7.0	7.0
Angola	0.5	0.2	0.4	1.1	2.5	0.9	1.1	1.1	—
Nigeria	1.1	1.6	1.5	1.1	1.0	0.9	1.1	1.0	—
South Africa	1.2	0.8	3.8	0.6	1.5	1.0	7.2	1.0	—

— Not available.
Note: e = estimate, *f* = forecast.

Table A.30 Net inward portfolio equity flows to developing countries, 1995–2003
(billions of dollars)

	1995	1996	1997	1998	1999	2000	2001	2002e	2003f
All developing countries	**20.2**	**33.6**	**26.7**	**7.4**	**15.0**	**26.0**	**6.0**	**9.4**	**13.0**
East Asia and Pacific	9.1	10.1	0.0	−2.8	4.6	19.3	2.9	5.4	7.0
China	3.3	4.1	9.3	1.4	3.8	21.4	3.0	4.0	—
Indonesia	1.5	1.8	−5.0	−4.4	−0.8	−1.0	0.2	0.2	—
Malaysia	2.2	0.8	−7.8	−0.4	0.1	−1.9	−0.7	1.0	—
Philippines	—	2.1	−0.4	0.3	0.5	−0.2	0.4	0.3	—
Thailand	2.1	1.2	3.9	0.3	0.9	0.9	0.0	0.0	—
Europe and Central Asia	1.7	4.3	4.0	4.0	2.0	1.2	0.3	1.4	2.0
Czech Republic	1.2	0.6	0.4	1.1	0.1	0.6	0.6	0.5	—
Hungary	0.0	0.4	1.0	0.6	1.2	−0.4	0.1	0.2	—
Poland	0.2	0.7	0.6	1.7	0.0	0.4	−0.3	−0.1	—
Russian Federation	0.0	2.2	1.3	0.7	−0.3	0.2	0.5	1.0	—
Turkey	0.2	0.2	0.0	−0.5	0.4	0.5	−0.1	0.1	—
Latin America and the Caribbean	4.8	12.2	13.3	−2.1	−3.6	−0.4	2.3	1.0	2.0
Argentina	1.1	1.0	1.4	−0.2	−10.8	−3.2	−0.1	−0.6	—
Brazil	2.8	5.8	5.1	−1.8	2.6	3.1	2.5	1.2	—
Chile	−0.2	0.7	1.7	0.6	0.5	−0.4	−0.2	−0.1	—
Mexico	0.5	2.8	3.2	−0.7	3.8	0.4	0.2	0.5	—
Venezuela, R.B. de	0.3	1.3	1.4	0.2	0.4	−0.5	−0.1	0.0	—
Middle East and North Africa	0.1	0.5	0.8	0.3	0.7	0.2	−0.1	0.0	−1.0
Egypt, Arab Rep. of	0.0	0.2	0.5	−0.2	0.7	0.3	0.0	0.0	—
South Asia	1.6	4.1	2.9	−0.6	2.4	1.7	1.6	0.8	2.0
India	1.6	4.0	2.6	−0.6	2.3	1.6	1.7	0.9	—
Sub-Saharan Africa	2.9	2.4	5.5	8.6	8.9	4.0	−1.0	0.7	1.0
South Africa	2.9	2.3	5.5	8.6	9.0	4.2	−1.0	0.7	—

— Not available.
Note: e = estimate, *f* = forecast.

Table A.31 Net inward debt flows to developing countries, 1995–2003
(billions of dollars)

	1995	1996	1997	1998	1999	2000	2001	2002e	2003f
All developing countries	**151.8**	**114.1**	**102.1**	**57.4**	**13.9**	**−1.0**	**3.2**	**7.2**	**5.0**
East Asia and Pacific	54.2	52.0	44.5	−32.5	−11.6	−18.0	−12.0	−8.3	−13.0
China	17.8	13.9	18.5	−14.2	−1.6	−5.3	0.0	—	—
Indonesia	9.9	12.3	10.1	−4.6	−3.8	−0.7	−6.0	—	—
Malaysia	5.1	6.4	8.4	−3.6	−0.7	0.3	3.6	—	—
Philippines	−0.7	4.5	7.5	−3.1	3.1	0.8	−0.2	—	—
Thailand	21.2	13.9	−1.3	−7.9	−9.4	−13.7	−9.8	—	—
Eastern Europe and Central Asia	23.4	22.7	32.6	40.4	15.8	22.0	3.3	11.2	17.0
Bulgaria	−0.2	0.0	0.0	0.1	0.7	0.4	−0.1	—	—
Czech Republic	4.8	4.1	3.2	1.4	−0.2	−1.7	−0.2	—	—
Hungary	2.8	−2.0	−1.4	2.7	2.0	0.5	1.6	—	—
Poland	0.3	1.0	2.5	4.2	1.7	3.5	0.1	—	—
Russian Federation	4.9	7.3	7.6	21.9	−4.2	−2.8	−2.2	—	—
Turkey	4.4	2.9	4.5	5.6	10.9	19.1	−3.3	—	—
Latin America and the Caribbean	61.3	36.0	24.3	37.9	12.3	−1.1	11.4	3.5	0.0
Argentina	22.0	14.1	17.1	11.7	6.3	4.3	−5.0	—	—
Brazil	8.8	19.2	−1.3	6.7	−5.9	−4.2	5.2	—	—
Chile	−0.3	1.2	2.0	4.8	2.1	2.4	1.4	—	—
Colombia	2.9	4.4	3.6	0.8	1.3	−0.2	3.3	—	—
Mexico	25.6	−4.9	−5.1	8.8	6.7	−8.4	1.6	—	—
Venezuela, R.B. de	−1.7	−0.2	2.3	1.7	0.2	0.9	−2.2	—	—
Middle East and North Africa	2.7	−2.5	−4.4	8.3	−2.2	−6.5	1.7	−0.3	2.5
Algeria	1.4	1.6	−0.4	−1.6	−1.9	−1.6	−2.0	—	—
Egypt, Arab Rep. of	0.1	−0.5	0.6	1.1	−0.6	−0.7	0.1	—	—
Lebanon	0.8	1.1	1.1	1.7	1.5	1.8	2.7	—	—
South Asia	2.5	2.6	0.6	4.7	0.5	3.4	−0.3	0.9	−1.0
India	−0.7	0.7	−1.6	3.0	−1.1	3.4	−2.4	—	—
Pakistan	2.6	1.1	1.6	0.7	0.7	−0.3	0.6	—	—
Sub-Saharan Africa	7.6	3.2	4.5	−1.4	−0.9	−0.9	−1.0	0.2	−0.5
South Africa	3.4	0.7	−0.4	−0.3	−0.7	1.2	−0.8	—	—

— Not available.
Note: e = estimate, f = forecast.

Table A.32 Net inward short-term debt flows to developing countries, 1995–2002
(billions of dollars)

	1995	1996	1997	1998	1999	2000	2001	2002e
All developing countries	**58.9**	**28.4**	**5.0**	**−64.2**	**−21.4**	**−9.4**	**−16.2**	**−6.1**
East Asia and Pacific	27.3	19.5	4.4	−43.9	−13.4	−10.2	−0.4	0.6
China	4.8	3.1	6.1	−14.1	−2.2	−2.1	1.8	—
Indonesia	6.5	6.3	0.6	−9.7	−1.6	1.5	−1.0	—
Malaysia	1.1	3.8	3.9	−6.5	−2.5	−1.4	0.5	—
Philippines	−0.4	2.7	3.8	−4.6	−1.4	0.2	0.1	—
Thailand	14.9	3.6	−9.9	−8.2	−6.2	−8.5	−1.7	—
Eastern Europe and Central Asia	9.0	6.7	8.5	4.4	−1.0	9.5	−5.3	−3.6
Bulgaria	0.1	0.3	−0.2	−0.3	0.1	0.1	−0.1	—
Czech Republic	2.2	0.7	2.4	−0.5	1.1	0.2	−0.1	—
Hungary	0.8	0.2	0.0	1.4	−1.2	0.6	0.5	—
Poland	1.3	0.6	1.1	2.4	−0.2	1.0	0.0	—
Russian Federation	−0.4	0.3	−1.4	−0.5	−1.0	2.0	4.5	—
Turkey	4.4	1.6	0.6	3.2	2.3	5.4	−12.6	—
Latin America and the Caribbean	14.8	−0.2	−8.6	−27.4	−7.9	−2.6	−9.2	−3.5
Argentina	14.2	2.1	8.5	−1.0	−1.5	−1.1	−8.3	—
Brazil	−0.4	4.3	−16.0	−24.0	0.7	1.8	−2.5	—
Chile	−0.4	−0.8	−1.3	0.3	−0.4	1.4	0.0	—
Colombia	1.1	0.3	−0.1	0.5	−2.3	−1.1	0.9	—
Mexico	−2.0	−7.5	−2.0	−1.5	−2.3	−5.1	−0.9	—
Venezuela, R.B. de	−0.6	−0.2	1.5	−2.0	−0.1	2.0	−0.3	—
Middle East and North Africa	2.7	−1.2	−0.6	4.6	1.3	−4.0	0.8	0.3
Algeria	−0.4	0.1	−0.2	0.0	0.0	0.0	0.0	—
Egypt, Arab Rep. of	0.4	0.0	0.6	1.3	0.0	−0.2	−0.7	—
Lebanon	0.0	0.3	0.1	0.2	0.2	0.3	0.1	—
South Asia	2.1	1.2	−2.1	−1.3	0.1	−1.0	−0.9	0.6
India	0.8	1.7	−1.7	−0.7	−0.4	−0.5	−0.5	—
Pakistan	1.3	−0.4	−0.3	−0.5	−0.1	−0.3	−0.2	—
Sub-Saharan Africa	3.0	2.4	3.5	−0.5	−0.6	−1.1	−1.1	−0.5
South Africa	1.9	1.2	0.1	0.5	−0.6	0.3	−1.2	—

— Not available.
Note: e = estimate.

Table A.33 Net inward debt flows to public-sector and publicly guaranteed borrowers in developing countries, 1995–2001
(billions of dollars)

	1995	1996	1997	1998	1999	2000	2001
All developing countries	**61.9**	**38.3**	**41.7**	**71.6**	**30.0**	**11.1**	**19.4**
East Asia and Pacific	16.2	12.8	28.9	19.3	11.3	3.0	−0.2
China	12.4	10.7	11.1	2.5	1.6	−1.1	0.0
Indonesia	1.0	−0.6	3.6	9.0	2.0	0.9	−2.2
Malaysia	2.4	0.3	1.7	0.5	0.9	1.3	3.1
Philippines	−1.1	0.3	1.8	1.3	4.6	1.6	0.6
Thailand	0.9	1.3	9.4	4.6	1.9	−0.2	−2.5
Eastern Europe and Central Asia	10.6	11.5	15.7	21.7	6.8	6.1	−1.7
Bulgaria	−0.3	−0.4	0.2	0.3	0.4	0.2	−0.1
Czech Republic	2.0	2.8	0.9	1.0	−1.0	−1.1	−0.8
Hungary	0.3	−3.1	−1.8	−0.4	1.5	−1.4	−0.8
Poland	−1.1	0.2	0.5	−0.1	−0.3	−1.4	−4.2
Russian Federation	5.3	7.0	7.1	16.2	−3.5	−3.8	−7.3
Turkey	−0.8	0.3	2.7	−0.9	4.6	12.3	10.4
Latin America and the Caribbean	31.7	13.7	−2.0	24.2	11.2	1.2	20.3
Argentina	6.7	10.1	4.9	8.3	8.7	6.4	7.3
Brazil	1.5	2.7	−0.3	12.1	0.5	−6.7	9.3
Chile	−2.2	−2.0	−0.3	0.6	0.6	−0.4	0.4
Colombia	−0.6	1.4	1.1	1.0	3.4	0.9	2.5
Mexico	26.4	0.6	−10.1	0.5	−3.8	−1.8	−1.9
Venezuela, R.B. de	−0.6	0.2	0.1	0.2	−0.6	−0.5	−1.7
Middle East and North Africa	−0.7	−1.8	−4.6	1.5	−2.5	−3.2	0.5
Algeria	1.7	1.5	−0.3	−1.6	−2.0	−1.6	−2.0
Egypt, Arab Rep. of	−0.3	−0.3	−0.1	−0.5	−0.7	−0.6	0.8
Lebanon	0.8	0.4	0.5	1.7	1.4	1.4	2.5
South Asia	−1.0	0.5	0.7	5.5	1.4	4.5	0.9
India	−2.5	−1.5	−1.5	3.6	−0.1	3.8	−1.3
Pakistan	0.9	1.1	1.6	0.9	1.2	0.3	1.2
Sub-Saharan Africa	5.1	1.6	2.9	−0.5	1.8	−0.5	−0.4
South Africa	2.0	0.6	1.1	−1.0	1.6	0.0	−0.4

Table A.34 Net inward debt flows to private-sector borrowers in developing countries, 1995–2001
(billions of dollars)

	1995	1996	1997	1998	1999	2000	2001
All developing countries	**89.8**	**75.8**	**60.5**	**−14.3**	**−16.1**	**−12.1**	**−16.2**
East Asia and Pacific	38.0	39.3	15.6	−51.8	−22.9	−21.0	−11.8
China	5.4	3.2	7.4	−16.7	−3.2	−4.1	−0.1
Indonesia	9.0	12.9	6.5	−13.6	−5.8	−1.6	−3.8
Malaysia	2.7	6.1	6.7	−4.0	−1.6	−1.0	0.4
Philippines	0.4	4.2	5.8	−4.3	−1.4	−0.8	−0.8
Thailand	20.4	12.6	−10.7	−12.5	−11.3	−13.5	−7.3
Eastern Europe and Central Asia	12.8	11.2	16.9	18.7	9.0	16.0	5.0
Bulgaria	0.1	0.4	−0.2	−0.2	0.3	0.2	0.1
Czech Republic	2.8	1.3	2.3	0.4	0.8	−0.6	0.6
Hungary	2.5	1.1	0.5	3.1	0.5	1.8	2.5
Poland	1.5	0.8	2.0	4.3	2.1	4.9	4.3
Russian Federation	−0.4	0.3	0.5	2.4	−0.7	1.1	5.1
Turkey	5.1	2.7	1.8	6.5	6.3	6.8	−13.7
Latin America and the Caribbean	29.6	22.3	26.3	13.7	1.0	−2.3	−8.8
Argentina	15.3	3.9	12.3	3.4	−2.4	−2.1	−12.3
Brazil	7.3	16.5	−1.0	−5.3	−6.4	2.4	−4.2
Chile	2.0	3.2	2.3	4.2	1.5	2.8	1.0
Colombia	3.5	3.0	2.5	−0.2	−2.1	−1.1	0.7
Mexico	−0.8	−5.5	5.0	8.3	10.5	−6.6	3.5
Venezuela, R.B. de	−1.1	−0.4	2.2	1.5	0.7	1.4	−0.4
Middle East and North Africa	3.5	−0.7	0.2	6.8	0.3	−3.4	1.2
Algeria	−0.4	0.1	−0.2	0.0	0.0	0.0	0.0
Egypt, Arab Rep. of	0.4	−0.2	0.6	1.5	0.1	−0.1	−0.7
Lebanon	0.1	0.7	0.6	0.1	0.1	0.4	0.2
South Asia	3.5	2.1	−0.1	−0.8	−0.9	−1.1	−1.2
India	1.8	2.2	−0.1	−0.5	−1.0	−0.4	−0.5
Pakistan	1.7	0.0	0.0	−0.2	−0.5	−0.6	−0.5
Sub-Saharan Africa	2.5	1.6	1.6	−0.9	−2.7	−0.4	−0.6
South Africa	1.4	0.1	−1.5	0.7	−2.3	1.3	−0.4

Table A.35 Net inward debt flows from public-sector creditors in developing countries, 1995–2003
(billions of dollars)

	1995	1996	1997	1998	1999	2000	2001	2002e	2003f
All developing countries	**38.8**	**3.8**	**13.0**	**34.1**	**13.5**	**−6.2**	**28.0**	**16.2**	**0.0**
East Asia and Pacific	9.1	3.6	17.3	14.7	12.5	7.0	3.5	−2.3	−8.0
China	7.9	4.4	4.3	2.3	3.4	1.5	2.2	—	—
Indonesia	1.1	−0.8	3.6	8.5	4.8	2.9	−0.8	—	—
Malaysia	0.4	−0.8	−0.2	0.2	0.6	0.6	2.1	—	—
Philippines	−1.1	−0.3	0.6	0.6	0.2	0.3	−0.2	—	—
Thailand	0.5	0.4	8.4	1.8	2.5	0.3	−1.3	—	—
Eastern Europe and Central Asia	6.8	8.6	6.7	7.4	−0.8	−0.1	2.8	3.9	2.0
Bulgaria	−0.2	−0.1	0.3	0.3	0.3	0.2	−0.4	—	—
Czech Republic	0.0	0.1	−0.1	0.0	0.0	0.1	0.2	—	—
Hungary	−0.9	−0.9	−0.1	−1.1	0.1	−0.2	−0.2	—	—
Poland	−1.5	0.2	−0.1	−0.5	−0.4	−0.5	−4.1	—	—
Russian Federation	5.6	6.8	4.2	6.3	−3.0	−3.3	−5.1	—	—
Turkey	−0.8	−0.8	−0.1	−0.3	−0.1	4.3	11.5	—	—
Latin America and the Caribbean	22.0	−10.7	−8.6	10.9	1.6	−11.1	20.2	12.6	6.0
Argentina	3.3	0.4	−0.1	1.0	−0.1	0.9	10.3	—	—
Brazil	−1.8	−0.8	−1.2	9.5	4.5	−8.5	9.5	—	—
Chile	−2.1	−0.6	−0.4	−0.1	−0.1	−0.1	−0.1	—	—
Colombia	−0.4	−0.1	−0.5	0.2	1.0	0.1	1.1	—	—
Mexico	22.5	−9.6	−8.0	−1.9	−5.4	−4.8	−0.7	—	—
Venezuela, R.B. de	−0.3	−0.1	−0.3	1.0	−0.1	−0.3	−1.1	—	—
Middle East and North Africa	−1.5	−0.8	−4.0	−1.7	−2.7	−2.9	−1.2	−1.6	0.0
Algeria	1.2	1.5	0.3	−0.3	−0.4	−0.4	−1.0	—	—
Egypt, Arab Rep. of	−0.1	0.0	0.0	−0.2	−0.5	−0.6	−0.6	—	—
Lebanon	0.1	0.2	0.1	0.2	0.1	0.1	0.1	—	—
South Asia	−1.2	1.0	0.3	2.3	2.5	0.5	2.5	1.9	−1.0
India	−2.8	−0.8	−1.0	0.6	0.8	−0.3	−0.3	—	—
Pakistan	1.0	0.9	0.7	0.9	1.2	0.3	1.4	—	—
Sub-Saharan Africa	3.5	2.0	1.4	0.5	0.4	0.5	0.3	1.6	1.0
South Africa	0.0	0.0	−0.4	−0.4	0.0	0.1	0.0	—	—

— Not available.
Note: e = estimate, f = forecast.

Table A.36 Net inward debt flows from private-sector creditors in developing countries, 1995–2003
(billions of dollars)

	1995	1996	1997	1998	1999	2000	2001	2002e	2003f
All developing countries	**113.0**	**110.3**	**89.1**	**23.3**	**0.5**	**5.1**	**−24.8**	**−9.0**	**5.0**
East Asia and Pacific	45.0	48.4	27.2	−47.2	−24.1	−25.0	−15.5	−6.0	−5.0
China	9.9	9.5	14.2	−16.5	−5.0	−6.8	−2.2	—	—
Indonesia	8.8	13.1	6.5	−13.0	−8.6	−3.6	−5.2	—	—
Malaysia	4.8	7.2	8.6	−3.8	−1.3	−0.3	1.4	—	—
Philippines	0.5	4.9	7.0	−3.7	2.9	0.4	0.0	—	—
Thailand	20.7	13.4	−9.7	−9.6	−11.9	−14.0	−8.5	—	—
Eastern Europe and Central Asia	16.6	14.1	25.9	33.1	16.6	22.2	0.5	7.2	15.0
Bulgaria	0.0	0.0	−0.3	−0.3	0.4	0.2	0.3	—	—
Czech Republic	4.8	4.0	3.2	1.4	−0.2	−1.7	−0.4	—	—
Hungary	3.7	−1.1	−1.3	3.8	1.9	0.7	1.8	—	—
Poland	1.8	0.7	2.6	4.7	2.2	4.0	4.2	—	—
Russian Federation	−0.7	0.5	3.4	12.3	−1.2	0.5	3.0	—	—
Turkey	5.2	3.8	4.6	5.9	11.0	14.8	−14.8	—	—
Latin America and the Caribbean	39.3	46.8	32.9	27.0	10.7	10.0	−8.7	−9.1	−6.0
Argentina	18.7	13.7	17.3	10.7	6.4	3.4	−15.3	—	—
Brazil	10.6	20.1	−0.1	−2.7	−10.4	4.3	−4.3	—	—
Chile	1.8	1.8	2.4	4.8	2.2	2.5	1.5	—	—
Colombia	3.3	4.5	4.1	0.6	0.2	−0.3	2.2	—	—
Mexico	3.1	4.8	3.0	10.7	12.1	−3.6	2.3	—	—
Venezuela, R.B. de	−1.4	0.0	2.6	0.7	0.3	1.2	−1.1	—	—
Middle East and North Africa	4.2	−1.7	−0.4	10.0	0.5	−3.6	2.9	1.3	2.5
Algeria	0.1	0.1	−0.7	−1.3	−1.5	−1.2	−1.0	—	—
Egypt, Arab Rep. of	0.1	−0.4	0.6	1.3	−0.1	−0.1	0.8	—	—
Lebanon	0.7	0.8	1.0	1.6	1.4	1.7	2.6	—	—
South Asia	3.7	1.6	0.3	2.4	−2.0	2.9	−2.7	−1.0	0.0
India	2.0	1.5	−0.6	2.5	−1.9	3.6	−2.1	—	—
Pakistan	1.6	0.1	0.9	−0.2	−0.6	−0.7	−0.8	—	—
Sub-Saharan Africa	4.1	1.2	3.1	−1.9	−1.2	−1.4	−1.3	−1.4	−1.5
South Africa	3.4	0.7	0.0	0.1	−0.7	1.2	−0.8	—	—

— Not available.
Note: e = estimate, *f* = forecast.

Table A.37 Gross market-based capital flows to developing countries, 1995–2003
(billions of dollars)

	1995	1996	1997	1998	1999	2000	2001	2002	2003f
All developing countries	**151.2**	**206.1**	**287.3**	**178.6**	**162.4**	**205.2**	**150.7**	**149.1**	**169**
East Asia and Pacific	60.0	71.5	76.2	27.3	28.2	48.7	20.7	41.0	50
China	15.2	16.1	26.4	10.1	8.7	29.0	6.6	16.0	—
Indonesia	17.5	24.2	21.1	1.2	2.8	1.1	1.0	1.4	—
Malaysia	10.4	10.9	11.9	3.4	6.8	6.9	5.6	12.7	—
Philippines	3.3	5.6	7.7	5.7	7.6	7.2	4.8	6.4	—
Thailand	12.5	14.1	8.9	6.7	2.2	4.3	2.5	3.7	—
Europe and Central Asia	21.9	26.9	51.2	43.4	31.0	40.7	27.7	35.5	44
Czech Republic	1.6	3.2	3.9	3.1	1.1	1.2	0.9	0.6	—
Hungary	5.2	3.5	4.2	4.0	3.9	2.1	3.1	1.8	—
Poland	1.5	0.9	4.5	4.6	5.0	4.5	5.4	6.6	—
Russian Federation	4.0	5.8	20.0	13.3	0.7	5.2	4.7	10.8	—
Turkey	7.1	8.6	10.3	9.8	12.9	22.1	6.9	7.3	—
Latin America and the Caribbean	42.8	84.9	120.6	84.5	75.3	89.9	75.8	45.3	44
Argentina	9.4	24.1	28.6	26.7	21.0	19.3	6.5	2.1	—
Brazil	7.1	14.5	32.3	18.0	14.6	28.0	23.6	14.6	—
Chile	2.6	5.5	8.9	4.8	9.0	6.5	6.9	3.8	—
Mexico	15.1	29.3	30.4	19.9	18.4	21.3	19.9	14.8	—
Venezuela, R.B. de	1.9	2.9	7.5	7.8	2.7	3.0	4.8	0.7	—
Middle East and North Africa	11.3	4.5	18.7	12.1	13.6	8.9	12.1	14.7	16
Egypt, Arab Rep. of	0.3	0.2	1.5	1.7	4.4	1.1	2.6	0.6	—
Lebanon	0.7	0.9	1.5	1.9	1.4	1.9	3.3	1.0	—
Saudi Arabia	3.1	0.8	9.7	6.5	4.4	2.4	1.9	5.7	—
South Asia	7.4	10.5	12.7	5.1	4.2	4.8	3.3	2.6	3
India	5.2	7.4	10.7	4.0	3.8	4.4	2.6	2.2	—
Pakistan	2.0	3.1	1.7	0.9	0.0	0.0	0.2	0.4	—
Sub-Saharan Africa	7.8	7.8	7.9	6.4	10.0	12.2	11.1	9.9	12
South Africa	4.2	5.8	5.7	3.0	7.8	9.2	6.9	6.5	—

— Not available.
Note: f = forecast.

Table A.38 Gross international equity issuance by developing countries, 1995–2003
(billions of dollars)

	1995	1996	1997	1998	1999	2000	2001	2002	2003f
All developing countries	**6.4**	**12.6**	**21.4**	**8.0**	**13.5**	**34.3**	**5.7**	**10.9**	**12**
East Asia and Pacific	4.1	5.2	10.7	4.0	6.2	22.1	3.5	7.2	9
China	0.8	2.1	9.1	1.2	3.7	21.9	2.9	5.5	—
Indonesia	1.4	1.3	0.9	0.0	1.2	0.0	0.3	0.3	—
Malaysia	0.6	0.6	0.4	0.2	0.0	0.0	0.0	1.2	—
Philippines	0.7	0.8	0.3	0.4	0.2	0.1	0.0	0.0	—
Thailand	0.5	0.2	0.0	2.2	1.0	0.0	0.2	0.1	—
Europe and Central Asia	0.6	1.3	3.1	2.6	1.4	3.4	0.3	1.6	2
Hungary	0.3	0.4	1.7	0.4	0.5	0.0	0.0	0.0	—
Poland	0.1	0.0	0.7	1.0	0.7	0.4	0.0	0.2	—
Russian Federation	0.0	0.8	0.1	0.0	0.0	0.4	0.2	1.3	—
Turkey	0.1	0.0	0.4	0.8	0.0	2.4	0.0	0.1	—
Latin America and the Caribbean	0.9	3.6	4.9	0.3	0.8	6.8	1.2	1.1	1
Argentina	0.0	0.4	1.1	0.0	0.3	0.4	0.0	0.0	—
Brazil	0.2	0.4	2.4	0.1	0.2	3.1	1.1	1.1	—
Chile	0.2	0.1	0.6	0.1	0.0	0.0	0.0	0.0	—
Mexico	0.0	0.7	0.8	0.0	0.2	3.3	0.0	0.0	—
Middle East and North Africa	0.0	0.4	0.7	0.4	0.1	0.4	0.0	0.0	0
Egypt, Arab Rep. of	0.0	0.2	0.3	0.1	0.1	0.3	0.0	0.0	—
Morocco	0.0	0.1	0.0	0.1	0.0	0.1	0.0	0.0	—
South Asia	0.3	1.3	1.1	0.1	0.9	0.9	0.5	0.3	0
India	0.3	1.3	1.0	0.1	0.9	0.9	0.5	0.3	—
Sub-Saharan Africa	0.4	0.8	1.0	0.7	4.2	0.6	0.3	0.7	1
South Africa	0.3	0.6	1.0	0.7	4.2	0.6	0.3	0.7	—

— Not available.
Note: f = forecast.

Table A.39 Gross international bond issues in developing countries, 1995–2003
(billions of dollars)

	1995	1996	1997	1998	1999	2000	2001	2002	2003f
All developing countries	**39.4**	**78.1**	**99.2**	**65.4**	**63.2**	**57.8**	**59.4**	**55.4**	**71**
East Asia and Pacific	9.9	20.8	20.2	4.5	8.6	5.1	7.1	12.4	18
China	1.6	4.1	6.1	1.8	1.7	1.3	2.6	0.9	—
Indonesia	2.5	5.5	5.6	0.5	0.0	0.0	0.1	0.9	—
Malaysia	2.8	2.5	3.1	0.0	2.2	1.4	2.4	6.0	—
Philippines	0.8	3.6	3.0	1.9	4.8	2.4	1.8	4.8	—
Thailand	2.2	5.1	2.4	0.3	0.0	0.0	0.3	0.0	—
Europe and Central Asia	6.5	6.8	15.7	21.7	13.6	14.0	11.1	15.0	24
Croatia	0.1	0.1	0.5	0.1	0.6	0.9	0.9	0.8	—
Hungary	3.3	0.3	0.4	1.8	2.4	0.5	1.2	0.1	—
Poland	0.3	0.3	1.2	1.9	1.7	1.6	2.8	2.7	—
Russian Federation	0.3	1.2	7.0	10.5	0.0	0.1	1.4	3.6	—
Turkey	2.4	2.9	4.2	3.4	5.8	8.5	2.2	3.5	—
Latin America and the Caribbean	19.8	46.8	57.4	36.6	37.3	34.8	33.6	22.2	21
Argentina	5.5	13.7	16.0	15.0	13.5	12.2	1.5	0.0	—
Brazil	4.7	10.9	15.0	6.5	7.6	11.2	11.9	7.0	—
Colombia	1.2	1.9	1.3	1.4	1.7	1.5	4.3	1.0	—
Mexico	6.9	18.0	14.9	8.4	9.5	7.2	8.2	7.4	—
Venezuela, R.B. de	0.7	1.0	5.9	3.3	2.2	0.5	1.7	0.0	—
Middle East and North Africa	1.0	1.0	2.1	1.5	1.9	2.4	5.3	2.7	4
Egypt, Arab Rep. of	0.0	0.0	0.0	0.0	0.1	0.0	1.5	0.0	—
Lebanon	0.4	0.5	1.3	1.5	1.4	1.9	3.3	1.0	—
Tunisia	0.6	0.1	0.5	0.0	0.2	0.5	0.5	0.7	—
South Asia	0.8	1.4	2.7	0.1	0.1	0.0	0.1	0.1	0
India	0.8	1.1	2.2	0.0	0.1	0.0	0.1	0.1	—
Pakistan	0.0	0.3	0.5	0.0	0.0	0.0	0.0	0.0	—
Sub-Saharan Africa	1.5	1.3	1.1	1.0	1.7	1.5	2.2	3.0	4
South Africa	1.3	1.0	1.1	1.0	1.7	1.5	2.2	3.0	—

— Not available.
Note: *f* = forecast.

Table A.40 Gross international bank lending to developing-country borrowers, 1995–2003
(billions of dollars)

	1995	1996	1997	1998	1999	2000	2001	2002	2003f
All developing countries	**105.4**	**115.4**	**166.6**	**105.2**	**85.7**	**113.2**	**85.7**	**82.8**	**84**
East Asia and Pacific	46.0	45.5	45.3	18.8	13.4	21.5	10.1	21.4	23
China	12.7	9.8	11.1	7.0	3.4	5.8	1.2	9.6	—
Indonesia	13.6	17.3	14.7	0.7	1.6	1.0	0.5	0.3	—
Malaysia	7.0	7.8	8.3	3.2	4.6	5.5	3.2	5.6	—
Philippines	1.8	1.2	4.4	3.4	2.6	4.7	3.1	1.5	—
Thailand	9.8	8.8	6.5	4.3	1.2	4.3	2.0	3.6	—
Europe and Central Asia	14.8	18.7	32.4	19.0	16.1	23.3	16.3	18.9	18
Czech Republic	1.6	3.2	3.5	2.4	0.6	1.2	0.8	0.2	—
Hungary	1.6	2.8	2.1	1.8	0.9	1.5	1.8	1.8	—
Poland	1.2	0.6	2.5	1.7	2.7	2.6	2.6	3.7	—
Russian Federation	3.6	3.8	12.9	2.8	0.7	4.7	3.1	5.9	—
Turkey	4.6	5.7	5.7	5.7	7.1	11.2	4.7	3.7	—
Latin America and the Caribbean	22.1	34.5	58.2	47.6	37.3	48.3	41.0	22.0	22
Argentina	3.8	10.0	11.5	11.8	7.2	6.7	5.0	2.1	—
Brazil	2.2	3.2	14.9	11.4	6.9	13.7	10.6	6.4	—
Chile	1.8	4.3	7.2	4.3	7.6	6.5	5.6	2.1	—
Colombia	3.2	2.3	4.9	1.8	2.0	2.2	0.6	1.2	—
Mexico	8.2	10.6	14.7	11.5	8.7	10.9	11.7	7.4	—
Middle East and North Africa	10.3	3.0	15.9	10.2	11.6	6.1	6.9	12.0	12
Egypt, Arab Rep. of	0.3	0.0	1.2	1.6	4.2	0.8	1.1	0.6	—
Iran, Islamic Rep. of	1.0	0.6	0.5	0.5	0.7	1.0	1.0	3.0	—
Saudi Arabia	3.1	0.8	9.7	6.5	4.4	2.4	1.9	5.7	—
South Asia	6.3	7.8	8.9	5.0	3.2	3.9	2.7	2.2	2
India	4.1	5.0	7.5	3.9	2.8	3.5	2.0	1.8	—
Pakistan	2.0	2.8	1.3	0.9	0.0	0.0	0.2	0.4	—
Sub-Saharan Africa	6.0	5.8	5.8	4.7	4.1	10.1	8.6	6.2	7
South Africa	2.6	4.1	3.6	1.3	1.9	7.1	4.4	2.8	—

— Not available.
Note: f = forecast.

Table A.41 Change in foreign exchange reserves of developing countries, 1995–2003
(billions of dollars)

	Gross foreign exchange reserves	Change (− = increase)								
	2001	1995	1996	1997	1998	1999	2000	2001	2002e	2003f
All developing countries	**778.5**	**−96.1**	**−90.4**	**−52.9**	**−16.6**	**−37.3**	**−55.1**	**−80.3**	**−110.0**	**−108.0**
East Asia and Pacific	320.3	−29.0	−45.2	−12.8	−20.7	−29.3	−10.1	−47.7	−57.0	−55.0
China	212.2	−22.0	−31.5	−34.9	−5.1	−9.7	−10.9	−46.6	—	—
Indonesia	27.0	−1.5	−4.5	1.7	−6.3	−3.8	−2.0	1.2	—	—
Malaysia	29.6	1.9	−3.2	6.1	−4.7	−4.9	1.0	−1.0	—	—
Philippines	13.3	−0.4	−3.7	2.8	−2.0	−4.0	0.2	−0.4	—	—
Thailand	32.3	−6.6	−1.7	11.5	−2.7	−5.4	1.9	−0.4	—	—
Europe and Central Asia	130.0	−41.0	−2.3	−7.3	−4.9	−6.5	−19.1	−10.3	−34.0	−25.0
Czech Republic	14.2	−7.7	1.5	2.6	−2.8	−0.3	−0.2	−1.2	—	—
Hungary	10.3	−5.2	2.3	1.3	−0.9	−1.5	−0.2	0.6	—	—
Poland	25.2	−8.9	−3.1	−2.6	−6.9	1.1	−0.2	1.2	—	—
Russian Federation	32.5	−10.3	3.0	−1.5	5.0	−0.7	−15.8	−8.3	—	—
Turkey	18.7	−5.3	−4.0	−2.2	−0.8	−3.7	0.9	3.6	—	—
Latin America and the Caribbean	155.9	−23.4	−28.0	−13.5	9.2	7.5	−2.9	−2.9	4.0	−10.0
Argentina	14.5	0.0	−4.0	−4.4	−2.3	−1.6	1.7	9.9	—	—
Brazil	35.7	−12.6	−8.6	7.5	8.2	7.8	2.3	−3.2	—	—
Chile	14.0	−1.0	−0.8	−2.3	2.0	1.1	−0.5	0.6	—	—
Mexico	44.4	−9.1	−3.9	−9.0	−3.3	0.5	−4.2	−9.2	—	—
Venezuela, R.B. de	8.8	1.7	−5.4	−2.9	2.4	−0.1	−0.9	3.8	—	—
Middle East and North Africa	85.2	−3.8	−11.5	−6.6	1.5	−2.6	−12.2	−8.8	−5.0	0.0
Algeria	18.0	0.6	−2.2	−3.8	1.2	2.4	−7.5	−6.1	—	—
Egypt, Arab Rep. of	12.9	−2.7	−1.2	−1.3	0.6	3.6	1.4	0.0	—	—
Morocco	8.3	0.8	−0.2	−0.2	−0.4	−1.1	0.9	−3.7	—	—
Saudi Arabia	14.8	−1.2	−5.7	−0.6	0.8	−2.8	−2.5	3.2	—	—
South Asia	52.8	4.1	−0.6	−5.2	−3.0	−5.0	−4.7	−10.2	−18.0	−15.0
India	45.3	1.9	−2.3	−4.6	−2.6	−5.0	−5.3	−8.0	—	—
Pakistan	3.6	1.2	1.2	−0.6	0.2	−0.5	0.0	−2.1	—	—
Sri Lanka	1.2	0.0	0.1	−0.1	0.0	0.4	0.6	−0.2	—	—
Sub-Saharan Africa	34.3	−3.0	−2.8	−7.6	1.4	−1.5	−6.0	−0.3	0.0	−3.0
Angola	0.7	0.0	−0.3	0.2	0.2	−0.3	−0.7	0.5	—	—
Nigeria	10.5	−0.1	−2.6	−3.5	0.5	1.7	−4.5	−0.5	—	—
South Africa	5.8	−1.1	1.9	−3.8	0.6	−1.9	0.3	0.0	—	—

— Not available.
Note: e = estimate; *f* = forecast.

Table A.42 Total external debt of developing countries, 1995–2001
(billions of dollars)

	1995	1996	1997	1998	1999	2000	2001
All developing countries	**2,065.6**	**2,126.0**	**2,188.8**	**2,395.2**	**2,427.0**	**2,363.6**	**2,332.1**
East Asia and Pacific	461.9	497.9	528.7	535.4	541.4	497.4	504.1
China	118.1	128.8	146.7	144.0	152.1	145.7	170.1
Indonesia	124.4	128.9	136.2	151.2	151.0	144.1	135.7
Malaysia	34.3	39.7	47.2	42.4	41.9	41.8	43.4
Philippines	37.8	40.1	45.7	48.3	53.0	50.4	52.4
Thailand	100.0	112.8	109.7	104.9	96.8	79.7	67.4
Eastern Europe and Central Asia	349.5	367.0	386.9	484.2	494.4	503.6	497.8
Bulgaria	10.3	10.0	9.8	10.0	10.0	10.1	9.6
Czech Republic	16.2	20.1	23.1	24.2	22.8	21.6	21.7
Hungary	31.6	27.2	24.5	28.5	29.9	29.5	30.3
Poland	44.3	43.5	40.4	55.5	60.7	63.3	62.4
Russian Federation	122.0	127.0	128.1	178.3	174.9	160.1	152.6
Turkey	73.8	79.6	84.8	97.1	102.2	118.3	115.1
Latin America and the Caribbean	649.6	670.9	702.2	774.3	794.8	782.9	764.9
Argentina	98.8	111.4	128.4	141.5	145.3	145.9	136.7
Brazil	160.5	181.3	198.0	241.0	243.7	238.8	226.4
Chile	22.0	23.0	22.8	30.2	34.3	37.0	38.4
Colombia	25.0	28.9	31.9	33.1	34.4	33.9	36.7
Mexico	166.6	157.5	148.7	159.9	167.3	158.5	158.3
Venezuela, R.B. de	35.5	34.5	35.4	37.4	37.3	37.8	34.7
Middle East and North Africa	211.8	203.7	195.0	209.8	213.9	202.1	200.6
Algeria	33.0	33.6	30.9	30.7	28.0	25.3	22.5
Egypt, Arab Rep. of	33.3	31.4	29.9	32.3	30.9	29.0	29.2
Lebanon	3.0	4.0	5.0	6.8	8.2	9.9	12.5
South Asia	157.3	155.2	155.0	163.0	167.4	165.1	161.7
India	94.5	93.5	94.3	97.6	98.3	99.1	97.3
Pakistan	30.2	29.8	30.1	32.3	33.9	32.8	32.0
Sub-Saharan Africa	235.5	231.3	220.9	228.5	215.0	211.4	203.0
South Africa	25.4	26.1	25.3	24.8	23.9	24.9	24.1

Table A.43 Total external debt of developing countries, as of December 2001, present-value basis
(millions of dollars)

	Total external debt (nominal terms)	Present value of total external debt	Present value as a percentage of total external debt
Albania	1,094	762	69.7
Algeria	22,503	21,694	96.4
Angola	9,600	9,348	97.4
Argentina	136,709	148,847	108.9
Armenia	1,001	654	65.4
Azerbaijan	1,219	994	81.6
Bangladesh	15,215	9,712	63.8
Barbados	701	739	105.5
Belarus	869	819	94.3
Belize	708	765	108.0
Benin	1,665	840	50.5
Bhutan	265	245	92.4
Bolivia	4,682	1,995	42.6
Bosnia and Herzegovina	2,226	1,591	71.5
Botswana	370	307	83.1
Brazil	226,362	237,596	105.0
Bulgaria	9,615	8,355	86.9
Burkina Faso[a]	1,490	716	48.1
Burundi	1,065	648	60.9
Cambodia	2,704	2,301	85.1
Cameroon	8,338	4,928	59.1
Cape Verde	360	231	64.3
Central African Republic	822	536	65.2
Chad	1,104	628	56.9
Chile	38,360	37,730	98.4
China	170,110	164,068	96.4
Colombia	36,699	37,554	102.3
Comoros	246	177	72.0
Congo, Dem. Rep. of	11,392	10,610	93.1
Congo, Rep. of	4,496	4,232	94.1
Costa Rica	4,586	4,799	104.7
Côte d'Ivoire	11,582	10,647	91.9
Croatia	10,742	10,708	99.7
Czech Republic	21,691	21,343	98.4
Djibouti	262	177	67.4
Dominica	206	181	87.8
Dominican Republic	5,093	4,836	95.0
Ecuador	13,910	14,505	104.3
Egypt, Arab Rep. of	29,234	25,075	85.8
El Salvador	4,683	4,593	98.1
Equatorial Guinea	239	193	80.8
Eritrea	410	235	57.3
Estonia	2,852	2,942	103.1
Ethiopia	5,697	2,915	51.2
Fiji	188	175	93.0
Gabon	3,409	3,335	97.8
Gambia, The	489	265	54.2
Georgia	1,714	1,066	62.2
Ghana	6,759	3,945	58.4
Grenada	215	190	88.5
Guatemala	4,526	4,333	95.7
Guinea	3,254	1,732	53.2
Guinea-Bissau	668	424	63.4
Guyana	1,406	882	62.7
Haiti	1,250	817	65.4
Honduras	5,051	3,157	62.5
Hungary	30,289	28,427	93.9
India	97,320	67,760	69.6
Indonesia	135,704	131,357	96.8
Iran, Islamic Rep. of	7,483	6,725	89.9
Jamaica	4,956	5,361	108.2

Table A.43 Total external debt of developing countries, as of December 2001, present-value basis
(millions of dollars)

	Total external debt (nominal terms)	Present value of total external debt	Present value as a percentage of total external debt
Jordan	7,480	6,894	92.2
Kazakhstan	14,372	14,265	99.3
Kenya	5,833	4,412	75.6
Kyrgyz Republic	1,717	1,326	77.3
Lao PDR	2,495	1,295	51.9
Latvia	5,710	5,548	97.2
Lebanon	12,450	13,451	108.0
Lesotho	593	406	68.5
Liberia	1,987	1,928	97.0
Lithuania	5,248	5,185	98.8
Macedonia, FYR	1,423	1,170	82.2
Madagascar	4,160	2,045	49.2
Malawi	2,602	1,486	57.1
Malaysia	43,351	46,030	106.2
Maldives	235	177	75.4
Mali	2,890	1,407	48.7
Malta	1,531	1,357	88.6
Mauritania[a]	2,164	1,407	65.0
Mauritius	1,724	1,658	96.1
Mexico	158,290	172,899	109.2
Moldova	1,214	1,126	92.7
Mongolia	885	606	68.5
Morocco	16,962	14,694	86.6
Mozambique	4,466	916	20.5
Myanmar	5,670	4,032	71.1
Nepal	2,700	1,567	58.0
Nicaragua	6,391	4,309	67.4
Niger	1,555	1,025	65.9
Nigeria	31,119	30,882	99.2
Oman	6,025	5,816	96.5
Pakistan	32,020	25,457	79.5
Panama	8,245	9,020	109.4
Papua New Guinea	2,521	2,188	86.8
Paraguay	2,817	2,666	94.6
Peru	27,512	28,114	102.2
Philippines	52,356	55,262	105.6
Poland	62,393	59,268	95.0
Romania	11,653	11,067	95.0
Russian Federation	152,649	146,725	96.1
Rwanda	1,283	670	52.2
Samoa	204	142	69.5
Sao Tome and Principe	313	100	32.0
Senegal	3,461	2,406	69.5
Seychelles	215	212	98.7
Sierra Leone	1,188	834	70.2
Slovak Republic	11,121	10,879	97.8
Solomon Islands	163	112	68.7
Somalia	2,531	2,277	89.9
South Africa	24,050	23,379	97.2
Sri Lanka	8,529	6,909	81.0
St. Kitts and Nevis	189	170	90.1
St. Lucia	238	229	96.3
St. Vincent and the Grenadines	194	156	80.2
Sudan	15,348	14,547	94.8
Swaziland	308	297	96.6
Syrian Arab Republic	21,305	20,837	97.8
Tajikistan	1,086	853	78.6
Tanzania	6,676	1,342	20.1
Thailand	67,384	66,760	99.1
Togo	1,406	999	71.1

(Table continues on next page)

Table A.43 Total external debt of developing countries, as of December 2001, present-value basis
(continued)
(millions of dollars)

	Total external debt (nominal terms)	Present value of total external debt	Present value as a percentage of total external debt
Tonga	63	42	66.9
Trinidad and Tobago	2,422	2,609	107.7
Tunisia	10,884	10,829	99.5
Turkey	115,118	116,685	101.4
Turkmenistan	—	—	—
Uganda	3,733	1,151	30.8
Ukraine	12,811	11,483	89.6
Uruguay	9,706	9,872	101.7
Uzbekistan	4,627	4,444	96.0
Vanuatu	66	37	55.6
Venezuela, R.B. de	34,660	37,467	108.1
Vietnam	12,578	10,933	86.9
Yemen, Rep. of	4,954	3,558	71.8
Yugoslavia, Fed. Rep. of	11,740	11,711	99.7
Zambia	5,671	4,036	71.2
Zimbabwe	3,780	3,493	92.4

— Not available.
Note: For definition of indicators, see Sources and Definitions section of *Global Development Finance 2003, II: Summary and Country Tables.* Numbers in italics are from debt sustainability analyses undertaken in the context of the HIPC Initiative. Present value estimates for these countries are for public and publicly guaranteed debt only. Export figures exclude workers' remittances.
a. Enhanced HIPC assistance will be accounted for in *Global Development Finance 2004.*

Table A.44 Total external debt of developing countries, medium- and long-term, 1995–2001
(billions of dollars)

	1995	1996	1997	1998	1999	2000	2001
All developing countries	**1,688.7**	**1,727.9**	**1,782.4**	**2,023.8**	**2,072.1**	**2,026.8**	**1,983.1**
East Asia and Pacific	351.8	367.9	395.8	449.1	466.7	433.3	411.3
China	95.8	103.4	115.2	126.7	136.9	132.6	126.2
Indonesia	98.4	96.7	103.3	131.1	131.0	121.4	113.9
Malaysia	27.1	28.6	32.3	33.9	35.9	37.2	38.2
Philippines	32.6	32.2	33.9	41.1	47.3	44.4	46.3
Thailand	55.9	65.1	71.9	75.3	73.4	64.8	54.2
Eastern Europe and Central Asia	305.1	314.7	330.8	413.3	422.1	423.2	422.1
Bulgaria	9.8	9.1	9.0	9.5	9.6	9.7	9.3
Czech Republic	11.1	14.3	15.0	16.6	14.0	12.6	12.7
Hungary	28.4	23.9	21.2	23.7	26.3	25.4	25.7
Poland	42.1	40.8	36.6	49.3	54.6	56.2	55.4
Russian Federation	111.7	114.9	122.1	163.3	159.1	144.5	131.7
Turkey	58.1	62.3	66.8	75.9	78.8	89.4	98.8
Latin America and the Caribbean	522.0	550.1	575.4	655.8	685.4	677.3	668.9
Argentina	77.4	87.9	96.4	110.6	115.9	117.6	116.7
Brazil	129.3	145.4	163.2	211.1	214.5	207.8	198.1
Chile	18.6	20.4	21.5	28.6	33.1	34.5	35.8
Colombia	19.5	23.0	26.2	26.9	30.5	31.1	33.0
Mexico	129.3	127.7	120.8	133.6	143.2	139.5	140.3
Venezuela, R.B. de	32.5	31.8	31.2	35.2	35.2	33.8	30.9
Middle East and North Africa	166.9	161.5	153.7	163.7	163.4	155.6	153.3
Algeria	32.8	33.3	30.7	30.5	27.8	25.1	22.3
Egypt, Arab Rep. of	31.0	29.0	26.9	28.0	26.6	24.9	25.9
Lebanon	1.6	2.3	3.2	4.8	6.0	7.3	9.8
South Asia	148.2	144.9	146.8	155.9	160.4	159.1	156.5
India	89.4	86.7	89.3	93.3	94.4	95.6	94.4
Pakistan	27.0	27.0	27.6	30.1	32.1	31.3	30.7
Sub-Saharan Africa	194.8	188.7	179.9	186.0	173.9	178.3	170.9
South Africa	15.7	15.2	14.3	13.3	13.1	15.3	15.7

Table A.45 Total external debt of developing countries, short-term, 1995–2001
(billions of dollars)

	1995	1996	1997	1998	1999	2000	2001
All developing countries	**376.9**	**398.1**	**406.4**	**371.4**	**354.9**	**335.8**	**349.0**
East Asia and Pacific	110.2	129.9	133.0	86.3	74.7	64.0	92.8
China	22.3	25.4	31.5	17.3	15.2	13.1	43.9
Indonesia	26.0	32.2	32.9	20.1	20.0	22.6	21.8
Malaysia	7.3	11.1	14.9	8.5	6.0	4.6	5.1
Philippines	5.3	8.0	11.8	7.2	5.7	5.9	6.0
Thailand	44.1	47.7	37.8	29.7	23.4	14.9	13.2
Eastern Europe and Central Asia	44.4	52.3	56.2	70.9	72.3	80.5	75.7
Bulgaria	0.5	0.9	0.7	0.4	0.4	0.4	0.3
Czech Republic	5.1	5.7	8.1	7.6	8.8	9.0	9.0
Hungary	3.2	3.4	3.4	4.8	3.5	4.2	4.6
Poland	2.2	2.7	3.8	6.2	6.0	7.1	7.0
Russian Federation	10.4	12.1	6.1	15.0	15.7	15.6	21.0
Turkey	15.7	17.3	18.0	21.2	23.5	28.9	16.3
Latin America and the Caribbean	127.6	120.8	126.8	118.5	109.4	105.7	96.0
Argentina	21.4	23.5	32.0	31.0	29.4	28.3	20.0
Brazil	31.2	35.9	34.9	29.9	29.2	31.0	28.3
Chile	3.4	2.6	1.3	1.6	1.2	2.5	2.6
Colombia	5.5	5.9	5.8	6.2	4.0	2.9	3.7
Mexico	37.3	29.8	27.9	26.3	24.1	18.9	18.0
Venezuela, R.B. de	3.1	2.7	4.2	2.2	2.1	4.1	3.7
Middle East and North Africa	44.9	42.2	41.3	46.1	50.4	46.5	47.4
Algeria	0.3	0.3	0.2	0.2	0.2	0.2	0.2
Egypt, Arab Rep. of	2.4	2.3	3.0	4.3	4.3	4.1	3.4
Lebanon	1.4	1.7	1.8	2.0	2.2	2.5	2.7
South Asia	9.1	10.3	8.2	7.1	7.0	6.0	5.1
India	5.0	6.7	5.0	4.3	3.9	3.5	3.0
Pakistan	3.2	2.8	2.5	2.2	1.8	1.5	1.3
Sub-Saharan Africa	40.7	42.6	40.9	42.5	41.1	33.1	32.1
South Africa	9.7	10.8	10.9	11.4	10.8	9.6	8.4

Table A.46 Total external debt of developing countries owed by public-sector and publicly guaranteed borrowers, 1995–2001
(billions of dollars)

	1995	1996	1997	1998	1999	2000	2001
All developing countries	**1,469.2**	**1,452.6**	**1,433.6**	**1,529.4**	**1,542.3**	**1,492.2**	**1,469.7**
East Asia and Pacific	263.0	263.1	278.3	295.4	314.2	294.3	289.0
China	94.7	102.3	112.8	99.4	99.2	94.8	91.7
Indonesia	65.3	60.0	58.8	76.4	83.7	80.3	77.5
Malaysia	16.0	15.7	16.8	18.2	18.9	19.1	24.1
Philippines	29.0	27.3	27.1	30.2	36.4	35.8	36.1
Thailand	16.8	16.9	24.7	31.3	34.7	32.5	28.1
Eastern Europe and Central Asia	286.9	286.9	289.0	321.0	316.1	305.2	291.0
Bulgaria	9.4	8.7	8.6	9.0	8.9	9.0	8.5
Czech Republic	9.7	12.2	12.8	11.6	7.7	6.6	5.9
Hungary	24.4	18.9	15.3	15.9	16.9	14.3	12.7
Poland	41.1	39.2	34.2	35.1	33.2	30.8	24.8
Russian Federation	111.7	114.9	120.2	141.1	136.6	122.7	109.4
Turkey	51.0	48.9	48.1	50.6	51.6	61.5	70.1
Latin America and the Caribbean	434.7	433.0	413.1	435.8	441.7	433.2	442.9
Argentina	61.4	68.8	73.0	82.7	88.6	91.7	99.3
Brazil	98.4	96.4	87.3	103.0	100.9	95.1	101.8
Chile	7.2	4.9	4.4	5.0	5.7	5.2	5.5
Colombia	13.9	14.9	15.4	16.7	20.2	20.8	21.8
Mexico	111.0	107.3	93.5	96.4	93.2	89.7	86.2
Venezuela, R.B. de	30.5	29.9	28.7	29.3	28.4	27.6	24.9
Middle East and North Africa	161.7	155.8	147.0	154.8	156.8	148.8	145.9
Algeria	32.8	33.3	30.7	30.5	27.8	25.1	22.3
Egypt, Arab Rep. of	30.7	28.9	26.8	27.6	26.1	24.4	25.2
Lebanon	1.6	1.9	2.3	4.0	5.3	6.6	9.0
South Asia	139.9	135.4	135.1	144.7	150.0	143.7	142.4
India	82.8	79.4	80.1	84.9	86.4	83.2	82.7
Pakistan	25.4	25.0	25.3	27.5	29.8	28.7	28.6
Sub-Saharan Africa	183.0	178.4	171.1	177.8	163.5	166.9	158.5
South Africa	10.7	11.2	11.9	10.7	8.2	9.1	7.9

Table A.47 Total external debt of developing countries owed by private-sector borrowers, 1995–2001
(billions of dollars)

	1995	1996	1997	1998	1999	2000	2001
All developing countries	**596.4**	**673.4**	**755.2**	**865.7**	**884.7**	**870.4**	**862.5**
East Asia and Pacific	198.9	234.8	250.5	240.0	227.2	203.1	215.1
China	23.4	26.6	33.9	44.6	52.9	50.9	78.4
Indonesia	59.1	68.9	77.3	74.8	67.3	63.8	58.2
Malaysia	18.3	24.0	30.4	24.3	23.0	22.7	19.3
Philippines	8.8	12.9	18.6	18.1	16.6	14.6	16.2
Thailand	83.2	96.0	85.0	73.6	62.0	47.2	39.3
Eastern Europe and Central Asia	62.6	80.1	97.9	163.2	178.4	198.4	206.8
Bulgaria	0.9	1.3	1.2	1.0	1.1	1.2	1.1
Czech Republic	6.5	7.8	10.2	12.7	15.1	15.0	15.8
Hungary	7.3	8.4	9.3	12.6	13.0	15.2	17.6
Poland	3.2	4.3	6.2	20.4	27.5	32.5	37.6
Russian Federation	10.4	12.1	8.0	37.1	38.3	37.4	43.3
Turkey	22.8	30.8	36.7	46.6	50.6	56.7	45.0
Latin America and the Caribbean	214.9	237.9	289.1	338.5	353.1	349.7	322.0
Argentina	37.4	42.6	55.4	58.8	56.7	54.2	37.4
Brazil	62.1	84.9	110.7	138.0	142.8	143.7	124.6
Chile	14.9	18.2	18.4	25.2	28.6	31.8	32.8
Colombia	11.1	14.0	16.5	16.3	14.2	13.1	14.9
Mexico	55.6	50.2	55.2	63.5	74.1	68.8	72.1
Venezuela, R.B. de	5.1	4.5	6.7	8.2	8.9	10.2	9.7
Middle East and North Africa	50.1	47.9	48.0	54.9	57.1	53.3	54.8
Algeria	0.3	0.3	0.2	0.2	0.2	0.2	0.2
Egypt, Arab Rep. of	2.7	2.5	3.1	4.6	4.8	4.7	4.0
Lebanon	1.4	2.1	2.7	2.7	2.9	3.3	3.5
South Asia	17.4	19.8	19.9	18.3	17.4	21.4	19.3
India	11.7	14.1	14.3	12.7	11.9	15.9	14.6
Pakistan	4.8	4.8	4.8	4.8	4.1	4.1	3.4
Sub-Saharan Africa	52.5	52.9	49.7	50.7	51.5	44.5	44.5
South Africa	14.6	14.8	13.3	14.1	15.7	15.8	16.1

Table A.48 Total external debt of developing countries owed to public-sector creditors, 1995–2001
(billions of dollars)

	1995	1996	1997	1998	1999	2000	2001
All developing countries	**919.3**	**885.3**	**842.9**	**906.1**	**922.2**	**880.3**	**866.7**
East Asia and Pacific	166.9	159.7	158.5	185.1	206.4	194.2	186.7
China	37.0	39.4	39.8	45.1	50.4	50.4	50.5
Indonesia	51.2	46.1	45.5	58.2	66.3	65.9	62.1
Malaysia	5.5	4.2	4.0	4.5	4.8	5.0	5.9
Philippines	23.1	20.8	19.5	21.9	23.4	21.8	19.7
Thailand	11.2	10.6	17.8	21.4	25.3	23.9	21.0
Eastern Europe and Central Asia	156.7	160.6	156.7	172.6	171.3	165.9	159.1
Bulgaria	3.6	3.3	3.3	3.8	3.8	3.8	3.4
Czech Republic	1.3	1.3	1.1	1.1	1.1	1.0	1.2
Hungary	4.8	3.7	3.3	2.3	2.3	1.9	1.6
Poland	32.2	30.5	26.6	27.1	25.1	23.7	17.8
Russian Federation	67.8	76.3	77.4	88.7	87.1	82.3	71.4
Turkey	18.0	15.9	14.3	15.0	13.8	17.3	27.7
Latin America and the Caribbean	217.3	194.2	176.0	180.5	183.0	169.8	181.3
Argentina	27.1	26.1	24.2	25.9	25.5	25.6	35.2
Brazil	28.0	25.4	22.2	32.7	37.7	31.1	37.2
Chile	3.6	2.7	2.2	2.2	2.1	1.9	1.8
Colombia	7.1	6.5	5.6	6.0	7.8	7.7	8.6
Mexico	54.8	42.6	32.1	31.4	26.3	20.8	19.9
Venezuela, R.B. de	6.9	6.3	5.5	6.7	6.6	6.1	4.9
Middle East and North Africa	117.8	117.2	109.2	112.3	107.5	101.2	98.2
Algeria	17.1	20.2	20.3	21.4	20.4	19.2	17.6
Egypt, Arab Rep. of	28.9	27.5	25.7	26.7	25.5	23.8	23.2
Lebanon	0.4	0.6	0.7	0.9	0.9	0.9	1.0
South Asia	114.5	109.7	104.3	110.1	118.8	108.0	106.7
India	59.5	55.9	52.8	53.9	58.6	50.6	49.7
Pakistan	24.3	23.8	22.8	25.1	27.7	26.7	27.3
Sub-Saharan Africa	146.1	143.9	138.1	145.6	135.2	141.1	134.6
South Africa	0.9	0.9	0.4	0.0	0.0	0.1	0.1

Table A.49 Total external debt of developing countries owed to private-sector creditors, 1995–2001
(billions of dollars)

	1995	1996	1997	1998	1999	2000	2001
All developing countries	**1,146.3**	**1,240.7**	**1,346.1**	**1,489.5**	**1,504.8**	**1,482.3**	**1,465.4**
East Asia and Pacific	295.1	338.1	370.2	350.3	335.1	303.1	317.4
China	81.1	89.4	106.9	98.9	101.6	95.3	119.6
Indonesia	73.1	82.8	90.7	93.1	84.7	78.1	73.6
Malaysia	28.9	35.5	43.2	37.9	37.1	36.8	37.4
Philippines	14.7	19.4	26.2	26.4	29.6	28.6	32.7
Thailand	88.9	102.3	91.9	83.5	71.5	55.8	46.4
Eastern Europe and Central Asia	192.8	206.4	230.2	311.6	323.1	337.7	338.7
Bulgaria	6.7	6.7	6.5	6.2	6.2	6.3	6.2
Czech Republic	14.9	18.7	22.0	23.1	21.7	20.6	20.5
Hungary	26.8	23.6	21.3	26.2	27.6	27.6	28.7
Poland	12.0	13.0	13.8	28.4	35.6	39.6	44.6
Russian Federation	54.3	50.7	50.7	89.6	87.8	77.8	81.2
Turkey	55.8	63.8	70.5	82.2	88.4	101.0	87.4
Latin America and the Caribbean	432.3	476.7	526.4	594.3	611.8	613.1	583.5
Argentina	71.7	85.3	104.2	115.6	119.8	120.3	101.5
Brazil	132.5	155.9	175.8	208.4	206.0	207.7	189.2
Chile	18.5	20.3	20.6	28.0	32.2	35.1	36.6
Colombia	18.0	22.4	26.3	27.1	26.6	26.2	28.1
Mexico	111.8	114.9	116.6	128.5	141.0	137.6	138.4
Venezuela, R.B. de	28.6	28.2	29.9	30.7	30.6	31.7	29.7
Middle East and North Africa	94.0	86.5	85.8	97.5	106.4	100.9	102.5
Algeria	15.9	13.5	10.6	9.2	7.6	6.1	4.9
Egypt, Arab Rep. of	4.4	3.8	4.2	5.5	5.3	5.2	6.0
Lebanon	2.5	3.4	4.3	5.9	7.3	8.9	11.5
South Asia	42.8	45.5	50.7	52.9	48.6	57.1	55.0
India	35.0	37.6	41.5	43.7	39.7	48.5	47.6
Pakistan	5.9	6.0	7.3	7.2	6.2	6.1	4.7
Sub-Saharan Africa	89.3	87.5	82.8	82.9	79.8	70.2	68.4
South Africa	24.4	25.2	24.9	24.8	23.9	24.7	23.9

Table A.50 Foreign exchange reserves of developing countries, 1995–2003
(billions of dollars)

	1995	1996	1997	1998	1999	2000	2001	2002e	2003f
All developing countries	**447.7**	**538.1**	**591.0**	**607.6**	**645.7**	**698.3**	**778.5**	**887.5**	**995.5**
East Asia and Pacific	154.5	199.7	212.5	233.2	262.5	272.6	320.3	377.3	432.3
China	73.6	105.0	139.9	145.0	154.7	165.6	212.2	—	—
Indonesia	13.3	17.8	16.1	22.4	26.2	28.3	27.0	—	—
Malaysia	22.9	26.2	20.0	24.7	29.7	28.6	29.6	—	—
Philippines	6.2	9.9	7.1	9.1	13.1	12.9	13.3	—	—
Thailand	35.5	37.2	25.7	28.4	33.8	31.9	32.3	—	—
Europe and Central Asia	81.1	83.4	90.7	95.6	102.8	119.6	130.0	164.0	189.0
Czech Republic	13.8	12.4	9.7	12.5	12.8	13.0	14.2	—	—
Hungary	11.9	9.6	8.3	9.2	10.7	10.9	10.3	—	—
Poland	14.7	17.7	20.3	27.2	26.1	26.3	25.2	—	—
Russian Federation	14.3	11.3	12.8	7.8	8.5	24.3	32.5	—	—
Turkey	12.4	16.4	18.6	19.4	23.2	22.3	18.7	—	—
Latin America and the Caribbean	125.1	153.1	166.7	157.5	150.0	152.9	155.9	151.9	161.9
Argentina	13.7	17.7	22.2	24.5	26.1	24.4	14.5	—	—
Brazil	49.7	58.3	50.8	42.6	34.8	32.5	35.7	—	—
Chile	14.1	14.9	17.3	15.3	14.2	14.7	14.0	—	—
Mexico	15.3	19.2	28.1	31.5	31.0	35.1	44.4	—	—
Venezuela, R.B. de	5.7	11.1	14.0	11.6	11.7	12.6	8.8	—	—
Middle East and North Africa	44.9	56.4	63.0	61.6	64.2	76.5	85.2	90.2	90.2
Algeria	2.0	4.2	8.0	6.8	4.4	11.9	18.0	—	—
Egypt, Arab Rep. of	16.0	17.2	18.5	17.9	14.3	12.9	12.9	—	—
Libya	5.0	5.0	5.0	6.2	6.2	11.4	13.7	—	—
Saudi Arabia	7.1	12.8	13.5	12.7	15.5	18.0	14.8	—	—
South Asia	24.2	24.8	30.0	32.9	37.9	42.6	52.8	70.8	85.8
Bangladesh	2.2	1.7	1.6	1.9	1.6	1.5	1.3	—	—
India	17.5	19.7	24.3	27.0	32.0	37.3	45.3	—	—
Pakistan	1.7	0.5	1.2	1.0	1.5	1.5	3.6	—	—
Sub-Saharan Africa	17.9	20.6	28.1	26.8	28.2	34.0	34.3	34.3	37.3
Botswana	4.6	5.0	5.6	5.9	6.2	6.3	5.8	—	—
Nigeria	1.4	4.1	7.6	7.1	5.5	9.9	10.5	—	—
South Africa	2.8	0.9	4.8	4.2	6.1	5.8	5.8	—	—

— Not available.
Note: e = estimate, f = forecast.

Table A.51 Key external debt ratios for developing countries
(percent, averages for 1999–2001)

	Total external debt (EDT) to Exports of G&S (XGS)	Present value (PV) of EDT as % of XGS	EDT as % of gross national income (GNI)	PV as % of GNI	Total debt service as % of XGS	Interest service as % of XGS
Albania	83	58	28	19	3	1
Algeria	114	110	46	44	22	6
Angola	140	136	147	143	27	3
Argentina	375	409	50	55	67	30
Armenia	176	115	50	33	10	3
Azerbaijan	60	49	25	20	7	2
Bangladesh	178	113	33	21	8	2
Barbados	46	49	29	30	5	3
Belarus	12	11	7	7	3	1
Belize	177	191	102	110	24	13
Benin	456	230	72	36	14	3
Bhutan	164	151	53	49	4	1
Bolivia	327	139	59	25	38	11
Bosnia and Herzegovina	134	96	46	33	18	6
Botswana	11	9	8	6	2	0
Brazil	337	354	43	45	81	24
Bulgaria	136	118	75	65	19	7
Burkina Faso[a]	569	273	61	29	14	4
Burundi	1,790	1,090	156	95	39	11
Cambodia	187	159	85	72	1	0
Cameroon	324	191	99	59	13	6
Cape Verde	151	97	63	41	6	2
Central African Republic	766	499	84	55	12	4
Chad	462	263	73	42	10	2
Chile	164	162	55	54	28	8
China	61	59	16	15	9	2
Colombia	214	219	45	46	37	15
Comoros	408	294	113	82	4	1
Congo, Dem. Rep. of	1,121	1,044	257	239	2	2
Congo, Rep. of	193	182	231	218	4	1
Costa Rica	57	59	31	32	9	4
Côte d'Ivoire	240	220	111	102	13	5
Croatia	111	111	55	55	31	6
Czech Republic	56	55	41	40	12	3
Djibouti	106	72	46	31	4	1
Dominica	143	125	87	76	11	7
Dominican Republic	49	47	28	26	6	2
Ecuador	198	206	102	107	22	10
Egypt, Arab Rep. of	140	120	30	26	9	4
El Salvador	86	85	36	36	7	4
Equatorial Guinea	9	8	54	44	0	0
Eritrea	142	82	61	35	2	2
Estonia	60	62	56	58	8	3
Ethiopia	598	306	91	46	19	6
Fiji	16	15	11	10	2	1
Gabon	111	108	87	85	15	6
Gambia, The	415	225	120	65	9	1
Georgia	190	118	56	35	9	4
Ghana	277	161	116	68	13	4
Grenada	89	79	59	52	7	2
Guatemala	112	96	26	23	10	5
Guinea	426	227	105	56	14	4
Guinea-Bissau	1,096	695	336	213	38	18
Guyana	210	131	218	137	7	3
Haiti	235	154	32	21	5	3
Honduras	210	131	88	55	14	3
Hungary	93	87	64	60	42	4
India	131	91	21	15	12	5
Indonesia	205	198	99	96	23	9
Iran, Islamic Rep. of	29	26	7	6	5	2
Jamaica	111	120	68	73	14	6

Table A.51 Key external debt ratios for developing countries
(percent, averages for 1999–2001)

	Total external debt (EDT) to Exports of G&S (XGS)	Present value (PV) of EDT as % of XGS	EDT as % of gross national income (GNI)	PV as % of GNI	Total debt service as % of XGS	Interest service as % of XGS
Jordan	127	118	89	82	11	4
Kazakhstan	153	151	79	78	35	7
Kenya	204	154	55	41	16	4
Kyrgyz Republic	292	225	131	101	30	8
Lao PDR	507	263	157	82	9	2
Latvia	165	160	80	78	15	6
Lebanon	428	463	71	77	50	27
Lesotho	108	74	55	37	13	3
Liberia	1,731	1,679	487	472	1	0
Lithuania	99	98	47	47	37	4
Macedonia, FYR	89	73	40	33	12	4
Madagascar	544	267	104	51	9	21
Malawi	556	318	151	87	8	3
Malaysia	41	44	56	59	6	2
Maldives	51	38	43	32	5	1
Mali	384	187	114	55	11	2
Malta	36	32	43	38	3	2
Mauritania[a]	568	369	222	144	23	7
Mauritius	63	60	40	38	7	2
Mexico	89	97	29	32	27	7
Moldova	144	134	88	82	22	6
Mongolia	150	103	92	63	8	2
Morocco	126	109	51	44	20	7
Mozambique	569	117	125	26	11	1
Myanmar	245	174	78	55	4	0
Nepal	159	92	49	28	5	1
Nicaragua	702	473	306	206	37	6
Niger	540	356	82	54	9	2
Nigeria	155	154	88	87	13	4
Oman	57	55	37	36	16	3
Pakistan	299	238	55	43	28	8
Panama	92	100	89	97	13	6
Papua New Guinea	113	98	80	70	12	4
Paraguay	86	81	37	35	11	4
Peru	284	290	53	54	23	14
Philippines	114	120	67	71	17	7
Poland	129	123	39	37	32	5
Romania	96	91	31	30	22	5
Russian Federation	140	134	63	60	16	7
Rwanda	910	475	71	37	13	4
Samoa	213	148	85	59	8	5
São Tomé and Principe	1,839	588	735	235	23	13
Senegal	252	175	77	53	16	4
Seychelles	46	45	37	37	3	1
Sierra Leone	1,100	772	178	125	89	12
Slovak Republic	79	77	56	55	19	5
Solomon Islands	98	68	58	40	4	2
Somalia	—	—	—	—	—	—
South Africa	65	63	20	19	12	3
Sri Lanka	117	95	54	43	10	3
St. Kitts and Nevis	123	111	65	58	13	7
St. Lucia	62	60	37	36	7	3
St. Vincent and the Grenadines	109	87	60	49	8	4
Sudan	710	673	156	148	3	0
Swaziland	28	27	22	22	2	1
Syrian Arab Republic	307	300	125	122	4	2
Tajikistan	138	109	109	86	10	3
Tanzania	500	101	75	15	11	3
Thailand	84	83	58	57	25	4
Togo	288	205	111	79	7	2

(Table continues on next page)

Table A.51 Key external debt ratios for developing countries *(continued)*

(percent, averages for 1999–2001)

	Total external debt (EDT) to Exports of G&S (XGS)	Present value (PV) of EDT as % of XGS	EDT as % of gross national income (GNI)	PV as % of GNI	Total debt service as % of XGS	Interest service as % of XGS
Tonga	67	45	42	28	2	1
Trinidad and Tobago	55	59	33	35	5	3
Tunisia	110	109	57	56	14	4
Turkey	207	209	65	66	40	11
Turkmenistan	—	—	—	—	—	—
Uganda	556	172	65	20	7	3
Ukraine	66	59	39	35	12	3
Uruguay	227	231	49	50	35	15
Uzbekistan	142	136	—	—	26	7
Vanuatu	37	21	31	17	1	0
Venezuela, R.B. de	113	122	30	33	25	9
Vietnam	76	66	41	36	7	2
Yemen, Rep. of	95	68	61	44	5	1
Yugoslavia, Fed. Rep. of	379	378	123	122	4	2
Zambia	626	445	178	127	14	4
Zimbabwe	174	161	54	50	6	3

— Not available.

a. Enhanced HIPC assistance will be accounted for in *Global Development Finance 2004*.

Table A.52 Classification of countries by levels of external indebtedness and income
(138 economies in World Bank Debtor Reporting System)

Severely indebted, low-income	Severely indebted, middle-income	Moderately indebted, low-income	Moderately indebted, middle-income	Less indebted, low-income	Less indebted, middle-income
Angola	Argentina	Bhutan	Bulgaria	Armenia	Albania
Benin	Belize	Cambodia	Bolivia	Azerbaijan	Algeria
Burkina Faso[a]	Brazil	Cameroon	Chile	Bangladesh	Barbados
Burundi	Ecuador	Ghana	Colombia	Equatorial Guinea	Belarus
Central African Republic	Gabon	Haiti	Croatia	Eritrea	Bosnia and Herzegovina
Chad	Guyana	Kenya	Dominica	Georgia	Botswana
Comoros	Jordan	Mali	Estonia	India	Cape Verde
Congo, Dem. Rep. of	Lebanon	Mongolia	Grenada	Lesotho	China
Congo, Rep. of	Panama	Papua New Guinea	Honduras	Mozambique	Costa Rica
Côte d'Ivoire	Peru	Senegal	Hungary	Nepal	Czech Republic
Ethiopia	Syrian Arab Republic	Tanzania	Jamaica	Solomon Islands	Djibouti
Gambia, The	Uruguay	Togo	Kazakhstan	Ukraine	Dominican Republic
Guinea	Yugoslavia, Fed. Rep. of	Uganda	Latvia	Vietnam	Egypt, Arab Rep. of
Guinea-Bissau		Uzbekistan	Malaysia	Yemen, Republic of	El Salvador
Indonesia		Zimbabwe	Philippines		Fiji
Kyrgyz Republic			Russian Federation		Guatemala
Lao PDR			Samoa		Iran, Islamic Rep. of
Liberia			Slovak Republic		Lithuania
Madagascar			St. Kitts and Nevis		Macedonia, FYR
Malawi			St. Vincent and the Grenadines		Maldives
Mauritania[a]			Thailand		Malta
Moldova			Tunisia		Mauritius
Myanmar			Turkey		Mexico
Nicaragua			Turkmenistan		Morocco
Niger					Oman
Nigeria					Paraguay
Pakistan					Poland
Rwanda					Romania
São Tomé and Principe					Seychelles
Sierra Leone					South Africa
Somalia					Sri Lanka
Sudan					St. Lucia
Tajikistan					Swaziland
Zambia					Tonga
					Trinidad and Tobago
					Vanuatu
					Venezuela, R.B. de

a. Enhanced HIPC assistance will be accounted for in *Global Development Finance 2004*.

Income and indebtedness classification criteria

	Indebtedness classification		
Income classification	PV/XGS higher than 220 percent or PV/GNI higher than 80 percent	PV/XGS less than 220 percent but higher than 132 percent or PV/GNI less than 80 percent but higher than 48 percent	PV/XGS less than132 percent and PV/GNI less than 48 percent
Low-income: GNI per capita less than $745	Severely indebted low-income countries	Moderately indebted low-income countries	Less indebted low-income countries
Middle-income: GNI per capita between $746 and $9,205	Severely indebted middle-income countries	Moderately indebted middle-income countries	Less indebted middle-income countries

Note: PV/XGS is present value of debt service to exports of goods and services. PV/GNI is present value of debt service to gross national income.

Table A.53 Classification of countries by region and level of income

		Sub-Saharan Africa		Asia		Europe and Central Asia		Middle East and North Africa		
Income group	Subgroup	East and Southern Africa	West Africa	East Asia and Pacific	South Asia	Eastern Europe and Central Asia	Rest of Europe	Middle East	North Africa	Americas
Low-income		Angola Burundi Comoros Congo, Dem. Rep. of Eritrea Ethiopia Kenya Lesotho Madagascar Malawi Mozambique Rwanda Somalia Sudan Tanzania Uganda Zambia Zimbabwe	Benin Burkina Faso Cameroon Central African Republic Chad Congo, Rep. of Côte d'Ivoire Equatorial Guinea Gambia, The Ghana Guinea Guinea-Bissau Liberia Mali Mauritania Niger Nigeria São Tomé and Principe Senegal Sierra Leone Togo	Cambodia Indonesia Korea, Dem. Rep. of Lao PDR Mongolia Myanmar Papua New Guinea Solomon Islands Timor-Leste Vietnam	Afghanistan Bangladesh Bhutan India Nepal Pakistan	Armenia Azerbaijan Georgia Kyrgyz Republic Moldova Tajikistan Ukraine Uzbekistan		Yemen, Rep. of		Haiti Nicaragua
Middle-income	*Lower*	Namibia South Africa Swaziland	Cape Verde	China Fiji Kiribati Marshall Islands Micronesia, Federated States of Philippines Samoa Thailand Tonga Vanuatu	Maldives Sri Lanka	Albania Belarus Bosnia and Herzegovina Bulgaria Kazakhstan Macedonia, FYR[a] Romania Russian Federation Turkmenistan Yugoslavia, Fed. Rep. of	Turkey	Iran, Islamic Rep. of Iraq Jordan Syrian Arab Republic West Bank and Gaza	Algeria Djibouti Egypt, Arab Rep. of Morocco Tunisia	Belize Bolivia Colombia Cuba Dominican Republic Ecuador El Salvador Guatemala Guyana Honduras Jamaica Paraguay Peru St. Vincent and the Grenadines Suriname
	Upper	Botswana Mauritius Mayotte Seychelles	Gabon	American Samoa Malaysia Palau		Croatia Czech Republic Estonia Hungary Latvia Lithuania Poland Slovak Republic	Isle of Man	Lebanon Oman Saudi Arabia	Libya Malta	Antigua and Barbuda Argentina Barbados Brazil Chile Costa Rica Dominica Grenada Mexico Panama Puerto Rico St. Kitts and Nevis St. Lucia Trinidad and Tobago Uruguay Venezuela, R.B. de

Table A.53 Classification of countries by region and level of income

		Sub-Saharan Africa		Asia		Europe and Central Asia		Middle East and North Africa		
Income group	Subgroup	East and Southern Africa	West Africa	East Asia and Pacific	South Asia	Eastern Europe and Central Asia	Rest of Europe	Middle East	North Africa	Americas
High-income	*OECD*			Australia Japan Korea, Rep. of New Zealand			Austria Belgium Denmark Finland France[b] Germany Greece Iceland Ireland Italy Luxembourg Netherlands Norway Portugal Spain Sweden Switzerland United Kingdom			Canada United States
	Non-OECD			Brunei French Polynesia Guam Hong Kong, China[c] Macao, China[d] New Caledonia N. Mariana Islands Singapore Taiwan, China		Slovenia	Andorra Channel Islands Cyprus Faeroe Islands Greenland Liechtenstein Monaco San Marino	Bahrain Israel Kuwait Qatar United Arab Emirates		Aruba Bahamas, The Bermuda Cayman Islands Netherlands Antilles Virgin Islands (U.S.)

Note: For operational and analytical purposes, the World Bank's main criterion for classifying economies is gross national income (GNI) per capita. Every economy is classified as low income, middle income (subdivided into lower middle and upper middle), or high income. Other analytical groups, based on geographic regions and levels of external debt, are also used.

Low-income and middle-income economies are sometimes referred to as developing economies. The use of the term is convenient; it is not intended to imply that all economies in the group are experiencing similar development or that other economies have reached a preferred or final stage of development. Classification by income does not necessarily reflect development status.

This table classifies all World Bank member economies, and all other economies with populations of more than 30,000. Economies are divided among income groups according to 2001 GNI per capita, calculated using the World Bank Atlas method. The groups are: low income, $745 or less; lower middle income, $746–2,975; upper middle income, $2,976–9,205; and high income, $9,206 or more.

a. Former Yugoslav Republic of Macedonia.
b. The French overseas departments of French Guiana, Guadeloupe, Martinique, and Réunion are included in France.
c. On 1 July 1997 China resumed its exercise of sovereignty over Hong Kong.
d. On 20 December 1999 China resumed its exercise of sovereignty over Macao.